LIVE FREE OR DIE

America (and the World) on the Brink

PG 87
BERNIE
MC GUICK?
1953-2022
43 2 2 6 CANCEL

SEAN HANNITY

THRESHOLD EDITIONS

NEW YORK   LONDON   TORONTO   SYDNEY   NEW DELHI

To God, the creator of everything.

To my family, I love you all dearly—especially my two kids, Patrick and Merri Kelly.

To the defenders of freedom, without whose sacrifice no book is possible.

Threshold Editions
An Imprint of Simon & Schuster, Inc.
1230 Avenue of the Americas
New York, NY 10020

First Threshold Editions trade paperback edition June 2022

THRESHOLD EDITIONS and colophon are trademarks of Simon & Schuster, Inc.

For information about special discounts for bulk purchases,
please contact Simon & Schuster Special Sales at
1-866-506-1949 or business@simonandschuster.com.

The Simon & Schuster Speakers Bureau can bring authors to your live event. For more information, or to book an event, contact the Simon & Schuster Speakers Bureau at 1-866-248-3049 or visit our website at www.simonspeakers.com.

Interior design by Jaime Putorti

Manufactured in the United States of America

10 9 8 7 6 5 4 3 2 1

Library of Congress Cataloging-in-Publication Data

Names: Hannity, Sean, 1961– author.
Title: Live free or die : America (and the world) on the brink / Sean Hannity.
Description: New York : Threshold Editions, 2020. | Includes bibliographical references. |
  Summary: "America's top rated cable news host and New York Times bestselling author offers his first book in ten years, a rousing look at contemporary politics in his trademark take-no-prisoners style"—Provided by publisher.
Identifiers: LCCN 2020019350 (print) | LCCN 2020019351 (ebook) | ISBN 9781982149970 (hardcover) | ISBN 9781982149987 (paperback) | ISBN 9781982149994 (ebook)
Subjects: LCSH: United States—Politics and government—21st century. | United States—Civilization—21st century.
Classification: LCC JK275 .H365 2020 (print) | LCC JK275 (ebook) | DDC 320.973—dc23
LC record available at https://lccn.loc.gov/2020019350
LC ebook record available at https://lccn.loc.gov/2020019351

ISBN 978-1-9821-4997-0
ISBN 978-1-9821-4998-7 (pbk)
ISBN 978-1-9821-4999-4 (ebook)

CONTENTS

? LOOK UP

FOREWORD

I wrote this book almost two years ago and warned that the socialist left, which now controls the Democratic Party, was determined to make this nation unrecognizable to previous generations of Americans. That may have sounded alarmist to some at the time, but I trust these skeptics will now see that my warning was hardly overstated.

In the body of the book I presented my case, documenting how the radical left had seized control of the Democratic Party and was hell-bent on enacting a horrifying agenda that would grow government exponentially and lead us into socialism, eviscerate America's prosperity, demolish our domestic energy industry, eradicate our borders, exploit COVID to suppress our liberties, coordinate with the mainstream media and tech oligarchs to censor, silence, and cancel conservatives, demonize and emasculate law enforcement, promote a two-tiered justice system, downsize our military and national defense, promote abortion on demand, further socialize our healthcare industry, justify raising taxes with appeals to class warfare, increase welfare benefits that would disincentive work and productivity, install left-wing activist judges, alienate and divide Americans on the basis of race, gender, and class, demonize our ancestors and our founding traditions, and undermine the integrity of our elections—all in the name of protecting "our democracy."

I feel compelled to remind you as well that I refuted the image of Joe Biden as a charming, harmless moderate who would unite Americans and reject the radical ideas of the Bernie Sanders wing of his party. The Never Trumpers were particularly adamant on this point, denouncing Trump's divisiveness and, by contrast, insisting ol' Joe was a wonderful, compassionate man who would govern from the center.

It didn't take a prophet to see what was coming. The signs were everywhere that Biden's administration would be far more radical than even Barack Obama's. After a year of Democratic rule, only die-hard leftist ideologues can deny that our nation has lurched leftward under Biden—or to be precise, under Biden's puppetmasters. I can't tell you how much I wish I had been wrong about all this but, regrettably, I wasn't. However, I have to admit that even I didn't think the Democrats would go this far and this fast. What Biden's handlers have done exceeds my worst fears.

They and their supporters have turned the American flag into a symbol of racism for many Americans. They have excused and even encouraged violent riots in our cities. They have gutted law enforcement and politicized criminal law, inviting lawlessness in our streets and looting in our stores. They have turned on its head the government's primary role of defending its citizens and promoting peace and domestic tranquility. Having sabotaged the Keystone XL Pipeline, they deliberately forfeited America's energy independence achieved under President Trump and are left begging rival nations to increase production—apparently, it's only American energy that contributes to the climate apocalypse they foresee.

Whether intentionally or not, they have engineered a border crisis by canceling Trump's wall and signaling that they'll shield illegal immigrants from prosecution, fly them in the dark of night to safe-haven communities, and shower them with government handouts. Pathetically, Vice President Kamala Harris, who is nominally in charge of the border, is doing nothing except pontificating about the "root causes" of this phenomenon. But it's hard to believe she hasn't realized that the true root causes of the border crisis are *her administration's own policies.*

Furthermore, the Biden administration's fiscal policy is utterly ruinous. They have already passed a $1.2 trillion misnamed "infrastructure bill" that nearly doubles the cost of Obama's grandiose socialist "stimulus" program. But of course, that extravagant price tag pales in comparison to their "Build Back Better" welfare bill, which was initially pegged at $3.5 trillion but has supposedly been trimmed to around $2 trillion. It may be the most expensive and wasteful socialist scheme in world history, but not to worry—the Democrats tell us the bill is fully paid for, it won't actually cost us a dime, and this spending orgy won't make inflation worse. It's hard to tell what's worse—the Democrats' policies or the ridiculous lies they expect us to believe about them.

In the meantime, this reckless administration is coddling China, our biggest geopolitical rival. Beijing is building new aircraft carriers, saber-rattling over Taiwan, expanding its capacity for space warfare, and quickly developing hypersonic aircraft and missiles. Even if this administration had the will to counter China, our ability to do so is rapidly eroding as Biden shrinks our military and his woke generals rapidly convert our military into a playground for leftist social experiments and indoctrination into critical race theory.

Although Biden held Trump responsible for 2020 COVID deaths, there were more COVID deaths under the Biden administration in 2021 than under Trump the previous year. So Biden's policies have been ineffective in stopping the virus but highly effective in eroding our freedom. They have weaponized the government against its citizens on vaccine mandates, masks, school closings, critical race theory indoctrination in our public schools, and anyone who questions the administration's ever-changing line or the shifting arguments of the megalomaniac Dr. Anthony Fauci. As this paperback is going to print, Faucists are hyping alarm over the Omicron variant, even though its symptoms have been mild. Now, Omicron still could become a major concern, but the Fauci regime has a clear pattern of always assuming the worst, promoting fear, and encouraging onerous mandates and restrictions as the solution, despite the past failure of those exact policies.

In light of all the above, conservatives can reasonably ask if there is any cause for optimism at all. My answer, unambiguously, is yes. This administration's extreme leftist agenda has already provoked a backlash like I've never seen before. I have talked to so many everyday Americans who are mortified by what's going on in this country and who can't wait to vote these anti-American extremists out of office. Even moderates can see the horrific effects of the leftist agenda. Conservatives have been extremely successful in Virginia and other states that have recently held elections, and Democrats themselves are expecting a bloodbath in the 2022 midterms. This trend will only increase as the administration arrogantly doubles down on its failed policies. They have no other cards in their hand.

Despite the left's arguments to the contrary, America is still the greatest, strongest, freest, and most benevolent nation in the world, and there is still time to ensure that it remains that way, provided that patriots remain united, fierce, and committed to restoring sanity to our federal and state governments. I believe that with God's help, America will come roaring back—but we can never take that for granted. Not much can turn victory into defeat like complacency can. Let us stay strong and dedicated to the ideas and principles that have made America unique, and together we will ensure that we preserve this land as a shining city on a hill.

God bless you all.

CHAPTER ONE

"A Republic—If You Can Keep It"

I begin the book with a brief history of America's foundation. I start here because if we don't understand where we came from, how this country was designed, and the principles that founded two hundred years of success, we will never be able to reestablish American greatness. This is crucial.

Sometimes we Americans act like we take our freedoms for granted—as though we've lost sight of our history and the sacrifices our ancestors made so that we could be free. Have we forgotten what it means to be free? Have we taught our kids the importance of our founding principles? Have we shown them the direct connection between preserving our Constitution intact and maintaining our liberties? Do they understand why the United States of America is strong and prosperous while other nations aren't? Have we sufficiently explained the miracles of a free market system and the evils of socialism? I make a point of emphasizing all these things on my radio and television programs day after day and night after night. And I intend to elaborate on them here.

I make no secret of my love for America and for its founding tradition and documents. Americans are committed to the individual as well as the greater good, to liberty, and to virtue.[1] I often quote one of the great founders and pioneers of talk radio, Barry Farber, who recently passed away: No country has ever accumulated more power and wealth, or abused them less, and, I would add, has used them to advance the human condition more than the United States. In the last twenty-five years, global poverty has decreased by two-thirds, largely due to free market capitalism that America has been instrumental in spreading.[2] Americans generously share our wealth with the world, both through government aid and private charities. America is still the world's beacon of freedom and the place where everyone wants to come, knowing they can pursue their aspirations and enjoy the guarantee of equal opportunity under the law.

This country paid the price for world freedom by defeating fascism, Nazism, communism, and Imperial Japan, and we are now leading the fight against radical Islamic terrorism. We emerged from World War II with far more power than any other nation in history, with the possible exception of Rome at the height of its empire. We had the world's strongest economy and a staggering superiority in military capacity, which included a monopoly on nuclear weapons and their delivery systems. Positioned to forcibly dominate the world, we instead exercised humble restraint.[3]

After our costly victory over Nazi Germany, we could have implemented the Morgenthau Plan—a strategy devised by Treasury secretary Henry Morgenthau Jr. to eradicate Germany's entire industrial base. Instead, under the leadership of U.S. secretary of state George C. Marshall, America included Germany in the Marshall Plan, providing $13 billion in aid to rebuild European cities, industries, and infrastructure and to stimulate U.S.–European commerce.[4]

America's critics deny our intentions were altruistic because we were also trying to shield Western Europe from Soviet expansion.[5] But protecting nations from the ravages of communism—a system responsible for nearly 100 million deaths worldwide in the last century alone[6]—*is* altruistic. Throughout the Cold War, the United States served as the bulwark for freedom and democratic principles against Soviet totalitarianism and its notorious slave labor camps, mass murder, and famines. Yes, the spread of freedom and prosperity worldwide also benefits us, but that does not diminish the benevolence of our world leadership. "Americans are as self-interested as any other people," writes historian Robert Kagan. "But for at least 50 years they have been guided by the kind of enlightened self-interest that, in practice, comes dangerously close to resembling generosity."[7]

Since the end of the Cold War, Americans have widely debated our rightful place in the world. Writing in 1998, Kagan observed that our generosity seemed to be fading—not due to arrogance but "because some Americans have grown tired of power, tired of leadership, and consequently, less inclined to demonstrate the sort of generosity that has long characterized their nation's foreign policy. What many in Europe and elsewhere see as arrogance and bullying may be just irritability born of weariness."[8]

Republicans are split on this question today, as many have indeed grown weary of America's protracted wars. President Trump reflects these tensions—he's no isolationist, but he clearly wants to reduce our global military footprint and prioritize our national interest in his foreign policy. As I've said many times, the president is tired of our country doing all the giving and getting little in return. He's tired of our brave soldiers sacrificing everything and other nations failing to contribute their fair share toward their own security, let alone ours. He is second to none in wanting the strongest possible military, and he has acted on his promises to rebuild our defenses. But he wants to use them wisely and efficiently. "Great nations do not fight endless wars," he said in his 2019 State of the Union address. "I got elected on bringing our soldiers back home."[9] Still, as shown by his victory over ISIS and his strike on Iranian archterrorist Qasem Soleimani, Trump doesn't hesitate to use military force when it directly strengthens our national security. And once again, these actions also benefit our allies and other nations.

America has been and continues to be exceedingly generous compared to any other nation in history. But according to the political left, nearly everything America does is selfish and oppressive. From John

Kerry's slandering our troops in Vietnam during Senate testimony in 1971 to Barack Obama's world apology tour, they blame America first and undercut this country at every opportunity. They are consistently trying to diminish our power and military.[10] They reject our nation's heritage, its values, and its very founding. They want to dilute our sovereignty by subsuming us in a larger international collective and by eradicating our borders.

This is the key to understanding the left today. They don't merely oppose specific American policies, they oppose our long-standing societal values, and they resent the institutions and culture that arose from those values. They have little use for liberty because it limits their ability to impose their political vision. They want to take more of your money and spend it on *their* priorities. And they want to dictate the most minute details of your life, decreeing what kind of straws you can drink from, what kind of lightbulbs you can use, and what kind of power your home can use.

The founders wisely worried that future generations might take liberty for granted. Going well beyond that, the left seeks to redefine liberty as selfishness. If you drive a car, or eat meat, or take a long shower, or fly to visit your relatives, or own a gun, you're not exercising your freedom, you're now sinning against our whole society. It's not easy to turn a nation against its founding ideals, but with its relentless assault on our liberty, traditions, and values, that is exactly what the left aims to do. This is a fairly new problem. Americans have always taken pride in this country's exceptionalism and its unusual goodness. But the left seems to be on a mission to erode our natural patriotism. As a result, Democrats increasingly denounce America in ways we've rarely heard from our leaders, such as New York governor Andrew Cuomo declaring that "America was never that great,"[11] former attorney general Eric Holder claiming, "This notion of [America's] greatness never in fact really existed,"[12] and Michelle Obama saying, "For the first time in my adult life, I am really proud of my country."

AN "INFORMED PATRIOTISM"

In his farewell address, President Ronald Reagan addressed the resurgence of national pride during his tenure in office, what he called the "new patriotism." While he was gratified that patriotism was rebounding, he knew that for this positive attitude to endure it must reach deep into our national soul. He clarified that patriotism is not blind love of country or a stubborn sense that your country can do no wrong. "This national feeling is good," he said, "but it won't count for much, and it won't last unless it's grounded in thoughtfulness and knowledge. An informed patriotism is what we want."[13]

This makes perfect sense. To maintain national cohesiveness, our citizens should unite in their love for the country based on the ideals that set this nation apart. Until relatively recently, this was not controversial. Immigrants seeking U.S. citizenship have to learn about our Constitution and our legal system so they'll develop an informed patriotism that ensures their loyalty to the values that underlie and guarantee our liberties.

The importance of an informed patriotism among our citizenry is one reason why I oppose amnesty for illegal immigrants and believe strongly that for America to retain a robust national identity, immigration should be a controlled and orderly process. The left, however, depicts this type of patriotism as racist and border enforcement as anti-American. They say a border wall contradicts who we are as a people. We should be an open refuge to all people at all times. Border enforcement advocates reject that notion outright, seeing the United States as a melting pot of different peoples united behind shared ideas—that is, assimilation.

A person does not have to be born in America to become American. Dinesh D'Souza became a citizen in 1991. Though born in India, he rightly considers himself American. He notes that an American could live in India for forty years and even become an Indian citizen, but he could not "become Indian," and Indians wouldn't consider such a person an Indian. Being an Indian, he says, "is entirely a matter of

birth and blood. You become Indian by having Indian parents." And
that's the norm throughout the world, but America is unique because
"becoming American is less a function of birth or blood and more a
function of embracing a set of ideas." [14]

National pride is a natural, wholesome, and even necessary sentiment. Our national security depends on our common love of
country—our collective commitment to the American idea and our
firm recognition that America is worth defending precisely because it
is exceptional. When you abandon the rule of law and grant amnesty to
those who are here illegally, you undermine the legal and orderly flow of
people into this country, their assimilation into our culture, the adoption
of our shared ideas, our common commitment to our national interests,
and our shared willingness to preserve and defend those interests.

But while our national ideals are universal in their truth, American
patriotism involves more than a consensus about a set of principles,
no matter how noble. It involves embracing our national identity as
well—our history as a nation. "We must know . . . not only our creed
but also our culture," wrote historian Wilfred McClay. "We need to take
aboard fully all that was entailed in our forbears' bold assertion that all
human beings are created equal in the eyes of the Creator and that they
bear an inherent dignity that cannot be taken away from them. But we
also need to remember, and teach others to remember, the meaning of
Lexington and Concord, and Independence Hall, and Gettysburg, and
Promontory summit, and Pointe du Hoc, and Birmingham, and West
Berlin, and countless other places and moments of spirit and sacrifice
in the American past. . . ." [15]

Already in the 1980s, President Reagan was distressed by the
inroads being made by "blame America first" types. He lamented the
dissemination of anti-American messages in our schools, culture, and
media. "Are we doing a good enough job teaching our children what
America is and what she represents in the long history of the world?"
he asked. He noted that people thirty-five years of age and older "grew
up in a different America." A love of country and for its institutions

was instilled in them. "If you didn't get these things from your family you got them from the neighborhood, from the father down the street who fought in Korea or the family who lost someone at Anzio," or even from the popular culture. "The movies celebrated democratic values and implicitly reinforced the idea that America was special. TV was like that, too, through the mid-sixties."[16]

Reagan continued, "But now, we're about to enter the nineties, and some things have changed." Younger parents, he said, weren't sure that it was right to teach their children to appreciate America in the same way. In the popular culture, "well-grounded patriotism is no longer the style. Our spirit is back, but we haven't reinstitutionalized it. We've got to do a better job of getting across that America is freedom—freedom of speech, freedom of religion, freedom of enterprise." Freedom, he noted, was the exception in history, not the rule, and it must be nurtured and defended. "Freedom is special and rare," he said. "It's fragile; it needs protection."[17]

Yes, patriotism must be based on something more than a reflexive loyalty to country, and our appreciation for freedom must be cultivated. That's why I've spent considerable time on my radio and television shows focusing on history and explaining the importance of our founding documents. I'm grateful for this opportunity because I am fascinated by our nation's origins and subsequent history. I am convinced that the more information Americans have about our actual history—not the revisionist version spewed by leftist writers and academics who want to tear down this country—the more they will appreciate America. I want to help set the record straight to promote our informed patriotism.

As I've said repeatedly, we must fight harder to protect what makes this country great: our Constitution, our values, the equal application of our laws, and the American people, who work hard every day, pay their taxes, and love their country.

While President Reagan is correct that freedom has been rare historically, it is at the crux of our own founding. It is who we are and what we've always been. It is a major part of our uniqueness. The colonists came to this land in search of religious and political liberty, and they established free, self-governing colonies. They eventually broke from the British not as rebels or revolutionaries but to recapture the freedom that Britain had previously afforded us through its "benign neglect" of the colonies. After the War of Independence, they were determined to form a government under which they could prosper as a free people. Throughout our history, preserving our liberty has been the bond that has united us as a people. Our ancestors sacrificed their lives to ensure they and their descendants would live in freedom.

I now want to take a closer look at why America is exceptional. Let's review how the colonists organized themselves into free, self-governing societies and the founding generation built freedom principles into our founding documents.

COVENANTAL SELF-GOVERNANCE

America's experience with democratic rule and consent of the governed long predated our formal break with Britain and our independence. This rich history of liberty was until relatively recently engrained in our body politic, and both major political parties were committed to the tradition. It was in that context that outgoing President Reagan noted the assaults on liberty that were routinely occurring in the United States, and reminded Americans of this nation's greatness and why reinvigorating its dedication to liberty was imperative if America was to remain exceptional. President Donald Trump has now taken up the mantle of defending America's liberty, reinforcing her greatness, and reigniting her entrepreneurial energy. Both Reagan and Trump are heirs to a legacy of freedom that began with the colonization of this land.

In 1620, the passengers of the *Mayflower* reached the New World five hundred miles north of their intended destination and outside the jurisdiction of the Virginia Company, from which they had obtained a land patent permitting them to form an English colony. The uncertainties of being remote from a higher government authority motivated

them to establish their own government, though they pledged continued loyalty to the British crown.[18] While still aboard the ship, forty-
one of the 102 passengers signed the Mayflower Compact, agreeing to
establish a colony dedicated to God's glory and the advancement of the
Christian faith.[19]

This was a "covenant" to combine themselves "together in a civil
body politic." As self-governing people, they would "enact, constitute
and frame such just and equal Laws, Ordinances, Acts, Constitutions
and Offices from time to time, as shall be thought most meet and con-
venient for the general good of the Colony, unto which we promise all
due submission and obedience." A century and a half before the Declaration of Independence affirmed the "self-evident" truth "that all men
are created equal," these bold pilgrims bound themselves together as
equal men to form their own civil government.[20] "What was remarkable about this particular contract," writes historian Paul Johnson,
"was that it was not between a servant and a master, or a people and a
king, but between like-minded individuals and each other, with God
as a witness and symbolic co-signatory."[21]

This compact for self-governance was modeled on church covenants
that empowered congregations to choose their ministers—a power that
came directly from Jesus Christ, not derivatively from a higher church
authority.[22] This pattern of government by social contract was common
throughout the New England settlements. In *The New England Clergy
and the American Revolution*, Alice Baldwin demonstrates "how the
New England clergy preserved, extended, and popularized the essential
doctrines of political philosophy, thus making familiar to every church-
going New Englander long before 1763 not only the doctrines of natural
right, the social contract, and the right of resistance but also the fundamental principle of American constitutional law, that government, like
its citizens, is bounded by law and when it transcends its authority it
acts illegally." Baldwin maintains there is "a direct line of descent from
seventeenth-century philosophy to the doctrines underlying the American Revolution and the making of written constitutions."[23]

John Winthrop, captain of the Puritan ship *Arbella*, articulated the Puritans' mission in his sermon "A Model of Christian Charity," which includes this now-famous passage: "For we must consider that we shall be as a city upon a hill. The eyes of all people are upon us. So that if we shall deal falsely with our God in this work we have undertaken, and so cause Him to withdraw His present help from us, we shall be made a story and a by-word through the world."[24] Thomas Hooker also articulated the connection between covenantal Christianity and governance—that early church governments modeled democratic government—in his Fundamental Orders of Connecticut in 1639: "[W]ell knowing where a people are gathered together the word of God requires that to maintain the peace and union of such a people there should be an orderly and decent government established according to God, [we] do therefore associate and conjoin ourselves to be as one public state or commonwealth; and . . . enter into combination and confederation together, to maintain and pursue the liberty and purity of the gospel of our Lord Jesus which we now profess. . . ."[25]

Likewise, theologian John Cotton of Massachusetts wrote in 1645, "It is evident by the light of nature that all civil relations are founded in covenant. . . . [T]here is no other way given where a people . . . can be united or combined together in one visible body, to stand by mutual relation, fellow-members of the same body, but only by mutual covenant. . . ."[26] Rhode Island also based its political governance on church covenantal doctrine. Its charter stated that its government should be "democraticall, that is a government held by the free and voluntary consent of all, or the greater part of the free inhabitants."[27]

During this period, observe Peter Marshall and David Manuel, the people "were beginning to discover a basic truth which would be a major foundation stone of God's new nation, and which by 1776 would be declared self-evident: that in the eyes of their Creator, all men were of equal value." It was when "we began to become aware of ourselves as a *nation*, a body of believers which had a national identity as a people chosen by God for a specific purpose: to be not just 'a city upon a hill,' but a veritable citadel of Light in a darkened world. . . . Americans were rediscovering God's plan to join them together by His Spirit in the common cause of advancing His Kingdom. Furthermore, they were returning to another aspect of His plan—that they were to operate not as lone individualists, but in covenanted groups."[28]

As you can see, our Constitution didn't arise in a vacuum. The framers sifted through and borrowed some of the greatest ideas for constitutional governance from Athens, Rome, Locke, and Montesquieu. But they also called upon the ideas of social contract and representative government that had developed in their churches from the time of their early colonization of this great land.

CHRISTIAN AND ENLIGHTENMENT INFLUENCES

The early American colonists were overwhelmingly Christian, but some academics downplay the importance of their faith, claiming America's founding documents were grounded more in secular enlightenment principles than in Christianity. By the time our nation was founded, these scholars claim, the people's religious spirit had given way to secular ideas sweeping over from Europe. While it's true that religious fervor waned in the beginning of the eighteenth century, America experienced a profound religious revival beginning in the 1730s called the Great Awakening, when the fiery sermons of evangelical preachers like Jonathan Edwards and George Whitefield rekindled the people's passion for Jesus Christ. This evangelical ethos continued through the Revolutionary War and our founding period. "The essential difference between the American Revolution and the French Revolution," notes Paul Johnson, "is that the American Revolution, in its origins, was a religious event, whereas the French Revolution was an anti-religious event. That fact was to shape the American Revolution from start to finish and determine the nature of the independent state it brought into being."[29]

University of Dallas professor M. E. Bradford extensively re-

searched the religious preferences of the signers of the Declaration
and Constitution and discovered that the great majority of them were
devout Christians. Fifty-two of the fifty-six signers of the Declaration
and the vast majority of the signers of the Constitution were church-
going, orthodox Christians.[30]

Admittedly the religious beliefs of some high-profile founders are
hard to pin down. For example, Thomas Jefferson may have been a
Unitarian, as he believed in a superintending God even if he doubted
the deity of Christ. And while Benjamin Franklin may have been a
Deist at some point in his life, some of his actions contradicted the
core Deist belief that God created the universe and then left it to its
own devices without his supervision. Franklin, at a difficult point during the Constitutional Convention, called the delegates to prayer, and
in the prayer asserted that God governs the affairs of men. This would
have been pointless had Franklin believed in the noninterventionist
god of the Deists. "I have lived, Sir, a long time and the longer I live,
the more convincing proofs I see of this truth—that God governs in
the affairs of men," said Franklin. "I therefore beg leave to move—that
henceforth prayers imploring the assistance of Heaven, and tis bless-
ings on our deliberations, be held in this Assembly every morning
before we proceed to business, and that one or more of the Clergy of
this City be requested to officiate in that service."[31]

Though Jefferson wrote the initial draft of the Declaration, it was
thoroughly edited by a congressional committee chaired by the pious
John Adams, resulting in some eighty edits and the deletion of almost
five hundred words.[32] Jefferson later admitted he was not seeking to
articulate his personal beliefs but to draft a corporate statement of
Congress "intended to be an expression of the American mind."[33]

While I believe the evidence shows that the Christian worldview
played the dominant role in the creation of America's founding documents, there's no question Enlightenment ideas were also an influence.
Beyond just getting our history straight, the reason this matters is that
leftists credit secular Enlightenment ideas for our freedom tradition.

They incorrectly see the Christian religion as authoritarian and incompatible with political liberty. If that's true and if our Christian faith and values were not instrumental in developing our liberties, then leftists have one more argument against preserving our traditional values and demonizing people of faith.

But the founders saw no contradiction between faith and reason, and I certainly don't, either. "For most of them, the Bible and plain reason went hand in hand, moral example for moral example," writes Michael Novak. "Even for those few (such as Thomas Paine) for whom common sense and the Bible were antithesis, plain reason led to belief in God. . . . Far from being contrary to reason, faith strengthens reason. To employ a poor analogy, faith is a little like a telescope that magnifies what the naked eye of reason sees unaided. For the founders, it was evident that faith in the God of Abraham, Isaac, and Jacob magnifies human reason, encourages virtue, and sharpens a zest for liberty."[34]

Similarly, historian Wilfred McClay argues, "It might seem logical to us today that there would be a necessary incompatibility and antagonism between the passionate Bible-based Protestant religious faiths of colonists like Edwards and the methodical new science embraced by the likes of Franklin . . . but this was not quite the way things looked to Americans of the time. In the Anglo-American world of the eighteenth century, the spirit of Protestantism and the spirit of science were not seen to be in fundamental conflict with one another. Belief in some version of the biblical God and belief in an ordered and knowable universe were not seen as at all incompatible."[35]

AMBITION MUST COUNTERACT AMBITION

Admittedly, I talk about the Constitution a lot. So I want to explain here in a little more depth why I think it is such an amazing document and how it gave rise to this nation's unrivaled greatness. What is so unique about our Constitution? The British, from which much of our freedom tradition is derived, do not have a formal, written constitution but rather a system that developed organically over centuries. British prime minister William Gladstone recognized this when he called the British constitution "the most subtle organism which has ever proceeded from progressive history."[36]

Our Constitution was different. It didn't evolve over centuries but was brilliantly crafted by a gifted group of men who were learned students of religion, history, political science, and comparative government. They understood the important distinction between pure democracies and republics, and they were aware of the shortcomings of the Athenian and Roman constitutions. Furthermore, as shown by Alexander Hamilton, James Madison, and John Jay in the *Federalist Papers*, they knew what had caused the failures of the Articles of Confederation, the colonists' first stab at a constitution when they broke from Britain. The drafters of the Articles were jaded by their experience with the British monarchy. They were so fearful that a robust federal government would lead to tyranny that they created a loose confederation of states with a central government so weak that it lacked a federal judiciary or the authority to tax citizens or raise an army. In trying to maximize their liberties, they imperiled them by not giving the federal government sufficient power to protect citizens against domestic and foreign threats.

George Washington believed the weakness of the federal government under the Articles was leading "rapidly to a crisis" and threatening the very existence of government. He feared we were running from one extreme to another. "What astonishing changes a few years are capable of producing," he observed. "I am told that even respectable characters speak of a monarchical form of government without horror. What a triumph for the advocates of despotism to find that we are incapable of governing ourselves and that systems founded on the basis of equal liberty are merely ideal and fallacious. Would to God that wise measures may be taken in time to avert the consequences we have but too much reason to apprehend."

When the delegates met in Philadelphia to re-form the Union, they understood their unique historical position in mankind's struggle for individual liberty.[37] They knew they faced a monumental challenge in trying to design a constitutional framework for republican government that would weather the test of time. Alexander Hamilton noted in Federalist 1 that many people at the time believed fate had placed upon the early Americans the challenge of determining whether "societies of men" were capable of establishing a good system of government by their own reasoned reflection or whether they were destined to adopt their governments by "accident and force."[38] "They were engaged in one of the great experiments in the annals of politics, attempting to use the example of previous republics to avert those republics' fate," McClay observes. "They used the new science of politics in trying to remedy the fatal flaws of republics past. They used history to defy history."[39]

They originally intended to amend the Articles to correct their deficiencies but soon realized they needed an entirely new constitution. They would design a system of government that would maximize individual liberties, not just because of their experience with British tyranny but because, as Christians, they firmly believed the words of the Declaration, "that all men are . . . endowed by their Creator with certain unalienable rights, that among those are life, liberty and the pursuit of happiness." That is, they recognized that their rights derived from God, not government, and embraced the scriptural revelation that men were created in God's image with intrinsic worth and dignity and were therefore entitled to liberty.[40] Or as Joe Biden says, "All men and women are created, by the, you know, you know, the thing."

They further believed that man is corrupted by sin and that, left to his own devices, he would subjugate other men. James Madison was clear on this point in Federalist 51: "Ambition must be made to counteract ambition. The interest of the man must be connected with the constitutional rights of the place. It may be a reflection on human nature, that such devices should be necessary to control the abuses of government. But what is government itself, but the greatest of all reflections on human nature? If men were angels, no government would be necessary. If angels were to govern men, neither external nor internal controls on government would be necessary. In framing a government which is to be administered by men over men, the great difficulty lies in this: you must first enable the government to control the governed; and in the next place oblige it to control itself."

Madison wasn't naive enough to believe that citizens' rights would be secured by virtue of a grant on a piece of parchment. The delegates would need to design a system that would ensure liberty by leveraging man's weaknesses instead of ignoring them—pitting men against other men and levels and branches of government against one another. These competing institutions under the control of fallen men would keep each other in check, thereby maximizing individual liberties. "This policy of supplying, by opposite and rival interests, the defect of better motives, might be traced through the whole system of human affairs, private as well as public," Madison explained. "We see it particularly displayed in all the subordinate distributions of power, where the constant aim is to divide and arrange the several offices in such a manner as that each may be a check on the other—that the private interest of every individual may be a sentinel over the public rights. These inventions of prudence cannot be less requisite in the distribution of the supreme powers of the State."

Had the framers crafted a pure democracy, there would have been no safeguards against encroachments on citizens' unalienable rights. The rights of the minority would have been subject to abuses at the hands of the majority—a concept Madison called the "tyranny of the majority."[41]

The delegates' challenge was to establish a federal government sufficiently strong to protect its citizens from domestic and foreign threats but without enough power to imperil the people's liberties. Their solution was to build into the Constitution a scheme of governmental powers and limitations. The government would have defined (enumerated) powers, but there would also be specific limitations on government to guard against its natural tendency to expand at the expense of individual liberties. They reserved for the states those rights not granted to the federal government and distributed federal power among three separate, coequal branches of government.

"VIRTUE IS OUR BEST SECURITY"

As realists, the framers understood that even with such institutional checks on government as federalism, the separation of powers, and subsequently the Bill of Rights, there was no absolute guarantee against tyranny. They knew liberty would not be self-sustaining. Though they understood man's sinful nature, they believed that by relying on God he could become more virtuous. They reasoned that the Constitution would have a greater likelihood of succeeding if the people adhered to Christian moral standards and aspired to a virtuous society. "A free society demands a higher level of virtue than a tyranny," writes Michael Novak, "which no other moral energy has heretofore proven capable of inspiring except Judaism and Christianity." [42]

In his Farewell Address, George Washington warned his fellow countrymen against adopting the militant antireligious philosophy of the French. "Of all the dispositions and habits which lead to political prosperity, religion and morality are indispensable supports," said Washington. "In vain would that man claim the tribute of patriotism, who should labor to subvert these great pillars of human happiness, these firmest props of the duties of men and citizens. The mere politician . . . ought to respect and to cherish them. . . . Let it simply be asked: Where is the security for property, for reputation, for life, if the sense of religious obligation desert the oaths which are the instruments of investigation in courts of justice? And let us with caution indulge the supposition that morality can be maintained without religion. . . . reason and experience both forbid us to expect that national morality can prevail in exclusion of religious principle." [43]

The founders strongly insisted on this point. "Our Constitution was made only for a moral and religious people," said John Adams. "It is wholly inadequate to the government of any other." He argued that "virtue must underlay all institutional arrangements if they are to be healthy and strong. The principles of democracy are as easily corrupted as human nature is corrupted."[44] Samuel Adams observed, "We may look up to Armies for our defense, but virtue is our best security. It is not possible that any state should long remain free, where virtue is not supremely honored."[45]

Almost half a century after the Constitution was ratified, in his famous *Democracy in America*, Tocqueville observed the strong connection between America's religious character and its political system. "It must never be forgotten that religion gave birth to Anglo-American society," he wrote. "In the United States religion is therefore commingled with all the habits of the nation and all the feelings of patriotism."

"OUR ENDURING CONSTITUTION"

Due to the brilliance and foresight of the framers and the American people's dedication to liberty, the Constitution survived the trials and tribulations of the growing republic, including the brutal Civil War, which tested it to its limits. In 1861 President Abraham Lincoln commented on the foundational importance of the liberty principle expressed in the Declaration of Independence to the endurance of the Constitution. The Declaration's expression "liberty to all," noted Lincoln, "was most happy and fortunate." He said we could have declared our independence from Britain with or without it, "but without it, we could not have secured our free government and consequent prosperity." Our forefathers wouldn't have pressed on if they'd had nothing more to fight for than "a mere change of masters." The expression of the principle of liberty has proved an "apple of gold," and "the Union and the Constitution, are the picture of silver subsequently framed around it. The picture was made, not to conceal, or destroy the apple but to adorn, and preserve it. The picture was made for the apple—not the apple for the picture."[46]

A few years later, in his Gettysburg Address, Lincoln might have had that metaphor in mind when he reaffirmed that the United States was "conceived in liberty, and dedicated to the proposition that all men are created equal." I noted above that in Federalist 1, Hamilton recognized that Americans saw themselves as having undertaken the responsibility of determining whether free people could establish a system of good government. Lincoln seemed to invoke that sentiment when he said, "Now we are engaged in a great civil war, testing whether that nation, or any nation so conceived and dedicated, can long endure." In his conclusion Lincoln answered the question: "we here highly resolve that these dead shall not have died in vain—that this nation, under God, shall have a new birth of freedom—and that government of the people, by the people, and for the people, shall not perish from the earth."[47]

Hamilton and the other framers believed that their designed structure of government would endure and that freedom would prosper under it. Lincoln was reporting that great Americans since the founding had vindicated the framers' vision. Now, in the midst of the Civil War, Americans and our Constitution were undergoing their greatest challenge yet, and we would meet the challenge by preserving our unique system of government and sparking a rebirth of the liberties it guaranteed. McClay summed it up nicely, saying that Lincoln redefined the war "not merely as a war for the preservation of the Union but as a war for the preservation of the democratic idea . . . which America exemplified in the world."[48]

In assessing the United States Constitution in 1878, British prime minister William Gladstone declared, "The American Constitution is, so far as I can see, the most wonderful work ever struck off at a given time by the brain and purpose of man. It has had a century of trial, under the pressure of exigencies caused by an expansion unexampled in point of rapidity and range; and its exemption from formal change, though not entire, has certainly proved the sagacity of the constructors, and the stubborn strength of the fabric."[49] Gladstone's point was that our Constitution had stood the test of time, surviving vast territorial expansion (with the Louisiana Purchase and territories acquired from Mexico) and deep internal conflicts.

Despite the myriad cautions the framers incorporated into the Constitution, they knew, as did Abraham Lincoln decades later, that political freedom would be difficult to sustain. Human nature being what it is, there would always be internal and external threats to our liberty. This is why, in his remarks to Kiwanis International in 1987, President Ronald Reagan said, "It is time that we ask ourselves if we still know the freedoms that were intended for us by the Founding Fathers and if we will pass on to these young people the freedoms we knew in our youth, because freedom is never more than one generation away from extinction. It has to be fought for and defended by each generation."[50]

THE PROGRESSIVE ERA

Over time well-meaning but pernicious forces began chipping away at the pillars of our constitutional system. I have come to believe that the momentum against our founding principles crystallized in the Progressive Era, roughly during the first two decades of the twentieth century, though the movement's political and intellectual roots stretched back into the preceding decades among journalists, novelists, political scientists, and social scientists.[51] I would strongly urge you to familiarize yourself with this period of our history. It will give you a much clearer insight into today's left.

Concerned by societal disruptions and wealth inequalities they believed were caused by the industrial revolution and capitalism's excesses, Progressives targeted corrupt trusts and mercenary capitalists.[52] For example, Henry Demarest Lloyd demonized Standard Oil Company in his book *Wealth Against Commonwealth*, and economist Thorstein Veblen denounced the wealthy in his *The Theory of the Leisure Class*.[53]

Socialists and social justice reformers focused on the problems of urbanization and advocated for the urban poor. Let me stress that I strongly believe in helping the poor, but I don't believe the answer is the government seizing control of the economy and suppressing individual freedom in the name of "equality." Of course there should be a safety net for the needy, but socialists constantly exploit the poor as a pretext for accumulating more power for themselves and confiscating more of society's wealth for their own ends.

Progressive academics pressed for social justice reforms following the example of European socialists. Advocates of women's suffrage joined in the struggle for social justice.[54] Progressives rejected the founders' belief in, and the biblical teachings on, the depravity of the human condition, believing instead that people are essentially good and perfectible, and that evil resulted from imperfect social systems and corrupt institutions that were impeding man from reaching his true potential.[55]

But despite their high view of man, they didn't believe the solution lay in empowering individuals with greater liberty or authority. They dismissed the notion of rugged individualism and laissez-faire capitalism, which were central to our founding and our subsequent history, and placed their faith in government.[56] Big business was the problem; big government was the answer. "This is the universal human purpose of the state," said John Burgess, a progressive political scientist. "We may call it the perfection of humanity; the civilization of the world; the perfect development of the human reason, and its attainment to universal command over individualism; the apotheosis of man. . . . The national state is the most perfect organ which has yet been attained in the civilization of the world for the interpretation of the human consciousness of right. It furnishes the best vantage ground as yet reached for the contemplation of the purpose of the sojourn of mankind upon earth."[57]

Progressives dismissed the founders' view that man was born free. Our rights were not God-given or inalienable. They were bestowed on us by government and could be denied when expedient or in the state's interests.[58] Progressive intellectuals dismissed the founders' conception of republican government as a social compact among free people—government by consent of the governed. "The present tendency, then, in American political theory is to disregard the once dominant ideas of natural rights and the social contract, although it must be admitted that the political scientists are more agreed upon this point than is the general public," wrote University of Chicago political scientist Charles Merriam, a leading progressive thinker. "The origin of the state is regarded, not as the result of a deliberate agreement among men, but as the result of historical development, instinctive rather than conscious; and rights are considered to have their source not in nature, but in law."[59] He further explained, "The notion that political society and government are based upon a contract between independent individuals and that such a contract is the sole source of political obligation is regarded as no longer tenable."[60]

Philosopher and educational reformer John Dewey was one of the Progressive movement's leading players. "The state is a moral organism, of which government is one organ," wrote Dewey. "Only by participating in the common purpose as it works for the common good can individual human beings realize their true individualities and become truly free."[61] He insisted that freedom is not "something that individuals have as a ready-made possession." Rather, "it is something to be achieved." Even more cynically, he wrote, "Natural rights and natural liberties exist only in the kingdom of mythological social zoology."[62]

As businessmen were successfully relying on scientific advancements, Progressives believed that government could do so as well, which also led to their increasing reliance on and expansion of the federal government.[63] As such, they saw the concept of natural rights, the Declaration of Independence, and the Constitution as obstacles constituting formidable, institutional restrictions on the power of government to address societal problems. They didn't conceal their desire to move beyond the Constitution's system of limited government toward a more energetic, centralized government to tackle social and economic conditions that, in their view, the founders didn't anticipate and provided no mechanism for handling in the Constitution.[64] "Progressivism . . . amounts to an argument in favor of progressing, or moving beyond, the political principles of the American founding," writes Hillsdale College professor Ronald Pestritto. "Progressives sought to enlarge vastly the scope of the national government for the purpose of responding to a set of economic and social conditions, that, it was contended, could not have been envisioned during the founding era, and for which the Founders' limited, constitutional government was inadequate."[65]

Progressives believed that government in the able hands of a self-appointed elite could advance mankind toward societal perfection.[66] They looked toward an administrative state, delegating government powers to federal bureaucracies and empowering them to more closely manage and control business and the affairs of men. The administrative bureaucracy was to consist of nonpartisan "experts" who would direct the restructuring of the social world and implement the larger goals of governing powers.[67] Why couldn't society's vast and varied problems be managed by these experts? These enlightened managers presumed that their expertise, backed by state power, could finally eradicate poverty and war.[68] "Progressivism was an outlook that cared deeply about the common people and knew, far better than they did, what was best for them," writes Wilfred McClay. "Thus there was always in Progressivism a certain implicit paternalism, a condescension that was all the more unattractive for being unacknowledged."[69]

Progressives nominally advocated a purer form of democracy in contrast to the founders' notion of republican government. For example, Progressives advocated the direct election of senators, while the Constitution originally mandated they be selected by state legislatures. However, Progressives actually diminished the people's power by delegating such extensive power to the administrative agencies.[70] They disfavored private property, and some were openly socialist. The federal government, they believed, should have greater powers to protect people against corporate abuses.

The reformers favored an expansion of the public sector and a corresponding shrinking of the private sector. The state had to expand its size, reach, and control in the name of protecting the individual.[71] Enlightened bureaucrats saw themselves as better equipped to spend people's money than the people themselves.[72] They also believed it was the government's duty to redistribute resources and control prices and methods of manufacture.[73] Accordingly, the government needed greater revenues, which gave rise to the federal income tax as codified in the Sixteenth Amendment to the Constitution, passed in 1913.[74] The Progressive movement thus chipped away at the founders' ideal of equal opportunity under the law in favor of equal outcomes.

PROGRESSIVISM BEGETS PROGRESSIVISM

Statist politicians continued to expand the federal government and undermine the Constitution throughout the twentieth century, particularly Presidents Woodrow Wilson, Franklin Roosevelt, and Lyndon Johnson. Then, in the 1960s and 1970s, a violent, extremist left-wing movement emerged. At that time, the radical left fought for outright revolution through such militant groups as the Weather Underground, the May 19 Communist Organization, and the Black Liberation Army. When their revolutionary dreams failed, leftists adopted a long-term strategy of the "long march through the institutions," implanting themselves in the education system, the media, much of the legal profession, and the entertainment industry, aiming to subvert these institutions from within and transform them into tools of the revolution.

Their patience has paid them huge dividends. Now firmly in control of these institutions as well as the formidable social media companies, the left subjects us to daily barrages of left-wing propaganda.[75] Along with many other conservative media personalities, I do my best to fight back against this torrent of disinformation and leftist dogma. However, although their arguments are often transparently false, the left's uniform control over these key institutions gives them a crucial advantage in spreading their message and limiting the circulation of opposing views. What we need is our own long march through the institutions, with courageous young conservatives wading back into what is now hostile territory and reclaiming a space for our dissenting views.

During the 1960s, profound changes occurred in societal attitudes and mores, characterized by a pronounced focus on self-discovery, including through recreational drug use and self-gratification. People abandoned traditional values for moral relativism. Instead of conforming to external societal norms, people embraced self-liberation and self-exploration, looking inside themselves for moral guidance.[76] This was a radical departure from the past, which had recognized that the inner self of flawed human beings was not a reliable moral compass.[77]

When a society rejects moral absolutes, it has no basis to protect individual rights against the tyranny of the majority—because without such standards, any action, no matter how good or evil, and any deprivation of our liberties, can be rationalized. As scholar M. Stanton Evans declared, "Moral relativism, however derived, must undermine the very possibility of freedom. No system of political liberty has ever been created from such notions, nor is it theoretically conceivable that one could."[78] All forms of despotism throughout history, Evans observed, have sprung from moral relativism. For freedom to exist there must be basic assumptions about the intrinsic dignity of human beings. It is this Judeo-Christian assumption that underlies the belief that our rights are God-given and must be protected not just against individual dictators and despots but against the tyranny of the majority.

STOPPING THE PROGRESSIVE JUGGERNAUT

It's no coincidence that today's leftists regard themselves as "progressives," as their ideas clearly trace back to the Progressive Era. But in fairness, it should be noted that while yesterday's Progressives seemed to share some of the utopian ends of their modern counterparts, they were less radical, seeking to achieve their goals gradually.[79]

Since the 1960s we've witnessed the steady advance of progressivism and statism and the corresponding erosion of our liberties. Progressives have continued to become more extreme yet have successfully tarred conservatives as the extremists just for striving to restore and preserve what is noble and good in society. The only antidote for this madness is to fight fire with fire—to match their energy and commitment with our own and to dedicate ourselves to reviving the freedom tradition of our founders.

Heritage Foundation scholar William Schambra attributes modern conservatism's success to its grounding in the founders' constitutionalism. There is no question about that. That is one reason I proudly identify as a constitutional conservative and why I strongly endorse the message of my friend Mark Levin, in his many books on constitutional principles. The left's assault on our ideals goes back to our country's first principles. They don't just reject conservative policy prescriptions; they reject freedom itself as it was understood by the framers.

For younger generations of Americans, the notion of liberty has become an abstraction. They don't regard big government as an enemy of their individual liberties because they have been raised during an era of big government, and neither their parents nor their schools have instilled in them a proper appreciation for liberty and the sacrifices required to sustain it. They see no downside in government—rather than individuals, churches, and other charitable entities—providing for the needs of others. They don't instinctively recoil at the idea of government regulating and even micromanaging the minutiae of our lives. They have become accustomed to the paternalistic attitude that they must be shielded from all adversity and disappointment—a world where everyone gets a trophy and where university campuses train students to be victims rather than self-reliant, constantly on the lookout for "trigger words" and "microaggressions" that could damage their psychic serenity.[80] We do truly have a generation of snowflakes now.

While yesterday's Progressives rejected the framers' structure of limited government, their modern leftist offspring have taken it to a new level, undermining our Constitution every day with legislative, executive, judicial, and administrative overreaches. They also wage war against the civil liberties enshrined in the Bill of Rights—freedom of speech and religion, the right to bear arms, and the protections of citizens concerning unreasonable searches and due process.

Our fight for control of the courts has become a crucial battlefield in our struggle against the left. The left rejects the Constitution itself, which is why their activist judges routinely overwrite its provisions by judicial fiat. If they control the courts they can undo any progress we make at limiting government and protecting our liberties. President Trump has appointed more originalist judges to federal courts than any of his predecessors. This, as much as any other presidential act, has given us hope that we can restore constitutional principles and our tradition of limited government and liberty.

History shows that great nations don't last forever. We must heed Ronald Reagan's warnings to never grow complacent about our liberties and remain ever vigilant against foreign and internal threats against them. The left, through the Democratic Party, is promoting an agenda so radical that if substantially implemented it would divorce America from its founding ideas.

A RISING SUN

Someone shouted an ominous question to Benjamin Franklin when he was leaving Independence Hall after the Constitutional Convention: "Doctor, what have we got? A republic or a monarchy?" Franklin presciently replied, "A republic, if you can keep it." Franklin was laying down the gauntlet to his fellow and future Americans. Would we realize the profundity of the gift we have been given—a governmental structure ingeniously designed to preserve our God-given liberties? Would we guard it with *our* lives, fortunes, and sacred honor? Throughout our history, great leaders have taken Franklin's baton, blessed and reaffirmed it, and passed it forward to future generations. It is now in our hands and we will determine whether our precious liberties will survive. Will we take them for granted or will we safeguard them with the sacred care they require?

With that in mind let me close this chapter with another inspiring anecdote involving Ben Franklin. In his notes summarizing the last day of the Constitutional Convention, James Madison reported, "Whilst the last members were signing [the Constitution], Doctor Franklin, looking towards the Presidents Chair, at the back of which a rising sun happened to be painted, observed to a few members near him, that painters had found it difficult to distinguish in their art a rising from a setting sun. I have, said he, often and often in the course of the Session, and the vicissitudes of my hopes and fears as to its issue, looked at that behind the President without being able to tell whether it was rising or setting: But now at length I have the happiness to know that it is a rising and not a setting Sun." [81]

It is our duty to ensure that our "sun" continues rising. I believe President Trump reveres this nation, its Constitution, and the unique liberty tradition it guarantees. He recognizes the forces that imperil our liberties and is fighting to defeat them every single day of his presidency. We Americans who value our constitutional heritage and who believe in our nation's benevolence and its divinely inspired founding must continue to support the president's efforts.

Having reviewed the importance of our founding principles, how we've slowly veered away from them through the years, and why we must dedicate ourselves to restoring them, I'll detail in the next two chapters the Democrats' thoroughly radical agenda and demonstrate how it will destroy everything that makes America unique unless we join together to thwart it.

CHAPTER TWO

Rise of the Radicals

We conservatives so often point to the extremism of today's Democratic Party that we might risk numbing ourselves to the seismic shift
that has taken place among its ranks. This is important, folks, and so in
the following pages I specify how deep and widespread it is, and how
much further left the party has moved even in the short years since
Obama's term expired—and it was already far too left then.

During the 2008 presidential campaign I repeatedly outlined
Barack Obama's radical past and his far-left views. Too many breezily
dismissed our warnings, and I pray that they do not do so today—or
the tattered flag shown on this book's cover will tear completely in two.

We did tons of investigative reporting on Obama's record—work
that the Obama-worshipping mainstream media mob wouldn't do. We
are one of the only TV shows anywhere that vetted Obama. We took
a deep dive into his associations with militants like Frank Marshall
Davis and ACORN, and revealed Obama's use of the cynical, manipulative tactics of community organizer Saul Alinsky. We also gave you
volumes about his close relationship with Rev. Jeremiah Wright, the
pastor behind the infamous "G-d d—n America" sermon, and an
adherent of the radical black liberation theology.

We reported in depth on Obama's links to leftist extremists Bill Ayers and Bernardine Dohrn, cofounders of the Weather

Underground—a communist revolutionary group that bombed public buildings, including the United States Capitol, the Pentagon, and New York police stations.[1] After the Pentagon bombing Ayers and Dohrn became fugitives. When the Weather Underground issued a "Declaration of a State of War" against the United Sates government in 1970, Dohrn was placed on the FBI's 10 Most Wanted List.[2] Obama claimed Ayers was just "a guy who lives in my neighborhood," but I told you differently, and I was proved right when it emerged that Obama and Ayers were partners in the Chicago Annenberg Challenge, an education foundation that funneled more than $100 million to community organizers and radical education activists.[3] With one exception, the media wholly ignored Obama's relationship with Ayers. Had Donald Trump had such a nefarious relationship, you can be sure the media would have asked him about it a thousand times, which is a perfect example of why American patriots don't trust the media mob.

Don't listen to anyone who tells you Obama wasn't a leftist president, and especially don't listen to the liberal media. They lied to you throughout the Obama years, and they're still lying today. I wish Americans had heeded our warnings because Obama was serious when he vowed to fundamentally transform the nation. He proved it during his eight long years in office by ramming through Obamacare on a party-line vote, appointing activist judges, issuing unconstitutional executive orders, downsizing our military, traveling the world apologizing for America, engineering long-term economic malaise, waging war on coal and coal miners, haranguing the cops, conferring legal status on more than one million illegal aliens via Deferred Action for Childhood Arrivals (DACA), and aggravating race relations in this country.

I'm not rehashing the Obama-Biden years out of some obsession. This book is about America's present and future, but we must learn from past mistakes—and as a society we made a major mistake in failing to recognize the threat Obama posed to the republic. Our battle against the left is a constant, never-ending struggle in which we must never lower our guard. Though Obama may seem less extreme than today's crop of hard-core leftists, his presidency paved the way for their ascendancy. He moved society as far left as was politically possible at the time. However, as shown by the backlash after the Democrats forced through Obamacare—when they lost sixty-three House seats, control of the House, and six Senate seats[4]—there were limits to how far Obama could take his transformation. We should remember this shellacking when Democrats and Never Trumpers gloat over the Republicans' loss of congressional seats in the 2018 midterms.

Even as Obama remade America, he sometimes projected a false image of moderation and bipartisanship that his media cheerleaders obediently amplified. He famously pretended to oppose same-sex marriage until he decided it was politically feasible to announce he had "evolved" on the issue. Even his adviser David Axelrod later admitted that during the 2008 campaign Obama lied in saying he opposed same-sex marriage—for reasons of political expedience.[5] He downplayed his health-care ambitions, claiming to reject a government-run, single-payer health-care system even though years earlier he'd privately told his labor union supporters that that was exactly what he wanted.[6] But try as he might, Obama couldn't always hide his militant partisanship.

I'll never forget his revealing utterances. While referring to his political opponents in a 2008 speech, he said, "If they bring a knife to the fight, we bring a gun."[7] All throughout Obama's first campaign for president, he mentioned me more than a dozen times—even threatening me by saying, "I'll put Mr. Burgess [an Obama supporter] up against Sean Hannity. He'll tear him up." He told his supporters they were "his ambassadors" and urged them to "argue with [their neighbors]; get in their face."[8] Implying Republicans were lazy obstructionists, he said, "We're down there pushing, pushing on the car. Every once in a while we'll look up and see the Republicans standing there. They're just standing there fanning themselves—sipping on a Slurpee."[9] Obama also often displayed his socialist leanings. He famously told Joe the Plumber, "I think when you spread the wealth around, it's good for everybody."[10] And let's never forget his infamous line: "If you've got a business, you didn't build that. Somebody else made that happen."[11]

Today's Democratic leaders and presidential candidates dispensed with even the pretense of moderation. Whereas Obama at least pretended you could keep your health insurance plan, which was named "Lie of the Year" by the left-leaning PolitiFact,[12] Senator Kamala Harris launched her presidential bid with a promise of eliminating private insurance. Every one of the Democratic presidential candidates on the stage at the July 30, 2019, Democratic presidential debate supported a public option for Obamacare that even the liberal 2010 Democratic Congress rejected.[13] All the candidates at the June 27, 2019, debate supported federally funded health care for illegal immigrants. Two of the top candidates, Bernie Sanders and Elizabeth Warren, supported "Medicare for All," an outright government-run socialized medicine scheme.

The Democrats' radicalism goes way beyond health care. Every candidate at the February 7, 2020, debate either cosponsored or supported the Green New Deal, Representative Alexandria Ocasio-Cortez's utopian plan to remake the American economy at a cost of unknown trillions of dollars. Indisputably, Democrats have become the party of socialism, open borders, sanctuary cities, the elimination of Immigration and Customs Enforcement (ICE), underfunding the military, abortion on demand, infanticide, environmental extremism, gun confiscation, higher taxes, radical identity politics, suppression of free speech and religious expression, and among some Democratic members of Congress, undisguised anti-Semitism. They're also the party of intolerance, smears, lies, character assassination, besmirchment, and fake Russian dossiers. They are singularly obsessed with their hatred for President Trump and his supporters. As the Brett Kavanaugh Senate Judiciary Committee hearings showed, they have abandoned any sense of fundamental decency, fairness, or common sense.

"THE LAST THING THEY WANT TO SEE IS A MIDDLE-OF-THE-ROAD DEMOCRAT"

What are Democrats thinking? Why are they showing their hand so openly? Have the American people taken a sharp turn to the left? They haven't, but there are worrying trends. Conservatives still outnumber liberals by 9 percentage points, but this gap has shrunk from 19 points in 1992. Gallup reported that in 2018, 35 percent of Americans described themselves as conservative, 35 percent as moderate, and 26 percent as liberal. The majority of Republicans call themselves conservative, but for the first time, a majority of Democrats identify as liberal.[14]

These numbers don't indicate socialism would be a winning message in the country overall. And of course, it's possible Joe Biden will suddenly moderate his message after winning the party primaries. However, he did the opposite to win the Democrat nomination over Bernie Sanders. It'll be nearly impossible for Biden to walk back his newfound radicalism. Besides, he seems to mean it. After all, the base of the party is very radical, as are their younger cohorts in Congress, led by AOC and her "squad" of like-minded extremists.

Like Obama, House Speaker Nancy Pelosi and other Democratic congressional veterans sometimes show they understand the need to *appear* more moderate, but when push comes to shove, their policy positions are not much different from the squad's. In fact, more than 25 percent of Democrat lawmakers voted with AOC 95 percent of the time in the first quarter of 2019, and even more damning, Pelosi initially held the coronavirus relief bill hostage to her demands for including Green New Deal provisions in the legislation.[15] There is simply no truth to Pelosi's dismissive claim that the party's AOC wing represents only "like five people."[16]

Indeed, as Karine Jean-Pierre of MoveOn.org made clear early on, it won't be easy for the Democrats' establishment wing to rein in the radicals. "[T]here's one thing we already know about the 2020 Democratic nominee: She or he must offer a clear, unapologetically progressive alternative to Donald Trump," writes Jean-Pierre. "Because [voters have] made it abundantly clear that the last thing they want to see in their nominee is a middle-of-the-road Democrat who won't go far enough to turn our country around."

Consider that for a second. Democrats controlled the executive branch for eight years under Obama and produced nothing but problems, from health-care chaos and unaffordability, to economic stagnation, to foreign policy aimlessness. Under President Trump, prior to the coronavirus panic, the nation was reinvigorated, with an unprecedented economic boom, strong foreign policy leadership, deregulation, exceptional judicial appointments, and energy independence. What, exactly, would the left have us turn around? Do they want a rebirth of malaise, executive overreach, and an America-last foreign policy? Do they want to reimpose the Obamacare mandate? In fact, yes, you can bank on it.

"Progressive candidates don't hesitate when it comes to supporting universal health care, or the fight for the $15 minimum wage, or the right to vote," says Jean-Pierre. "I can tell you this: [the Democratic presidential nominee] will be the most progressive candidate the Democratic Party has ever seen."[17] Do you hear an implied "or else" at the end of that sentence? You should, because it's there. The party's ultimate rejection of Sanders in favor of Biden doesn't disprove Jean-Pierre's prophecy. Considering where the party is today and Biden's leftward turn, Biden will be the most progressive candidate the party has nominated. The Democratic base is feeling emboldened and uncompromising. Even if the party leaders were open to a more moderate course—and there's no evidence of that—their base wouldn't allow it.

Early in 2019, Congresswomen AOC and Rashida Tlaib made Pelosi squirm as they presented their radical proposals. AOC announced her plan to raise income taxes to help pay for her delusional "Green New Deal" to end the use of fossil fuels in about a decade. Without a hint of self-consciousness, she compared her program to President Lincoln's Emancipation Proclamation. "If that's what radical means, call me a radical," she said.[18] But eventually we saw Democrat leaders, one by one, fall in line behind AOC's crazy ideas.

Naturally, impeaching Trump was a top priority for the newcomers. Hours after being sworn in to Congress, Tlaib told a cheering
crowd at a MoveOn.org event that "we're going to go in there and we're
gonna impeach the mother——r." [19] That quote became pretty famous,
though some people forget she was retelling what she'd said to her
thirteen-year-old son. But forget Tlaib's inappropriate way of talking to
children. Notice that the crowd went crazy for a vow to impeach Trump
before his phone call with Ukrainian president Volodymyr Zelensky
even occurred. And why not? The exit polls from the 2018 midterm
elections showed that almost 80 percent of Democratic voters favored
Trump's immediate impeachment—and some 6.5 million Democrats
had already signed a petition to impeach him. [20] Some party veterans,
like the late Elijah Cummings, cringed at the newcomers' unmasked
radicalism and militancy, knowing the country wasn't ready for it, but
their nods to restraint were mere posturing. The party was dead set
on impeachment, just waiting on a suitable pretext, as we quickly saw.

AOC, Tlaib, and the rest of the squad are in sync with the Democratic base, and they are the party's future. They are not outliers,
and—truth be told—they are not that far apart from the old guard
except in their style and bluntness. "I was not sent to Washington to
play nice," said Congresswoman Ayanna Pressley. [21] Still, the stylistic
differences are enough to provoke skirmishes between the two wings.
Retired Democratic senator Joe Lieberman said, "With all respect, I
certainly hope [AOC is] not the future and I don't believe she is." [22]
AOC responded with a flippant tweet: "New party, who dis?" [23]

Even when the old guard occasionally distances itself from the
upstarts, we often find them forced to backtrack and fall in line. For
example, Pelosi initially opposed impeachment. Earlier in 2019 she
announced that Trump is unfit for office "ethically," "intellectually,"
and "curiosity-wise," but insisted impeachment would be too divisive.
"I'm not for impeachment," said Pelosi, claiming it's "so divisive to the
country that unless there's something so compelling and overwhelming and bipartisan, I don't think we should go down that path, because

it divides the country. And he's just not worth it."[24] Though not one House Republican supported impeaching Trump for the Zelensky call, she caved to the leftists' demands, morphing from reluctant veteran to enthusiastic general of the rabid neophytes.

"WELL TO THE LEFT OF WHERE THE PARTY WAS A FEW YEARS AGO"

So it's hard to deny that the newcomers are driving the agenda.[25] And they are working hand in hand with their base to purge any actual moderates from their ranks—even some who identify as progressive. "You don't just get to say that you're progressive," warned Congressman Pramila Jayapal, cochair of the Congressional Progressive Caucus.[26] *Politico* reporter David Siders explained during the primaries, "So many Democratic presidential prospects are now claiming the progressive mantle in advance of the 2020 primaries that liberal leaders are trying to institute a measure of ideological quality control, designed to ensure the party ends up with a nominee who meets their exacting standards."[27] Progressive donors, said Siders, are also conspiring to ensure they fund candidates who are committed to pet leftist causes, such as "Medicare for all, debt-free college education, and non-militaristic foreign policy."[28] Bernie Sanders helped the purge by responding, after being asked whether there's such a thing as a pro-life Democrat, "I think being pro-choice is an absolutely essential part of being a Democrat."[29] The Democratic Party used to have a significant pro-life contingent, but now the party has no use for them.

The radicalism on display by the Democratic candidates this past year worried James Carville, a spin doctor and attack dog for President Bill Clinton. "We have candidates on the debate stage talking about open borders and decriminalizing illegal immigration," he complained. "They're talking about doing away with nuclear energy and fracking. You've got Bernie Sanders talking about letting criminals and terrorists vote from jail cells. It doesn't matter what you think about any of that, or if there are good arguments—talking about that is not how you win a national election."[30] Note that Carville didn't actually condemn these extremist proposals—in fact, he said there may be "good arguments" for them. He just thought it was politically damaging that Democrats were advocating them publicly.

It's not just the Democrats' policy positions that are extreme. They have embraced an extreme form of political correctness. Obama, who as I mentioned has more political savvy than his would-be successors, has warned his party against their tendency to shut down debate. "This idea of purity, and you're never compromised, and you're always politically woke, and all that stuff, you should get over that quickly," Obama warned in October 2019. "The world is messy. There are ambiguities. People who do really good stuff have flaws."[31]

Given his track record, it's doubtful that Obama has had an awakening on policy, but he clearly understands, like James Carville, that the more Democrats display their extremism and the more they try to shut down debate, the worse their electoral prospects. But the party won't listen. It's amazing how quickly the Democrats have dropped the mask—just a few short years ago, in Obama's second term, Democrats were advocating immigration policies that President Trump was pushing in his first term, such as constructing new barriers on the southern border,[32] yet they now decry Trump's policies as a fascist attack on the inalienable right of the entire world's population to cross our borders.

Even a couple of self-described New York Times "fact-checkers" admitted that the policy positions of many in the Democratic presidential field were "well to the left of where the party was just a few years ago."[33] They acknowledged that every one of the candidates supported health-care plans that "would generally require substantially more government spending, higher taxes, an increased public-sector role in private markets and a reversal of the deregulatory push championed by Trump." Yet they unconvincingly disputed Trump's claim that these would-be Democratic Party presidential nominees are socialists—mainly because only Senator Bernie Sanders self-identified as one. "Even Senator Elizabeth Warren of Massachusetts, who is the most ideologically aligned with Mr. Sanders among the 2020 contenders, says she is not a socialist," insisted the fact-checkers. "When she is asked about the difference between her and Mr. Sanders, her stock answer has been that she is 'a capitalist to my bones.' "[34]

Seriously? They expected us to take Warren's word for it? She wanted a complete government takeover of health insurance, a Green New Deal to exponentially expand the government's power over much of the rest of the economy, and a new wealth tax, and we're expected to believe she is a die-hard capitalist? Also, have these diligent fact-checkers forgotten about "democratic socialists" AOC and Rashida Tlaib—as if so-called "democratic socialists" are less socialistic than "socialists." And what reasonable observer could deny that former candidates Kamala Harris, Beto O'Rourke, and the others leaned far left?

Some Democrats try to deflect the socialist label, but the party's policies speak for themselves. "The progressive wing of the new House Democratic majority has lost no time in pushing radical proposals that are far out the mainstream of American politics, but which accurately reflect their hard-left worldview," writes columnist James S. Robbins, a former Department of Defense official. "It is refreshing to see them being so open about promoting socialism in America. The days of President Bill Clinton's 'New Democrats,' " he notes, "are long gone."[35]

Even certain reliably progressive media commentators voiced concern over the Democrats' leftward drift. The *New York Times*' Thomas Edsall feared that the Democratic presidential contenders were embracing "bold progressive policy initiatives" that would appeal to liberal primary voters but not to the general electorate. He offered one possible explanation, first proposed by University of Mississippi political scientist Julie Wronski: Democrats are more diverse than the mostly "homogenous white, Christian conservative" Republican Party. To appeal to African Americans, Latinos, environmentalists, and others, "[T]heir candidates need to start embracing boutique policies for these groups that may not align with a general election 'median voter' model of espousing moderate policies."[36]

However, there's a simpler explanation: the Democratic base, which especially reigns in the primaries, is in fact extreme, and primary candidates had to cater to that extremism. Additionally, Democratic strategists were surely aware of Pew polling data showing that "consistently liberal" Democrats have a 70 percent turnout rate in elections compared to 47 percent of "mostly liberal" and 41 percent of those with "mixed views."[37] In short, if a Democrat wanted to win the primary, catering to the left was virtually the only option.

"ONE'S RIGHT TO HEALTH CARE DOESN'T DEPEND ON ONE'S ZIP CODE"

Democrats today are also decidedly left on social issues and are indignant toward any who disagree with their superior values, treating them as moral reprobates simply for embracing ideas that supermajorities of Americans have held for centuries. At CNN's LGBTQ Equality Town Hall in Los Angeles in October 2019, Elizabeth Warren was asked how she'd reply to an old-fashioned supporter whose faith teaches that marriage is between one man and one woman. "I'm going to assume it is a guy who said that," she remarked. "And I'm going to say, 'Well, then just marry one woman. I'm cool with that.'" After a pause she added, "Assuming you can find one."[38]

Keep in mind that leftists like Warren claim conservatives are the bullies. We are the mean and intolerant ones, not progressives. And yet, here's Warren ridiculing religious believers for clinging to those "old-fashioned biblical" values—you know, the ones Jesus taught. In her follow-up from moderator Chris Cuomo, Warren cast "people of faith" who disagree with her on this issue as hateful, insisting *she* is the one who follows the true teachings of the church. "I mean, to me, it's about what I learned in the church I grew up in," said Warren.

I ever remember singing is, 'They are yellow, black, and ...y are precious in his sight, Jesus loves all the children of the world.' . . . And the hatefulness, frankly, always shocked me, especially for people of faith, because I think the whole foundation is the worth of every single human being."[39] Former Democratic presidential candidate Beto O'Rourke went even further, vowing to strip colleges, churches, and other charities of their tax-exempt status if they refuse to support same-sex marriage.[40]

Even Joe Biden, the falsely billed "moderate," shows the difficulty in trying to buck the leftists controlling his party. As a senator he had supported the Hyde Amendment, which prohibits federal funding for abortion except in cases of rape or incest, but under an onslaught of leftist criticism he shamelessly reversed himself in June 2019. "Women's rights and women's health are under assault like we haven't seen in the last 50 years," said Biden. "If I believe health care is a right, as I do, I can no longer support an amendment that makes that right dependent on someone else's zip code."

Interestingly, the month before, Biden had announced his reversal on this issue to an ACLU volunteer, but his campaign preposterously claimed he'd misheard the question. "He has not at this point changed his position on the Hyde Amendment," his campaign clarified.[41] But he just couldn't go the distance. Maybe just a month earlier Biden didn't quite view "health care as a right," or maybe he had a different feeling about certain zip codes. Who knows? But this is the type of left-wing ideological purity we've come to expect from a party being consumed by its own radicalism.

THE THIRD LEFT

The Democrats may be courting electoral suicide with their radicalism, but their extremist proposals often resonate with the younger generation, which has a growing affinity for socialism. This is alarming but not surprising, seeing as today's young people have been thoroughly indoctrinated in leftist ideals in both popular culture and in the education system.

In 2014, the Pew Research Center found that 43 percent of 18 to 29-year-olds positively respond to the word "socialism." Older generations are less favorably disposed, with 33 percent of 30 to 49-year-olds, 23 percent of 50 to 64-year-olds, and 14 percent of those 65 and older reacting positively.[42] More recent polling is even worse. A 2018 Gallup poll showed that young Americans not only view socialism positively but dislike capitalism. Only 45 percent view capitalism favorably, while 51 percent view socialism positively.[43] Incredibly, since 2010, Gallup polling has shown that a majority of Democrats view socialism positively. Its 2018 poll put that number at 57 percent.[44]

A 2019 Gallup poll showed that 43 percent of Americans overall say socialism would be a good thing for the country, while just 51 percent say it would be a bad thing.[45] That's shocking—and we can't let this stand. Taken together, all these polls show that capitalism is being systematically discredited in America.

We can take some comfort from recent polls revealing that the majority of socialism supporters don't even understand what socialism means. But that won't help unless conservatives do a better job of reaching them and disabusing them of their warped ideas.[46] We old folks have our work cut out for us. We must ensure Americans can define socialism and understand its devastating impact historically. Socialist policies have failed everywhere they've been tried. I flesh this out in Chapter Four.

Patriots can never rest easy with so many Americans warming up to socialism, even while a slim majority still reject it. History shows that leftists don't need majority support to bring about radical economic and social change. In a December 2018 analysis, progressive writer Peter Beinart applied this lesson to the Trump era. He argued that left-wing candidates don't necessarily even have to win elections to exert their influence. "Who wins an election is often less important than who sets the agenda," writes Beinart. "And, ideologically, the Democratic Party has veered so sharply left that 'establishment' or 'centrist' Democrats now frequently support larger expansions of government, and more vehemently scorn Big Business and Big Finance, than most liberal Democrats did a few years ago. . . . For the first time in more than 40 years, the left is shaping the Democratic Party's identity."[47]

For Beinart, what distinguishes a leftist from a liberal or progressive—though all three terms are often used interchangeably—is that leftists are committed to "radical equality," believing that "economic inequality renders America's constitutional liberties hollow."[48] Only twice in American history has the left had enough power to force Democrats to adopt its ideas—in the 1930s and 1960s. Both times the left derived its power "through mass movements that threatened the public order." Both movements began outside the Democratic Party. To keep order and prevent further extremism, Beinart says, "Democrats passed laws that made America markedly more equal"[49]—in other words, America was blackmailed by the radicals.

Both these leftist successes were possible because the American left mobilized behind them, Beinart argues. That's why we should take seriously the left's current mobilization. The "third left," as Beinart calls it, began in 2011 with Occupy Wall Street—young people protesting the financial crisis. Other triggers followed, such as George Zimmerman's acquittal for killing Trayvon Martin, which "launched Black Lives Matter." Bernie Sanders, he notes, went outside the Democratic Party structure for support—principally from the Occupy network and eventually Black Lives Matter. This was significant, because Sanders's "campaign became a funnel through which the activist left entered the Democratic Party's mainstream." Since then the left has gained greater control of the party and "remade" it in certain respects.

Beinart also notes that today's Democrats "are embracing Big Government policies dismissed as utopian or irresponsible only a year or two ago," such as tuition-free college and federal job guarantees.[50] He imagines that if Democrats regain the presidency and Congress and try to enact ambitious leftist policies, they'll likely meet stiff resistance from a conservative minority that would rely on the filibuster and the Supreme Court to obstruct the Democrats' agenda. He contends that the history of the 1930s and '60s shows that if such an impasse occurs, Democrats will succeed only through outside pressure from leftist activists, which is likely to occur because the activists are more mobilized today than they have been in decades.

If activist pressure doesn't work to soften GOP opposition, says Beinart, Democrats may resort to legislative trickery to advance their agenda. They could expand the use of the "reconciliation" process to pass legislation, limit the use of the filibuster, or even try to pack the Supreme Court like FDR attempted. We should pay attention to this warning, coming from a leftist sympathizer, that Democrats could bend or break the rules to get their way. In fact, they've been a party of lawlessness for some time. Obama demonstrated this with his unconstitutional executive orders (his "phone and pen"), his administration's harassment of conservative groups and taxpayers through the IRS, and his abuse of counterintelligence programs to illegally spy on the Trump campaign. Obviously, as the Democrats see it, to achieve a goal as ambitious as fundamentally changing America, they may have to take some liberties here and there with the rules, laws, and constitutional rights of American citizens. The current slate of Democratic candidates and their supporters look ready to do whatever is necessary—legal or illegal—to finish the job.

Beinart anticipates a further GOP backlash in the event Democrats resort to such measures. With the two sides thoroughly polarized and vying for their respective positions, Beinart says this "third left" movement will prevail only if it can "convince Americans that the true cause of radicalism is injustice, and the best guarantee of social peace is a more equal country."[51]

"HIJACKING THE ELECTORAL COLLEGE"

The Democrats' elaborate schemes to abuse their power are ironic considering their main complaint against President Trump is that he maliciously "abuses his power" and "interferes" with "our democracy." In fact, this leftist Democratic Party has no respect for the system they pretend to uphold. If they did, they wouldn't be attacking it with designs from abolishing the Electoral College, to packing the Supreme Court, to effectively eliminating our borders, to stripping our civil liberties. While complaining about alleged Republican corruption they are active agents of chaos, trying to undermine the system itself at every turn—whatever it takes to make America "more equal." Just as the Democrats themselves were the ones interfering with the 2016 presidential election while falsely accusing Trump of having done so, they are the ones threatening our constitutional order while pointing the finger at Republicans.

Democrats tirelessly accuse Trump of being a tyrannical autocrat—an authoritarian who flouts the Constitution and believes he is above the law. During the impeachment trial, Congressman Jerry Nadler even accused Trump of being a "dictator,"[52] apparently unaware that dictators don't allow themselves to be impeached. Once again, the Democrats are projecting—it is *they* who refuse to accept elections they lose, pay for phony dossiers falsely accusing their political opponents of treason, and skew our constitutional norms for their own political benefit.

In fact, Beinart's prediction that Democrats might try to pack the Court has already come true. Frustrated that President Trump has appointed justices and judges who will uphold the Constitution rather than bend it to the left's political ends, multiple Democratic presidential candidates proposed adding justices to the Court. Beto O'Rourke, Pete Buttigieg, Elizabeth Warren, Kamala Harris, and Kirsten Gillibrand all said they would add judges or consider the move.[53] While Biden didn't join the Democratic field on this issue, he has shown his flexibility under party pressure, so we have no assurance he won't eventually come on board.

Similarly, in light of Presidents George W. Bush and Donald

Trump becoming president without winning the popular vote, Senators Cory Booker, Kamala Harris, and Elizabeth Warren support, or would consider, abolishing the Electoral College. Here again, Biden didn't join the pack, but we can't rely on him not bending later. The framers wisely designed the Electoral College to establish republican government instead of pure democracy in order to bolster the power of the states, reduce electoral fraud, and protect minority rights. "Our founders so deeply feared a tyranny of the majority that they rejected the idea of a direct vote for President," says legal scholar Tara Ross. "That's why they created the Electoral College. For more than two centuries it has encouraged coalition building, given a voice to both big and small states, and discouraged voter fraud." [54]

But Democrats don't like the results that the Electoral College sometimes yields, so they are attacking this institution from numerous angles. Senators Brian Schatz, Dick Durbin, Dianne Feinstein, and Kirsten Gillibrand introduced a constitutional amendment to abolish the Electoral College and elect presidential candidates by national popular vote. [55] Knowing this proposal had little chance of succeeding, progressives proposed the National Popular Vote Interstate Compact (NPV) to circumvent the Electoral College and the Constitution's high bar for amendments. Under the plan, states would agree to ignore their own voters' choice and select their presidential electors based on the national popular vote. [56] "If you think that through, it really . . . hijacks the Electoral College . . . to do exactly what the American Founders rejected, which is to create a direct election system, a national popular vote, a direct election for president of the United States, rendering state lines irrelevant, rendering state governments and state laws potentially irrelevant in the process," says Trent England, director of Save Our States, a program to preserve the Electoral College. [57]

England helped launch the organization in 2009 after several states adopted the NPV from 2007 to 2009. This effort worked well until Trump's Electoral College victory over Hillary Clinton in 2016, which revived the momentum for NPV. Now some fifteen states, plus the District of Columbia, with a total of 196 electoral votes, have joined the compact.[58] The agreement won't take effect unless the signatory states have a total of 270 electoral votes. If that happens, the Electoral College will be effectively nullified and presidents will be elected by national popular vote, despite the fact that it's unconstitutional. The framers viewed the Electoral College as a crucial constitutional safeguard, but since it's not working to the Democrats' advantage, it has to go.

THE FLAWED PREMISE OF EQUAL OUTCOMES

Beinart apparently believes leftist militancy is justified because the "third left" will effect transformational change only if it can convince Americans that its radicalism is a natural response to society's injustices and that its goal is "a more equal country." Beinart is not considered radical compared to many on the left, so his justification of this militancy is an ominous sign that should serve as a wake-up call to conservatives.

As long as patriots resolve to defend this nation's guarantees of liberty, the left will have difficulty extorting the electorate to cater to their demands in exchange for social peace. Progressives are free to try to persuade Americans that socialism is a superior and fairer system, but not through threats of violence. Such tactics would meet resistance in any period of American history, but today, leftists will find it even harder to prevail because grassroots conservatives and the Republican Party have never been more united. Awakened to leftist extremism, hatefulness, and intolerance, and fully aware of what is at stake, we have begun to fight back under the leadership of Donald Trump. We must continue to do so. I believe that we will win this battle if we conservatives make the case relentlessly and convincingly to the American people, especially younger people, that America's founding principles are no less worthy now than when conceived by the framers and that the system of government they gave us is still the best guarantee of liberty and prosperity.

Conservatives must refute Beinart's flawed premise. The promise of this country has never been income equality. Its guarantee has always been, and must continue to be, opportunity for all. Forced equal outcomes are themselves unfair and destroy liberty and prosperity. We must never let the American people or their elected representatives be held hostage to radical mobs who threaten social unrest unless their socialist demands are met, and who offer social peace only in exchange for our abandonment of the American dream.

Prior to the coronavirus outbreak, economic conditions for all income groups improved under President Trump, and wages were at an all-time high, which would have made the left's task of seducing voters into accepting socialism that much tougher. Regardless of what impact the virus-induced economic slowdown will have on voters, conservatives must continue to explain the dangers of socialism. Income inequalities have always existed, and not because of capitalism. Under a socialist system income may be more evenly distributed, but only because everyone has less except for the ruling class, which has existed in every socialist country throughout history.

There's also something more basic we should consider. Conservatives and progressives have fundamentally different outlooks on economic growth and opportunity. The left generally believes economies are finite, which means that if the wealthy get wealthier there will be less for everyone else. Free market advocates know that economic growth expands the pie, and that one person's gain is not necessarily another's loss. Indeed, studies show that even when there are increases in income inequality, there is not generally a decline in upward mobility.[59] That is, Bill Gates growing rich does not keep other Americans from improving their own standard of living. If anything, it opens doors of opportunity for them. "Standards of living have increased for everyone—as have incomes—and mobility, however one measures it, remains robust," write Heritage Foundation scholars Rea Hederman and David Azerrad. "Simply put, how much the top 1 percent of the population earns has no bearing on whether the bottom 20 percent can move up."[60]

We have direct evidence of this with the Trump economy. To the chagrin of class warfare demagogues, under Trump's economy—again, prior to the coronavirus downturn—Census Bureau records show that while Americans' standard of living is improving across the board, the share of income for the top 20 percent fell by the largest amount in a decade, and households between the 20th and 40th percentile had the largest increase in average household income in 2018.[61]

But the facts don't matter to Democrats. They focus on income inequality because they have no ideas to help the poor, argues Akhil Rajasekar in the *Federalist*. And make no mistake, Biden has been pandering to middle-class voters on income inequality like the rest of his rivals—while simultaneously raking in money from his rich donors.[62] Even if the income gap between rich and poor or between rich and middle class increases with free market policies, should you oppose those policies if everyone's living conditions improve? If socialist policies decrease the income gap but all groups are worse off, what have you gained? "Here is the problem with thinking in terms of inequality," writes Rajasekar. "By focusing on closing the gap, one is only concerned with the *differential* between the two classes, regardless of how each class is doing independently. . . . Diverting existing wealth by force of government will close any economic gap, no matter how large. But, as the post-revolutionary French will attest, pulling down those at the top is never a sustainable solution to inequality. Instead we must seek to raise our overall economic health so that bridging the wage gap becomes a natural side-effect of market conditions, not a forced outcome."[63]

That's true. The left's economic policies kill economic growth, so they resort to class warfare. But they can't have it both ways: if they foment jealousy and resentment among Americans and pursue policies to equalize outcomes, they will shrink the economic pie. Increasing taxes and transfer payments smothers economic growth, which explains why Democratic icons Jimmy Carter and Barack Obama urged us to lower our expectations and accept permanent economic malaise. Each time, their respective conservative successors—Reagan and Trump—proved them wrong. But as long as the left, when in power, implements radical policies based on class envy, they'll never preside over a robust economy. To embrace growth policies, they'd need to abandon class warfare, and that's not in their DNA.

Conservatives also generally believe it's morally corrupting and biblically forbidden for people to dwell on other people's possessions. Thus, the left's obsession with class conflict is detrimental not only to our economy but to our moral and spiritual health. The American dream involves the freedom to work hard and prosper—it is not about coveting your neighbor's property and having the government seize it for you.

RADICALS ARE A MOB—
NO MATTER WHO DENIES IT

I have highlighted Beinart's piece because I think it's revealing about the left and the Democratic Party—written by a progressive connected to their thinking and inner workings. It's one thing for us conservatives to speculate about the motives and future intentions of the left and the Democratic Party. It's another to let the words of their thought leaders illuminate their mind-set.

I believe it's important we take seriously his view that leftist radicals are more mobilized than they've been since the 1960s and that they are exerting enormous influence over the Democratic Party. Now we face a double threat from activists mobilizing their fellow leftists outside the party structure and from those inside the party itself. Even when these radicals get blowback, they are undeterred and do whatever it takes to advance their agenda. For the left, the end justifies the means, and that's even more true of leftists today, because the greater their ideological intensity, the less their respect for democratic norms, the Constitution, and the rule of law.

Beinart defends the activists against Republican claims that they act like a "mob," such as during the Kavanaugh hearings. He suggests it is Trump who has encouraged his crowds to commit violence. It's been a common ploy of Democrats and Never Trumpers to paint Trump and his supporters as violent, but Trump supporters are overwhelmingly law-abiding, Constitution-respecting patriots. In fact, a sting video by James O'Keefe's Project Veritas showed that fights at Trump rallies, which were breathlessly hyped by the media during the 2016 elections, were being deliberately provoked by left-wing provocateurs who were running a dirty tricks operation for the Hilary Clinton campaign.[64] We are not the ones hounding people out of public places or denying youths a dissenting voice on college campuses. We are not the ones dressed in black beating our political opponents in the streets. That is the province of the left—today, just as it was in the 1960s.

We have watched endless bullying from our political opponents and their malcontent community organizers and activists. We have witnessed their unwillingness to live and let live. We have seen their vilification of all who don't kowtow to their agenda and demands. They no longer fool us with their simulated anguish over President Trump's threats to our system. They are the ones who threaten the system. They are the ones who interfere with elections. They are the ones who disrespect the Constitution and undermine the checks and balances that hold it in place. They are the ones whose political candidates are dedicated to overthrowing American values, traditions, and institutions.

And we are the ones who must stand in their way. That not only requires our ongoing vigilance but our studied awareness of precisely how they intend to achieve their goals. We must not only promote "informed patriotism"—fully understanding what is so wonderfully unique about America and why it is worth preserving. We must also fully inform ourselves of the ideas and policies that threaten it—meaning the particulars of the leftist agenda this current crop of Democratic leaders intends to advance. We must do a better job convincing our fellow Americans that Democrats mean business and must be defeated.

To be honest, it's laughable to suggest that the Democratic Party isn't radical and out of control. It's undeniable if you look at their policy proposals—a true horror show in the making. So let's do that now.

CHAPTER THREE

Welcome to Fantasyland:
The Democrats' 2020 Agenda

It's important that the American people understand exactly what the Democrats are offering them: radical changes to our economic system and a severe disruption of the American social fabric. Their outlandish plans are not the result of careful consideration of their costs and benefits to the nation. Instead, they stem from a mix of the Democrats' extreme leftist ideology, their maniacal hatred of President Trump, and a neurotic angst that has robbed them of all reason and fairness. These qualities have diverted them from pursuing any constructive agenda and rendered them generally unfit to lead this nation—which is ironic considering their constant harping on Trump's alleged unfitness for office.

Just about everything the Democrats do and say today stems from their animosity toward Trump. They refused to stand or applaud for great American achievements during either of Trump's State of the Union addresses—it was more important to display their contempt for the president than, for example, to celebrate rising wages for the middle class, historic lows in black unemployment, or even a schoolgirl who earned an opportunity scholarship. Even their approach to the coronavirus pandemic was focused on undermining Trump. Trump Derangement Syndrome is an amazingly powerful force that has completely overwhelmed the Democratic Party. Out of this toxic stew of rage and resentment, the Democrats have produced a preposterous agenda that would transform our country beyond all recognition.

THE JOYLESS PARTY

You can bank on one thing: I, for one, won't let the Democrats divert attention from Trump's policy successes, which I highlight in Chapter Nine and which are not diminished by the economic slowdown resulting from the coronavirus pandemic. The amazing Trump economy stands on its own merit, making it clear that it is Trump—not the whining leftists—who is best suited to lead our post-coronavirus recovery.

Seriously, how will the Democrats find an audience for their utopian schemes when Trump had already proved, before the pandemic, his ability to raise America to new heights of prosperity? Minorities were doing better than ever under the Trump economy, which made the left palpably nervous.[1] As I pointed out on my show, Obama official turned commentator Van Jones warned that Trump's 2020 State of Union speech was a "wake-up call" for Democrats because Trump was helping African American communities "in real life."

It's easy to forget that Trump's election victory sparked catastrophic economic predictions from the left. Remember when economist Paul Krugman warned in the *New York Times* that Trump's election would cause a global recession and the stock market would "never" recover?[2] Yeah, with both the stock market and the economy breaking new records seemingly every day before the virus, it's safe to say that one didn't quite pan out. But in an effort to sell their grandiose economic reprogramming plans, the Democrats tried to convince the American people that the economy at its pinnacle was actually terrible for everyone except the villainous 1 percent, even if the American people somehow failed to notice it. But it's horrifying to consider how devastated the economy would be today if Trump hadn't put it in the best possible position to withstand the economic dislocations caused by the virus.

During the first Democratic presidential primary debate on June 26, 2019, Beto O'Rourke lamely scrambled to explain away Trump's successes. "This economy has got to work for everyone and right now we know that it isn't and it's going to take all of us coming together to make sure that it does," O'Rourke said. "Right now, we have a system that favors those that can pay for access and outcomes, that is how you explain an economy that is rigged to corporations and to the wealthiest."[3] How can this message resonate when it glaringly contradicted reality? Unemployment rates were at record lows and wages were rising for people at all income levels, not just the wealthy. So O'Rourke was relegated to complaining that some people have more than others.

We heard some version of this class warfare appeal from nearly all the Democratic presidential candidates. During one presidential debate, Senator Warren at least five times accused American businesses of wanting to "suck" profits from consumers and boasted about her plans to eliminate private health insurance providers because they too have "sucked billions of dollars out of our health-care system."[4] In Warren's grim world, our economy comprises countless greedy, immoral companies whose primary activity is exploiting the American people, who in turn can be saved only by the government—with Warren at the helm.

Similarly, Bernie Sanders accused the fossil fuel industry of intentionally wrecking the environment to line their pockets. "What do you do with an industry that knowingly, for billions of dollars in short-term profits, is destroying this planet?" asked Sanders. "I say that is criminal activity that cannot be allowed to continue."[5] Earth to Bernie: oil is the lifeblood of the world's economy, and it creates the highest potential for high-paying career jobs for Americans. Without fossil fuels, the entire American economy would grind to a halt, and the nation would largely deindustrialize—not to mention that alternative energy sources can't power a modern economy. Yet according to Bernie, the entire industry is a criminal enterprise. "So legally drilling for oil and gas, employing millions of people, and providing cheaper energy for hundreds of millions is now criminal?" asked the *Wall Street Journal* editors. "And they say Donald Trump is demagogic."[6]

The Democrats' gloom and despair were so at odds with our economic reality that occasionally they'd wander off script and argue the opposite of what they were supposed to be saying. For example, on February 17, 2020, former president Obama tweeted, "Eleven years ago today, near the bottom of the worst recession in generations, I signed the Recovery Act, paving the way for more than a decade of economic growth and the longest streak of job creation in American history."[7] Oops—instead of harping on the rank injustices that permeate our economy, Obama jumped off the sidelines to *claim credit* for Trump's economic achievements. The Democrats' doom-mongering also contradicted the rekindled patriotism stoked by President Trump's "America First" agenda.[8] They were so confounded by Trump's "winning" and so bankrupt of positive ideas, they had no believable answer for Trump's brilliant economic record. The pandemic, politically speaking, fell into their laps as they seek to directly blame Trump for the damage done by a pernicious virus originating in China.

Prior to the outbreak, my friend Bill O'Reilly predicted on my radio show that President Trump would win reelection handily if he uses the stature of his office to communicate his message to voters. Why? Well, because he's got a strong record and the "Democrats don't have anybody." Bill was right, but he didn't go far enough. It's not just that they don't have *anybody*—unless you count Sleepy Joe Biden, which I don't; the problem is they don't have *anything*. They have no credible policy agenda. What they have is rage, extremism, and the bogus claim that Trump botched the response to the virus, which I detail later.

The indignant Democrats have become the joyless party, characterized more by anger than a loving spirit, which is also ironic, since they hold themselves out as loving and compassionate. They never get off their moralistic high horses, always pointing their fingers of judgment while basking in their false sense of superior compassion and humanity. Everyone is evil but them. No one cares about their fellow man but them.

The leftist-controlled Democratic Party isn't interested in improving people's lives. It wants to *control* them, through the instrument of government. Democrats believe they know better than the people do what's in the people's best interests. They want to pick the winners and losers among businesses and entire industries. For them, it's a class struggle, which is what socialism and communism have always been. They must demonize and punish the rich. As we'll see in the next chapter, they are willfully blind to the failed record of socialism.

The discontent and rage of the sixties radicals now dominate the Democratic Party and the millions of people indoctrinated by leftist propaganda since that turbulent decade. You saw their anger in the presidential debates. You see it in their late-night "comedians." You see it in their radical foot soldiers, from Occupy Wall Street to Antifa. You see it in their demand for intellectual conformity—their refusal to permit dissenting opinions in their ranks. And you see it course through their entire agenda, which is more geared toward singling out and punishing scapegoats than it is helping anyone achieve a better life for themselves.

TRUMP DERANGEMENT SYNDROME

Democrats and Never Trump Republicans sometimes argue that even if you believe Trump's policies have improved people's lives, it's not worth sullying the presidential office with such a vile man. But we're not going to let them get away with that, either. No president in the modern era has had to take these unprecedented sustained attacks by both liberal Democratic socialists and the media mob in an attempt to destroy him and tear him down. As I've outlined on my programs, and as we'll see in the myriad examples below, *they* are primarily responsible for the partisan rancor and for coarsening our political debate with their never-ending stream of personal attacks against the president. Democrats and the media have so ruthlessly derided Trump that people seem to overlook the astoundingly unpresidential behavior of the Democrats who campaigned to replace him. They denounce him for his alleged rudeness and vulgarity, hoping we'll overlook the enormous planks in their own eyes. Their outrage rings hollow when they constantly attack Trump, his family, and even his everyday supporters in the most crude and vicious ways.

Trump Derangement Syndrome permeated the entire Democratic presidential field. They could say anything they want about him without the liberal media batting an eye. At the CNN Democratic debate on July 30, 2019, the candidates seemed to be competing with each other to hurl the most over-the-top invectives at Trump. Senator Warren declared, "We live in a country now where the President is advancing environmental racism, economic racism, criminal-justice racism, health-care racism."[9] She claimed Trump "is a part of a corrupt, rigged system that has helped the wealthy and the well-documented and kicked dirt in the faces of everyone else." Bernie Sanders jumped in the fray, calling Trump "a pathological liar" and declaring, "We have got to take on Trump's racism, his sexism, [and] xenophobia."[10]

The second-tier candidates chimed in as well. Senator Michael Bennett called Trump a "bully" who "doesn't give a damn about your kids or mine." Representative Tulsi Gabbard said that "Donald Trump is not behaving like a patriot," "is continuing to betray us," and "is supporting al-Qaida." Washington governor Jay Inslee called Trump a "white nationalist." Julian Castro called him "a racist." Senator Kirsten Gillibrand said, "The first thing that I'm going to do when I'm president is I'm going to Clorox the Oval Office. Donald Trump has really torn apart the moral fabric of this country, dividing us on every racial line, every religious line, every socioeconomic line he can find."[11]

Hypocritical senator Kamala Harris said Trump "has a predatory nature and predatory instincts. . . . And predators are cowards."[12]

Nonsense. Harris herself, however, has engaged in predatory behavior. She calls herself a "progressive prosecutor." But as law professor Lara Bazelon noted, she "fought tooth and nail to uphold wrongful convictions that had been secured through official misconduct that included evidence tampering, false testimony and the suppression of crucial information by prosecutors."[13]

The overwrought accusations continued to flow unabated. New York City mayor Bill de Blasio accused Trump of committing "crimes worthy of impeachment," adding that Trump is "the real socialist. The problem is, it's socialism for the rich."[14] Former Colorado governor John Hickenlooper said that Trump "is malpractice personified." Beto O'Rourke claimed that Trump "uses fear to try to drive us further apart." Mayor Pete Buttigieg said, "When [former Ku Klux Klan leader] David Duke ran for Congress, ran for governor, the Republican Party 20 years ago ran away from him. Today, they are supporting naked racism in the White House or are, at best, silent about it." And Marianne Williamson added her trademark cosmic take on Trump, declaring, "The racism, the bigotry and the entire conversation that we're having here tonight, if you think any of this wonkiness is going to deal with this dark psychic force of the collectivized hatred that this president is bringing up in this country, then I'm afraid that the Democrats are going to see some very dark days."[15]

Former Maryland congressman John Delaney made a particularly noteworthy remark: "Donald Trump is the symptom of a disease and the disease is divisiveness."[16] Delaney's jab says it all, does it not? After participating in a debate that involved more personal attacks against Trump in a few hours than he could level against his opponents in a month, Delaney blamed Trump for divisiveness. Are these Democrats, even the allegedly mild-mannered and less radical among them, incapable of recognizing they've become consumed with hatred? Trump is no wallflower, but he usually doesn't start these skirmishes. Legions of Democratic opponents, haters, and detractors have blasted him without provocation since the moment he announced for the presidency.

Neither they nor their media co-conspirators have any standing to accuse him of polarizing behavior.

We also saw an unvarnished display of TDS at the 2020 State of the Union address, where House Speaker Nancy Pelosi dramatically ripped up her copy of Trump's speech. But what was supposed to appear as a spontaneous act of righteous indignation was quickly revealed as an orchestrated stunt—film clips circulated of Pelosi, earlier in the address, hiding her copy of the speech under a table and slightly pre-ripping the pages to ensure they tore properly when her dramatic moment arrived.[17] House Republicans sought to reprimand her ridiculous conduct, but failed by a vote of 224 to 193.[18]

An unrepentant Pelosi excoriated Trump again at her weekly news conference, attacking his State of the Union address, his record on health care, his economic policies, and his impeachment defense efforts. Pelosi also took a cheap shot at my friend Rush Limbaugh, who has been the leading conservative voice in the country for a generation now, having paved the way for me and many others to follow, a patriot who's done more to advance freedom in this country than Pelosi and all her colleagues combined. Trump awarded Rush with the Presidential Medal of Freedom during the SOTU speech a few days after Rush announced he has advanced lung cancer. At her news conference, Pelosi flippantly said that when Trump mentioned a cancer diagnosis, she thought he was getting ready to honor Congressman John Lewis, who suffers from pancreatic cancer and has already received the Presidential Medal of Freedom. Pelosi and her friends have been demonizing Rush for years with false accusations of racism and other horrendous slanders, but her disparagement of Rush, his award, and his illness was a new low.

Pelosi also doubled down on tearing up Trump's speech. "It's appalling the things that he says. And then you say to me, 'Tearing up his falsehoods, isn't that the wrong message?' No, it isn't. I feel very liberated. I felt that I've extended every possible courtesy. I've shown every level of respect." This sounds delusional, since Pelosi has shown

Trump nothing but scorn. She treated him contemptuously during negotiations on the border wall and helped impeach him on a transparent hoax, reneging on her vow that impeachment could not advance on purely partisan lines because it would be too divisive.[19] In fact, at her press conference Pelosi displayed malicious glee over impeaching Trump, bragging, "He's impeached forever, no matter what he says. You're never getting rid of that scar."[20] Considering Trump was acquitted in the Senate, this is like declaring that a person indicted on a phony charge and then found not guilty is "indicted forever."

THE DEMOCRATS' NIGHTMARE VISION FOR AMERICA

We can't let Democrats get away with changing the subject when we compare our respective agendas. But when they're forced to discuss the issues, they try to dupe Americans into thinking they're not as extreme as they sound. Every American must understand that if Trump is defeated by any Democrat, even one mistakenly thought of as a "moderate," America will never be the same again.

Don't be fooled if presumptive nominee Joe Biden pretends to distance himself from some of his party's more radical proposals. The party has embraced a radical agenda, and that will be America's agenda if they regain control. Biden, as we've seen, has already shown his willingness to bend to the radicals' will, and he would be putty in their hands. When Bernie Sanders dropped out of the race and endorsed Biden, they both announced that they were working together to form six working groups to focus on education, criminal justice, climate change, immigration, the economy, and health care policy during the 2020 campaign. More ominously, Biden told the socialist Sanders, "I think people are going to be surprised that we are apart on some issues, but we're awfully close on a whole bunch of others."[21]

Anyone who thinks a vote for Biden is a vote for the Obama administration platform is mistaken. How do I know? Because Obama himself said so. In his speech endorsing Biden, Obama declared, "If I were running today, I wouldn't run the same race or have the same platform as I did in 2008," adding, "Joe already has what is the most progressive platform of any major party nominee in history."[22] As radical as Obama policies really were, Obama is already indicating that more progressivism is in order.

So let's now turn to the specific policy proposals of today's Democratic members of Congress, senators, and former presidential hopefuls, which are nightmarish on their face and which, if properly understood by the American people, would spell electoral disaster for Democrats. None of these proposals was treated as radical by the Democratic establishment, and if Biden is elected, he will be pursuing most of them. If empowered, Democrats have promised to take or consider taking the following actions:

- Enact the Green New Deal
- Ban fracking, thereby reversing our newfound energy independence
- Subordinate some of our sovereign authority to international bodies like the UN
- Pack the Supreme Court with additional justices
- Appoint leftist activist judges throughout the judicial branch
- Gut the Second Amendment and confiscate our firearms
- Suppress our First Amendment speech and religious freedoms
- Expand the federal administrative bureaucracy and erode states' rights
- Abolish or nullify the Electoral College
- Downsize the military
- Promote federally funded abortion on demand including, in some instances, infanticide

- Abolish private health insurance and wholly socialize medicine through Medicare for All
- Impose a wealth tax
- Increase the death tax
- Raise taxes on individuals and businesses by reversing the Trump tax cuts
- Increase the top marginal income tax rate to 70 percent
- Abolish student debt and tuition
- Enact a universal basic income (also called a citizen's income, guaranteed minimum income, or basic income)—the idea that the federal government should pay a federal cash subsidy to certain groups of Americans or all Americans regardless of their work status
- Greatly increase the minimum wage
- Abolish the border and grant mass amnesty
- Abolish ICE
- Make it easier for immigrants with criminal records to enter our country, including criminal illegal immigrants who were already deported
- Expand welfare benefits and provide free education and health care to illegal immigrants
- Recalibrate our foreign alliances away from Israel and toward Iran
- Make transgenderism the "civil rights issue of our time,"[23] including mandating gender-neutral restrooms, allowing biological males to compete in female sports, and making gender identity a protected class under federal civil rights laws
- End all new drilling and mining on federal lands
- Provide slavery reparations
- Legalize voting for convicted felons
- Enact "race-conscious laws"
- Empower the government to micromanage what we can eat and drink

It's an impressive list of bizarre and destructive proposals, but let's begin by looking at the granddaddy of them all—the Green New Deal.

SOCIALISM DISGUISED AS ENVIRONMENTALISM: THE GREEN NEW DEAL

While AOC claims she is concerned about the environment, it's hard to distinguish her concern for the earth from her passion to impose socialism on America. There's no denying that many environmentalists truly believe much of the apocalyptic lunacy they preach, but it's also clear that they use fearmongering to advance their statist agenda. AOC's former chief of staff, Saikat Chakrabarti, admitted as much in connection with his boss's climate agenda. "The interesting thing about the Green New Deal," he said, "is it wasn't originally a climate thing at all. Do you guys think of it as a climate thing? Because we really think of it as a how-do-you-change-the-entire-economy thing." [24]

Notice that Chakrabarti didn't say the GND is about both climate and the economy, but that it originally had *nothing* to do with climate. He also said it's about "the entire economy." That's not code for socialism, it's a naked admission—they want to control the economy from top to bottom, which should horrify adherents of free markets everywhere. It's a ruse to trick us into giving up our liberty and our wealth so leftists can realize their vision of a socialist utopia. If they succeed, people won't just be leaving New York, New Jersey, Illinois, and California—they'll be leaving America.

AOC and her loose-lipped aide are not the only ones who see climate hysteria as a Trojan horse for socialism. In *Curbed*, writer Diana Budds explains that the GND "is really about designing an entirely new world. It involves unbuilding our mistakes—and building an equitable, just, and sustainable future." [25] *Roll Call* writers Benjamin Hulac and Elvina Nawaguna argue, "At its core, the Green New Deal is an economic stimulus plan designed to use climate change, as it accelerates and its effects come into sharper view, as a springboard to confront issues such as income inequality that a warming world will aggravate."[26] So the real concern isn't that climate change will kill us all in ten years, but that it will make the rich richer? You can't make this up.

No one should doubt the connection between environmental alarmism and socialism. Environmentalist and author Bill McKibben confidently asserts that President Trump and the Republicans are completely out of sync with the American people on the environment. "That's why all the thinking that falls under the general rubric of the Green New Deal is so smart," writes McKibben. "It understands the climate crisis as a lens through which to view the world—a change to address not only its rising temperature but the rising inequality that roils our politics. If your own life is insecure, it's harder to imagine change of the kind we need to deal with this moment. Ideas like a federal job guarantee for anyone who wants to help with the renewables transition are important precisely because they give people a chance to get their feet on the ground."[27]

The Green New Deal is horrifying, ambitious, reckless, and fiscally incoherent. But it cannot be dismissed as some pie-in-the-sky leftist fantasy, because Democrats are dead serious about it. It's not just activists promoting this, but intellectuals, commentators, journalists, and Democratic Party officials.[28] Ninety-eight House representatives cosponsored the bill. In my research, however, I've found there's not much objective analysis of the plan. Google search pages are filled with links to leftist reports, from think-tank analyses to opinion pieces, praising the scheme as a practical blueprint for saving the planet. So whatever you do, don't take this plan lightly.

In *Politico*, Michael Grunwald recalls that the GND has been tried before. As if to prove my point that Obama is no moderate, Grunwald notes that Obama "signed a prototype Green New Deal into law in February 2009, pouring an unprecedented $90 billion into clean electricity, renewable fuels, advanced batteries, energy efficiency, a smarter grid, and a slew of other green initiatives."[29] Look how that turned out with Solyndra—the solar panel manufacturer that went bankrupt after receiving half a billion dollars in federal loan guarantees—and the rest of Obama's green boondoggles! Grunwald says we may not have realized what Obama was really doing because the green scheme was hidden in Obama's $800 billion stimulus package. "People don't understand how forward-leaning the stimulus was on climate issues," said Congresswoman Kathy Castor.[30] "There was an incredible amount of green stuff in it that people didn't see," says progressive activist Sean McElwee.[31]

So what exactly is the GND? The congressional resolution, sponsored by AOC and Senator Edward J. Markey, declared that it is the federal government's "duty to create a Green New Deal" to accomplish specified goals "through a 10-year mobilization."[32] An "overview" of the resolution stated, "The Green New Deal resolution [is] a 10-year plan to mobilize every aspect of American society at a scale not seen since Word War 2 to achieve net-zero greenhouse gas emissions and create economic prosperity for all."[33]

The GND resolution's "mobilization" includes, among other things:

- "Guaranteeing a job with a family-sustaining wage, adequate family and medical leave, paid vacations, and retirement security to all people of the United States."
- "Providing all people of the United States with—(i) high-quality health care; (ii) affordable, safe, and adequate housing; (iii) economic security; and (iv) access to clean water, clean air, healthy and affordable food, and nature."
- "Providing resources, training, and high-quality education, including higher education, to all people of the United States."
- "Meeting 100 percent of the power demand in the United States through clean, renewable, and zero-emission energy sources."

- "Upgrading all existing buildings in the United States and building new buildings to achieve maximal energy efficiency, water efficiency, safety, affordability, comfort, and durability, including through electrification."
- "Overhauling transportation systems in the United States to eliminate pollution and greenhouse gas emissions from the transportation sector as much as is technologically feasible, including through investment in—(i) zero-emission vehicle infrastructure and manufacturing; (ii) clean, affordable, and accessible public transportation; and (iii) high-speed rail." [34]

Try to wrap your mind around this. The GND would summarily scrap America's oil and gas drilling industry and its hundreds of thousands of employees just when this industry and its shale revolution have made us a net exporter of oil for the first time in seventy-five years.[35] America is now the largest oil-producing nation in the world.[36] Not Russia. Not Saudi Arabia—the United States of America. Donald Trump launched this revolution by reversing leftist environmental policies and unleashing fracking, opening the Keystone Pipeline, the Dakota Pipeline, and ANWAR. The GND would undo all this progress by banning all fossil fuels—all oil and natural gas, and nuclear energy—the most affordable sources of energy and prosperity. It would, according to the sponsors' overview, "totally overhaul transportation by massively expanding electric vehicle manufacturing, build charging stations everywhere, build out high-speed rail at a scale where air travel stops becoming necessary, create affordable public transit available to all, with [sic] goal to replace every combustion-engine vehicle."[37] You read that correctly—no more planes and no more gas-powered cars.

"Right from the outset, the six-page document laying out the 'Green New Deal' seemed like a joke," quipped columnist Joseph Curl, "something a few devious wags in the Republican Party whipped up to parody an expansive environmental plan conjured by Democratic Socialist Rep. Alexandria Ocasio-Cortez. . . . Apparently, a sixth-grader was given a homework assignment that read: 'What would you do if you had a gazillion dollars to make the world shiny and perfect?' "[38] President Trump captured the absurd grandiosity of the plan in a tweet a few days after its release. "I think it is very important for the Democrats to press forward with their Green New Deal," Trump tweeted. "It would be great for the so-called 'Carbon Footprint' to permanently eliminate all Planes, Cars, Cows, Oil, Gas & the Military— even if no other country would do the same. Brilliant!"[39]

But in fairness to AOC, she's trying her best not to be unrealistic. After all, according to a document released by her office, "We set a goal to get to net-zero, rather than zero emissions, in 10 years because we aren't sure we'll be able to fully get rid of farting cows and airplanes that fast, but we think we can ramp up renewable manufacturing and power production, retrofit every building in America, build the smart grid, overhaul transportation and agriculture, plant lots of trees and restore our ecosystem to get to net-zero."[40] On another occasion, she suggested the world will end within twelve years. So what's the point of saving it? Might as well just have one big good-bye party. Can you see why Curl thought the GND seemed like a Republican parody of environmental nuttiness?

I'm not sure where PETA stands on getting rid of all farting cows, though they'd probably be thrilled with eliminating airplanes. But just think about retrofitting every home and building in this country (there are 136 million homes) for energy efficiency![41] Imagine waving your magic wand and creating a good-paying job for every American, "high-quality education, including higher education and trade schools," and "economic security for all who are unable or unwilling to work."[42] Why didn't President Trump think of that? Don't overlook the word "unwilling" in that sentence. As a thought experiment, let's assume you think it's moral for the government, using taxpayers' money, to support sluggards who refuse to support themselves. In your wildest dreams, do you think there are enough simultaneously stupid and industrious people in America to pull that off? Yet many on the left treat this absurd fantasy as a legitimate economic and environmental blueprint.

As for the plan's price tag, "I think we really need to get to $10 trillion to have a shot," said AOC. "I know it's a ton. I don't think anyone wants to spend that amount of money . . . but it's just the fact of the scenario."[43] Well, if $10 trillion is a "ton," then a more realistic estimate of the cost by the American Action Forum—from $51 trillion to $93 trillion—is between five and nine tons.[44] A study by Power the Future and the Competitive Enterprise Institute calculated that the GND would cost a typical American household more than $70,000 in its first year, $45,000 per year for the next four years, and $37,000 a year thereafter.[45]

But here's the kicker: the Green New Deal would have barely any impact on the climate. In fact, even if the United States outlawed all carbon emissions, the earth's temperature would decrease by less than 0.2 degrees Celsius by the year 2100. If the entire world joined in— which it won't (major emitters like India and China are reluctant to sabotage their own economies)—the temperature would decrease by less than 0.4 degrees.[46] These stunning facts tell us all we need to know about AOC and her band of climate zealots. If we do everything they demand, we'll end up with totalitarian socialism and the same "climate emergency" they claim exists today. And it's a safe bet that even the vast societal transformation envisioned by the GND is not the end point but just the beginning. As Elizabeth Warren exclaimed at a CNN town hall event on February 20, 2020, the Green New Deal "is not enough."[47]

For his part, Biden, under pressure from the left, released a twenty-two-page climate plan in June 2019, embracing the Green New Deal "framework." Though some leftists didn't believe Biden went far enough because his initial proposal called for eliminating the nation's carbon footprint by 2050 instead of AOC's and Markey's 2030 deadline, the *Washington Post* reported that his plan "adopts the rhetoric— and at times, many of the actual policy proposals—of the Green New Deal resolution."[48]

Demonstrating both his tendency to pander to his party's radicals and that he still hasn't fully repented for his history of plagiarism, Biden admitted through his campaign that portions of his climate plan had been lifted word for word, without credit, from publications of environmental groups.[49] As the campaign proceeded Biden drifted further left on the issue, suggesting the Democrats push for Green New Deal provisions in the second coronavirus stimulus bill. "We're going to have an opportunity, I believe, in the next round [of economic aid] here to use . . . my Green New Deal to be able to generate both [sic] economic growth as consistent with the kind of infusion of monies we need into the system to keep it going," said Biden.[50]

MEDICARE FOR ALL AND OTHER FREEBIES

The GND's promise to provide "high-quality health care" for "all people of the United States" is laughable way before you analyze its probable cost. You simply cannot legislatively guarantee high-quality universal care, when all proposals promising it decimate supply and demand and free market incentives that lead to higher quality at lower costs. But when you consider the projected costs, you're entering the Twilight Zone. Bernie Sanders took a stab at socialized medicine by concocting his Medicare for All plan, which would cost an inconceivable $32 trillion over a decade, according to the Urban Institute, a liberal group whose estimates are nearly identical to those of the Mercatus Center at George Mason University.[51]

Elizabeth Warren proposed an arguably more ambitious Medicare for All plan that some say could cost $52 trillion over a decade. Others estimate the price at $34 trillion,[52] but why quibble over a mere $18 trillion when Warren insisted her plan would not entail any tax increase on middle-class families?[53] Both plans would be government run and provide comprehensive health coverage for every American with almost zero deductibles, copayments, or premiums. "At the heart of the 'Medicare for all' proposals championed by Senator Bernie Sanders and many Democrats is a revolutionary idea: Abolish private health insurance," wrote the *New York Times*' Reed Abelson and Margot Anger-Katz.[54] "There's no precedent in American history that compares to this," said Paul Starr, a sociology professor at Princeton University.[55]

Biden initially criticized the cost of Medicare for All, proposing instead a public option to compete with private health insurance. After Sanders's withdrawal from the race, Biden predictably moved left on this issue and suggested lowering the Medicare age to sixty. That wasn't far enough to spare him harsh criticism from AOC and other leftists whose support is critical to rally the party behind Biden. "The trouble is, of course, that even if rank-and-file Democrats don't act as though they think there's a big difference between [Medicare for All] and Biden's public-option scheme, the progressive opinion leaders they need to unite the Democratic Party most definitely do, and, like Sanders and AOC, they're not going to be quiet about it," notes liberal writer Ed Kilgore.[56] He adds that Biden must begin to make "serious concessions to the left on health-care policy or let it be known quietly that he's gone as far as he can."

Disturbingly, Kilgore observes that a silver lining of the coronavirus pandemic is that it's created a "new context" for "policy proposals thought to be too extravagant earlier."[57] This is how progressives think—as Rahm Emanuel famously said, "Never let a crisis go to waste." Biden already exploited this "new context" in pushing for Green New Deal provisions in the stimulus bill, as noted. As his party's leader, he can never be trusted to reject Medicare for All, even if he doesn't endorse it during the election campaign.

Of course, the Democrats' fiscally ruinous proposals don't end with Medicare for All. Warren also proposed "a bold new Universal Child Care and Early Learning plan" to "guarantee high-quality child care and early education for every child in American from birth to school age." She claimed, "In the wealthiest country on the planet, access to affordable and high-quality child care and early education should be a right, not a privilege reserved for the rich." Under her plan, free child care would be provided to all families with income below 200 percent of the federal poverty line. A family with income above the line would pay no more than 7 percent of its income.[58] The plan would cost $700 billion over ten years, which Warren would finance with her new wealth tax.[59]

Sanders proposed a plan for tuition-free college, which would cost $807 billion over a decade, according to the Tax Policy Center. Warren and Sanders had separate plans to cancel all student debt, which would cost a staggering $1.6 trillion[60]—though perversely, the outrageous price tags of the Green New Deal and Medicare for All make this scheme seem cheap by comparison. And that's to say nothing of its unfairness. One voter at an Iowa campaign event gave Warren a piece of his mind. "I just wanted to ask one question. My daughter is getting out of school. I've saved all my money. She doesn't have any student loans. Am I going to get my money back?" Warren responded, "Of course not." The man shot back, "So you're going to pay for people who didn't save any money and those of us who did the right thing get screwed." Warren had no answer beyond huffing and puffing.[61]

We need more such displays of common sense. Democrats preach about fairness but don't know the first thing about it. This man's indignation resonates with middle-class voters, and the Democrats have no answer for it—so we must frame the Democrats' giveaways just as this outraged voter did. Further proving his pandering flexibility, as soon as Sanders suspended his presidential bid, Biden also said he would erase undergraduate student debt for anyone earning $125,000 a year or less.[62]

Many of the Democrats' other plans are similarly couched in terms of fairness but wholly unfair, unworkable, and fiscally catastrophic. Their federal job guarantee for every American at the increased minimum wage of $15 per hour plus benefits would cost almost $7 trillion over a decade, according to the Center on Budget and Policy Priorities, a liberal group.[63] Additionally, economists have long agreed that big minimum wage hikes harm the people they're designed to help by incentivizing businesses to cut their workforce—the last thing we need as we try to recover from the economic damage of the coronavirus. Then there was Sanders's Social Security expansion plan, at a projected cost of nearly $200 billion over the next decade, and $270 billion for his paid family and medical leave program.[64]

It must be easy for socialists to sleep at night. If you think money grows on government trees, why not promise that the state will provide, free of charge, for all the main expenses in a person's entire life and guarantee a job to boot? Of course, no government on earth has the funds to pay those expenses, especially when you consider the many millions of newcomers who would be entitled to these benefits if the Democrats succeed in abolishing the border.

FINANCING THE INSANITY

As I've told you, the Democrats view the economy as a zero-sum game and legislate as if their policies will have no impact on taxpayers' incentives to produce, save, or spend. So to them, it's a matter of simple math (more like Common Core math), where any amount of government spending can be financed by tax increases. They recognize virtually no legal or practical restraints on taxing and spending—the only criterion is whether it will serve their ends.

The framers never intended the government to act as a giant wealth redistribution factory. The original Constitution, says constitutional scholar John O. McGinnis, didn't allow Congress to redistribute wealth.[65] Even the power to tax income, for example, didn't become part of the Constitution until 1913, with the Sixteenth Amendment. But the left couldn't care less about the framers' intentions. They view government as a vehicle to reallocate resources according to a central plan, while the people are entitled to keep only the money they earn that's not needed to fulfill the plan. Remember, leftists are socialists, and socialists reject private property. Have you ever heard a leftist wrestling with the morality or constitutionality of any tax or spending increases—other than for the military or a border wall?

Government spending and taxing do affect saving, investing, spending, and economic growth. Even if it were consistent with the American idea for government to tax and spend with reckless abandon, the government couldn't finance unlimited spending increases through unlimited taxes because burdensome taxes stunt economic growth, and the government can't finance projects by printing money it doesn't have. The more the government taxes and spends, the more it restricts our liberties.

But these objections fall on deaf leftist ears. This is clear when you consider the impossible tax burden needed to fund the Democrats' Green New Deal, Medicare for All, and the rest of their statist wish list. The enormous government spending necessitated by the coronavirus shutdown is alarming, but can you imagine how much worse that spending would be—for all kinds of projects totally unrelated to the virus—had Democrats been in control of both the White House and Congress? Many Americans rightly criticized the inclusion in the stimulus of frivolous spending such as $25 million for the Kennedy Center for the Performing Arts in Washington, D.C., but just consider some of the items Democrat House Speaker Nancy Pelosi tossed into her own proposed stimulus bill: eliminating $11 billion of U.S. Postal Service debt; creating a cash-for-clunkers program for airplanes; providing $1.2 billion for "sustainable aviation fuels"; allocating $1 billion for a new version of the failed Obamaphone program; providing pension funding relief for newspapers; and $300 million each for the National Endowment of the Humanities and the National Endowment of the Arts.[66]

AOC has proposed taxing income above $10 million at 70 percent, whereas the top marginal rate today is 37 percent, which begins at $500,000. While AOC is correct that the top rates were this high between World War II and the Reagan era, she omits that the effective rates—the percentage of income that people actually pay once exemptions, deductions, and other tax-code incentives are accounted for[67]— were substantially lower then because more deductions, exemptions, and shelters were available.[68] Leftists disregard critics who say such taxes will raise little revenue because, for them, higher taxes have a higher purpose. "A slew of articles have since debated whether higher tax rates would actually raise much revenue," says Vanessa Williamson of the Brookings Institution. "But these articles miss the point. Taxes on the very wealthy are corrective taxes, like tobacco taxes, that should be judged by their societal impact, not simply their revenues." And here's the punch line: "The purpose of high tax rates on the rich is the reduction of vast fortunes that give a handful of people a level of power incompatible with democracy."[69] Once again, it all boils down to class warfare.

Warren proposed a new wealth tax ("ultra-millionaire tax")—an annual tax of 2 percent on household wealth above $50 million and 3 percent above $1 billion. Sanders had a similar plan beginning with a 1 percent tax on household wealth above $32 million, graduating to 8 percent above $10 billion.[70] Such schemes have been tried before with dismal results. New York University professor Edward Wolff says that since the 1970s, thirteen advanced economies have imposed a wealth tax, and eight of them have abandoned it while the other five have yielded disappointing outcomes. Wolff reports that European wealth taxers found that many of the rich hid their assets, avoided the tax illegally, or left the country.[71] Well, even if her tax doesn't raise much revenue, Warren can rest easy knowing she has engineered a "corrective tax" to punish the wealthy.

Sanders would also have taxed stock trades at 0.5 percent, bond trades at 0.1 percent, and derivative transactions at 0.005 percent. Sanders too appeared to view this more as an act of class warfare than a means to raise revenue. "This bill targets Wall Street investment houses, hedge funds, and other speculators," he boasted.[72] He claimed his tax would raise some $3 trillion over a decade, but the Tax Policy

Center, analyzing his earlier, similar plan, estimated it would earn only $400 billion. Investors would likely respond to this punitive measure either by moving to lower-taxed overseas markets or just trading less. Naturally, the less they invest, the less revenues the taxes will generate.[73]

Democrats also want to raise the death tax, which taxes wealth that people pass on to their families or other beneficiaries when they die. The estate tax, as it's officially called, was passed by Congress in 1916 as much to redistribute wealth as to raise revenue. But if leftists are really motivated by compassion, they should support abolishing this tax because it harms grieving family members. The tax is also unjust since it applies to assets that were acquired with money that was already taxed. The death tax, reports Heritage Foundation policy expert Curtis Dubay, inflicts "serious harm on family business, workers, and the economy." It "slows economic growth, destroys jobs, and suppresses wages because it is a tax on capital and on entrepreneurship." It also discourages savings and investment and undermines job creation.[74] Nevertheless, Sanders would have reduced the death tax exemption from its current level of $11 million per person ($22 million for married couples) to $3.5 million per person and $7 million per married couple. He would have taxed estates above $1 billion as high as 77 percent—a massive government confiscation of wealth.

Democrats would increase capital gains tax rates as well. Joe Biden would double the top rate from 20 percent to 40 percent for taxpayers with incomes of more than $1 million.[75] He would also raise taxes on corporations and expand the payroll tax to income over $400,000—the exact kind of policies that encourage companies to move their operations overseas. "While Wall Street may view Biden as more moderate than self-declared democratic socialist Sen. Bernie Sanders, investors would still face dramatic tax increases under his proposals, including higher rates on both ordinary income and capital gains," writes Ylan Mui. "Corporations would also be subject to a significant rise in taxes at home and overseas."[76]

Democrats refuse to learn the lessons of history—or simply don't care—because waging class warfare is critical to securing their base's support, which is more important to them than serving the nation's best interests. History shows that capital gains taxes discourage investment and slow economic growth, raise unemployment, and reduce personal income.[77] The higher the rates, the greater the damage. When rates are high, investors will be less likely to sell or trade their stock for more profitable investments because they pay tax only when the stock is sold. This "lock-in" effect reduces economic output.[78]

There are similarly outrageous proposals from many other Democrats, but you get the idea—elect Democrats and watch the economy shrink along with our liberties. An economic slowdown, of course, is most damaging to the poor, who have the fewest resources to deal with unemployment and slowing wage growth, but this is acceptable collateral damage in the Democrats' mania for class warfare.

ABOLISHING BABIES AND BORDERS

Nothing better illustrates the Democrats' extremism and cultural depravity than their position on abortion. After surveying the Democratic presidential field, the *New York Times*' Maggie Astor found that the group "coalesced around an abortion rights agenda more far-reaching than anything past nominees have proposed." Every candidate "supports codifying Roe v. Wade in federal law, allowing Medicaid coverage of abortion by repealing the Hyde Amendment, and removing funding restrictions for organizations that provide abortion referrals."[79] Almost all supported abortion on demand throughout pregnancy and opposed the Born-Alive Abortion Survivors Protection Act, which requires that babies who survive botched abortions receive medical care.[80] You can't get much closer to infanticide than that. Or maybe you can. The left's extremism is seen crystal clear in Virginia governor Ralph Northam's comments about abortion after delivery:

"If a mother is in labor, I can tell you exactly what would happen. The infant would be delivered. The infant would be kept comfortable. The infant would be resuscitated if that's what the mother and the family desired. And then a discussion would ensue between the physicians and the mother."

Though the Democratic Party has typically denied applying a litmus test to judicial nominees, almost all the Democratic candidates said they would, and would nominate only judges who support abortion rights. Almost all the candidates opposed any restrictions on late-term abortions. Even Biden, formerly more cautious, tilted full left on abortion. "The 2020 candidates' responses reflect a fundamental change in the Democratic Party's approach [to abortion]," writes Astor. Planned Parenthood's Jacqueline Ayers boasted that the candidates were no longer allowed merely to claim they're pro-choice. They had to go on offense, specify how abortion access "is being undermined in this country," and propose "plans to protect and expand rights."[81] Astor notes that the candidates were far more unapologetic in their abortion advocacy—and who could deny that, with Democrats lighting up buildings in celebration of abortion and proudly promoting the hashtag #ShoutYourAbortion? While a few candidates still paid lip service to President Clinton's mantra that abortion should be "safe, legal and rare," most abandoned even the pretense that they want to make it rare. "Abortion should be safe, legal, and accessible to every person who chooses it," wrote Bernie Sanders.[82]

The Democrats' position on immigration is similarly extreme—minimal to zero restrictions. They not only oppose additional border walls on the southern border; they want to take down existing ones. "A wall is an immorality," said Nancy Pelosi. "It's not who we are as a nation."[83] Let me correct Pelosi's statement: "Without a wall we are not a nation." That's what she should have said, because we cannot protect our national sovereignty without controlling our borders and having a regulated, lawful, and orderly immigration process.

But Democrats have gone off the rails on this issue as well. Many of them would abolish or severely restrict U.S. Immigration and Customs Enforcement (ICE)—the agency that protects our borders. They support sanctuary cities that, in defiance of federal law, refuse to cooperate with federal law enforcement to locate and deport illegals, and they often sabotage these efforts. " 'Abolish Ice' has become a slogan of the progressive wing of the Democratic Party," writes Dara Lind. "It's impossible to imagine anything like that happening 10 years ago, when immigration was still an issue that split both parties."[84] Again trying to position himself as the more moderate choice, Biden opposed abolishing ICE but still advocated overhauling the system and undoing Trump's immigration policies.[85] Let's be honest, those who oppose securing our borders, who support sanctuary cities and states, are damaging America immeasurably. Our lax border enforcement costs our criminal justice system billions of dollars annually, let alone the other staggering burdens it imposes on taxpaying Americans.·

Some argue that the party has recently backed away from its immigration extremism, but don't count on it.[86] Democrat moderation preceding an election can never be trusted. If anything, the party, under increasing control of the radical left, is getting more extreme on immigration. Many Democrats support full amnesty for the estimated 11 million illegal immigrants and providing them free government health care and college, as noted, and free housing and other benefits. Democrats increasingly oppose Kate's Law, ending chain migration, ending the visa lottery, deporting MS-13 gang members and other violent criminals, and mandates for private employers to use E-verify to check employees' legal status.[87] While they claim that compassion drives their positions on immigration, the hard truth is that most of them are power-hungry posers, cynically angling to create millions of new Democratic voters.

REPARATIONS

It seems like a lifetime ago, but just a few years back both Hillary Clinton and Barack Obama spoke out against slavery reparations. For the left, which thrives on racial conflict, identity politics, and perpetual victimhood, the Civil War, civil rights laws, and even the election of an African American president are irrelevant. There can never be sufficient atonement, but attempts must be made in the form of cold, hard cash.

The idea of slavery reparations has been around since the 1860s, and demagogues have given the proposal new life in recent years. It's an awful idea that prioritizes race over individual character and fosters an "us against them" mentality, which the left thrives on but which greatly damages race relations. It is patronizing, and treats people as perpetual victims.

Reparations divide the country. And it's impossible to believe that the left would be satisfied with mere slavery reparations—in fact, Elizabeth Warren advocated for reparations for Native Americans as well.[88]

This entire idea is impractical and racially inflammatory—it could be supported only by leftists who traffic in racial conflict. The proposal is also economically impossible—a study in *Social Science Quarterly* estimated the cost of a reparations program at between $5.9 trillion and $14.2 trillion. This was based on the total number of hours slaves worked in the country since 1776. What's more, creating a new, racially exclusive government handout would do nothing to improve anyone's life—it's a textbook example of giving people fish rather than teaching how to catch them. Our goal should be to increase opportunity for all and expand the economy to maximize employment, raise wages, and improve everyone's standard of living, which is precisely what President Trump is doing.

Predictably, an increasing number of prominent Democrats are giving this destructive idea serious consideration. The House of Representatives held a hearing on Sheila Jackson Lee's H.R. 40 bill, which calls for a commission to "study and consider a national apology and proposal for reparations for the institution of slavery, its subsequent de jure and de facto and economic discrimination against African-Americans." Meanwhile, pandering Democratic presidential candidates liked the idea.[89] Senators Corey Booker, Kamala Harris, and Elizabeth Warren announced support, and Castro, Biden, Buttigieg, Gabbard, Klobuchar, Sanders, and others were open to studying the concept.[90]

Indeed, Biden demanded immediate action to address racism in America. "We have to look at institutional racism that exists in this country," said Biden. I've "spent my whole life trying to do away with institutional racism . . . [and] systemic racism that exists in the United States."[91] But in fact, Biden has a checkered history of making borderline racist comments. For instance, in 2006, he told a voter, "You cannot go to a 7-Eleven or a Dunkin' Donuts unless you have a slight Indian accent. I'm not joking." In 2007, he called Obama "articulate and bright and clean." In 2012, he claimed to a largely black audience that Romney and Wall Street were "going to put y'all back in chains." In 2019, he said, "Poor kids are just as bright and just as talented as white kids." And just recently, on the *Breakfast Club* radio show, he told host Charlamagne tha God, "If you have a problem figuring out whether you're for me or Trump, then you ain't black." On the same program, he lied about receiving an endorsement from the NAACP.

Compare all this with the history-making areas of opportunity President Trump has created for black Americans and other minorities. He has been a major supporter of historically black colleges, and prior to coronavirus, his economic policies led to record low unemployment for African Americans.

GUN CONTROL

It's self-evident that the left wants to emasculate the Second Amendment and take our guns. Every time there's a horrific mass shooting, especially in a public school, Democrat demagogues rush to the microphone and, blaming the weapons instead of the shooters, clamor for gun control. This attempt to emotionally manipulate people reeling from tragedy is extremely disingenuous, as they know gun control measures would have little effect on stopping school shootings. Consider these statistics:

- Some 94 percent of public mass shootings since 1950 have occurred in "gun-free zones."[92]
- The average age of mass public shooters is thirty-four,[93] indicating there would be little benefit in increasing the minimum age for buying guns.
- Most American mass shooters used guns owned by a family member rather than one they had purchased.[94]
- The Heritage Foundation reports that some 80 percent of gun-related crimes are carried out with illegally owned firearms. The vast majority of gun-related homicides are committed with handguns, with rifles being responsible for only 3 percent of such killings. More people are stabbed to death every year than are murdered with rifles. And almost two-thirds of America's annual gun deaths are suicides.[95]
- Mass killings account for 0.2 percent of homicides every year.[96]
- In countries with more restrictive gun laws, mass killers find other methods to kill—bombings, stabbings, and car attacks. For example, Australia's ban on assault weapons failed to reduce homicides, suicides, or unintentional firearms deaths, and its effect on mass shootings is disputed.[97]

True to form, Democrats demand that we believe them instead of our lying eyes. The trouble is, our eyes aren't lying. They want our weapons—as they've made clear for decades. Beto O'Rourke came right out and said it during a Democratic presidential debate. "Hell, yes, we're going to take your AR-15, your AK-47." When accepting O'Rourke's endorsement, Biden hailed his gun control advocacy. "I want to make something clear: I'm going to guarantee this is not the last you're seeing of this guy," said Biden. "You're going to take care of the gun problem with me. You're going to be the one who leads this effort. I'm counting on you. We need you badly, the state needs you, the country needs you, you're the best."[98] Former Democratic presidential candidates O'Rourke, Harris, and Booker support mandatory buybacks for certain guns, and other Democrats would ban them outright.[99] In response to a Twitter user who asserted that former candidate Eric Swalwell risked provoking a war by his plan to prosecute gun owners who refuse to comply with his proposed mandatory gun buyback scheme, Swalwell charmingly asserted that the government could use nuclear weapons "on noncompliant citizens."[100]

I suspect nearly every Democratic presidential candidate would have supported some form of gun confiscation if they thought they could get away with it politically. Their favorite boogeyman is the National Rifle Association, which they treat as a satanic organization that has all Republicans under its spell and financial control. Democrats have consistently shown us they support severe restrictions on the Second Amendment. When asked about the issue, Buttigieg said, "Look, right now we have an amazing moment on our hands. We have agreement among the American people not just for universal backgrounds checks, but we have a majority in favor of red-flag laws, high-capacity magazines, banning the new sale of assault weapons. This is a golden moment to finally do something."[101]

DEBT AND ENTITLEMENTS

Most Americans are concerned about the national debt, but not many Democratic politicians appear to be—they've never met a federal dollar they wouldn't spend except for national security purposes. Admittedly, deficits are still too high under President Trump, especially since the coronavirus stimulus expenditures, but his deficits pale next to the budget-busting effect of the Democrats' multitrillion-dollar schemes. What's important to understand is that entitlements—Social Security, Medicare, and Medicaid—are by far the principal drivers of the deficits and debt. If we don't restructure them soon, we won't be able to balance the budget no matter how much we restrict discretionary spending. Though Trump didn't campaign on entitlement reform, I've always been confident he would eventually tackle the problem, as he understands their exponential growth, and he sincerely wants deficit reduction to be part of his legacy. But the problem every Republican president faces is that Democrats are steadfastly opposed to entitlement reform. The mere mention of the subject sends them into dyspeptic spasms and brings out their inner demagogue.

When Trump said he would examine possible cuts in entitlements "at some point," Democrats accused him of harboring a sinister second-term plan to gut the programs. "Even as the impeachment trial is under way, Trump is still talking about cutting your Social Security," Senator Chuck Schumer warned. This put Trump on the defensive, leading him to tweet that he would save Social Security, as promised. It was Democrats who were going to destroy it.[102]

This rings true because these programs are going insolvent, and the only way to save them is to restructure them. The Democrats' position is dishonest and illogical, for their obstruction of entitlement reform guarantees that the programs will go broke. Reforming these programs will cause some sacrifice in the short run, but failure to do so will cause catastrophic fiscal problems. Republicans have tried to tackle the issue and failed because the left successfully demonized the reformers, portraying them as murdering madmen pushing a wheelchair-bound grandmother off a cliff.[103] We do need reform and we must support President Trump in his efforts to restructure—and thus save—these programs.

IDENTITY POLITICS

I can't conclude a discussion of the Democrats' agenda without m.
tioning the elephant in their room—identity politics, which perme-
ates every policy idea they have. They used to tout themselves as the
party of inclusiveness, but today they demand we obsess over race,
gender, sexual orientation, and other group identities. In fact, their
dramatic move to the left is tied to their fixation on identity politics.
It overshadows everything. "The Democrats' focus on identity politics
is ruining any semblance of meaningful principle in the party," noted
Owen Mason in the *Washington Examiner.* "After all, isn't defining
someone as *what* they are and not *who* they are the very opposite of
liberal?"[104]

Biden has been among the most shameless practitioners of identity politics. "I commit that if I'm elected president and have an opportunity to appoint someone to the [Supreme Court], I'll appoint the
first black woman to the court," said Biden. "Secondly, if I'm elected
president, my Cabinet, my administration will look like the country.
And I commit that I'll pick a woman to be vice president."[105] Law professor Jonathan Turley was appalled. "Biden's promise to appoint a
black female to the Court is a remarkable moment for the presidency,"
Turley tweeted. "It is saying that there will be a race and gender pre-
requisite for appointments to the Court. This follows the pledge in the
earlier debate to impose a litmus test on nominees."[106]

Any Democratic debate on policy descends into an argument
about identity politics. Democrats can't offer any policy solutions without falsely accusing Republicans of bigotry. They never claim Republican policy proposals are simply deficient—it's that all our policies,
from the economy to abortion, are grounded in hatred for some group.
Democrats have gone to the well too many times with this tactic—to
the point of parody—and it's bound to backfire as ordinary Americans
grow weary of being constantly accused of prejudice every time they
disagree with some left-wing policy prescription. Instead of uniting us

as a people, it divides us as oppressors and oppressed, whites versus minorities, gays versus straights, and men versus women. The Democrats can't win an argument on the merits, so they resort to inflammatory accusations in a desperate and socially destructive attempt to conceal their lack of constructive ideas.

During the Democratic presidential primaries, the party proved it has no practical plan to improve social harmony, boost the American economy, or competently address any other important issue. On virtually every topic, the Democratic position can be summed up in a single word: socialism. So let's take a look at the origins of that concept and the disastrous results it's had over the last century.

CHAPTER FOUR

Socialism: A History of Failure

For the nearly two-hundred-year history of socialism, its core problem has always been its dishonesty and broken promises.

Socialist parties and leaders don't declare that if empowered, they'll build an authoritarian police state, suppress dissent, rip away every vestige of freedom from society, run the economy into the ground, and transform their nation into an unlivable hellhole that specializes only in producing refugees. Yet time and again, that is exactly what has happened under the rule of socialist planners.

The ability of socialism to wreck an economy is actually pretty incredible—it's an awesome force of nature, like a tornado or a tsunami. Socialism managed to turn Soviet Russia from the world's largest grain exporter into a major importer, humiliatingly forced to turn to its chief geostrategic rival—the United States—to help feed its own people.[1] In Venezuela, oil production has dropped 75 percent since the socialist revolution began there in 1999, despite the country having the world's largest proved oil reserves.[2] And just look at the former East Germany—thanks to socialism, the nation stopped producing anything extraordinary except steroid-infused athletes, a gigantic internal spying apparatus, and a massive wall designed to keep its captive subjects from fleeing their centrally planned dystopia. Socialism found a way to do what Germany's enemies for nearly a century could not achieve—it made Germany poor.

Unsurprisingly, the Russian, Venezuelan, and German socialists

people that that's what they'd do. To the contrary,
where promise to bring about a bright, shining future
e's needs and desires will all be fulfilled for the grand
of zero dollars. There will be fantastic free health care for
all, to free housing, wonderful free college education, and guaranteed jobs for everyone. They don't promise to snuff out opposing viewpoints or strangle entrepreneurship or micromanage your life. No, it's rainbows and unicorns and justice for everyone. All that's asked of you, as a citizen, is to trust the government with most of your money and all your liberties.

Bafflingly, thirty years after the free world celebrated the collapse of communism behind the Iron Curtain, socialism has become trendy in America. For decades we were the world leader in the Cold War between communism and freedom, but as discussed earlier in this book, rising numbers of people, particularly young people, now want our nation to be more like the giant prison systems we helped to liberate.

Despite once again losing the Democratic presidential primaries, the popularity of the Bernie Sanders campaign is a flashing red warning sign. After spending decades in Congress as a freakish left-wing oddball, Bolshevik Bernie attracted crowds of ten thousand people or more to hear him preach class warfare and promise to abolish all student debt, make health care free, reengineer the U.S. economy through the Green New Deal, and adopt countless other impossible programs that would bankrupt the country many times over.

We have to take the Bernie phenomenon seriously. That's where the Democratic Party's energy is, that's where its passion is, and that's where its youth are. Although Bernie is not the Democratic presidential nominee, it's clear his socialist ideas are having a huge effect on Democrats nationwide.

So it's worthwhile here to review the history of socialism—what it is, where it came from, and how it's worked out when it's been tried. Since it's not a new phenomenon, we have a lot of evidence to work with in many different countries and contexts.

DRENCHED IN BLOOD FROM THE VERY BEGINNING

In short, socialism is a political system in which the government owns and runs the key elements of the economy. But there isn't universal agreement on what defines socialism—socialists everywhere have always had a tendency toward schisms, infighting, and factionalism, as they battle one another over the minutiae of their destructive ideology and repudiate each other as heretics. As such, there have developed many kinds of socialism—utopian socialism, anarcho-syndicalism, Nazi-style national socialism, to name a few—but the dominant form is Marxism.

Karl Marx and his collaborator, Friedrich Engels, set out the basic principles of socialism in many different articles and books, their most influential work being *The Communist Manifesto* of 1848. According to them, all of history has been dominated by conflict between economic classes. The main conflict of their own time, they said, was the struggle between the proletariat, or factory workers, and their oppressors—the bourgeoisie, or the wealthier middle and upper classes. They predicted that the workers would inevitably seize power through a violent revolution and establish the "dictatorship of the proletariat," in which the newly empowered workers would suppress their class enemies, seize control of the economy, and bring about socialism, in which the workers run the economy for their own benefit. Eventually, after some period of time, the other social classes would be wiped out, economies would begin functioning much more productively, and people would be working because they get satisfaction from it, not because they are compelled to do so. After this system reached its final stage—communism—everything would work so well, said Engels, that the government and the state itself would wither away, having become unnecessary for the functioning of society.

This scenario is ridiculous utopianism. Yet socialists would spend the next 170 years squabbling over the meaning and application of

Marx's statements as if they were the word of God come down from Mount Sinai. The godfather of the Soviet Union, Vladimir Lenin, drew from Marx that the whole economy should be organized along the lines of the post office[3]—which helps explain the Soviet Union's seventy-year record of economic dysfunction.

Some of the core problems of Marxism were mocked by Marx's rivals at the time. For example, the anarchist Mikhail Bakunin noted that it's impossible to have a "dictatorship" of an entire social class. He predicted Marx's "dictatorship of the proletariat" would really be a dictatorship of a small group of Marxists who refuse to surrender power, leading to an authoritarian one-party state[4]—which is exactly what has happened just about everywhere Marxists have gained power.

When one socialist country after another turned out to be a horrific police state instead of the promised utopian paradise, socialists began arguing that the problem wasn't socialism itself but that no one was implementing it correctly. But the seeds of authoritarianism and violence are right there in socialist philosophy. Socialists these days cite "social justice" as their goal, but socialism is not focused on achieving justice of any kind. Instead, its main impulses are rage, envy, scapegoating, a thirst for vengeance, and a desire to violently overturn the entire existing order. *The Communist Manifesto* demonized the so-called bourgeoisie, characterizing them as merciless and fiendish exploiters of the workers, whom they supposedly kept as "slaves."[5] The workers "have nothing of their own to secure and to fortify; their mission is to destroy all previous securities for, and insurances of, individual property," said Marx and Engels.[6] Communists, they declared, "support every revolutionary movement against the existing social and political order of things," and "[t]hey openly declare that their ends can be attained only by the forcible overthrow of all existing social conditions."[7]

So socialist revolutions were envisioned from the beginning as bloody insurrections that don't just change governments but violently overturn all of society by abolishing private property—essentially, the workers seize control of the government, and then the government steals the property of their enemies and eliminates them as a social class. A class of people is scapegoated for causing everyone else's misery, and open season is declared on them. People are promised that not only will their lives get better, but they'll achieve utopia if they annihilate their class enemies. Once you understand this, you understand why socialism so often degenerates into mass murder.

The utopian end goal also helps explain the inherent violence of socialism. If you're promised not just better living conditions, or higher wages, or more equality but instead a whole new stage of development for mankind in which all exploitation and inequality are permanently ended, then you can justify using extreme means to achieve that miraculous end. Anyone who stands in the socialists' way can easily be demonized as an exploiter and a reactionary who is thwarting utopia.

Take, for example, an order issued by Lenin concerning "kulaks," which is a term of abuse the Russian communists used for wealthier peasants. Lenin wrote this order to his fighters in 1918 during the civil war that followed the communists' seizure of power in Russia the previous year: "1) Hang (and I mean hang so that the *people can see*) *not less than 100* known kulaks, rich men, bloodsuckers. 2) Publish their names. 3) Take *all* their grain away from them. 4) Identify hostages as we described in our telegram yesterday. Do this so that for hundreds of miles around people can see, tremble, know, and cry: they are killing and will go on killing the bloodsucking kulaks. Cable that you have received this and carried out (your instructions). Yours, Lenin. P.S. Find tougher people."[8]

Note that Lenin is not ordering his men to hang a hundred random people—he's ordering them to hang *at least* a hundred. There's a minimum but no maximum. But if you really believe in socialism, why not kill all these peasants and seize their grain and take hostages? Regardless of who they are or what good things they've done in life, they're class enemies. By definition, they're reactionaries who are hindering mankind's progress.

Of course, Bakunin's observation also came true—that once a regime enters a "dictatorship" phase, it doesn't give it up voluntarily. And if revolutionaries are following Marx's blueprint, then dictatorship is their immediate goal. There's no need for democratic elections, or freedom of the press, or freedom of speech, or freedom of religion when a nation is being ruled by a cabal who, in their own minds, have unlocked the secret to history, society, economics, and politics. Dissenting views become unacceptable temptations to go down the wrong path. The dictators know all the answers, so all that's left is to implement them, not to debate them.

BACK IN THE USSR

Socialism got its first chance to prove itself in practice, on a mass scale, with the Bolsheviks' seizure of power in Russia in 1917 and their transformation of Russia into the Union of Soviet Socialist Republics (USSR). As is the case with many socialist power grabs that the left hails as popular revolutions, the October Revolution really wasn't a revolution at all—it was a coup secretly planned and executed by paramilitary forces of the Communist Party. In the standard way that coups unfold, armed Bolsheviks seized communications hubs, the post office, and other key points in the capital, imprisoned the ruling authorities, and declared themselves the new authorities. They cynically claimed they were acting to guarantee that democratic elections could be held to a new body called the constituent assembly. But when those elections didn't turn out well for the Bolsheviks, they shut down the assembly after its first meeting.[9]

The Bolshevik coup sparked a years-long civil war that the communists eventually won. As they set about implementing socialism, they made clear that they took seriously Marx's demand for a dictatorship. In a series of moves that would be repeated in socialist countries worldwide, they first suppressed the nonsocialist parties, then they eliminated the other socialist parties, and finally they banned dissent—or "factions," as they called it—within the Bolshevik Party itself.[10] The USSR quickly became a totalitarian, one-party state in which the views of the party leadership were the only acceptable views. All other political parties were wiped out, the free press was crushed, and even trade unions—which represented the workers who supposedly now ran the country—were abolished or made subservient to the Communist Party. Religious expression and churches were also attacked with furious energy, inspired by Marx's denunciation of faith as "the opiate of the masses." There was simply no space for any other viewpoints or initiatives in society than those of the all-powerful party, and in particular, the small group surrounding Lenin who led the party.

To smother any expressions or actions that might conflict with the party, the rulers created what would become a hallmark of socialist governments: a gigantic secret police force with nearly unlimited power. People lived in fear of a dead-of-night visit that could result in the victim's disappearance into a forced labor camp. These camps for those deemed enemies of the party began under Lenin and were expanded under his successor, Joseph Stalin, into the sprawling, nightmarish gulag system that imprisoned an estimated 18 million people.[11] According to the Russian historian Dmitri Volkogonov, at the time of Stalin's death in 1953, "there were eleven million people employed in one way or another on the task of watching the rest of the population. There had never been anything like it in history. . . ."[12]

As I mentioned, a key element in constructing the socialist paradise was to ruthlessly suppress the Bolsheviks' class enemies. They abolished private property, confiscated citizens' wealth, and nationalized most of the economy. Volkogonov explained how the so-called bourgeois were systematically humiliated, abused, starved, and murdered:

In December 1919 there was a fuel crisis in the country. Lenin appointed A. Eiduk to deal with the problem, and
all manner of "bourgeois" were mobilized to gather and load
wood onto trains: clerks, intellectuals, tsarist officers—any "ex-
person" whom the new order had impoverished and as a rule
denied a ration card. It was a common sight to see frail people,
wrapped in what remained of a once-fine coat, clumsily loading
frozen logs under the watchful eye of some "authorized" com-
rade. Later harried by a rule of 20 April 1921 under which their
apartments could be packed out with poor and homeless people,
or taken over altogether, these desolate individuals sought any
excuse to avoid the drudgery of manual labour. Religious holi-
days were one such excuse. On 25 December 1919 Lenin told
Eiduk: "it is stupid to tolerate 'Nikola' (i.e., St Nicholas' Day); all
Chekists [secret policemen] have to be on alert to shoot anyone
who doesn't turn up to work because of 'Nikola.'"[13]

Leon Trotsky, Lenin's right-hand man, made clear how pitiless
the Bolsheviks' class warfare would be: "There is nothing immoral
in the proletariat finishing off the dying class. This is its right. You
are indignant . . . at the petty terror which we direct against our class
opponents. But be put on notice that in one month at most this terror
will assume more frightful forms, on the model of the great revolutionaries of France. Our enemies will face not prison but the guillotine."[14]

The communists didn't show the peasants any mercy, either. In a
bloody operation under Stalin, agriculture was collectivized, meaning
government agents seized control of the peasants' land, equipment,
and animals, and forced peasants to surrender however much of their
harvest the party deemed necessary. An estimated 7 million people
died in the resulting famine, mostly in Ukraine[15]—a catastrophe of
unimaginable proportions. This is the calamity that *New York Times*
correspondent and Soviet sympathizer Walter Duranty, reporting
from the USSR, famously denied was occurring. In 1990, the *New York*

Times called Duranty's reports on the USSR "some of the worst reporting to appear in this newspaper" [16]—which is really saying something.

As have socialist regimes everywhere, the USSR subscribed to the
cult of planning. The free market—allowing people to freely trade their
goods and services with each other and to set prices for them—was
viewed as a tool of the rich for exploiting the workers. Trotsky was explicit
about the need to totally replace free commerce with government-
controlled planning: "The socialist organization of the economy begins
with the liquidation of the market, and that means the liquidation of its
regulator—namely, the 'free' play of the laws of supply and demand. The
inevitable result—namely, the subordination of production to the needs
of society—must be achieved by the unity of the economic plan, which,
in principle, covers all the branches of productivity." [17]

But what's left when you abolish the free market? In Marxist theory, under a socialist regime, the workers *as a class* are running the
economy for their own benefit. But in practice, party bureaucrats are
in charge. They decide where factories will be built, what goods they'll
produce, and what price they'll charge. The problem is, it's impossible
to efficiently plan a mass industrial economy. There are just too many
variables for even the wisest among us—much less some corrupt,
power-hungry party hacks—to be able to allocate the correct resources
to the right places and to set the proper prices in a modern economy.

In the USSR, the centralized planning mania took the form of five-
year plans, which in the late 1920s and the '30s guided the country through
a crash industrialization program that fundamentally transformed life in
the Soviet empire. Starved and suppressed in the countryside by collectivization, peasants poured into the cities to work in factories. Meanwhile, now that the government directly controlled newly collectivized
farms, it could seize the remaining peasants' production and use it to
feed the workers to support the industrialization program.

In the end, although the USSR did industrialize quickly, it was
achieved at the cost of millions of lives. What's more, socialist planning
resulted in severe economic problems that plagued the entire economy

until its collapse in 1991. There were constant shortages of everyday consumer goods, leading to a pervasive black market. Manufactured goods were poorly made, and agriculture was inefficient, as farmers had little motivation to work hard to grow crops to be confiscated by the government at whatever price the party dictated. To paper over the problems, the government manufactured fake economic statistics that were not taken seriously anywhere in the world.

Meanwhile, because the state-guaranteed wages weren't enough to live on, the entire economy worked on bribes. The writer David Remnick, who worked in the USSR in the late 1980s and early '90s as a reporter for the *Washington Post*, told how his son's Russian nanny showed up to work one day "exhausted and depressed," and then explained what she just had to go through to bury her mother, even though the funeral and burial were supposed to be provided free of charge by the government:

> First, Mother's body had to be taken to the morgue. We were told that the morgues were all filled up, and they wouldn't take her. But when we paid two hundred rubles to the attendants, they took her. Then there was the fifty rubles for her shroud. Then the funeral agent said he had no coffins my mother's size and that we could only buy something eight feet long. My mother was five feet tall. For eighty rubles he came up with the right size. Then the gravediggers said they could not dig the grave until two p.m., even though the funeral was set for ten a.m. So that took two bottles of vodka each and twenty-five rubles each. The driver of the funeral bus said he had another funeral that day and couldn't take care of us. But for thirty rubles and a bottle of vodka we could solve the problem. We did. And so on with the gravesite and the flowers and all the rest.[18]

Remnick explained that this sort of dishonesty and corruption was everywhere. "[I]n the Soviet Union, no economic transaction was untainted. It was as if the entire Soviet Union were ruled by a gigantic mob family; virtually all economic relations were, in some form, mafia relations. . . . No one could avoid at least a certain degree of complicity. That was one of the most degrading facts of Soviet life: it was impossible to be honest."[19]

The system was so corrupt and hopeless that both the USSR and its Eastern European socialist satellites had to ban their citizens from emigrating. If they allowed it, there wouldn't have been anyone left to populate their paradise. The USSR tightly restricted its own citizens' travel to nonsocialist countries—if someone could secure the party's permission to travel abroad, he typically had to leave immediate family members behind in order to increase the odds he would return home.[20] Neither the Soviet Union nor any other communist government wanted a repeat of the embarrassment communist Hungary had suffered in 1956, when *forty-eight* of its Olympians—nearly half its team—defected during the Olympics in Melbourne, Australia.[21]

Viktor Belenko, a Soviet fighter pilot who escaped to Japan in a MiG-25 jet in 1976 and defected to America, compared leaving the USSR to leaving prison. "After my arrival [in America], the hardest thing for me to understand was freedom of choice," he said. "When you are in a closed society and the government is making [the] decision where you live, what you do for a living, and even where you die, it is very hard to understand freedom of choice. Those people who spend many years in U.S. in jail have a hard time after their release. But when I discovered the freedom of choice in the U.S. it became the best part of my life today."[22]

SOCIALIST DISASTERS WORLDWIDE

Socialism spread worldwide throughout the twentieth century based on the Soviet model. The USSR actively encouraged socialist revolutions—both because socialist governments tended to become client states of the USSR and because Marxist theory imagines socialism as a worldwide phenomenon, reflected in Marx's catchphrase "Workers of the world, unite!" The USSR directly funded socialist uprisings, created an international organization—the Comintern, later reestablished as the Cominform—to advance socialist causes, and unleashed a worldwide propaganda campaign touting the joys of socialism and criticizing the free world in general and America in particular. Soviet premier Nikita Khrushchev discussed many of these efforts, and the resulting tensions between the United States and USSR, in his memoirs. It is the ultimate irony that, because Khrushchev was overthrown in a coup and largely erased from official Soviet history, he had to smuggle his memoirs to America in order to get them published.[23]

The USSR had its first big success spreading socialism in Eastern Europe, mainly thanks to the Soviet Red Army marching through the region on its way to Germany in World War II. In Hungary, Yugoslavia, East Germany, Romania, Poland, Albania, Czechoslovakia, and Bulgaria, communists seized power and went to work constructing their own socialist paradise. The communists nationalized industries, eviscerated freedom of speech, suppressed churches, set up vast secret police forces, and created one-party authoritarian states featuring ridiculous cults of personality around the leaders.

Eastern Europe became a giant jail imprisoning its own citizens. Occasional rebellions against these oppressive conditions were suppressed with ruthless force, sometimes directly by occupying Soviet troops. A 1953 revolt in Eastern Germany, eventually involving nearly a million people,[24] was particularly embarrassing because it ended with Soviet troops violently suppressing industrial workers in whose name the Soviet regime supposedly acted. A major anticommunist revolution in Hungary three years later was also violently put down by Soviet troops. In 1968, the USSR decided it could not tolerate the Prague Spring—internal reforms in Czechoslovakia designed to allow more freedom within the communist system—and so army units from the USSR and other Eastern Bloc regimes invaded Czechoslovakia and put an end to it. Claiming they were trying to avoid yet another Soviet intervention, Poland's communist regime declared martial law in 1981 and suppressed workers' protests led by a workers' union called Solidarity.

These rebellions are easy to understand—socialism throughout the Eastern Bloc had created sickening conditions similar to those in the USSR. James Bovard wrote about his experience traveling through Romania as a reporter in 1987. In "The Daily Hell of Life in the Soviet Bloc" he described Romania—which had, prior to World War One, been a top grain exporter—deep in the throes of a food crisis:

> Children could not get milk without a doctor's prescription. It was forbidden for foreigners to send food to Romanians. The government responded to food shortages with a publicity campaign on the danger of overeating. . . . Food shortages became so bad that the lion in the Bucharest Zoo was converted into an involuntary vegetarian and lost his teeth as a result.
>
> The communists destroyed hundreds of square miles of prime farmland to erect factories and open pit mines. Hundreds of villages were razed and the residents corralled into cities and conscripted to work in factories.

Government investment had shifted almost entirely to heavy industry. Romania nevertheless produced poor quality products and industry was "extremely inefficient, consuming up to five times as much energy per unit of output as western factories. The government compensated by cutting off electricity to people's homes for up to six hours during the winter, and permitting only one 25-watt light bulb per room."

Bovard wrote that the Romanian healthcare system nosedived. The government consistently cut off hospitals' electricity, causing a staggering number of preventable deaths, and infant mortality was "so high the government refused to register children as being born until they survived their first month."[25]

Closer to home, Cuba was put on the road to socialism in 1959, when Fidel Castro's guerrillas seized power. Much like the Bolsheviks did, Castro took charge promising to hold free elections but quickly broke his promise. He destroyed the free press, cracked down on workers' unions, subjugated churches, and created a massive secret police force. During the 1960s alone, the regime killed between 7,000 and 10,000 people and imprisoned around 30,000 for political crimes.[26] As cited in *The Black Book of Communism*, forced labor camps were established by the Military Unit of Production Assistance (MUPA) to handle the huge load of political prisoners.

The organization, which endured from 1964 to 1967, established concentration camps that incarcerated "socially deviant people" who were considered a danger to society. The group included religious prisoners, pimps, and homosexuals, many of whom were forced to build the camps and "were subjected to military discipline, which quickly degenerated into poor treatment, undernourishment, and isolation. Many detainees mutilated themselves to escape this hell; others emerged psychologically destroyed by their experiences."[27]

One of Castro's most fanatical accomplices was Che Guevara. Nigel Jones of Britain's *Telegraph* summed up his bloody career: "Guevara was jailer and executioner-in-chief of Castro's dictatorship. As boss of the notorious La Cabaña prison in Havana, he supervised the detention, interrogation, summary trials and execution of hundreds of 'class enemies.'" Ernest Hemingway, who was then living in Cuba, invited an acquaintance to see the execution of prisoners by Che's tribunals. "They watched as the men were trucked in, unloaded, shot, and taken away."[28]

When it came to executions, Che wasn't worried about little

details like evidence. "To send men to the firing squad, judicial proof is unnecessary," Che declared. "These procedures are an archaic bourgeois detail. This is a revolution! And a revolutionary must become a cold killing machine motivated by pure hate."[29] After Castro was forced to abandon efforts to install Soviet nuclear weapons in Cuba during the Cuban Missile Crisis, Che revealed what the regime would have done if the efforts had succeeded: "If the missiles had remained, we would have used them against the very heart of America including New York. We must never establish peaceful coexistence. In this struggle to the death between two systems we must gain the ultimate victory. We must walk the path of liberation even if it costs millions of atomic victims."[30]

And yet Che became an international youth icon, with Che T-shirts becoming popular on college campuses throughout the Western world. Unsurprisingly, Hollywood is a big fan of Che's, though actors don't seem very knowledgeable about him. Benicio Del Toro, who played this psychopath in the hagiography *Che*, excitedly told a reporter what first captured his attention on this subject: "I hear of this guy and he's got a cool name. Che Guevara!" The reporter noted, "Del Toro as good as swoons when he says it. And the appeal does seem as simple as that—groovy name, groovy man, groovy politics." Del Toro also denounced the execution of Che by soldiers in Bolivia, where Che was raising an army to fight for another socialist revolution. "He was killed like a war criminal, man, and he was not a war criminal. He should have been given a fair trial,"[31] Del Toro said, either not knowing or not caring that Che himself didn't believe that fair trials were groovy at all.

If socialism's body count in Cuba was bad, it was just a drop in the ocean compared to China. After Mao Zedong led the communists to power in 1949, the Chinese effort to implement socialism was so catastrophic that it nearly defies belief. Even aside from the typical socialist horrors—the mass murder of political opponents, suppression of all freedoms, unrestrained class warfare—just one element of Mao's program, "the Great Leap Forward," was one of the greatest tragedies in world history.

The Great Leap Forward was Mao's attempt to rapidly industrialize China and to collectivize agriculture to make that possible. Based on information from Chinese Communist Party archives, historian Frank Dikköter compiled a devastating account of the Chinese people being systematically robbed of their "work, homes, land, belongings, and livelihoods," as the government forced peasants onto giant communal farms, seized control of the food supply, and used it as a weapon to impose its will in the ensuing famine. During the campaign, reports Dikköter, "between two and three million victims were tortured to death or summarily killed, often for the slightest infraction. When a boy stole a handful of grain in a Hunan village, local boss Xiong Dechang forced his father to bury him alive. The father died of grief a few days later." According to Dikköter's study, the Great Leap Forward resulted in at least *45 million* deaths. This makes Mao, in Dikköter's view, "one of the greatest mass murderers in history." [32]

To understand the true lunacy of these socialist frenzies, let's look at an account of just one aspect of the Great Leap Forward provided by Li Zhisui, who traveled extensively with Mao during this period, serving as Mao's personal doctor. In order to increase steel production, the Communist Party ordered that small furnaces be built in fields and courtyards throughout the country. What was used to fuel these contraptions, which spit out small, useless globs of steel? People's steel household implements—pots and pans, knives, shovels, and doorknobs. What's more, because there wasn't enough coal to fuel the furnaces, families were forced to feed their wooden furniture—tables, chairs, and beds—into them. Meanwhile, because so many peasants were transferred to work with the furnaces, the harvest in many villages was left to rot in the fields, contributing to one of the worst famines in human history. Liu noted, "Mao said that China was not on the verge of communism, but in fact some absurd form of communism was already in place. Private property *was* being abolished, because private property was all being given away to feed the voracious steel furnaces."[33]

In Cambodia, the communist Khmer Rouge regime led by Pol Pot seized power in 1975 and upped the ante on socialist utopianism, declaring they were resetting time to a mythical "year zero" in which Cambodian society and culture would begin completely anew. Suspicious of urban living, they emptied out their own cities, including the capital of Phnom Penh, and forced the residents into the countryside. The Cambodia Tribunal Monitor, which was established to document the later trials of Khmer Rouge leaders, provides a short summary of the regime's bizarre totalitarian rule. In order to bring about a classless society, the Khmer Rouge

abolished money, free markets, normal schooling, private property, foreign clothing styles, religious practices, and traditional Khmer culture. Public schools, pagodas, mosques, churches, universities, shops and government buildings were shut or turned into prisons, stables, reeducation camps and granaries. There was no public or private transportation, no private property, and no non-revolutionary entertainment. Leisure activities were severely restricted. People throughout the country, including the leaders of the CPK, had to wear black costumes, which were their traditional revolutionary clothes.

The government deprived individuals of basic human rights, prohibiting them from congregating in public or leaving their cooperatives. If even three people were to gather to have a discussion, "they could be accused of being enemies and arrested or executed."

The government also profoundly intruded on personal and familial relationships: "People were forbidden to show even the slightest affection, humor or pity. The Khmer Rouge asked all Cambodians to believe, obey and respect only Angkar Padevat [the Communist Party leadership], which was to be everyone's 'mother and father.'"[34]

The Khmer Rouge was responsible for an estimated 1.2 million–2.8 million deaths—or 13–30 percent of the country's entire population at the time[35]—from execution, starvation, and other causes. In early 1979 they were overthrown in an invasion by Vietnam, a fellow socialist country. Some of the regime's criminals fled into the jungles of Thailand. Although Pol Pot died in 1998 without facing justice, others were put on trial years later. It's not often that an everyday victim of genocidal socialism gets to confront his tormentors in court, but during the trials some Cambodians got that chance.

One was Bou Meng, who was among just fifteen prisoners who survived Tuol Sleng prison, from where sadistic Khmer Rouge maniacs took at least twelve thousand prisoners to various locations for execution. In 1977, despite being a Khmer Rouge supporter, Bou Meng was arrested with his wife, Ma Yoeun, for no apparent reason. They were taken to Tuol Sleng, where Ma Yoeun, who had worked as a midwife, was quickly executed, a tragedy that still brings tears to Bou Meng's eyes. He was tortured and forced to falsely confess to working for the CIA. His life was spared, though, because the prison chief, a notorious Khmer Rouge operative known as Duch, learned he was an artist and put him to work drawing portraits of Pol Pot and other international communist leaders.

In the 1980s, after the Khmer Rouge were overthrown and the prison was converted into a museum, Bou Meng returned there to search for the photo his captors took of Ma Yoeun when she was processed into the prison. In 2015 he told a BBC reporter that he could still see her standing in front of him, and that he wanted to be able to pray over her grave. His tormentor, Duch, was put on trial in 2009 by a special court established to try Khmer Rouge officials. Bou was given the opportunity to ask Duch one question during the trial, so he asked where his wife was killed. Duch was unable to answer the question.[36]

A more recent socialist experiment occurred in Venezuela under Hugo Chavez, a former military officer who'd been imprisoned for staging a failed coup in 1992. Elected president in 1998, Chavez presided over the "Bolivarian Revolution," a socialist movement inspired by nineteenth-century Venezuelan revolutionary Simon Bolivar. As president, Chavez centralized power, cracking down on oppositional media outlets and packing the Venezuelan Supreme Court. He realigned his nation's foreign policy and cultivated Castro's Cuba as a close ally while denouncing then-president George W. Bush as "the devil" at the United Nations.[37]

Chavez introduced many programs to fight poverty and assist the poor, including low-income housing projects, literacy programs, free health care, and food subsidies. While those programs were touted by his leftist international supporters, they proved to be utterly unsustainable when his overall socialist economic program wrecked the economy. Forced land transfers, land expropriations, and increasing state control in agriculture led to a 75 percent drop in food production over the following two decades as the Venezuelan population increased 33 percent. A vast program of nationalizing industry spread corruption and dramatically suppressed operations in electricity, water, banks, supermarkets, construction, and other industries.[38]

A core problem was that Chavez never diversified the Venezuelan economy from its dependence on oil. With the price of oil skyrocketing from $20 a barrel when he became president to $110 when he died in office in 2013,[39] Chavez's social programs survived during his tenure, even though they were piling up an enormous debt load. But Chavez planted the seeds of catastrophe when he included the oil industry in his massive program of seizing and nationalizing businesses. He seized private oil fields and gave them to the national oil company, PDVSA. After the company's employees joined an anti-Chavez general strike in 2002, he fired nineteen thousand oil workers. Their replacements were Chavez loyalists who lacked the knowledge and experience to competently run the company. Many foreign experts were later chased out of Venezuela when Chavez seized control of oil projects run by ExxonMobil and ConocoPhillips, and confiscated their assets.[40] The result was a long, steep decline in Venezuela's oil output that outlasted Chavez's reign, with output falling from 3.5 million barrels per day in 1998, when Chavez was elected, to just 760,000 in February 2020.[41]

Chavez responded to the economic deterioration by socializing the economy even more, implementing price controls and exchange controls that only made the problems worse, creating more shortages and an extensive black market in foreign currencies.[42]

Chavez's successor, Nicolàs Maduro, continued the economic policies of the Bolivarian Revolution, resulting in a shattering economic collapse. Due to food shortages, the average Venezuelan lost twenty-four pounds in 2017, while 90 percent of the population lived in poverty—compared to 33 percent in 2015, the last time the Venezuelan government published poverty statistics.[43] The health care system has been decimated by a lack of medicine and equipment and the emigration of doctors. Women about to give birth must endure what they call "the roulette": traveling to multiple hospitals to find one that will accept them. According to the *New York Times*, "They sometimes hitchhike, or walk for miles, or take buses over roads whose ruts and bumps seem designed just to torture them. In rare cases, they are rejected over and over until finally giving birth in the street, on a hospital's steps—or in its lobby."[44] The economic meltdown has created a huge outflow of refugees, with around 5 million people[45]—more than 15 percent of the population—having fled their socialist paradise.

Hyperinflation of the Venezuelan currency, the bolivar, reached epic proportions. Because the Venezuelan government stopped publishing the inflation rate, Bloomberg news service created its own estimate based on the price of a cup of coffee at one bakery. In January 2018, its gauge measured an annualized inflation rate of 448,025 percent.[46] In August 2018, a Bloomberg journalist reported paying 20 million bolivars for lunch at Burger King.[47] The previous month she wrote, "With inflation soaring above 60,000 percent, a top-shelf liter of Scotch can set you back 1 billion bolivars—a sum that a minimum-wage worker would have to toil 16 years to earn."[48] The currency has become so worthless that state officials are increasingly demanding that citizens pay them their bribes in dollars.[49]

Bloomberg filed a series of reports from correspondents in the capital city of Caracas that offers a glimpse into the bizarre, hellish landscape of Venezuela's collapse. The dispatches included the following observations:

- Due to constant water shortages, "Dishes are brushed off and reused, and clothing is not something regularly laundered. . . . You ask friends whether it's okay to flush. You often do not. We're sweaty and, yes, smelly. . . ."[50]
- In a report titled "Everyone I Know Is Depressed and Medicated," a reporter described the explosion of the use of anti-anxiety and depression medications, adding, "Our country has been so short on meds that some people buy drugs made for pets."[51]
- Because Venezuela no longer produces auto spare parts, importers have shut down, public transport has "fallen into ruin," and any public transport that does work is crime ridden, people are forced to hitchhike to work.[52]
- A correspondent described obstacles to dating in Caracas, including hyperinflation, the closing of bars and restaurants, condom shortages, rampant crime, rolling blackouts, tear-gas smoke, and the constant emigration of possible partners.[53]
- Starving child beggars have appeared "seemingly everywhere" in Caracas. A reporter described Andrea, a nine-year-old juggling limes on a street corner: "She kept her

collections in a pink-plastic purse: 24 bolivars, less than a penny, and a packet of strawberry-flavored wafers. By 11 a.m., that was all she'd had to eat." [54]

Mind you, these are the miserable conditions in the country with *the largest proved oil reserves in the entire world*. It's hard to think of any system of government other than socialism that could accomplish that feat. As I said, the destructive power of socialism is like a force of nature.

FEEL THE BERN OF SOCIALISM

As you see, socialists have a long record of promising utopia for the poor and then delivering economic destruction, famine, oppression, forced labor camps, and mass killings. Their horrific record speaks for itself. Yet, as I noted earlier, the popularity of socialism is having a resurgence in America, particularly among young people. Democrats in the current Congress have a high-profile "squad" of socialists whose proposals are quickly entering the mainstream of the Democratic Party, and avowed socialist Bernie Sanders became so popular among the Democratic grassroots that for a time he was the front-runner for the 2020 Democratic nomination for president.

Socialists have an endless supply of excuses for all the misery that governments have inflicted in their name. As I mentioned earlier, a primary one is to argue that the architects of all the socialist nightmares we've discussed just weren't doing socialism right. In other words, there's nothing wrong with central planning per se, it's just that people keep getting the plan wrong. And if some socialist regime becomes a big enough embarrassment, socialists will simply deny that it was socialist at all. However, leftists inevitably praise these regimes as they're implementing socialism and disown them only years later, once the disastrous consequences have become undeniable.

In an essay titled "But That Wasn't *Real* Socialism," Kristian Niemietz, head of political economy at the United Kingdom's Institute of
Economic Affairs, provides numerous examples of left-wing Western
intellectuals and politicians praising Maoist China, the USSR, Eastern European communism, and other socialist disasters in their early
years, only to repudiate them later. One example is renowned left-wing
academic Noam Chomsky. On a trip to Venezuela in 2009 he gushed
about the Bolivarian Revolution: "[W]hat's so exciting about at last visiting Venezuela is that I can see how a better world is being created. . . .
The transformations that Venezuela is making toward the creation of
another socio-economic model could have a global impact." But eight
years later, Chomsky was singing a different tune: "I never described
Chavez's state capitalist government as 'socialist' or even hinted at such
an absurdity," he claimed. "It was quite remote from socialism. Private capitalism remained. . . . Capitalists were free to undermine the
economy in all sorts of ways, like massive export of capital."[55]

Bernie Sanders did a similar about-face on Venezuela. In 2006,
he participated in a Hugo Chavez stunt in which Bernie bought
discounted Venezuelan heating oil for distribution to Vermonters
through government assistance programs.[56] But in 2015, when Hillary
Clinton supporters began attacking him over that deal, he denounced
Chavez as a "dead communist dictator."[57] That makes it really hard
to explain why, during the Venezuelan general strike of 2002–2003,
Bernie signed a letter along with eighteen Democratic members of
Congress expressing support for the dictator and opposing efforts to
remove him from office.[58]

Today's crop of socialists in Washington claims they don't support
communist or authoritarian socialism, insisting they have something
more peaceful in mind. Bernie insists Denmark is his inspiration—
which upset the Danish prime minister, who noted that Denmark
actually isn't socialist at all.[59]

Despite these claims, Bernie can't seem to stop himself from
blurting out praise for communist regimes. This is no one-time slip-

up, it's a decades-long habit. In 1988 he honeymooned in the USSR and returned to America declaring, "There are some things that [the USSR does] better than we do and which were, in fact, quite impressive," going on to rave about the wonders of the Moscow subway system.[60]

True to form, after the USSR collapsed, Bernie's messaging was noticeably different. At a 2020 CNN town hall, an audience member told Bernie that his father's family had fled the USSR and asked, "How do you rectify your notion of democratic socialism with the failures of socialism in nearly every country that has tried it?" Bernie answered, "Is it your assumption that I supported or believe in authoritarian communism that existed in the Soviet Union? I don't and never have. And I opposed it. . . . What do I mean when I talk about democratic socialism? It certainly is not the authoritarian communism that existed in the Soviet Union and in other communist countries."[61]

If that's the case, it's strange that Bernie continually praised the actions of the communist regimes he supposedly opposes. In 1985 he traveled to Nicaragua for celebrations commemorating the sixth anniversary of the communist Sandinista regime. According to the *New York Times*, "At the anniversary celebration, a wire report described a chant rising up: 'Here, there, everywhere, the Yankee will die.' If Mr. Sanders harbored unease about the Sandinistas, he did not dwell on it." After returning to Vermont, Bernie wrote a letter to Sandinista leader Daniel Ortega inviting him to Burlington and bemoaning the U.S. media's supposed bias against his regime. But today, with Ortega again ruling Nicaragua as Amnesty International and other human rights groups denounce him for committing crimes against humanity, Bernie voices concern about Ortega's "anti-democratic policies."[62]

Similarly, after returning from a trip to Cuba in 1989, Bernie babbled, "I did not see a hungry child. I did not see any homeless people." He admitted Cuba was "not a perfect society," but insisted that the communist nation "not only has free health care but very high-quality health care. . . . The revolution there is far deeper and more profound than I understood it to be. It really is a revolution in terms of values."[63] When asked by *60 Minutes* during the 2020 presidential campaign about his praise of the Castro regime, he again changed his tune, claiming, "We're very opposed to the authoritarian nature of Cuba." But Bernie just couldn't help himself, following that statement by lauding Castro's "massive literacy program."[64] So Castro may have thrown dissidents into prison camps and murdered them, but at least some of those who didn't resist learned how to read—and mostly government-sanctioned "news" and books.

Despite his halfhearted attempts to distance himself from hard-core communism, Bernie has a long history of supporting radical Marxist organizations. In the 1980 and 1984 U.S. presidential elections, Bernie campaigned for the Socialist Workers' Party, a fringe communist group. As the *Washington Examiner* reported,

> In 1980, Sanders "proudly endorsed and supported" Andrew Pulley, the party's presidential candidate, who once said that American soldiers should "take up their guns and shoot their officers." Sanders was one of three electors for Pulley on the Vermont ballot, stating in a press release: "I fully support the SWP's continued defense of the Cuban revolution."
>
> Four years later, he backed and campaigned for the SWP presidential nominee Mel Mason, a former Black Panther, saying it was important for there to be "fundamental alternatives to capitalist ideology." During the campaign, Mason praised the Russian and Chinese revolutions and said: "The greatest example of a socialist government is Cuba, and Nicaragua is right behind, but it's still developing."[65]

And if Bernie now projects himself as merely supporting peaceful assistance for the poor, some of his followers haven't got the message. In video stings, Project Veritas captured multiple Bernie campaign workers and volunteers declaring support for "extreme action," warning of mass violence if Bernie doesn't win the Democratic nomination, discussing the need to keep quiet about Marxist-Leninists and anarchists participating in the campaign, and advocating sending their class enemies to Soviet-style forced labor camps.[66]

Bernie's ideological instincts are obvious. His proposal to abolish private health insurance through his Medicaid for All scheme is similar to his policy proposals from years ago, when he was less guarded about his program than he is today. In the 1970s, he called for "placing doctors on salaries" and implementing a 100 percent tax rate for income over a million dollars a year. He also advocated for the government to seize control of the energy industry, electricity and telephone utilities, banks, "corporations" in general, and drug companies.[67] In other words, he called for state control over the main levers of the economy.

That is what socialists want, because that's what socialism means. According to socialism, free individuals can't be trusted to run industries; only the government can be trusted. Why government bureaucrats are smarter or less selfish or less corrupt than businesspeople remains to be seen. But if a socialist gains power, this state of affairs has the benefit of concentrating far more power in his or her own hands.

People can reasonably ask what would be needed to discredit socialism if the centuries-long record of disaster after disaster isn't enough. The answer, clearly, is that for true believers, *nothing* can discredit the ideology. No number of famines, mass murders, or economic collapses will ever be enough to make them question their socialist faith. To the contrary, *everything* is proof of the need for socialism. When the U.S. economy is doing poorly, they claim capitalism is broken and socialism will do better. When the economy is doing well, they say we need socialism to eliminate inequality between the rich and poor. For most reasonable people, the spread of the coronavirus showed the need to be more wary of communist China, but for Bernie and his supporters, it simply proved the need for more socialism.[68]

Although socialists often spend entire lifetimes arguing over the trivial details of their philosophy, it's possible that no one has understood socialism better than Margaret Thatcher. She was elected prime minister of Britain in 1979 as a backlash against socialists, who had conducted a decades-long experiment on the British economy. The wide-scale nationalization of industry and other collectivist policies had produced the typical results—economic stagnation, labor unrest, and social strife. But Thatcher understood that the problem with socialism is not just that it fails to meet its goal. The problem is the goal itself. Leveling society to make everyone equal is not only impossible, it's inherently destructive, it breeds corruption, and it's totally incompatible with freedom and limited government. In 1976 Thatcher declared,

One of our principal and continuing priorities when we are returned to office will be to restore the freedoms which the socialists have usurped. Let them learn that it is not a function of the State to possess as much as possible. It is not a function of the State to grab as much as it can get away with. It is not a function of the State to act as ring-master, to crack the whip, dictate the load which all of us must carry or say how high we may climb. It is not a function of the State to ensure that no-one climbs higher than anyone else. All that is the philosophy of socialism. We reject it utterly for, however well-intended, it leads in one direction only: to the erosion and finally the destruction of the democratic way of life.[69]

So long as socialists continue to fight for their destructive policies, the rest of us will have to remind people, especially young people, about socialism's miserable real-life record. We have to recognize socialism's sinister appeal—its promise of utopian equality, and its relentless scapegoating and encouragement of class warfare. We have to emphasize not only socialism's failures throughout the world, but the dilution of freedom that socialism requires.

With her stunning victory over socialism in Britain, Thatcher provides an example of how to argue our case—relentlessly, factually, fearlessly, and passionately. Never allow socialists to claim moral superiority—they have none. Never apologize for free markets and freedom, which produced the greatest system of wealth creation in human history. Instead let's put *them* on the defensive and make *them* justify their adherence to a failed, freakish ideology and their mystical faith in government planning that has resulted in anguish and squalor throughout the world.

Considering the American left's long fascination with socialist regimes and its romance with the USSR, it was a stunning turnaround when they suddenly decided in 2016 and 2017 that Russia was our chief enemy worldwide—a country so powerful and evil that it could supposedly corrupt a U.S. presidential election just by putting up some broken-English Facebook and Twitter posts. But if that's the argument they thought would get rid of President Trump, then that's the argument they had to make, and we turn to that topic in the next chapter.

CHAPTER FIVE

Deep State I: Russian Collusion—
The Hoax of the Century

On December 9, 2019, Department of Justice Inspector General Michael Horowitz reported that FBI officials had perpetrated a massive fraud on a federal surveillance court when they applied for a warrant and three renewals to spy on Trump campaign aide Carter Page. The report was proof that a cabal of rogue agents in the Obama administration spied on the Trump campaign, its transition team, and the presidency. For us at the Hannity team, it was proof of something else as well: that we had been right every step of the way.

Democrats and the media mob for three years had peddled lies, propaganda, and conspiracy theories. They started in the fall of 2016, with claims that Carter Page was working with the Kremlin to influence the election.[1] By January 2017 they had made public Christopher Steele's infamous dirty dossier, with its wild claims that Trump campaign manager Paul Manafort was at the heart of a "well-developed conspiracy of cooperation" between Trump and the Kremlin, and that the Trump team had promised foreign policy changes if the Russians helped Trump win the 2016 election. It even claimed the Russians had compromising information on Trump, showing him with hookers in the Ritz-Carlton hotel in Moscow.[2]

The accusations grew wilder with each day. The left accused Trump of working with Russia to spread misinformation. They claimed to have proof that Trump lawyer Michael Cohen snuck into Prague to discuss paying hush money to Russian hackers.[3] They claimed Trump Tower hosted a shady server that connected to Russia's Alfa Bank.[4] Donald Trump Jr. was supposedly in on the Russia plot. So were Attorney General Jeff Sessions, National Security Adviser Michael Flynn, half of Congress, and even the National Rifle Association. Every day it was "Russia, Russia, Russia."

This crazed narrative inflicted terrible harm on both the country and specific individuals. The FBI's investigation destroyed the reputations of patriotic American citizens like Flynn and Page. It inspired the appointment of a special counsel, Robert Mueller, who reigned as a dark shadow over 675 days of the Trump administration, tyrannizing Washington with a flood of subpoenas and witness demands. Mueller never found any Trump-Russia "collusion," but he jailed more than a half dozen people for unrelated crimes. A corrupt media establishment abandoned its most basic duties to truth and fairness, even as the liberal elite abandoned that most core American concept: innocent until proven guilty.

Yet it was all a giant hoax—one unlike anything we've ever seen in our lives. It was brought to you by the very same people who rejected the 2016 election results. They hated that Donald Trump won that election fair and square, and were willing to spin any fantasy to take him out. And they stick to that fantasy even after four separate investigations have proven them wrong. The FBI found no evidence of Russian collusion. Neither did a House Intelligence Committee probe run by California's Devin Nunes. Nor has a bipartisan Senate Intelligence Committee investigation. Mueller, too, struck out.

Even as the mob peddled their lies, an all-star cast on my radio and TV shows was providing Americans the real story. Mark Levin, Dan Bongino, Sara Carter, John Solomon, Gregg Jarrett, Alan Dershowitz, David Limbaugh, Joe diGenova, Victoria Toensing, and many other standouts joined us to document how a corrupt upper echelon of law enforcement and intelligence officials abused their powers to spy on a campaign and presidency they didn't like. They relied on phony intel, listened in on conversations, used undercover informants, and leaked bogus claims. We the people gave them powerful intelligence tools to protect us, and they turned that weaponry back on the man whom Americans duly elected to office. The Fake News Media trashed our Hannity ensemble cast every day for reporting these truths. But we never relented. We covered this very real abuse of power, and the 434-page Horowitz report was vindication. We were dead-on right.

ANATOMY OF A WITCH HUNT

We were right, for instance, that the FBI had launched a counter-intelligence investigation into the Trump campaign in July 2016 on the thinnest of suspicions. Forget all the crazy later conspiracy claims. According to the IG report, the FBI started with one paltry piece of information: a tip from Alexander Downer, an Australian diplomat then based in the United Kingdom.[5] For some unknown reason, Downer arranged to have a drink in May 2016 with a lower-level Trump campaign aide, George Papadopoulos. Downer later claimed Papadopoulos told him the Russians intended to release information that would hurt the Hillary Clinton campaign.

Papadopoulos later testified that he didn't even remember saying that to Downer. But suppose he did. So what? A lot of people at the time were talking about the secret server Clinton kept as secretary of state and whether it had been hacked by foreign governments. What we have here is our crack FBI admitting it launched a full-fledged probe on the basis of worldwide gossip.

Making this story even more mysterious is that Papadopoulos remembers a Maltese professor named Joseph Mifsud telling him in April 2016—right before he met with Downer—that the Russians had Clinton emails. In his report, Mueller claimed Mifsud had "connections to Russia," to make it sound as if the FBI had good reason to investigate all this.[6] (Notably, Mueller stopped short of FBI director James Comey's characterization of Mifsud as a "Russian agent"[7] or House Intelligence Committee chairman Adam Schiff's description of him as a "Russian cut-out.")[8] But reports show Mifsud is actually connected to all kinds of Western intelligence agencies, making him an unlikely Russian asset. The bottom line is that the FBI's claim that it had good reason for starting a full-fledged counterintelligence investigation into a political campaign doesn't wash.

We were also right that the FBI used the dirty dossier in their investigation. For nearly a year, Democrats and the media described the dossier as a series of high-value "intelligence reports," passing off its author, Christopher Steele, as a "well-placed Western intelligence source,"[9] a "Russia expert,"[10] and "a veteran spy" for Britain's MI6 who "spent almost two decades on Russian intelligence matters."[11] NBC News actually ran this headline: "Christopher Steele, Trump Dossier Author, Is a Real-Life James Bond."[12] Comey would later insist Steele was "a credible source, someone with a track record, someone who was a credible and respected member of an allied intelligence service during his career."[13]

America learned the ugly truth in October 2017, thanks to the Nunes investigation in the House Intelligence Committee. We reported on it, and the Horowitz report confirmed it. The dossier wasn't the work of a well-meaning intel professional. It was a political dirty trick, a hit job paid for by the Clinton campaign and fed to the FBI to sabotage Trump.[14] It was the source of all those claims that Page and Manafort were at the heart of a Trump-Russia "conspiracy."

The dossier was funded by the Clinton campaign and the Democratic National Committee, which paid more than $12.4 million during the 2016 campaign to a law firm called Perkins Coie. That legal outfit funneled cash to Fusion GPS, a political strategist firm, which in turn hired Steele.[15] The Clinton campaign claimed all this as a legal expense and hid from the public its hiring of a notorious opposition research firm to dig up Russian dirt on Trump. Some people would call that a campaign finance violation, but Clinton got away with it—as usual.

The FBI went running with its dossier to the Foreign Intelligence Surveillance Court to get a surveillance warrant on Carter Page, who in early 2016 joined the Trump campaign as a foreign policy adviser. The FISA court not only granted a warrant against Page in October 2016, it agreed to three additional renewals—putting Page under surveillance for nearly an entire year. The surveillance was extremely intrusive, including physical searches and authorization to spy on Page when he traveled abroad.[16] And as former federal prosecutor Andrew McCarthy explained, FISA warrants don't just cover "forward-going communications." The Page warrants freed the FBI to snoop through any *past* Page calls, texts, or emails. "They were hoping to get a motherlode of communications involving Page and Trump campaign people," McCarthy told radio's Hugh Hewitt in 2018.[17]

We were right that the dirty dossier was the only reason the FBI could get its warrants. Comey obfuscated the facts about that early on, to protect the FBI. He told Fox News's Bret Baier that "there was a significant amount of additional material about Page and why there was probable cause to believe he was an agent of a foreign power, and the dossier was part of that but was not all of it or a critical part of it, to my recollection."[18] Comey's Fake News Media pals kept up that fiction for years.

We already knew Comey's statements did not reflect reality, thanks to the Nunes memo, which was issued in February 2018 after House Intel members finally were allowed to review the FBI's applications against Page. The memo said that the dossier "formed an essential part" of the Page applications, and that former FBI deputy director Andrew McCabe testified to the committee in December 2017 that "no surveillance warrant would have been sought from the [FISA court] without the Steele dossier information."[19] It confirmed the FBI had hid from the FISA court the Clinton-DNC connection to the dossier (even though FBI officials knew about the shady connection and had been warned that Steele had a bias against Trump). It revealed that the FBI had given the court the dossier before it was vetted.

We also reported on a criminal referral of Steele from Senators Lindsey Graham and Chuck Grassley that was declassified the same month. The Grassley-Graham document confirmed key sections of the Nunes memo, noting that the Page applications "relied heavily on Mr. Steele's dossier claims"; that the FBI had failed to get "meaningful corroboration" of the dossier; and that the Bureau didn't tell the FISA court about the Clinton cash or Steele's bias. But the Grassley-Graham referral also delved into Steele's credibility, tearing up the FBI's claim to the court that Steele was a reliable source. Like the Nunes memo, the referral noted that the FBI had in fact fired Steele in October 2016 for leaking his dossier details to the press.[20]

Liberals and their press cheerleaders had a meltdown over both the memos and claimed Nunes, Grassley, and Graham were either lying or exaggerating. They were egged on by the top Democrat on the House Intelligence Committee, the fact-challenged Adam Schiff, who issued a rival memo to the Nunes memo that bluntly declared, "FBI and DOJ officials did *not* 'abuse' the [FISA] process, omit material information, or subvert this vital tool to spy on the Trump campaign." It repeated Comey's unsubstantiated statement, saying the FBI had made "only narrow use" of the dossier, and also claimed DOJ had been transparent about the Clinton connection.[21] The press circled the wagons and presented his memo as truth.

In December 2019, the report by DOJ Inspector General Horowitz confirmed everything we'd reported on the FISA warrants on Carter Page:

1. No dossier, no warrants.
2. The dossier was unverified garbage.
3. The FBI knew the dossier was a political hit job.
4. The FBI nonetheless used it to spy on the Trump campaign, duping the FISA court.

The details were gorier than even we expected. Comey had insisted that the FBI had behaved perfectly. "I have total confidence that the FISA process was followed and that the entire case was handled in a thoughtful, responsible way by DOJ and the FBI," he said.[22] Even former Trump deputy attorney general Rod Rosenstein made it sound as if it would be impossible for the FBI to hoodwink the court. In May 2018, he lambasted House Republicans who were investigating the FBI and boasted, "There's a lot of talk about FISA applications. Many people I've seen talk about it seem not to recognize . . . In order to get a FISA warrant, you need an affidavit signed by a career federal law enforcement officer who swears that the information is true. . . ."[23]

Or not. Inspector General (IG) Michael Horowitz blew up this narrative, reporting that the Clinton-bought-and-paid-for dossier "played a central and essential role in the FBI's" decision to get the warrant to spy on Page.[24] The FBI had wanted a warrant in August 2016, but government lawyers said the Bureau didn't have enough evidence. It was only when the FBI investigating team (code name Crossfire Hurricane) obtained the Steele dossier on September 19, 2016, that the lawyers gave the green light.

The IG meanwhile went on to describe seventeen "significant inaccuracies and omissions" in the FBI's applications.[25] That's a bureaucratic way of saying that the FBI repeatedly engaged in a premeditated fraud on the FISA court.

It turns out the Steele "intelligence" was little more than lies and conspiracy theories based largely on a single source who denied to the FBI that he had a network of sub-sources, as Steele repeatedly claimed.[26] Steele himself described one supposed sub-source to the FBI as a "boaster" and an "egoist" and someone who "may engage in some embellishment."[27] The FBI didn't bother to do any vetting of this source prior to submitting its application on Page. And when it finally got around to speaking to this person (starting in January 2017), the source said that he/she never even expected Steele to include "statements in reports or present them as facts" since "it was just talk." The source "explained that his/her information came from 'word of mouth and hearsay;' 'conversation that [he/she] had with friends over beers;' and that some of the information, such as allegations about Trump's sexual activities, were statements he/she heard made in 'jest.'"[28] In other words, the FBI's source was relaying bar gossip.

Possibly even worse, declassified footnotes in the Horowitz report revealed that the FBI had multiple indications that the dossier was contaminated with Russian disinformation. It turns out that Steele had close connections with five Russian oligarchs who tried to use him as an intermediary to connect with the FBI. Meanwhile, sources providing information for the dossier had connections with Russian intelligence, and the FBI thought Russian agents may have targeted Steele's private intelligence company.[29] So when you heard about dossier allegations from all the media mobsters, leaking FBI agents, and Trump-hating Democrats like Shifty Adam Schiff, there's a good chance they were spreading Russian disinformation.

The report also confirmed the FBI could never verify any of the dossier's insane accusations. Why? Because—as we noted all along—they were unverifiable. As the IG wrote, the "Crossfire Hurricane team was unable to corroborate any of the specific substantive allegations regarding Carter Page contained in Steele's election reporting."[30] As we reported much earlier, the FBI put together a spreadsheet containing each of Steele's allegations; it failed to confirm any of them. And that included the allegations it presented to the FISA court as proof that Page was a Russian asset. Pretty much the only thing the FBI ever managed to confirm, said the IG, was "publicly available information" such as dates or names. The dossier was a pack of lies.

The FBI never told any of this to the FISA court. It knowingly suppressed the damning facts about the reliability of this principal source and of Steele himself. The IG reported that in later FBI interviews, Steele couldn't keep straight where he'd gotten all his information. His own primary source said Steele exaggerated or misstated claims. And when Bureau agents finally got around to talking to Steele's former colleagues about the quality of his work, they were told repeatedly that Steele demonstrated "lack of self-awareness" and "poor judgment."[31] Yet instead of fessing up to the FISA court its discovery that its source and material were all a fraud, the FBI in application after application continued to present the Steele dossier as rock-solid.

Then there's all the exculpatory information the FBI purposely left out of its application, facts that would have destroyed its case against Page. The FBI in the summer and fall of 2016 had sent "confidential human sources"—or what honest people call "spies"—to talk to Trump campaign members, including Page. In one conversation, Page told the FBI spy that he'd "literally never met" Paul Manafort. Page also denied ever having met two Russians who the dossier claimed were his collusion points of contact.[32] Both these statements directly contradicted the dossier's claims. But the FBI purposely didn't tell the FISA court about these denials, despite a requirement to do so.

Worse, the FBI deliberately kept hidden from the court the crucial information that Page had actually been approved as an "operational contact" for the CIA from 2008 to 2013 and that he'd reported information to that agency about interactions he'd had with Russian intelligence officers. The man the FBI had accused of being "an agent of a foreign power" had actually worked with the CIA, serving the country he loves. The FBI didn't just hide this crucial detail; it turned Page's service *against him*, using his contact with the Russian officers as more "proof" that he was colluding. The IG reported that an FBI lawyer even went so far as to doctor an email from the CIA, to keep hidden from the court that Page had worked as a CIA source. Horowitz has referred that attorney, Kevin Clinesmith, for possible criminal prosecution.

Finally, Horowitz confirmed we were right that the FBI had been warned every which way that Steele was a political operator, out to take down Trump. Comey spun propaganda to the nation on this, too. In his interview on Fox, Baier asked Comey when he found out the dossier had been paid for by the Clinton rabble. Comey responded, "I still don't know that for a fact. I've only seen it in the media."[33]

Really, Comey? The IG report explains that Justice Department official Bruce Ohr—whose wife worked for Fusion GPS—went to FBI and DOJ officials with warnings that "Steele's reporting was going to Clinton's presidential campaign and others," and that Steele was "desperate that Donald Trump not get elected and was passionate about him not being the U.S. president."[34] Steele also met in October 2016 with State Department officials, where he again rattled off his dossier conspiracy theories. Deputy Assistant Secretary of State Kathleen Kavalec told the FBI about her Steele meeting and pointed out that he had some information wrong—Steele had told her a conspiratorial ring of election saboteurs was being paid out of the Russian consulate in Miami, but there is no Russian consulate there.[35]

So the FBI was well aware even before it filed its application that Steele had credibility problems and was violating FBI rules by shopping his dossier to other Washington players.

One omission after another; one lie after another. Why lie about Page's work for the CIA, the fact that he'd worked undercover and risked his life? Why not tell the court about the exculpatory statements Page made to an undercover FBI informant? Why not say up front that the Clinton campaign paid for this information? Why? Because the FBI knew that if they were truthful, if they were transparent, the court would have denied the application. The only way to view this is that the FBI engaged in a criminal conspiracy to commit fraud on the FISA court.

Not that the media mob will ever present it that way. When the devastating Horowitz judgment finally hit, the press largely ignored the parts about the FBI's lies and distortion. It instead went into overdrive to distort two pieces of the report. First, it focused on Horowitz's finding that the investigation had "sufficient predicate." The media spun this to mean that the FBI was justified in launching a defcon investigation into a presidential campaign.

In fact, Horowitz went out of his way in the report to note several times that the "threshold" for starting an FBI probe is so "low" as to be nonexistent. The FBI has sweeping authority to probe pretty much anything. Horowitz also made a point of expressing his concern at finding that there were no existing rules requiring the FBI to get senior approval before launching a probe into a "sensitive" matter like a "major party presidential campaign."[36]

The media's second obsession was the following line in the report: "We did not find documentary or testimonial evidence that political bias or improper motivation influenced the decisions to open" the investigation. "Report On F.B.I. Russia Inquiry Finds Serious Errors But Debunks Anti-Trump Plot," screamed the *New York Times* headline. The report was a "triple rebuke to Trump's conspiracy theories," wrote Aaron Blake at the *Washington Post.*

This is the classic example of Fake News Media lying, lying, lying. Take apart that Horowitz statement. All he is saying is that his team didn't find any *smoking-gun email* in the form of Comey saying the goal of his probe was to remove Trump.

But Horowitz found plenty of bias and included it in his findings. That included the text messages of disgraced former FBI agent Peter Strzok and his paramour, Lisa Page, a former FBI lawyer. The duo refers to Trump as a "loathsome human" and an "utter idiot." In August 2016 a frantic Page texted the following to her lover: "[Trump's] not ever going to become president, right? Right?!" Strzok responded: "No. No he's not. We'll stop it."[37] Strzok only a week later texted about the FBI's need for an "insurance policy" in case Trump was elected. This was the man who was front and center on the anti-Trump probe, and his texts make more than clear that his "insurance policy" was an FBI investigation designed to undo the 2016 election.

In his congressional testimony, Horowitz himself directly contradicted the media claims of "no bias." "There is such a range of conduct here that is inexplicable. And the answers we got were not satisfactory. That we are left trying to understand how could all these errors have occurred over a nine month period, among three teams, handpicked, in one of the highest profile if not the highest profile case in the FBI, going to the very top of the organization, involving a presidential campaign." Horowitz also said this: "On the one hand, gross incompetence, negligence? On the other hand, intentionality? And where in between? We weren't in a position, with the evidence we had, to make that conclusion [of intentionality], but I'm not ruling it out."[38]

Attorney General William Barr put it more starkly in an NBC interview: "The core statement, in my opinion, by the IG, is that these irregularities, these misstatements, these omissions were not satisfactorily explained. And I think that leaves open the possibility to infer bad faith." Barr summed up the broader findings this way: "Our nation was turned on its head for three years based on a completely bogus narrative that was largely fanned and hyped by a completely irresponsible press. I think there were gross abuses of FISA, and inexplicable behavior that is intolerable in the FBI."[39]

REVENGE OF THE SWAMP CREATURES

How did this happen in our great country? How does one political party get away with feeding disinformation to our law enforcement and provoke a counterintelligence probe into a rival campaign? How does the FBI get away with turning its powerful tools on the man the United States citizenry elected as president? How do we end up with a special counsel who completely ignores FBI abuse and instead spends two years tyrannizing the Trump White House? How do we get stuck with a media horde that reports lie after lie, all to help the Democratic Party?

The answer: this is the swamp. The nation was put through hell for three years because a cabal of politicians, investigators, and media liars decided to put their own political agenda ahead of the country's institutions and well-being. They ignored the rules, they trampled on the Constitution, and they threw over basic decency, all so that they could take out a president who had vowed to clean up that swamp.

Let's be clear: there are specific individuals who are responsible for this epic scandal. The FBI is and remains the premier law enforcement agency in the world, and 99 percent of its agents are heroes. They are out protecting this country every day. The Russia witch hunt was instead about the 1 percent who abused their power for corrupt reasons.

At the top of that list is Mr. Super Patriot himself, Jim Comey. He spent his entire Washington career parading around as holier-than-thou. The guy even had the gall, after Trump fired him for incompetence, to write a book titled *A Higher Loyalty: Truth, Lies, and Leadership*. We rely on individuals in powerful positions to guard the government against political dirty tricks like the Clinton dossier. Comey instead invited the bad guys in and put his FBI at their disposal.

Consider that word: "leadership." After Comey was fired, he was the subject of two other Horowitz reports even before the inspector general released his one on FISA abuse. The first excoriated Comey for his handling of the Hillary Clinton server case. You remember the one? Where the FBI treated the Clinton campaign with kid gloves even after Clinton mishandled classified information, deleted subpoenaed emails, and acid-washed her hard drive with BleachBit to disappear whatever she was hiding. Instead of charging Clinton with a crime, Comey broke the chain of command, going around his superiors to call a press conference at which he spent fifteen minutes slamming her for being "extremely careless."

That IG report found that Comey was no leader. It denounced him for being "insubordinate," usurping Attorney General Loretta Lynch's authority by doing that press conference.[40] It rebuked him for using the media conference to make derogatory statements about a person the DOJ was declining to prosecute. The report was perfectly consistent with Deputy Attorney General Rod Rosenstein's memo recommending Comey be fired, in which Rosenstein wrote, "[Comey] laid out his version of the facts for the news media as if it were a closing argument, but without a trial. It is a textbook example of what federal prosecutors and agents are taught not to do."[41]

The second Horowitz report on the former FBI director, issued in August 2019, destroyed Comey's infamous claims that he doesn't leak or do "weasel moves." Turns out that after Trump fired Comey, Mr. Super Patriot had swiped four government memos detailing his private conversations with the president and stashed them in his home safe. Comey leaked the memos to his private attorneys, including one containing classified information, and also had a buddy leak the contents of one to the *New York Times*. These documents were so sensitive that FBI agents showed up at the disgraced former director's front door to retrieve them.

Horowitz found, "By not safeguarding sensitive information obtained during the course of his FBI employment, and by using it to create public pressure for official action, Comey set a dangerous example for the over 35,000 current FBI employees—and the many thousands more former FBI employees—who similarly have access to or knowledge of non-public information."[42] The IG found Comey's handling and dissemination of the memos violated FBI policies and his own employment agreement, and Horowitz referred Comey for federal prosecution for mishandling classified information. Only the DOJ declined to prosecute. Why? Because Comey made certain none of the memos were "marked" as classified when he was director; only after he was fired did the memos undergo a classification review. So Comey could claim that nothing was officially classified at the time he mishandled the information. How's that for a weasel move?

Speaking of weasel moves, also consider this: Comey admitted the entire reason he leaked that memo information to the *New York Times* was to pressure the DOJ to appoint a special counsel to investigate Trump-Russia collusion. Thanks to all the Horowitz digging, however, we now know that by that time, Comey and his corrupt FBI cronies knew the collusion claim was a lie. They knew Clinton was behind the dossier, that Steele was a dirty political operator, that his own main source admitted the dossier was unconfirmed gossip, and that they hadn't verified a single accusation. Yet Comey still schemed to appoint a special prosecutor, who spent two more years putting the country through hell. This one leak alone shows how political Comey was from the get-go. This was an FBI director out to get President Trump.

Or how about his underhanded ensnaring of former Trump national security adviser Michael Flynn? Only a few days after Trump was sworn into office, the FBI sent agents to interview the general about his transition-period conversations with Russian ambassador Sergei Kislyak. They'd discussed U.S. sanctions on Russia and a UN resolution condemning Israel. The FBI concocted the outrageous theory that Flynn might have violated the Logan Act, a law that bars U.S. citizens from engaging with foreign governments without sign-off. No serious person prosecutes the Logan Act. Only two people have ever been indicted for violating the act, and the last one was in 1852.

Comey later bragged that he took advantage of the "chaos" of the new administration by sending agents to interview Flynn without following protocol. That FBI interview was something "I probably wouldn't have done or maybe gotten away with in a more organized investigation, more organized administration, in the George W. Bush administration, for example, or the Obama administration," Comey boasted in 2018. "In both of those administrations, there was a process. And so, if the FBI wanted to send agents into the White House itself to interview a senior official, you would work through the White House counsel and there would be discussions and approvals, and who would be there. And I thought, it's early enough. Let's just send a couple guys over." [43]

The sick reality is that Comey didn't need to ask Flynn about those conversations. The FBI already had the transcripts. The only reason to interview Flynn was to set him up for a perjury trap. This was confirmed by handwritten notes taken after a meeting consisting of Comey, McCabe, and FBI counterintelligence chief Bill Priestap, in which the note taker—presumably Priestap—asked if the goal of the Flynn interrogation was "to get him to lie, so we can prosecute him or get him fired."[44] And McCabe admitted that he lulled Flynn into thinking he didn't need a lawyer present for the interview and purposely omitted the standard warning against lying to the FBI. They wanted Flynn "relaxed."[45] It later emerged that the FBI had decided to close its investigation of Flynn weeks before his interview, having found no derogatory information on him, but Strzok intervened, saying his superiors wanted it kept open.[46]

Flynn had conducted hundreds of discussions during the presidential transition, and his recollections of the Kislyak conversation didn't match what was in the transcript. The FBI interviewing agents nonetheless said they saw "nothing that indicated to them that he knew he was lying."[47] And why would he intentionally lie? Flynn had headed the Defense Intelligence Agency and surely knew the FBI was monitoring Kislyak's calls. Despite all this, Mueller went after Flynn for "lying," driving him to the edge of bankruptcy and threatening to indict Flynn's son on unrelated issues. Flynn fell on his sword for his family and pleaded guilty to lying.

This is how the FBI and a special prosecutor treated a thirty-three-year veteran who protected his country over many years in combat. They set him up, put the screws to him, and gloated over their "plea deal." The case was drenched in malfeasance and could proceed only as long as the evidence of the government's abuses stayed hidden. Once Attorney General Barr appointed prosecutor Jeff Jensen to review the case, and Jensen began producing that evidence, the case disintegrated. Despite the judge's outrageous resistance, the Department of Justice then sought to drop the prosecution, admitting there was no legitimate reason for the FBI to have interviewed Flynn in the first place.

How about Saint Jim's claims that he doesn't lie? Comey signed off on the very first FISA application against Page and then two more renewals. Every one of those warrant requests was marked "verified" at the top of the document. He swore three times that the evidence in those applications was true, accurate, and verified. None of it was.

He also misled President-elect Trump when he went to "warn" him about the dossier in January 2017. Comey outright told Trump that he was not the target of an investigation. But one of the Horowitz reports revealed that Comey was using that meeting to probe Trump for information and to get his reaction to the dirty dossier. He didn't tell Trump that just a couple of months earlier he'd signed a FISA into one of his campaign aides. He instead told Trump the very dossier that he'd verified as truthful in that application was "salacious and unverified." [48]

About the only FBI official who even competed with Comey on the liar front was his deputy. Andrew McCabe was also fired from the FBI for lying. Horowitz issued a separate report about McCabe's behavior in February 2018, a seething rebuke of the fired deputy director. It examined McCabe's role in disclosing the existence of an FBI investigation into the Clinton Foundation. McCabe's wife had run for state election in Virginia and taken money from a Clinton ally, and McCabe was getting questioned over his impartiality. So he authorized the release of information to the *Wall Street Journal*, resulting in a story that suggested McCabe was heroically pushing forward a Clinton investigation.

The Horowitz report slammed him for a leak designed solely to "advance his personal interests at the expense of Department leadership" and for lying about the leak. The IG said McCabe was guilty of "lack of candor"—that's "lying" in FBI-speak—at least three times under oath in talks with investigators. He also told Comey he didn't know who was behind the leak. And he was unclear with investigators about what he'd told Comey.[49] And he blamed FBI colleagues for his own leak. This troubled relationship with the truth is presumably why Fake News CNN hired McCabe as a commentator—he fits right in.

This is the same McCabe who says that in the spring of 2017 he discussed with Rosenstein a plan to have the deputy attorney general wear a wire during conversations with Trump and secretly try to recruit cabinet members to remove the president under the Twenty-Fifth Amendment.[50] Assuming McCabe's being honest just this once, let's call this what it was: McCabe was actively working to stage a coup against the commander in chief.

Yet McCabe also skipped out of jail time. Washington prosecutors ended his case in February 2020, after the same disgraced FBI cabal that caused this mess came to his rescue. The *New York Times* earlier reported, "A key witness in the case—Lisa Page, the former FBI lawyer whom Mr. McCabe authorized to speak to the *Wall Street Journal* reporter—also told the grand jury that he was not motivated to lie about the episode. . . . Her sympathetic testimony to Mr. McCabe would most likely be a problem for prosecutors."[51]

These FBI officials weren't the only government players engaged in mass corruption. They had help from the intel community. Never forget Senate Minority Leader Chuck Schumer's warning to Trump in January 2017. The Obama intel groups had rushed to release their official "assessment" of Russian interference in the 2016 election and to distort intelligence to claim that Putin had interfered specifically to get Trump elected. The president-elect correctly pointed out that intelligence forces were playing politics. Schumer crowed that Trump would rue the day he said that. "Let me tell you: You take on the intelligence community—they have six ways from Sunday at getting back at you," Schumer told MSNBC.[52]

They were already sabotaging Trump under the direction of partisans like former CIA head John Brennan. Intel community leaders were part of the plot to gin up the investigation into Trump, his associates, his campaign, his transition, and later his presidency. And they were likely behind the leaks of raw intelligence designed to sabotage Trump team members like Flynn.

Since crawling from the CIA straight into the arms of NBC News and MSNBC, Brennan has repeatedly made vicious, bitter accusations against Trump. He's called the president's behavior "treasonous" and once raged on Twitter at Trump, "When the full extent of your venality, moral turpitude, and political corruption becomes known, you will take your rightful place as a disgraced demagogue in the dustbin of history." Maybe no surprise then that in a May 2017 congressional hearing, Brennan claimed he was the guy behind the Trump investigation. He said the CIA discovered intelligence about contacts between Russian officials and Americans and made sure every "bit" of it was shared with the FBI. He claimed those details "served as the basis for the FBI investigation."[53]

Brennan is also the reason the story exploded on the public in the fall of 2016. Brennan kept pushing through the spring and summer of 2016 for the intel community to take the line that Russia was working to get Trump elected, but he couldn't convince some of his colleagues to go that far. So he used an August meeting with former Senate minority leader Harry Reid to voice his conspiracy theory. And sure enough, Mr. Reid instantly sent a letter to Comey—which leaked— asking about the "direct connection between the Russian government and Donald Trump's presidential campaign." He demanded the FBI launch a full investigation, just as Brennan had hoped.[54]

THE FINAL STEP: ACCOUNTABILITY

It was law enforcement and intel figures who perpetrated the corruption. But we also need to hold to account the people who then aided it and covered it up, pursuing their own agenda against Trump. Mueller is at the top of that list. Mueller had the opportunity—the obligation— to get to the truth about the political corruption, the dossier, the FBI's abuse of power, and its lies. He instead kept alive the FBI's collusion hoax for years, feeding the fevered anti-Trump press and undermining the Trump administration's ability to govern.

The fix was in the minute Mueller chose for his team the same Obama holdovers who had worked side by side with Comey and McCabe and former deputy attorney general Sally Yates on their Trump takedown. That included prosecutors like Andrew "Pit Bull" Weissmann and Jeannie Rhee, both fervent Democrats. Of the seventeen attorneys whom Mueller had publicly appointed by 2018, thirteen were registered Democrats and half of those had donated to Clinton's presidential campaign.[55] This group hired an army of investigators, subpoenaed millions of documents, and spent more than $30 million in a desperate attempt to prove a collusion accusation that the FBI already knew was false.

Mueller's team left a trail of devastation. It went after Flynn and other Trump officials for "lying" to the FBI or the special counsel. That included George Papadopoulos, who from the start had cooperated with the FBI and the special counsel investigation but was sentenced to two weeks in jail anyway. The team jailed former Trump campaign manager Paul Manafort for unrelated financial crimes. Ditto former Trump lawyer Michael Cohen. Manafort—who was never accused of any violent crimes—was held in solitary confinement and locked in a cell for twenty-three hours a day as part of an intense pressure campaign to get him to plead guilty. Roger Stone endured a predawn raid by more than a dozen armed FBI agents at his house, where a CNN news crew just happened to be positioned at the time. This is not how our American democracy and system of justice are supposed to work.

And yet here's what Mueller never found: a single case of a Trump person conspiring with Russians. His final 448-page report had to admit he failed to discover a shred of evidence to support the insane conspiracy theories of the prior three years.

Still, Mueller's team couldn't leave it at that—his report included an entire second section meditating on whether President Trump had committed "obstruction of justice" throughout the Mueller probe. The team was furious Trump had questioned their motives and denounced their probe as a "witch hunt." So they devoted 187 pages to Trump's tweets and whether he had ordered Mueller fired. The very fact that Mueller completed his project—and was provided every resource he needed—was proof there was never any obstruction. Unable to recommend prosecution for a nonexistent crime, Mueller left it to DOJ superiors to decide whether his obstruction "evidence" was worthy of an indictment. The DOJ determined there was absolutely no ground for a case, but Mueller's real interest was in providing Democrats in Congress a road map for impeachment.

Cue the Mueller House testimony of July 2019. Democrats vowed the special counsel would bring his report "to life."[56] They promised Mueller would swoop in and prove that Trump remained an "unindicted co-conspirator" in a separate Mueller prosecution—thereby laying the groundwork for impeachment. Instead, Mueller's stumbling, incoherent House testimony was an epic embarrassment. He spent the day confused and dazed, unable to remember basic facts, slow to comprehend questions, and evasive or clueless on anything to do with Hillary, the dossier, or obvious FBI malfeasance. "I'm not going to get into that" was his favorite line. By the end, the media was in mourning, the most depressed they'd been since Trump was elected.

Republicans on the House Judiciary and Intelligence Committees did their job: they highlighted just how badly Mueller had failed in his most basic mission. The special counsel's job was to look at Russian interference in the 2016 election, but he failed to investigate what the FBI itself strongly suspected: that the Russians interfered in the election by feeding disinformation into Christopher Steele's dossier. In fact, Mueller's team was so intent on protecting the FBI, it refused to investigate the dossier at all. "Can you state with confidence the Steele dossier was not part of Russia's disinformation campaign?" Florida congressman Matt Gaetz asked the special counsel during the hearing. Mueller dodged, saying questions about the dossier "predated" him.[57]

Another hype-and-cover-up award goes to crazed congressional Democrats. To serve as one of the country's elected congressional representatives is one of the highest honors in the land. Sure, we expect the political parties to engage in spin and politics. But we also expect them to play by the rules of the game, abide by the Constitution, and tell the truth.

Democrats for decades positioned themselves as the party of "civil liberties," the party that cared the most about intrusive government surveillance. Some of them probably really believed it. But that's

what makes their actions throughout the Russian hoax all the harder
to stomach. They were willing to abandon every principle they'd ever
claimed—cheering on the FBI's violations of Carter Page's liberties and
its manufacturing of process crimes against other wrongly accused
Trump aides—in order to hide their party's role in the dossier trick
and to try to remove Trump from office.

When Congressman Devin Nunes in March 2017 uncovered
evidence that the Obama White House had in its waning days been
unmasking the names of Trump transition officials in intelligence
reports, he held a press conference. He was convinced his news that an
outgoing administration had been surveilling an incoming one would
provoke strong bipartisan condemnation. Yet even the seasoned
Nunes—who was used to partisan warfare—was shocked by Democrats' response. Instead of joining him to ask for answers, they accused
him of mishandling classified information. They were still in a rage
about the Trump win and willing to say or do anything to protect the
corrupt actions of Obama officials.

Leading the Democratic assault on Nunes was none other than his
counterpart on the House Intelligence Committee, Adam Schiff. I'll
have a lot more on Shifty Schiff in the next chapter on impeachment.
But suffice it to say the Russian hoax was where Schiff first cemented
his reputation as a congenital liar.

After Trump was inaugurated, Schiff spent more than two years
distorting and perverting Intel Committee information, misleading the
public into believing the dossier hoax. The more Nunes and Republican
members of the committee unraveled the truth of the dossier-FBI lies,
the more Schiff publicly doubled down, telling Americans he had proof
that Trump was a Manchurian candidate. As early as March 2017—
before Comey was fired or Mueller hired—Schiff told NBC's Chuck
Todd that "there is more than circumstantial evidence" of the Trump
campaign colluding with Russia.[58] In December 2017, he revealed the
supposed details to CNN's Jake Tapper: "The Russians offered help, the
campaign accepted help. The Russians gave help and the president made

full use of that help."[59] The Mueller report proved every word of this Schiff statement a lie, but the public wouldn't get that truth for another eighteen months. Schiff engaged in the same pattern of deception with his memo on the Carter Page FISA applications, claiming the FBI committed no abuses whatsoever and that the dossier information used in the applications was corroborated. But again, the country had to wait nearly two years for Horowitz to set the record straight.

While Schiff was publicly hoodwinking the nation, behind the scenes he was working to obstruct and hinder Republican efforts to get to the truth. He objected to nearly every element of Nunes's FISA abuse investigation—including the subpoena that eventually revealed that the Democrats had funded the dossier—and his legal staff objected to Republican questions during depositions to help shield witnesses (like Fusion GPS's Glenn Simpson) from answering. Schiff's steady stream of falsehoods was designed to undercut Republican facts, to give the media mobsters new, shiny tales to chase.

Most damaging, Schiff acted as chief spokesman for the Democratic campaign to present the entire Republican effort to get to the truth as nothing more than damaging partisan politics. Asked about GOP concerns about bias on the Mueller team, Schiff in that same December Tapper interview said, "The intent here is nothing short of discrediting Mueller, then discrediting the Justice Department, then discrediting the FBI, then discrediting the judiciary . . . this is an effort to tear at the very idea that there is an objective truth."[60]

Schiff's colleague in the Senate, Intelligence Committee vice chairman Mark Warner, was no better. At the center of the Senate's bipartisan Russia investigation, Warner must have known there was never any evidence of Trump-Russia collusion. Yet to this day, he insists Trump may have been conspiring with Putin to win the election. They all do. Democrats promised Mueller would be the final word on their conspiracy theory. But now that we have the truth, have any of them accepted that judgment? Have any of them apologized? Not at all. The Russia conspiracy theories go on.

Aided, of course, by the final, fraudulent players in this scandal: the media. The press continues to pretend to be arbiters of truth and facts. But the Russia hoax showed them to be nothing more than a propaganda arm of the Democratic Party. They spent three years peddling baseless conspiracy theories simply because they fit a vengeful, psychotic, anti-Trump narrative.

For more than a thousand days, it was Russia, Russia, Russia, with minute-by-minute headlines. Americans were told Trump campaign members had engaged in repeated interactions with Russian intelligence; that Trump Jr. and Michael Cohen and Carter Page and Roger Stone were all Russian cutouts; that the Russians had a server in Trump Tower; that Manafort secretly met with WikiLeaks founder Julian Assange in the Ecuadorian embassy in London; that the National Rifle Association laundered Russian money for the Trump campaign. All complete lies. And all from supposedly legitimate "news" outfits: the *New York Times*, *Washington Post*, *Guardian*, McClatchy, CNN, MSNBC, and many others.

And when the press isn't lying, it's busy spinning its narrative—again, all to undermine Trump. They promised us that Steele was a brilliant spymaster and that the FBI was motivated by nothing but good intentions. They assured that the government had fail-proof safeguards to protect against surveillance abuse and that anybody who suggested otherwise was spinning a "conspiracy theory."

We at the Hannity TV and radio shows were among the people most frequently accused by this preening press corps of floating those conspiracies. And again, that's why the Horowitz report was so valuable. We never went out with a story until we had corroboration; we crossed every "t" and dotted every "i." We told the country the truth.

It was the swamp that perpetrated a massive fraud on the nation.

For all we learned from the Horowitz report, there's still much we don't know. Horowitz couldn't issue subpoenas or empanel a grand jury. He was entitled to speak only to currently employed members of the DOJ and FBI, which meant he had to rely on the cooperation of former employees. Some weren't very helpful. Horowitz reported, for instance, that "loyal" Jim Comey refused to have his security clearance renewed as part of his interview—a clear attempt to evade tough questions related to classified information.[61] Horowitz also couldn't interview witnesses in other intel agencies or private or political actors.

But current U.S. attorney John Durham has no such constraints. Attorney General William Barr in May 2019 assigned the Connecticut prosecutor the job of investigating the origins of the Trump investigation. Durham's reputation is that of a crack investigator, with a history of probing government malfeasance. His past jobs included looking into accusations of CIA abuse of detainees and the FBI's ties to mob figures in Boston. He's widely respected as tough and no-nonsense.

There are already indications Durham is digging into the spring of 2016, the crucial months prior to the FBI opening up its "official" counterintelligence investigation. Indeed, when Horowitz issued his report, Durham took the rare step of issuing a public statement that took issue with the IG's claim of sufficient "predicate." While he had "utmost respect" for the work Horowitz put into his report, Durham's team did "not agree with some of the report's conclusions as to predication and how the FBI case was opened."[62]

Durham will hopefully get to the truth about whether the United States was outsourcing intelligence gathering to friendly countries like Italy, Great Britain, and Australia in order to circumvent laws against spying on Americans. He needs to look into the political side of this equation, and what role Fusion GPS, Democrats, and Obama officials had from the start, and what they knew as it went along. What were the roles of Brennan, former director of national intelligence James Clapper, former national security adviser Susan Rice, and former attorney general Loretta Lynch? What, for that matter, did Barack Obama know? We now know that Brennan, Clapper, Biden, former ambassador Samantha Power, former Obama chief of staff Denis McDonough, and dozens of other Obama officials unmasked Flynn's name in intelligence reports. We need to know which other Trump associates were unmasked and who criminally leaked information on them.

By October 2019 Durham had transitioned his probe into a full-fledged criminal investigation, giving him subpoena power and the ability to empanel a grand jury and file charges. That announcement is excellent news, because it finally holds out the potential for equal justice.

The Russia hoaxers did great damage to the country. They weaponized our most powerful intelligence tools, committed a fraud on an intelligence court, killed faith in our institutions, destroyed the reputations and lives of American citizens, and attempted to remove a duly elected president. But the great casualty has been equal justice.

I like to use the WWHTH standard. What Would Happen To Hannity? If an inspector general determined I was a liar and leaker, I'd go to jail. If I deliberately deceived a court, presenting it with "verified" information that I knew wasn't true, I'd be behind bars. Or imagine if Trump had a private server containing classified material and chose to delete 33,000 subpoenaed emails and destroy the evidence? The media mob would be howling for his removal.

But Hillary Clinton never faced any charges for mishandling top secret material and acid-washing her hard drives. Mueller went after Manafort and Papadopoulos and Cohen and Flynn for lying. Some may spend years in jail. But James Comey cashes in on a book, and McCabe lands a cushy job at CNN. We have laws against leaking classified information. We have laws against spying on Americans. And so far, not one person has yet been held to account.

If we don't have equal application of our laws, we might as well shred the Constitution. We cannot have dual justice in this country. We cannot have one system that applies to corrupt actors in the upper echelons of government, and one that applies to the rest of us. The Durham investigation will not only provide us information, but, hopefully, will answer the crucial question of whether we can still have faith in our system of government.

CHAPTER SIX

Deep State II: Impeachment—
The Failed Attempt to Decapitate
the Trump Presidency

On December 18, 2019, Democrats did to Donald J. Trump what they'd promised from the moment he was elected: they impeached him.

That vote had nothing to do with telephone calls to the Ukrainian president, or quid pro quos, or obstruction of Congress. It had nothing to do with high crimes or misdemeanors—or even impropriety. It was not about "protecting national security," or "upholding the Constitution," or any of the dishonest arguments Democrats gave for their vote.

Impeachment was instead the foreordained outcome of the left's psychotic rage against President Trump. They were unable to accept that he won the 2016 election. This president, as a result, lives rent-free in their heads, every second of every day. It's become a sickness.

The Ukraine allegations were actually just a subset of the much bigger trap the left was laying—what would become the Russia witch hunt. Even as Trump prepared to take office, Comey was doubling down on the Clinton dossier, Obama officials were unmasking transition team members, and the Obama DOJ was pursuing its crazy Logan Act claims. The Obama and Washington-bureaucrat and media machines were out to destroy Trump from the very beginning.

The radical left spent nearly three years on the Russia hoax, betting, as I explained earlier, that Robert Mueller would give them the goods to undo the 2016 election. Democrats were so convinced of their win that in early March 2019—before Mueller finished his work—Judiciary chairman Jerry Nadler laid the groundwork for impeachment by opening an investigation of "alleged obstruction of justice, public corruption, and other abuses of power by President Trump" and his associates.[1] And even after the special counsel proved an utter dud, Nadler and his comrades kept it up. They held more hearings, issued more subpoenas. They expanded their impeachment "proceedings" into Trump's finances, pardons, inaugural committee, and Stormy Daniels. It wasn't just rage fueling this gutter politics, it was escalating Democratic worry that they might lose to Trump again. Here's how Al Green, a Texas congressman, put it in May 2019: "I'm concerned that if we don't impeach this president, he will get re-elected."[2]

And that's how Russia, Russia, Russia became Ukraine, Ukraine, Ukraine. On August 12, a Deep State Democrat working in the intelligence bureaucracy filed a "whistle-blower" complaint alleging Trump was "using the power of his office to solicit interference from a foreign country in the 2020 election." By mid-September, Democrats had leaked the outlines of the Ukraine story and the media mob was spinning it 24/7. So it went for nearly five more hysterical months.

DEMOCRATS—THE REAL PURVEYORS
OF CORRUPTION IN UKRAINE

The Trump impeachment was actually two stories. The hate-Trump press wanted America to hear only one of these—the fantasy claim that Trump abused his power by pressuring Ukraine for dirt on Joe Biden. But it's the other story that matters, since it puts everything into context.

That's the story of Ukrainian corruption. The media never covered this reality because it vindicated Trump. That story also centered on the front-runner for the Democratic nomination: former vice president Joe Biden. It particularly spotlighted Biden's second son Hunter, a lawyer and lobbyist. Hunter was acutely aware of the sway of the Biden name, and Ukraine gave him the opportunity to cash in on it.

Ukraine had a revolution in 2014, which led to the ouster of its pro-Russian president, Viktor Yanukovych. Obama in early 2014 dispatched Joe Biden to lead the administration's work with that new government. Sleepy Joe became a regular visitor to Ukraine, traveling there frequently from 2014 to 2016, getting to know all the major players. This position also gave Biden a say over how to direct Western aid dollars to the country.

So imagine the coincidence when in spring 2014—just a few months after Joe got his Ukraine job—Hunter Biden scored a lucrative position on the board of Burisma Holdings, a Ukrainian energy company. Hunter had zero experience in the energy industry. Zero experience in the oil and gas sector. Zero experience with the country of Ukraine. And yet according to reports, Burisma started paying Hunter up to $50,000 a month for his non-expertise.[3] Hunter's business partner, Devon Archer, was also named to the board. According to one report, Burisma paid a total of $3.4 million to a Biden-Archer firm over eighteen months.[4]

What exactly did Hunter bring to the company? At the time it hired him, Burisma was swamped by corruption allegations. Investigators in Ukraine, the United States, and Great Britain were all looking at its operations. Its owner, a Ukrainian oligarch, had been accused of embezzling public funds and steering government contracts to his companies.[5] Nice time to have a Biden on your side, right?

The press downplays it now, but the Hunter appointment was immediately news in Washington and caused a stink. John Kerry was secretary of state at the time, and his stepson, Christopher Heinz, was invested in the Biden-Archer firm. When Hunter's board position was made public in May 2014, Heinz wrote an email to Kerry's top aides distancing himself from the decision.[6] A Heinz spokesman later admitted that "the lack of judgment in this matter was a major catalyst for Mr. Heinz ending his business relationships with Mr. Archer and Mr. Biden."[7]

Aides within Vice President Biden's office discussed whether "Hunter's position on the board would be perceived as a conflict of interest."[8] The *Washington Post* admitted that "one former adviser was concerned enough to mention it to the vice president . . . but the conversation was brief."[9] And the concerns didn't die. George Kent, a career State Department official, testified that in early 2015 he raised Hunter's position with the vice president's staff, saying it was a potential "conflict of interest" given Joe Biden's Ukrainian portfolio. "The message that I recall hearing back was that the Vice President's son Beau was dying of cancer and that there was no further bandwidth to deal with family-related issues at that time," Kent testified.[10] Amos Hochstein, the Obama energy czar, also raised the issue directly to Joe Biden.[11]

Ol' Joe now claims he knew nothing about his son's business dealings. We know that's not true. Discussing Hunter's position with Burisma, "Dad said, 'I hope you know what are doing,' " Hunter told the *New Yorker* in a story written before the impeachment drama.[12] There is also a public picture of Joe Biden golfing with Devon Archer in 2014. And on December 8, 2015, the *New York Times* wrote a story blowing the whole issue into the open. It noted Hunter Biden's appointment and Burisma's corruption problems, and questioned whether they "undermined" Joe Biden's "anticorruption message" in Ukraine. The story explained that "Kate Bedingfield, a spokeswoman for the vice president, said Hunter Biden's business dealings had no impact on his father's policy positions in connection with Ukraine."[13]

Joe knew all about his son's work and that Burisma was under investigation by Ukrainian authorities. Yet also in December 2015, Biden traveled to Ukraine and demanded the government fire the very prosecutor who was investigating Burisma, threatening to withhold $1 billion in U.S. loan guarantees to Ukraine unless that firing happened. Joe even bragged about the moment at a Council on Foreign Relations event in January 2018: "I looked at them and said: I'm leaving in six hours. If the prosecutor is not fired, you're not getting the money. Well, son of a bitch. [Audience laughter]. He got fired."[14]

This is the kind of despicable nepotism and influence-peddling that is all too common in Washington and that Trump promised to stop. Joe Biden was leveraging his role in the White House—and your tax dollars—for a get-rich-quick scheme for his family. Hunter Biden and his Burisma buddies were facing a major corruption investigation by Ukraine's top prosecutors. Who came to the rescue? Daddy, the vice president, ensuring his son would continue to benefit from his get-rich scheme.

Let's also call this for what it was: a quid pro quo. Biden was giving Ukrainian officials the message: you will not get over a billion dollars' worth of American aid unless you get rid of a prosecutor who is investigating the company my son is profiting from. This was Quid Pro Quo Joe exploiting his position to keep his son in the cash.

And the Biden corruption doesn't stop at Ukraine. Even before the Burisma scandal, Hunter Biden in December 2013 jumped on Air Force Two, making a trip with his father to Asia. They stopped in China, where Joe had talks with the Chinese president. Hunter ran off to a few business appointments. Around the same time, a Hunter Biden–connected firm landed a private-equity deal with a subsidiary of the Bank of China, owned by the Chinese government.

As Peter Schweizer, author of *Secret Empires*, has pointed out, this was a deal unlike others given to Western firms. Why would it go to Hunter Biden? As with Ukraine, he had no experience or expertise in China. He had limited expertise in private equity.[15] Financial giants like Goldman Sachs, Deutsche Bank, Bank of America—they aren't getting deals like this. So what did Hunter bring to the table? What did he have to offer beyond being the son of America's second-most-powerful decision maker?

Even Hunter has admitted that the only thing he brought to the

Burisma board was his dad's influence. In an October 2019 interview with ABC News, Amy Robach asked, "If your last name wasn't
Biden, do you think you would have been asked to be on the board
of Burisma?" Hunter answered: "I don't know. I don't know. Probably
not. I don't think there's a lot of things that would've happened in my
life if my last name wasn't Biden." [16]

At least ABC News asked the question, which is ten times more
than most of the press corps has been willing to do. Prior to the Trump
impeachment putsch, the media was happy to write about the Hunter-
Ukraine story, since it helped Democratic presidential candidates
whom the press preferred over Joe Biden. But once Trump asked about
the Biden corruption, the media declared it a dead issue. Instead of
digging further into the Hunter affair, the press proclaimed the Bidens
innocent of any wrongdoing and the story off-limits.

The press engaged in the same cover-up when it came to another
example of corruption: Democratic efforts to enlist Ukraine to help
defeat Trump in 2016. We know some of the details of this story
because, again, the press was interested—right up until it preferred the
story be only about Trump and Russia.

On January 11, 2017—before the Russia collusion hoax truly
engulfed the public—*Politico* ran a story by Kenneth P. Vogel and David
Stern. The headline: "Ukrainian efforts to sabotage Trump backfire:
Kiev officials are scrambling to make amends with the president-elect
after quietly working to boost Clinton." The first line: "Donald Trump
wasn't the only presidential candidate whose campaign was boosted by
officials of a former Soviet bloc country."

According to the piece, "Ukrainian government officials tried to
help Hillary Clinton and undermine Trump by publicly questioning
his fitness for office. They also disseminated documents implicating
a top Trump aide in corruption and suggested they were investigating the matter, only to back away after the election. And they helped
Clinton's allies research damaging information on Trump and his
advisers." [17]

The story detailed how a contractor for the Democratic National Committee (DNC), Alexandra Chalupa, had asked the Ukrainian embassy in 2016 to get dirt on Donald Trump and his campaign manager, Paul Manafort, in hopes of inspiring a congressional investigation in the run-up to the election. She even asked the embassy to arrange an interview with then–Ukrainian president Petro Poroshenko, to grill him for ugly details on Manafort. That sounds an awful lot like Democrats requesting a foreign government to interfere in our election.

Writing at *The Hill*, reporter John Solomon built on this story, in 2019 getting the former Ukraine ambassador to the United States to confirm this DNC pressure campaign had occurred. Solomon also reported that two top Ukrainian officials provided dirt to the U.S. media that smeared Manafort, forcing him to step down as Trump's campaign manager. And he noted that Nellie Ohr, a contractor for Fusion GPS (which was behind the infamous dossier), testified to Congress that some of her opposition research against Trump came from a Ukrainian parliament member.[18]

Our Trump-hating media insists that the Ukraine election meddling story has been debunked. They want to pretend that Russia was the only meddler. That's a lie. Ukraine's involvement was real and consequential, which is why three Senate committee chairmen—Chuck Grassley, Ron Johnson, and Lindsey Graham—are investigating the matter. Unlike Democrats, these Republicans care about interference in our system, regardless of which country is meddling.

These two issues—Biden corruption in Ukraine and Ukraine's election meddling—are essential to understanding the Trump impeachment. Democrats ignored these realities, instead shamefully twisting a routine conversation into something nefarious—for their own political gain. These issues also highlight the absurdity of the impeachment "articles" the House brought against the president. The left doesn't care about corruption or election interference. All it cares about is weaponizing any tool at its disposal against Trump.

A FAKE WHISTLE-BLOWER
SPARKS A MEDIA FRENZY

On April 21, 2019, Ukrainians elected forty-one-year-old Volodymyr Zelensky, a lawyer and comedian, as their new president. Zelensky ran against rampant Ukrainian corruption, promising to bring honest people to power. He won by a landslide. Ukraine is ranked one of the most corrupt countries in Europe, and Western leaders were excited about the reformer. They watched anxiously to see if Zelensky's party would win enough seats in the July 21, 2019, parliamentary elections to allow him to push through his agenda. His party won an absolute majority, the first time in Ukrainian history.

On July 25, 2019, President Trump called to offer Zelensky his congratulations on this "fantastic achievement." The call transcript shows a conversation that from the first second focused on Ukraine's biggest problem: corruption.[19] Zelensky promised Trump that he was working to "drain the swamp here in our country." He said he'd "brought in many, many new people. Not the old politicians, not the typical politicians, because we want to have a new format and a new type of government." He thanked Trump for U.S. assistance and for making available Javelin antitank missiles.

It's in the context of this corruption discussion that Trump asked Zelensky to "do us a favor." He explained that "our country has been through a lot," and "Ukraine knows a lot about it." He mentioned the cybersecurity company CrowdStrike—which first linked Russians to the 2016 DNC server hack—and wondered if Ukraine might have a missing server. Trump asked if Attorney General William Barr could call to "get to the bottom of it." Trump was clearly talking about both Russian and Ukrainian interference in the 2016 election (he at one point references the Mueller probe) and was asking Zelensky to cooperate with the Barr-Durham investigation.

Zelensky later brought up how much he also hoped to meet with former New York mayor and Trump lawyer Rudy Giuliani. Giuliani by this time had publicly announced he was investigating the Biden-Burisma corruption. Trump mentioned that Biden "went around bragging that he stopped the prosecution" of Burisma and said "it sounds horrible to me." Zelensky assured Trump that he was appointing a new prosecutor who would be looking into the situation.

In an interview I did with President Trump on October 21, 2019, he laid out the simple reasons for this discussion. "When you look at what's going on, and then you see all this horrible stuff . . . I heard Clinton was involved. I heard—they got somebody who wrote the fake dossier. Was it out of—out of Ukraine? . . . I would like the attorney general to find out what's going on, because you know what? We're investigating corruption," Trump said.[20]

None of this was wrong or scandalous—much less impeachable. Quite the opposite—it was necessary. The president of the United States has a sworn, constitutional duty to investigate crimes. The United States has a treaty with Ukraine, just like it has treaties with allies like Australia or Great Britain. Those documents require cooperation between countries in investigations.

And then there's the Constitution, which states that the president "shall take Care that the Laws be faithfully executed." We also have the Foreign Corrupt Practices Act, which makes it illegal for a U.S. person to coerce or to influence foreign officials through extortion. And we have a bribery statute, which forbids corruptly giving offers or promises of anything of value to a public official in order to influence an official act.

It was Biden who had threatened Ukraine in 2018. He threatened to withhold a billion dollars from that country unless it fired the prosecutor who was investigating his son. Does that count as a corrupt practice or bribery? Do Democrats become immune from laws by virtue of running for president? Hillary Clinton got the same special treatment over her private server and her mishandling of classified information in 2016. Trump has a very different view: that the laws should apply equally to all Americans, even elitist Democrats.

Trump's call with Zelensky was routine; the president was asking lots of other world leaders to cooperate with Barr's probe. In fact, America would never have even heard about this nonissue were it not for the infamous "whistle-blower." Eighteen days after the Trump-Zelensky call, an unnamed CIA officer filed a complaint with the inspector general of the intelligence community, accusing Trump of abusing his power for political gain by pressuring Zelensky to investigate the Bidens and 2016 election meddling.

By September, Democrats and the media had swirled this trivial call into a full-blown "scandal," adding even more allegations. Trump had pressured Zelensky to dig up "dirt" on a rival! Trump had threatened to withhold aid to Ukraine unless he got his demands! Trump was hiding the evidence! Quid pro quo! Extortion! Foreign interference! Impeach!

It was a classic example of the Deep State at work, another instance of the intel world getting back at Trump "six ways from Sunday." It turns out the "whistle-blower" was never a real whistle-blower. His own complaint acknowledged he hadn't been on the call—he had no direct knowledge of the conversation—and that everything he alleged was hearsay.[21] Conveniently, shortly after receiving this complaint, Michael Atkinson, the intelligence community inspector general who was later fired by Trump, secretly changed the guidance language on whistle-blower submission forms to eliminate the ban on hearsay information.[22] Of course, Atkinson should not have been advancing this complaint in the first place, since it had nothing to do with intelligence and was therefore outside his jurisdiction.

It's worth underscoring: the so-called whistle-blower was not a whistle-blower at all—he was a political saboteur, a partisan Trump hater, ground zero of the Democrats' new Ukraine hoax. The inspector general had to acknowledge the non-whistle-blower had a "political bias" in favor of Trump's Democratic rivals.[23] Later reporting determined he was a registered Democrat who had worked in the Obama White House alongside then–vice president Joe Biden and then–CIA director John Brennan.[24] He also hired as his attorney Mark Zaid, a prominent Trump-despising political operative who had been ranting about impeachment since Trump's first days in office. Here's a Zaid tweet from January 30, 2017, just ten days after Trump's inauguration: "#coup has started. First of many steps. #rebellion. #impeachment will follow ultimately. #lawyers." He kept it up, fantasizing for months about removing Trump from office.

It also turned out that this hearsay whistle-blower had plotted with Schiff from the start. In an obvious preemptive leak by Schiff's team, the *New York Times* reported that "the CIA officer approached a House Intelligence aide" days before he filed his official complaint. This allowed Schiff a head start on his impeachment march. The Schiff team even gave the fake whistle-blower advice on how to prepare the complaint and get a lawyer.[25] Schiff would go on to lie about this, telling MSNBC on September 17, "We have not spoken directly with the whistle-blower."[26]

All these damning facts explain why Schiff abandoned his demand that the whistle-blower testify to Congress. He knew Republicans would expose the political bias, the hearsay nature of the complaint, and the ties to Schiff's office. It would have early on exposed this as the latest Democratic scheme to bring down the president.

Not that Americans ever needed to hear the wild speculations of a partisan non-whistle-blower. Within days of the media mob latching on to the complaint, the Trump White House decided to set the record straight. On September 25, it released the full, unredacted transcript of the president's call with Zelensky, allowing Americans to see for themselves the absurdity of the left's claims.

The hyperpartisans on the left were so alarmed by this transparency that their first reaction was to deny the transcript's authenticity— they argued it was only a "rough" or "reconstructed" version.[27] [28]And Schiff the next day felt compelled during a televised congressional hearing to "read" a purely fabricated, fictionalized version of the transcript, disingenuously saying it was the "essence of what the president communicates." This is what the biggest liar in Congress claimed the president said on the call: "We've been very good to your country, very good. No other country has done as much as we have. But you know what? I don't see much reciprocity here. I hear what you want. I have a favor that I want from you, though. And I'm going to say this only seven times, so you better listen good: I want you to make up dirt on my political opponent, understand?"[29] The actual transcript was so exonerating, Schiff had to make up an entirely different version to keep his narrative.

The transcript, coupled with several other realities, blew the Democratic accusations out of the water. Ohio representative Jim Jordan made a point throughout the impeachment saga of repeating four basic facts. Those four truths were clear, irrefutable, and unchanging—and they obliterated all the Democrats' claims. Let's go through them.

Fact #1: The transcript proved there was no "quid pro quo." The president asks Zelensky to "do us a favor." That's a phrase President Trump has used hundreds of times since taking office; it's how he talks. Moreover, he asks the favor for "us"—we, the people—not for him personally. Most important, at no point in the transcript does the president ever demand something in return for that "favor" or threaten to withhold anything unless he gets it. He laid out no conditions whatsoever.

Not in that call—and not in any other. In November, the White House released the full, unredacted transcript of the president's previous conversation with Zelensky—which followed Zelensky's presidential election in April 2019. The president asks for nothing, threatens nothing. He instead goes out of his way to offer: "When you're settled in and ready, I'd like to invite you to the White House."[30] The clear words of these transcripts demolished the central Democratic claim in impeachment. No quid pro quo.

Schiff, whom I like to call Corrupt Compromised Schiff, claimed he didn't need transcripts and that the administration's brief summer hold on foreign aid to Ukraine was itself evidence of extortion. But there were many reasons for the White House to delay the aid, none of which had anything to do with requests for investigations.

Trump has never made any secret of his dislike for foreign aid. He has slowed or blocked financial assistance to many countries, demanding to know whether it is being spent wisely. Trump was hugely concerned about corruption in Ukraine and was trying to assess if Zelensky was the real deal. He was also annoyed that Europeans weren't providing their fair share of financial help to Ukraine. This was a point he made to Zelensky on the July call. Trump may well have been negotiating to get the Europeans to step up more. The Office of Management and Budget explained in December 2019 that it had temporarily paused the aid while the administration engaged in a "policy process" over Ukraine and that this was a common occurrence before aid went out the door.[31]

Democrats spent weeks secretly interviewing witnesses, auditioning them for later congressional hearings. Yet not one of the Deep State actors they dragged on national television could provide a shred of quid pro quo evidence. State Department official George Kent. Lieutenant Colonel Alexander Vindman. U.S. diplomat William Taylor. Former ambassador to Ukraine Marie Yovanovitch—remember these characters? Americans were forced to listen to their Trump smears for hours. But in the end, the only thing they all said that mattered was this: none had ever spoken to Trump about his Ukraine decisions. They had no knowledge of his thinking and zero evidence he'd withheld the aid in order to pressure Ukraine into doing investigations. It was all hearsay, opinion, speculation, and gossip.

Even the Democrats' supposed "bombshell" witness bombed. Democrats hyped the testimony of former European Union ambassador Gordon Sondland, who *had* spoken with Trump about Ukraine. And they were gleeful when in his opening statement he declared there *was* a quid pro quo and that "everyone was in the loop"—Schiff even paused the hearing to hold a press conference in the hallway to brag about Sondland's supposed smoking gun. But during Republican questioning, Sondland admitted that he simply *presumed* this without evidence. Sondland was asked, "So the president never told you about any preconditions for the aid to be released?" He replied, "No."[32] Sondland admitted again and again that his nefarious beliefs about Trump's motivations were all "presumption" and "my own personal guess." In fact, Sondland testified, Trump told him directly that he wanted "nothing" from Ukraine and specifically "no quid pro quo."[33]

Fact #2: The only other person on the call with Trump was Zelensky. And he, too, confirmed there was no pressure, no threats, and no quid pro quo. Speaking at the United Nations General Assembly in New York on September 25, Zelensky said, "We had, I think, a good phone call. It was normal. We spoke about many things. And so, I think, and you read it, that nobody pushed—pushed me."[34] In a December interview with Germany's *Der Spiegel* magazine, Zelensky again affirmed the straightforward nature of the call. "I did not speak with U.S. President Trump in those terms: you give me this, I give you that," he said.[35]

Ukraine's foreign minister also rejected Democrats' impeachment theory. "I know what the conversation was about and I think there was no pressure," Vadym Prystaiko said in September.[36] And this wasn't the Zelensky administration just trying to play nice with the Trump White House after everything exploded. During his impeachment testimony, Ambassador Taylor admitted that he'd asked Zelensky about the call not long after it happened and that Zelensky had said even then that "the call was fine."[37]

Fact #3: At the time of the July call, Ukraine had no idea that aid had been withheld. It's impossible to extort or threaten a person who isn't aware there is a threat or extortion. Zelensky himself made this point in an October interview. "There was no blackmail. I had no idea the military aid was held up," he said.[38]

According to a Ukrainian deputy foreign minister, the country didn't find out about the hold until nearly a month after the call. Even when the Ukrainians did find out, they had no idea why the aid had been delayed—Ukrainian officials did not connect it to any demands for investigations.[39]

Fact #4: The Ukrainians didn't have long to wait—the Trump administration released the aid on September 11. So the Ukrainians got the money, despite never announcing or starting an investigation into Burisma or the Bidens. The Trump administration has been immensely more supportive of Ukraine than the Obama White House. Trump has supported Ukraine with lethal aid in its fight against Russian aggression, which his predecessor would not do. And yes, Trump sent Ukraine its aid in 2019, a show of support for the country's young reformer. He released that money without any conditions. Even as the House held its partisan impeachment vote, even as the Senate conducted its impeachment trial, Ukraine had the money despite never having taken a single act to benefit the president.

Those are the facts.

Indeed, every single witness in the sham impeachment hearings was either a hearsay witness or an opinion witness, which is disgraceful in a proceeding of such monumental import. The sole fact witness who actually talked to the president said there was no quid pro quo.

THE IMPEACHMENT FARCE

The Democrats' impeachment was, by contrast, pure fiction—a fiction that did enormous damage to our country, our Constitution, our core values, equal justice, transparency, and future presidencies.

As previously noted, Speaker Nancy Pelosi in the spring of 2019 told the *Washington Post*, "Impeachment is so divisive to the country that unless there is something so compelling and overwhelming and bipartisan, I don't think we should go down that path, it divides the country."[40] Correct, Madame Speaker.

But Pelosi doesn't run the Democratic Party; it's run by their radical, socialist base, the likes of Alexandria Ocasio-Cortez, Ilhan Omar, and Rashida Tlaib. They give the orders, and they demanded impeachment. So Pelosi chose to rip up the fabric of the nation and drag its citizens through an exhausting, polarizing spectacle.

The Trump impeachment was the first in modern history to be conducted entirely on partisan lines. The House vote to authorize an impeachment inquiry into Richard Nixon was 410–4. Thirty-one Democrats joined Republicans to authorize the House Judiciary Committee to investigate Clinton's perjury. But Pelosi initially refused to even hold a vote for a formal impeachment inquiry; she worried she didn't have a majority. When she finally got around to it—on October 31, 2019—she couldn't even keep all her own people on board. Two Democrats—Collin Peterson of Minnesota and Jeff Van Drew of New Jersey—voted with every Republican against the farce. Both also voted against the final impeachment of the president, and Van Drew was so disgusted he switched parties. Pelosi, by contrast, spent the "solemn" (her word) hours after she signed the impeachment articles handing out commemorative pens and mugging for pictures.

The Democratic impeachment process was an assault on fairness and due process. The left decided it wasn't going to make the same mistake it did with Mueller—wait three years, only to be disappointed. Schiff and Nadler made sure to control every last choreographed aspect of their narrative, even though that meant robbing Republicans and President Trump of basic rights.

In the Clinton impeachment, the president had the right to have his counsel present, to cross-examine, to call witnesses, to submit evidence, and to build a defense. Schiff conducted his witness depositions in a basement of Congress—secret testimony recorded in secret transcripts. He barred most Republicans from attending and from reading the documents. Those Republicans who were allowed to take part were barred from calling their own witnesses or issuing their own subpoenas. Even when they were allowed to ask questions, Schiff often directed witnesses not to answer.

Schiff likewise barred the president's attorneys from attending. The White House was therefore unable to present evidence, or call witnesses, or cross-examine those Schiff summoned, or defend itself in any way. Senator Lindsey Graham was so offended by the House's sham process that he collected fifty Senate cosponsors for a resolution condemning it as a farce.

Ironically, this Soviet-style proceeding was conducted by the same Democrats who a few months earlier had screamed for the right to see a "fully unredacted" Mueller report. Their secrecy allowed Schiff to mine his depositions for juicy tidbits and leak them to the media mob to spin his one-sided narrative. Only after Schiff had conducted his entire, illegitimate investigation did he send his impeachment "report" to Nadler's Judiciary Committee. And only then did the White House get an invitation: Would the president's lawyers like to come to Judiciary's two public hearings—one of which would feature a panel mostly comprising far-left, sanctimonious law professors—and explain why the president shouldn't be impeached? The White House correctly declined. Democrats had made a mockery of due process.

The House's final two articles of impeachment were an assault on constitutional principles and a threat to future presidencies. Democrats had started out with accusations of quid pro quo. Then they used focus groups to determine that the words "bribery" and "extortion" sounded better! Their problem was that our federal laws provide real definitions of "bribery" and "extortion," and nothing Trump did came close to measuring up.

So Democrats instead impeached him for two fictional "high crimes"—acts that don't exist in the Constitution, in any statute, or any prior impeachments. Their first article vaguely claimed an "abuse of power." That definition is so broad that any Congress could use it against any president. Remember when Obama in 2012 got caught in a hot-mic moment asking the Russians to lay low on missile defense until after he got reelected? Obama was asking that as a personal political favor, to help him in his race against Mitt Romney. Under the

Democrats' "abuse of power" standard, Republicans would have been in their rights to immediately impeach him.

The second article was even wilder. It accused the president of "obstruction of Congress" for refusing to hand over documents Democrats wanted for their impeachment inquiry. Every modern president has exerted executive privilege and refused to comply with certain congressional document demands. We have a remedy for these stand-offs: the courts. The judicial branch exists to resolve disputes between the two other branches of government. But Democrats didn't want to take the time to resolve this dispute in court. They were in a rush to get impeachment done before their own Democratic presidential primary. As Democrats had openly stated, they also feared if they didn't impeach Trump, they might lose the election.

Constitutional scholar Jonathan Turley, the only sane professor invited to Judiciary's impeachment hearings, put it this way: "I can't emphasize this enough, and I'll say it just one more time. If you impeach a president, if you make a high crime and misdemeanor out of going to the courts, it is an abuse of power. It's *your* abuse of power. You are doing precisely what you are criticizing the president for doing."[41]

Pelosi couldn't even *transmit* the articles of impeachment in a constitutional fashion. Democrats jammed through impeachment in record time, holding a final vote on December 18. They told us impeachment was urgent; they said their case was rock-solid. Yet Pelosi said she wouldn't formally deliver the articles to the Senate unless Majority Leader Mitch McConnell agreed to her demands to call new witnesses and subpoena new documents. Democrats in particular wanted the Senate to haul in former national security adviser John Bolton and Secretary of State Mike Pompeo—neither of whom the House had itself bothered to subpoena for testimony.

McConnell set up a Senate trial based entirely on the precedent of the Bill Clinton trial. But Pelosi suddenly wanted to dictate to the U.S. Senate its job. Her very suggestions were an offense to the Constitution. That founding document gives the House the sole power to impeach—to investigate, produce evidence, and vote on articles. It was the House's job to call Bolton and any other witnesses. The Constitution gives the Senate the sole power of a trial. The Senate had no business assisting or legitimizing Pelosi's warped and twisted impeachment investigation, which she herself was now apparently admitting was inadequate. And Pelosi had no business telling the Senate what to do.

Pelosi held on to the articles for nearly a month. Even Senate Democrats lost patience with her theatrics and demanded a start to the trial. But the Pelosi pressure campaign raged on. The House continued issuing new "evidence," which they claimed bolstered their demands for new Senate witnesses. Senate Minority Leader Chuck Schumer held daily press briefings, insisting that only new witnesses would result in a "fair trial" and that anything less would amount to a Republican "cover-up." "Leader McConnell is plotting the most rushed, least thorough and most unfair impeachment trial in modern history," complained Schumer, even as he simultaneously claimed he had a slam-dunk case.[42]

The Witness Games hit their hysterical peak on January 26, with a perfectly timed leak courtesy of the New York Times. The paper claimed—based, as usual, on unnamed sources—that Bolton was accusing Trump of a Ukrainian quid pro quo in a new book he was writing. It didn't matter to Democrats that the Times gets everything wrong, or that the paper didn't have a draft of Bolton's book. (Its information came from sources who claimed to have seen it.) It didn't matter that Bolton's attorneys refused to confirm the contents of the report.[43] Nor did it matter that Bolton was on record describing Trump's calls with Zelensky as "warm and cordial."[44] Democrats bellowed that a trial without Bolton was no trial at all.

Senate Republicans remained true to their constitutional duties, and none of them except Mitt Romney fell into this trap. Some of them deserve extra credit, since Schumer's witness campaign was about more than just smearing Trump. He also hoped to use impeachment to take back the Senate by undercutting vulnerable Republicans up for reelection in 2020. The media assisted this ploy by writing nonstop articles claiming that senators like Colorado's Cory Gardner and Arizona's Martha McSally risked losing their seats if they didn't capitulate to Schumer's demands.

Also worthy of extra credit were those Republican senators who made clear to the Senate the ramifications of Democrats' witness demands. Texas senator Ted Cruz insisted that if the Senate sent out subpoenas, he'd demand "witness reciprocity." For every witness Democrats called, Republicans would get to call one, too. GOP senators floated the idea of subpoenas for Quid Pro Quo Joe and Hunter Biden. They also debated calling the whistle-blower and potentially even Schiff—whose early interaction with the whistle-blower made him a fact witness in the case. The reciprocity demands rightly worried a number of Democrats. And they reminded the entire chamber that reopening the House's partisan work by calling new witnesses would add months to the trial.

In the end, nearly every Republican senator stood for truth, facts, and fairness—despite having to suffer a trial based on a warped and wholly partisan impeachment. They listened to Shifty Schiff and his fellow Democrat impeachment managers as they spent days on monotonous, repetitive talking points, indulging in their unhinged hatred of the president. The Schiff sham-show left even Democrats bored. Senator Elizabeth Warren was spotted during the proceedings playing a game on a piece of paper.

The hardest part was listening to Democrats accuse Trump of all their own despicable behavior. The hypocrisy was rank. To this day, precisely one guy in Washington has been caught on tape trying to elicit dirt from foreigners on a political rival: Adam Schiff. In 2017, during Congress's Russia collusion investigation, a Russian prankster called Schiff, pretending to be a Ukrainian official. The prankster claimed to have "pictures of naked Trump." Schiff asked the caller if Putin was "aware" of the "compromising material." He asked for the spellings of names.[45] And he had his staff contact the prankster after the call to try to arrange delivery of the material.⁴⁶ Democrats care about "foreign interference" only when it suits their political agenda.

They impeach Trump for allegedly making threats against Ukraine? He never did. Read the transcript. But in September 2019, Democratic senator Chris Murphy actually bragged that he had threatened Ukraine's new president with consequences if he dared looked into the Biden-Burisma scandal. "I cautioned [Zelensky] that complying with the demands of the President's campaign representatives to investigate a political rival of the President would gravely damage the U.S.-Ukraine relationship," Murphy told John Solomon.⁴⁷

This is also the same Democratic Party that had a paid operative, Alexandra Chalupa of the Democratic National Committee, working with the Ukrainian government in 2016 to spread dirt on Donald Trump.

Republicans did confront the House impeachment team with its hypocrisy at least once, and the response was priceless. Senator Richard Burr submitted the following question for Chief Justice John Roberts to read to Hakeem Jeffries, a Democrat impeachment manager: "Under the House managers' standard, would the Steele dossier be considered as foreign interference in a U.S. election, a violation of the law and/or impeachable offense?" Jeffries was totally taken off guard. He finally replied that the "analogy" wasn't right, since Democrats had paid for the dossier.⁴⁸ Got that? It's okay to solicit foreign dirt, so long as you get a receipt.

Republican senators did at least get to hear, for the first time, the president's legal team make its defense. And they crushed it. They included White House counsel Pat Cipollone; the president's personal attorney Jay Sekulow; former independent counsel Ken Starr; former Florida attorney general Pam Bondi; and Harvard law professor emeritus Alan Dershowitz.

This group methodically and overwhelmingly destroyed the Democrats' two bogus articles of impeachment. They hammered home that the nebulous "abuse of power" article was nothing more than a made-up theory—one that "supplants the Framers' standard of 'high Crimes and Misdemeanors.'"[49] And they pointed out the terrifying precedent it set. Dershowitz on the Senate floor listed more than thirty American presidents (including George Washington and Abraham Lincoln) who'd also been accused of abuse of power. "None of them was impeached," Dershowitz said on my show. "Which shows you how vague and open-ended and selective that criteria is. It can be weaponized and used against anybody or nobody, depending on the whim of Congress."[50]

They also explained that the second article of impeachment—"obstruction of Congress"—was a blatant attempt to destroy the critically important concept of "executive privilege." That's a tool that allows the president to withhold sensitive information from Congress. The White House exercised the privilege during the impeachment drama, refusing to just roll over for every Democratic document demand—especially because most of those Democratic document subpoenas were fishing expeditions. As the president's legal team explained, it is "essential to protect the President's ability to secure candid and confidential advice and have frank discussions with his advisers."[51] Equally important, it is up to the judiciary to define when it applies. The House impeachment article was an unconstitutional claim that it was up to the House to decide.

The case was thorough and compelling and convinced even wavering Republicans—like Alaska's Lisa Murkowski—that there was no need for further witnesses. On January 31, 2020, fifty-one GOP senators voted to kill that Democratic ploy. They lost only Maine's Susan Collins and Utah's Mitt Romney.

Five days later, the Senate acquitted the president of the United States. The vote on "abuse of power" was 52–48. The vote on "obstruction of Congress" was 53–47. Both fell dramatically short of the sixty-seven votes needed to convict. The only Republican defector was, once again, Romney—who voted for the "abuse of power" charge. Unfortunately, Romney can't get over the fact that he lost in 2012, and he cares too much about parading around as a media hero. He forgets that the media who lauded him for his "brave" impeachment vote was the same media that spent 2012 calling him a racist, a misogynist, and a cruel capitalist.

All that really mattered in the end was that the president was vindicated. He'd won again. The three-year-long Democratic campaign to impeach was over. The American voters had emerged victorious.

MAKING DEMOCRATS PAY A PRICE— ELECTION 2020

We can't get back what Democrats lost the country during their long impeachment march and temper tantrum. President Trump wanted to talk about infrastructure. He wanted to do a deal on lower drug prices. He wanted a debate on border security, and how best to protect the country. He proposed trade deals that would help our manufacturers. Democrats had no interest in dealing with these pressing concerns or in concentrating on the new coronavirus that was spreading out of China. They were too obsessed with their vendetta against Trump and their rage against this White House.

The good news is that America still gets the opportunity in Election 2020 to judge them for this failure of leadership. Democrats always knew they wouldn't be able to convict and remove Trump from office. Pelosi understood the risk of impeachment, but she caved to her radical socialist base. Democrats then threw everything they had at slandering Trump in hopes of at least softening him up for an election defeat.

It didn't work. The longer impeachment went on, the better the Trump reelection campaign did. Trump and the Republican National Committee raised a staggering $125 million in the third quarter of 2019;[52] it raised a whopping $154 million in the fourth quarter.[53] Both numbers were a direct response to impeachment—Trump supporters rejecting the Democrats' appalling abuse of their House powers.

Democrats never moved the polling needle on impeachment, despite months of slander and lies. Quite the opposite. In the days following impeachment, Trump's approval rating moved to an all-time high in his presidency.[54]

By contrast, the American people aren't feeling great about Democrats' rage-fueled approach to everything. At particular risk in this upcoming election are the thirty-one Democrats who in 2018 won districts that voted for Trump. They campaigned as moderates and as Democrats able to work with the president on a bipartisan basis. They instead spent months working to impeach him. Nearly all voted to proceed to a formal inquiry, and nearly all voted for both impeachment articles. Also up for judgment will be senators like Democrat Doug Jones, who voted to convict the president. Jones represents Alabama, a state that voted 62 percent for Trump.

Elections allow for that voter judgment, and they remain this country's greatest tool for accountability. Democrats can play their destructive political games. But the American people are the ultimate deciders. And come November 3, 2020, they will get to shock the world—again.

CHAPTER SEVEN

Enemy of the People:
The Hate-Trump Media Mob

I'm not trying to be cute when I call the liberal press the "Fake News Media." They collude with the leftist Democratic Party and spread lies, distortions, and propaganda. They don't even try to hide it anymore. Even media watcher Howard Kurtz argues the media's hatred for Trump is unprecedented. Their attacks are "more personal" and "visceral" than against any other president. "None of us have ever seen anything like this, just the sheer intensity of it," said Kurtz. "If you only consumed a lot of the mainstream media, particularly places like MSNBC, you would think that the Trump presidency is an absolute disaster, that he's ruining the entire world. . . ."[1]

The liberal media uniformly claim Trump is deliberately dividing the nation. "Trump's theory of politics is that it's okay to offend five voters if seven voters approve," wrote *Washington Post* columnist Robert J. Samuelson. "Dividing the country is the name of the game. The object is to create a coalition of the resentful. Polarization is not only the consequence. It also is the underlying purpose and philosophy." In Samuelson's view the media are Trump's "scapegoats for assorted disappointments."[2]

That message surely resonated with Samuelson's fellow Trump-hating journalists. But it conveniently ignores how the media mob has dropped all semblance of objectivity and now serves as a loyal mouthpiece for the so-called Resistance. They have gone to the most extreme lengths imaginable to undermine Trump since he was a candidate. *They* are the polarizing figures. *They* are the ones dividing the country.

They are the ones who, more than three years into Trump's presidency, still refuse to accept the legitimacy of his election—after responding with sputtering outrage when then-candidate Trump said he'd wait to see the election results before committing to accepting them. CNN's take—and this was in a news report, not an opinion piece—was typical. Trump's comments, said CNN, "marked a stunning moment that has never been seen in the weeks before a modern presidential election. The stance threatens to cast doubt on one of the fundamental principles of American politics—the peaceful, undisputed transfer of power from one president to a successor who is recognized as legitimate after winning an election."[3] Of course, when Hillary Clinton spent the next three years claiming the election had been stolen from her by diabolical Trump officials colluding with Russia—a hoax *her own campaign* helped create by funding the phony Steele dossier—the media dropped its dire warnings about the sanctity of election results and parroted Clinton's accusations.

The media's motivation here is obvious. True, they don't like Trump's personality, his brashness, and his ridiculing of his opponents. But let's face it, if Trump were a left-wing president criticizing conservatives, they'd have no problem with those qualities. No, they hate Trump because he campaigned on a conservative agenda that they find abhorrent, and now he's implementing it. Even *Baltimore Sun* columnist David Zurawik, no conservative himself, acknowledged the liberal media's anti-Trump bias. "With some folks it seems as if there is only one allowable position when it comes to Donald Trump: He's the most dangerous president ever, and nothing good can come of his tenure," writes Zurawik. "Trump is being treated unfairly in some parts of the media, and unless we deal with it honestly and openly, we are the ones who will wind up losing credibility even as we point our fingers at Trump for his lies."[4]

Early on in Trump's term, Zurawik commented that Trump's conflict with the press wasn't nearly as unjustifiable as Obama's was. The Trump administration "has not yet come close to doing what President Obama's administration did in making the act of reporting itself criminal behavior," said Zurawik—referring to the Obama administration prying into the phone and computer records of reporter James Rosen, then with Fox News, and calling Rosen "an aider, abettor and/ or co-conspirator" and a flight risk in court documents. Zurawik also recounted how the Obama administration excluded Fox News from interviews with government officials, denounced the network as a "wing of the Republican Party," and announced that the White House would stop treating us as a "news network."[5] Yet the media worships Obama like the Messiah and portrays Trump as a dictator. Go figure.

The media pathologically hate Trump, but they're dependent on him. Their sensational Trump coverage sells newspapers, resuscitating some that were on life support, and boosts ratings for cable and broadcast news. This success comes at a price, though, because their bias has turned nearly all of conservative America against them. A 2016 Gallup poll found Republican trust in the media is at an all-time low of 14 percent,[6] mainly because they portray Trump in particular and conservatives generally as stupid bigots.[7]

I'm not anti-media. I work in the media. From the time of our founding Americans have recognized the media's crucial role in holding our leaders accountable—as another important check against tyranny. But we shouldn't assume the media's watchdog function guarantees their integrity, fairness, or objectivity. Collectively, they wield enormous power—not just in keeping presidents, congressmen, and governors honest, but in influencing elections and policy, so much so that the press is often referred to as the fourth estate or fourth branch of government.[8] The media's influence is vast enough that they can even bring down a president, as the *Washington Post* did with President Nixon—a model countless reporters hope to emulate today.

The Hoover Institution's Bruce Thornton observes that the media has been partisan almost from the inception of the nation, but earlier in our history, the variety of outlets with competing partisan views prevented a major imbalance in the news. That balance was lost, says Thornton, during the sixties, when journalism became a "profession" credentialed by university degrees. "Before then . . . journalism was a working-class trade." Most of the newsroom veterans didn't have college degrees, and their biases "tended to reflect those of class as much as political ideology." But journalism school graduates reflected "the leftist perspective of those institutions. . . . Now the old progressive view that the press should not just report fact, but mold public opinion to achieve certain political ends, served an ideology fundamentally adverse to the free-market, liberal-democratic foundations of the American Republic." [9]

We saw this play out in the media's adoring coverage of the Obama administration. For instance, after Obama halted America's "wet foot, dry foot" policy, which had permitted Cuban refugees who reached our shores to enter the country, the next morning the three major broadcast networks spent a scant sixty-eight *seconds* covering the story. But when Trump issued an executive order temporarily banning immigration from several Middle Eastern and African countries, they spent sixty-four *minutes* on the news. As NewsBusters noted, "The coverage of Trump's executive order has been overwhelmingly negative, with NBC's *Today* even suggesting a link between Trump's immigration ban and a mass shooting at a mosque in Quebec, despite a complete lack of evidence." [10]

There you go—when Obama blocks refugees, it's a nonstory. When Trump does it, it's a form of mass murder.

THE MEDIA'S LOVE AFFAIR WITH OBAMA

To fully understand media bias, it's useful to reflect on media coverage of the Obama administration. The media literally deified Obama, often depicting him adorned with a halo. Magazine covers idolized

him as "God of All Things," and "The Second Coming."[11] *Newsweek*
editor Evan Thomas marveled, "In a way Obama is standing above the
country, above the world. He's a sort of God. He's going to bring all different sides together."[12] Barbara Walters said "we" thought Obama was
"the next Messiah."[13] *SF Gate* columnist Mark Morford was even more
over-the-top: "Barack Obama isn't really one of us. Not in the normal
way, anyway. . . . It's not merely his youthful vigor, or handsomeness,
or even inspiring rhetoric. It is not fresh ideas or cool charisma or
the fact that a black president will be historic and revolutionary in
about a thousand different ways. It is something more. Even Bill Clinton, with all his effortless, winking charm, didn't have what Obama
has, which is a sort of powerful luminosity, a unique high-vibration
integrity . . . that rare kind of attuned being who has the ability to lead
us not merely to new foreign policies or health care plans or whatnot,
but who can actually help usher in a new way of being on the planet, of
relating and connecting and engaging with this bizarre earthly experiment."[14] Chris Matthews famously took his fawning in a more obscene
direction. "I have to tell you," he gushed, ". . . the feeling most people
get when they hear Barack Obama's speech. My, I felt this thrill going
up my leg. I mean, I don't have that too often."[15]

Of course, the entire idea that Obama was some transcendent
uniter was a fantasy manufactured by the press itself. As I pointed out
at the time, Obama was partisan, divisive, and radical, he vilified his
opponents, and he went into snits when things didn't go his way. He
had thin skin and repeatedly singled me out by name as his administration tried to sideline Fox News, the one network that didn't believe
he walked on water. But he was the media's long-awaited liberal savior,
so they protected him at every turn.

The media were even complicit in the Obama administration's
scapegoating of an obscure producer of an internet video, who was
blamed for the 2012 attack on our embassy in Benghazi. The media
dutifully echoed the administration's false claim that the attack
began as a protest against an anti-Islamic video, whose producer

was promptly arrested in America, when in fact it was a preplanned assault by al Qaeda–linked terrorists.[16] The Obama administration, however, had been bragging about its victories over al Qaeda, so it was inconvenient for al Qaeda to sack our embassy and murder four Americans, including an ambassador. "This unsavory relationship between the media and the Democrats has long existed, but the political career of Barack Obama marks a quantum leap beyond the media's traditional liberal preferences and biases—which in the past had at least a patina of objectivity and neutrality—to blatant advocacy, double standards, and explicit partisan hatred," Thornton commented at the time.[17]

The media was so subservient to Obama that his "foreign policy guru" and speechwriter, Ben Rhodes, bragged that he had led them by the nose to do the administration's bidding. During negotiations for the Iran nuclear deal, as with other important events, Rhodes coordinated policy, politics, and messaging for the administration. *New York Times Magazine*'s David Samuels admitted, "The way in which most Americans have heard the story . . . was largely manufactured for the purpose of selling the deal."[18] They sold it as Obama seizing the opportunity to make a deal with newly empowered Iranian moderates to dismantle the mullahs' nuclear weapons program. But in fact Obama had been "eager to do a deal with Iran as far back as 2012, and even since the beginning of his presidency," as part of his wider foreign policy vision.[19]

To push their false narrative, the administration set up a "war room" inside the White House quarterbacked by Rhodes, which operated as "the nerve center for the selling of the Iran deal to Congress."[20] They mounted a sophisticated operation to spread their message online. "By applying 21st-century data and networking tools to the white-glove world of foreign affairs, the White House was able to track what United States senators and the people who worked for them, and influenced them, were seeing online—and make sure that no potential negative comment passed without a tweet," wrote Samuels.

As this plan played out, "legions of arms-control experts began popping up at think tanks and on social media, and then became key sources for hundreds of often-clueless reporters. 'We created an echo chamber,' " said Rhodes. " 'They were saying things that validated what we had given them to say.' "[21] Rhodes admitted he was scared by the prospect of such an elaborate spin campaign being run by some other administration, but that didn't seem to bother him. "I mean, I'd prefer a sober, reasoned public debate, after which members of Congress reflect and take a vote," said Rhodes. "But that's impossible."[22]

The main thing I want you to take away from this is not that Obama and his inner circle were deceitful and manipulative, though they absolutely were. What is most striking is the casual treatment of this saga by the *New York Times*—its reaction, through Samuels's story, of adulation rather than disgust at being deceived and manipulated by Obama. The media were so enamored of Obama's progressive staffers that they appeared grateful for the honor of being duped by them. There was no outrage from the mainstream media and no demands for Rhodes's head.

Obama's lackeys sold Obamacare in a similarly dishonest way. Massachusetts Institute of Technology professor Jonathan Gruber, Obamacare's principal architect, openly bragged about deceiving the American people by writing the Obamacare law "in a tortured way" to ensure favorable scoring from the Congressional Budget Office. Gruber essentially admitted the public would have rejected Obamacare had it been properly understood. "Lack of transparency is a huge political advantage," said Gruber. "And basically, call it the stupidity of the American voter or whatever, but basically that was really, really critical for the thing to pass."[23] Again, there was no indignation from the mainstream media, whose entire reason for being is supposed to be preventing this kind of fraud from being perpetrated on the American people.

Remember these examples the next time you hear the Fake News Media whining about Trump's treatment of the press. The hate-Trump media don't care about keeping government officials honest; their primary concern is advancing the left's agenda, and they'll hype, bury, or skew their stories accordingly.

TAKING AIM AT CANDIDATE TRUMP

The media's fawning coverage of Obama could not stand in starker contrast to the daily beatings they meted out to Donald Trump throughout his campaign. They've been obsessed with the man since June 16, 2015, when he descended the escalator at Trump Tower in New York City to formally announce his candidacy. Having quickly decided that he's a racist, the media were noticeably excited when former Ku Klux Klan leader David Duke endorsed him. When Trump was asked about this, he said he didn't know anything about Duke, his endorsement, or white supremacists. This simple and straightforward answer sparked a media frenzy. The *Daily Beast*'s headline was typical of the hysterical coverage: "Trump won't denounce KKK support."[24] Meanwhile, they didn't show the slightest concern about Obama's *documented ties* to domestic terrorist Bill Ayers.

The media mob's different treatment of the 2016 Republican and Democrat conventions is another damning indictment of their bias. The Media Research Center found that journalists described the Republican convention negatively *twelve times* more often than its Democratic counterpart. Most media reactions to Democratic speakers were positive and "often enthusiastic." There was also a marked difference in the amount of airtime they gave leaders of the opposing party during the respective conventions—Democratic figures received far more time to comment during the Republican convention than Republicans were given to sound off during the Democratic convention.[25]

During the campaign, the *New York Times*' Jim Rutenberg made a shocking plea for reporters to abandon journalistic standards when covering Trump. In an August 7, 2016, column he asked how "a working journalist" was supposed to cover candidate Trump, "a demagogue playing to the nation's worst racist and nationalistic tendencies." If you believe that, he said, "you have to throw out the textbook American journalism has been using for the better part of the past half-century, if not longer, and approach it in a way you've never approached anything in your career. . . . If you view a Trump presidency as something that's potentially dangerous, then your reporting is going to reflect that. You would move closer than you've ever been to being oppositional." He admitted that covering Trump as abnormal and potentially dangerous "upsets balance, that idealistic form of journalism with a capital 'J' we've been trained to always strive for. But let's face it: Balance has been on vacation since Mr. Trump stepped onto his golden Trump Tower escalator last year to announce his candidacy."[26] Typical of leftists, Rutenberg was arguing that their noble ends (defeating Trump) justify terrible means (eviscerating journalistic standards).

How would these corrupt hacks feel about conservatives arguing that normal journalistic standards shouldn't have applied to covering President Obama because his ideas are dangerous to the republic? Who's to say which president is more "dangerous"? It used to be journalists' job to report the facts and let the American people decide those kinds of questions. Now they're convinced the people can't be trusted to make the "right" decision.

As the media played up Trump's alleged vileness on the campaign trail, they played down his chances of winning. An October 18, 2016, article by Stuart Rothenberg in the *Washington Post*, which was not designated as an opinion piece, was brazenly headlined, "Trump's Path to an Electoral College Victory Isn't Narrow. It's Nonexistent." He insisted that Trump "trails badly with only a few weeks to go until Nov. 8, and he must broaden his appeal to have any chance of winning. That is now impossible."[27] Rothenberg called Trump "a disaster as a presidential nominee" and "his own worst enemy," and cemented his place in history as the world's worst political analyst by including this line: "Pennsylvania, Michigan and Wisconsin, once part of the Trump scenario, have never been 'in play.' "[28]

With just three weeks to go until the election, Trump had not received a single major newspaper endorsement, according to the Media Research Center, while sixty-eight papers had endorsed Clinton.[29] Despite Trump supposedly having no shot at winning, however, an MRC study showed that in the twelve weeks following the party conventions, the media devoted substantially more airtime to Trump than Clinton—and 91 percent of it was "hostile."[30]

The media arrogantly assumed they were pulling Trump's strings— forcing him to the front of the Republican primaries while believing he didn't have a chance to win the general election. But it turns out that Trump understands the media better than they understand themselves. In fact, Trump was manipulating *them*, enticing them to cover him whether they wanted to or not.

Politico's Jack Shafer figured it out, noting that Trump shrewdly ran "a media campaign directly against the media, helping himself to the copious media attention available to a TV star while disparaging journalists at every podium and venue." Other presidents had attacked the media, said Shafer, but Trump baited them at a whole new level, running against them even more than he was against Hillary Clinton and ceaselessly hammering their pro-Clinton bias. "The most powerful weapon deployed by the Clintons is the corporate media," said Trump. "The reporters collaborate and conspire directly with the Clinton campaign on helping her win the election all over." By suckering the media mobs into covering him even while he was attacking them, noted Shafer, Trump could operate a lean campaign, ignoring "all the orthodoxies, eschewing the traditional campaign-building, almost ignoring the field offices and a 'ground game.' By April [2016] his campaign had only 94 payrolled staffers compared to Hillary Clinton's 795."[31]

RealClear Media fellow Kalev Leetaru observed that the press devoted so much attention to Trump that in some ways it helped revive American journalism.[32] "In the end, for media outlets that spend so much of their time attacking Trump, it is clear that they simply cannot live without him," wrote Leetaru. CNN full-time Trump, Hannity, and FNC hater and Jeff Zucker stenographer—or as I affectionately call him, Humpty Dumpty—Brian Stelter made a similar admission. "Trump is the media's addiction," said Stelter. "When he speaks, he is given something no other candidate gets. That's wall-to-wall coverage here on cable news. He sucks up all the oxygen."[33]

Regardless of which was the tail and which the dog, the spotlight was on Trump—constantly—and the attention legitimized his candidacy even though most of it was openly hostile. "Donald Trump's surge to the front of the GOP presidential polls has occasioned not a little media attention and endless speculation as to why," wrote George Washington University political science professor John Sides. "The answer is simple: Trump is surging in the polls because the news media has consistently focused on him since he announced his candidacy on June 16."[34]

The professor's view was common on the left. It was comforting for them to attribute Trump's popularity solely to the media attention. That allowed them to avoid acknowledging that his positions— cracking down on illegal immigration, renegotiating unfavorable trade deals, and reviving American manufacturing, to name a few—were finding widespread support. "It is tempting to attribute Mr. Trump's surge to something more than media coverage, to assume that his positions must have unusual resonance with Republicans voters, or to infer that Republicans are clamoring for an anti-immigration candidate," wrote *New York Times* political analyst Nate Cohn. "Those factors do play a role, but the predominant force is extraordinary and sustained media coverage."[35]

So the media played a tortured role in the 2016 campaign. They posed as guardians of the public trust warning us of Trump's evils, yet by their own account they played a key role—in fact, *the* key role— in promoting his campaign. Once he rode this notoriety all the way to the White House, one would think the media would do a bit of self-reflection and cover him differently in order to stop inadvertently helping him. But that didn't happen. Their obsession with Trump is so deep that they're simply incapable of reporting on him fairly and reasonably, even when they know he thrives on their delirious hatred.

PEAK FAKE NEWS: THE MEDIA AND THE TRUMP PRESIDENCY

It's hard to imagine a more acute form of media bias than Trump Derangement Syndrome/Psychosis. After Trump won election, the *Washington Post* welcomed our new president by adopting the official motto "Democracy Dies in Darkness." "We thought it would be a good, concise value statement that conveys who we are to the many millions of readers who have come to us for the first time over the last year," said the paper's spokeswoman. The *Post* insisted that the motto has nothing to do with Trump,[36] laughably, given that it was adopted just one month after he took office. With its anti-Trump coverage, you see, the *Post* is saving democracy from the Trumpian "darkness." A tweet from *The Federalist*'s Mollie Hemingway captured the absurdity: "I thought people were joking about this new WP motto: 'democracy dies in darkness.' They were not. I shouldn't be laughing so hard."[37]

The Pew Research Center analyzed the media's coverage of Trump's first sixty days and found it was far more biased than it was for the three preceding presidents. The Trump coverage was 62 percent negative, compared to 20 percent negative for Barack Obama and 28 percent for both George W. Bush and Bill Clinton. Only 5 percent of the Trump coverage was positive versus 42 percent positive for Obama, 22 percent for Bush, and 27 percent for Clinton.[38] "And it's not a case of overwhelmingly negative coverage on one subject drowning out some moderately positive coverage on other matters," wrote blogger Allahpundit about the media's Trump reporting. "It was resoundingly negative across the board."[39]

The Democrats and the media will weaponize almost any news story to demonize Trump. Consider two shooting incidents, one in El Paso by a white supremacist and another in Dayton by a socialist. The media used the El Paso shooting to smear Trump as a white nationalist and connect him to the shooting of more than twenty innocent people, with the *New York Times* claiming the shooter's manifesto "echoes" Trump's language. Meanwhile, the Dayton shooter's ideology was downplayed and ignored, including his expressed support for Elizabeth Warren and his rants about "concentration camps" at the border that mimic the rhetoric of Alexandria Ocasio-Cortez and other Democrats.[40] And of course, you'd have to look a long time before finding a mainstream news article blaming Bernie Sanders because a fan of his shot up a Republican softball practice, wounding Congressman Steve Scalise—nearly mortally—and three others.

The media doesn't just portray Trump as a white supremacist; it routinely describes his everyday supporters the same way. Their smearing of Nick Sandmann and his fellow Covington High School students who attended a March for Life rally in Washington, D.C., was a prime example. Without any facts, the media castigated the students, getting almost everything wrong in their stories and never apologizing when their lies were uncovered. They described the students as mocking and mistreating an elderly Native American who, as it turns out, was the aggressor in a confrontation with the Covington students. A video of the event exonerated the students and exposed the media's lies. A sampling of the media mob's slanderous coverage of the incident: "Boys in 'Make America Great Again' Hats Mob Native Elder at Indigenous People's March," said the *New York Times*; "The Catholic Church's Shameful History of Native American Abuses," declared the *Washington Post*. "Covington Catholic High School students surrounded, intimidated and chanted over Native Americans singing about indigenous people's strength and spirit," read the lead paragraph in a piece from the *Cincinnati Enquirer*.[41] Lin Wood, who is representing Sandmann, will likely make the kid a billionaire due to all the lies and slander told about him by major media outlets. CNN has already had to settle for an undisclosed amount. [42]

In their self-defeating war against Trump, the media have compromised their journalistic integrity in countless, often bizarre ways. In September 2018 the *New York Times* informed its readers, "The Times is taking the rare step of publishing an anonymous Op-Ed essay. We have done so at the request of the author, a senior official in the Trump administration whose identity is known to us and whose job would be jeopardized by its disclosure." The anonymous author then revealed, "The dilemma—which he [Trump] does not fully grasp—is that many of the senior officials in his own administration are working diligently from within to frustrate parts of his agenda and his worst inclinations. I would know. I am one of them." [43]

So the *Times* gave a platform to an alleged senior administration official who is working secretly to sabotage the agenda that the American people elected Trump to implement. Instead of denouncing this direct attack on democracy, the media and the left hailed the traitor, now known as "Anonymous," who was quickly treated to a book deal. Ironically, the person's claims, if true, prove the existence of the Deep State and fully justify Trump's efforts to purge disloyal officials. Yet the media continues to ridicule the Deep State as a right-wing conspiracy theory and furiously condemn Trump as a dictatorial tyrant whenever he tries to remove officials who are actively conspiring against him.

For example, when Trump removed National Security Council employee Alexander Vindman—who during impeachment hearings described his dismay at how Trump sometimes pursues his own policies and ignores the advice of bureaucrats like Vindman himself—the media mourned over the end of American democracy. A *New York Times* column bemoaned Vindman's "petty" and "vindictive" removal and the "Trumpification" of the National Security Council [44]—because it's apparently a travesty that Trump wants to work with officials who implement his policy instead of sabotage it. CNN's Chris Cuomo called the firing of Vindman, who was tossed along with his brother Yevgeny and ambassador to the EU Gordan Sondland, another "Friday Night Massacre."[45] CNN also ran a column declaring that the firing was a criminal act and musing about prosecuting Trump after he leaves office.[46]

Trump Derangement Syndrome is so severe in the Fake News outlets that they'll reflexively support anything Trump is against—even terrorists. When U.S. forces killed ghoulish ISIS leader Abu Bakr al-Baghdadi—a man who led a murderous cult that burned people alive and operated as a gigantic sex slavery ring—the *Washington Post* headline called him an "austere religious scholar." Congressman Steve Scalise tweeted, "Every day the Washington Post uses harsher words against @realDonaldTrump than they do in writing about one of the world's most evil terrorists. Yet we're supposed to take them at face value. Let that sink in."[47]

But the hate-Trump media just can't help themselves. When Trump ordered the killing of Iranian Revolutionary Guard commander Qasem Soleimani on January 3, 2020, *Time* magazine absurdly offered advice for "concerned parents" who might need help talking to their poor snowflake children about the terrorist's death. In fact, *Time* couldn't even bring itself to call him "a terrorist," instead noting that he was "called a terrorist by President Trump." Along the same lines, the Associated Press explained that it would not call Soleimani's killing an assassination because the term is "politically freighted," and so they called it a "slaying," which is typically synonymous with murder. *Spectator* columnist Dominic Green was having none of it. "The political freight that the pro-Democratic media carry is not fear for the lives of American servicemen and women, or even concern at the epic fail of American nation-building in the Middle East," wrote Green. "The Americans who do the fighting live as they die, far in social and physical geography from the pampered quasi-aristocrats of the media elite. The freight is a loathing of Donald Trump—for the vulgarity which embarrasses them in front of their European friends, for the coarseness with which he has pricked every bubble of their conceit, for the glee with which he overturned every monument to their fetish object, Barack Obama."[48]

If this wasn't enough, when U.S. guards sprayed tear gas at rioters who stormed the U.S. embassy compound in Baghdad, MSNBC host Joy Reid called the incident "Trump's Benghazi"—a direct comparison to the Obama administration's feebleness when terrorists murdered four Americans in Libya. A disgusted Ted Cruz replied, "What's wrong with you? Is partisan hatred really that deep? We root for American soldiers, not against them." [49] Donald Trump Jr. noted that Trump's response to the Baghdad incident "was really the anti-Benghazi response"—decisive action that kept a bad situation from spiraling into worse violence. [50]

Sharyl Attkisson, a frequent guest on my show, is as close as it gets to a nonpartisan investigative journalist. She has kept a running tally of major media mistakes in the Trump era that is now up to 131 examples. [51] Attkisson draws attention to many of the media's typical deceits and deceptions in covering Trump: depicting his opinions as "lies"; taking his statements and events out of context; "reporting secondhand accounts" against him "without attribution as if they're established fact"; relying on untruthful, conflicted sources; and "presenting reporter opinions in news stories—without labeling them as opinions." According to Attkisson, "formerly well-respected, top news organizations" are making "unforced errors" in volumes that "were unheard of" just a few years ago. [52] It particularly annoys her that the media parade their mistakes as virtues because they sometimes correct them, and that they blame Trump for their own errors. "It's a little bit like a police officer taking someone to jail for DUI, then driving home drunk himself: he may be correct to arrest the suspect, but he should certainly know better than to commit the same violation," writes Attkisson. [53]

I deeply admire Attkisson's work but think she's a bit charitable in calling these egregious incidents "mistakes," because it's impossible to believe this many "mistakes" just happened to all go in the same direction—against Trump. The media is doing something different with Trump than they've done with any other president. Progressive Ezra Klein admitted this as early as August 2016. "Increasingly, the press doesn't even pretend to treat Trump like a normal candidate: CNN's chyrons fact-check him in real time; the *Washington Post* reacted to being banned from Trump with a shrug; *BuzzFeed News* published a memo telling reporters it was fine to call Trump 'a mendacious racist' on social media; the *New York Times* published a viral video in which it simply quoted the most vile statements it heard from Trump's supporters," wrote Klein. "That is not normal. . . . The media has felt increasingly free to cover Trump as an alien, dangerous, and dishonest phenomenon."[54]

Incredibly, after Trump withstood an unprecedented three-year media assault on his presidency, in February 2020 the *Washington Post*'s Margaret Sullivan scolded reporters for not treating Trump *harshly* enough. "Some will argue that many journalists . . . normalized Trump at every turn and never successfully conveyed to the public a clear and vivid picture of how he has toppled democratic norms and marched the country toward autocracy," wrote Sullivan.[55] Which mainstream journalists "normalized" Trump? Name one! Can she point to a single one of her Fake News colleagues who didn't panic over Trump's alleged autocracy? Has she read a single article since 2017 in the paper she works for?

What is Sullivan's prescription for the fake problem she presents? Just like Rutenberg, she wants journalists to shed their standards—as if they have any left. "First, we need to abandon neutrality-at-all-costs journalism, to replace it with something more suited to the moment," she writes. "Call it Fairness First." That means "describing the world we report in honest and direct terms." Outraged that Trump claims vindication over his impeachment trial acquittal, she insists the press must "apply more scrutiny and less credulity to his increasingly extreme actions and statements." Traditional "just the facts" reporting, she says, might be good in theory but not in practice. The mainstream media is failing its audience by "not getting across the big picture or the urgency."

Sullivan's flight from reality is alarming. How could the media treat Trump news with greater urgency? It sounds like she wants the media to expressly declare all-out war against him instead of waging that war while pretending not to. She closes, "With Trump unbound, the news media need to change. Yes, radically. The stakes are too high not to." Unlike the Fake News Media, you just can't make this stuff up!

FAKE NEWS VS. FOX NEWS

If you listen to my radio show and watch my TV program, then you know about the Fake News Media's obsession with Fox News—and their false claims that the network is politically biased. There are major differences between Fox and the Fake News networks. Our news division and opinion divisions are separate, and our news reporters and broadcasters present the news with objectivity and journalistic integrity. Our programs, in both the news and opinion divisions, have both conservative and liberal guests. My friend Juan Williams is a passionate liberal, yet day in and day out he's on the network presenting his positions. Bret Baier reliably includes liberals on his all-star panel. We on the opinion side are open about our views. I'm up front that I'm a conservative and a Trump supporter, and I present facts to back up my opinions. The same can't be said for my Fake News counterparts.

I am very up-front about what I do for a living. As a talk show host, I sometimes present straight news, other times opinion, and often a combination of both. With my trusted team of journalists, I also offer extensive investigative reporting. But unlike certain hosts of many other biased networks who falsely hold themselves out as journalists, I don't pretend that my opinions are excluded from my commentary. Every listener and viewer knows where I stand, because I am honest about my opinions. Contrast this with the numerous pseudo-journalists of other networks who laughably pretend to be objective reporters.

You will rarely find conservative guests on the Fake News. But you'll find a slew of Never Trumpers, many of whom, in their maniacal hatred for Trump, have abandoned everything about conservatism.

Yet the title in the chyron falsely identifies them as conservatives. If any real conservatives, like Jeff Lord, find their way onto those networks, they're eventually fired for bucking the party line, as Lord was in 2017.[56] They fired him after he said that Media Matters members were behaving like fascists in promoting a boycott of my show, and he posted "Sieg Heil!" on Twitter to mock Media Matters president Angelo Carusone. CNN summarily fired Jeff over the post, saying that "Nazi salutes are indefensible."[57]

I hate Nazis, of course. But any reasonable person would understand Jeff was mocking Media Matters for the way they conduct themselves, not promoting Nazism. By the way, did any Fake News outlets demand firings, for example, when news surfaced that a high school history lesson at Loch Raven High School near Baltimore had compared President Trump with Nazis and communists?[58] Of course not. It all depends on whose ox is being gored—and as long as the ox belongs to President Trump, you may gore away.

Fox's reporting of the news might seem biased to Fake News viewers because they hear only one side of the story—the liberal, hate-Trump version. They object that we present both sides, because liberals tend to believe there is only one reality—the liberal reality—and all other perspectives are false. The Fake News networks have no clear division between news and opinion, yet they pretend their "news" reports are unbiased and objective. Back before Rush Limbaugh and Fox News, it was nearly impossible to get the other side of the story. But the rise of the alternative media has robbed the Fake News of their monopoly.

The Media Research Center found that the three major Fake News networks—ABC, CBS, and NBC—devoted almost seven times more coverage to news that former attorney general Jeff Sessions, when he was a U.S. senator, had met with a Russian ambassador than they did in June 2012 when Congress held Attorney General Eric Holder in contempt of Congress.[59] The Holder contempt citation involved serious misconduct—stonewalling Congress about the Obama administration's gun-walking program, which allowed U.S. weapons to fall into the hands of Mexican drug cartels. The Sessions meeting, by contrast, was a momentary encounter with the Russian ambassador at a cocktail party. But that was useful for the fake Russian collusion narrative, so the media mob manufactured so much hysteria over the incident that Sessions was forced to recuse himself from the Russia investigation.

Altogether, the three major Fake News evening newscasts spent more than half their news coverage on Trump and his administration during the first thirty days of his term—and a whopping 88 percent of it was negative.[60] How is that even possible during what is typically a "honeymoon" period? Well, it didn't get any better afterward. In the first ninety days of his presidency, Trump got 89 percent negative coverage from the Fake News broadcast networks,[61] and it got even worse during the summer, with 91 percent negative coverage of Trump.[62]

The networks despise Trump, but the Fake News cable stations have found a way to exceed the networks' bias. Take MSNBC, for example. The Media Research Center found that MSNBC interviewed congressional Democrats *thirteen times* more often than Republicans and that 81 percent of the policy questions directed at Democrats were supportive versus just 3 percent supportive for Republican guests.[63] Meanwhile, there's an endless list of crazy anti-Trump and anti-conservative outbursts on the network. A short sampling of lowlights would include:

- Lawrence O'Donnell announcing, "The president is a Russian operative."[64]
- Chris Hayes claiming Trump's support for a border wall is rooted in pandering to his racist supporters, who prefer an "ethnically pure America."[65]
- Chris Matthews denouncing President Trump's inauguration speech as "Hitlerian."[66]
- Roland Martin saying, "White conservative evangelicals are Christian frauds."[67]

- Joe Scarborough claiming, "Donald Trump is either an agent of Russia or he's a useful idiot," and that Trump "pledged his fealty and loyalty to Vladimir Putin."[68]
- Chris Matthews comparing Trump to Lincoln assassin John Wilkes Booth, Ugandan dictator Idi Amin, North Korean dictator Kim Jong-un, communist Ethiopian dictator Mengistu Haile Mariam, and the Romanov dynasty in Russia, and suggesting Trump could channel Italian dictator Benito Mussolini and execute his own son-in-law, Jared Kushner.[69]

Viewers can easily get the impression that with invective like this, MSNBC doesn't even take itself seriously. CNN, however, amusingly fronts as a bona fide news network. But whatever credibility it built up since its founding in 1980 has been completely destroyed by its jihad against President Trump. Its obsession with the man is constant, disturbing, and self-destructive. An MRC analysis of a typical day's "news" coverage found that CNN filled its day entirely with Trump stories, and that its coverage was "heavily skewed" with "anti-Trump guests and on-air commentators."[70] Focusing on a single day of CNN coverage—May 12, 2017—MRC analysts found that an incredible 92 percent (13 hours, 27 minutes) of its coverage centered on the Trump presidency, with all other news combined occupying only 8 percent of its network's airtime. MRC concluded that 78 percent of the guests were Trump critics and just 6 percent were pro-Trump. A similar anti-Trump imbalance was displayed by CNN's own talent, as well as in the "frequent editorializing of CNN's hosts and anchors."[71]

If anything, the MRC survey downplayed CNN's bias. The network is filled with miserable mopes who do nothing but nip at the president's heels. They provide a platform for imbeciles like Brian "Humpty Dumpty" Stelter. Now, I should probably have a little sympathy for a poor guy who's somehow managed to get every major story wrong in recent memory: Richard Jewell, Michael Brown, the Duke lacrosse rape hoax, Freddie Gray, Russia collusion, FISA abuse, the Deep State, and the Covington kids, to name a few. Humpty's judgment is so bad he became enamored with, of all people, Michael Avenatti, the Trump-hating porn star lawyer who is now a convicted felon. After Avenatti went to jail, I reminded Americans that Humpty had touted him as a potential presidential candidate. "Was that stupid on my part?" Stelter asked in response.[72] Hey, Humpty, I think you're on to something.

I've long accused CNN personalities of being stenographers for CNN president Jeff Zucker. They didn't seem to like that comment—which is strange, because this was proven true by James O'Keefe's Project Veritas sting video that featured recordings of Zucker's morning calls with CNN executive producers and news staffers. In these calls, Zucker sets the day's focus for the network, such as ordering his employees to criticize Fox News, to stop being friendly with Republican senator Lindsey Graham, and to ignore other stories in favor of impeachment. In the videos, CNN's own employees complain about Zucker's direction and his all-encompassing obsession with Trump.[73]

The entire CNN network has incredibly thin skin. CNN reporter Donie O'Sullivan denounced the *Babylon Bee*, a satirical publication, after a *Bee* story ridiculing the Democrats' response to the killing of Soleimani drew as much attention on social media as top stories by the *New York Times* and CNN.[74] The *Bee* struck back with a satirical piece titled, "CNN Attacks Babylon Bee: 'The Internet Is Only Big Enough for One Fake News Site.' " The *Bee* offered up a fake quote from Humpty: " 'They're obviously amateurs over there at The Bee,' said Brian Stelter. 'A lot of times, their reporting comes true. If you're gonna do fake news, do it right—100% fake, guaranteed, 24/7. They really should learn from the pros over here at CNN.' 'Stay out of our territory,' he growled."[75]

And that's how you fight the Fake News, folks. Call them out. Ridicule their bias. Don't back down, and don't let them intimidate you. There's a reason why Fox News generates headlines like "FOX News Channel Dominates Basic Cable for 41 Consecutive Months in Total Day,"[76] while CNN gets headlines like "Fox Wins Cable Battle—CNN

Loses to Cartoon Network."[77] It's because more and more Americans are deciding they're not going to tolerate Fake News anymore.

THE RUSSIA HOAX: "ONE OF THE GREAT POLITICAL SMEARS OF ALL TIME"

My team of investigative reporters and I have consistently broken news that the Fake News outlets won't cover. We have been on the cutting edge of reporting, exposing the lies of the Deep State and the mainstream media. Over the last three years, there was one story above all others that was pushed forward by the media with maximum hysteria, which we attacked as false from the very beginning, and for which we took the most abuse by the hate-Trump outlets we were questioning and contradicting. But in time we were vindicated, and now the real story is crystal clear to the American people: there was no Trump-Russia collusion.

It really wasn't hard to figure out that Russian collusion was a hoax. Days before Trump was inaugurated, *BuzzFeed* published the Steele dossier, supposed intelligence reports in which anonymous sources—mostly Russians—detailed a years-long collusion conspiracy between Trump and the Russians, including a plot to hack the 2016 presidential election. The allegations ranged from merely stupid to totally ridiculous, topped off by the asinine report that Trump, a notorious germophobe, had hired prostitutes to perform a "golden shower" urination show in a Moscow hotel room to defile a bed once used by Barack Obama. The story sounds like it's straight out of an episode of *South Park*.

Even before Congressman Devin Nunes forced out the revelation that the dossier was bought and paid for by the Hillary Clinton campaign and the Democratic National Committee, it was obvious the whole thing was an outrageous fraud. Even journalists directly involved in the initial reporting on the dossier could see the problems. *BuzzFeed* editor in chief Ben Smith not only failed to corroborate the dossier, but in an internal memo he said there was "serious reason to doubt" the report's claims.[78] What's more, hours before *BuzzFeed* published the dossier, CNN posted a story in which anonymous Deep State stooges revealed that President Obama and President-elect Trump had been briefed on dossier allegations. We later learned that Jake Tapper, a coauthor of the CNN story, emailed Ben Smith and blasted him for printing the dossier, claiming it made the CNN story "less serious and credible."[79] That's right—Tapper feared if Americans could read the dossier themselves instead of relying on CNN's characterization of it, they wouldn't take it seriously. Amid all the hysteria and lies, ABC's Brian Ross managed to utter a true statement on *Good Morning America*: "If true [the dossier allegations] are a grave national security issue. If false, one of the great political smears of all time."[80]

Despite all the dossier's credibility problems, the entire mainstream media recklessly promoted its claims. In just a five-day period, CNN mentioned "the pee tapes" *seventy-seven* times.[81] However, although the entire Washington press corps seems to have tried to confirm the dossier's collusion allegations, no evidence turned up anywhere. The *Washington Post* sent investigators to every hotel in Prague to vindicate the dossier's claim that Trump lawyer Michael Cohen had gone there for a secret meeting with Russian conspirators—and the *Post* came up empty.[82]

But the media had no restraint, dropping "bombshell" after "bombshell" of new allegations of Trump campaign members colluding with Russians. Adam Schiff and other Democrat miscreants became constant fixtures on TV news shows, giving credence to the dossier and to whatever happened to be the most recent collusion fabrication.

The media ignored all the indications that the entire story was false, and they spit venom at those of us who pointed out that the dossier was a joke and that the rest of the case was built on unverifiable lies from anonymous Deep State idiots. They wouldn't even listen to their fellow Trump hater, FBI director James Comey, who testified to the Senate Intelligence Committee in June 2017 that "there've been many, many stories purportedly based on classified information, about—

well, about lots of stuff, but especially about Russia that are just dead wrong."[83] Comey described as "almost entirely wrong" a key *New York Times* story reporting that phone records and intercepted calls showed Trump associates had "repeated contacts with Russian intelligence." Not only did the *Times* refuse to retract that story, but in a stunning sign of the total corruption of the mainstream media, the article was among twelve stories on Trump-Russia collusion for which the *Times* won a prestigious George Polk Award.[84]

Unsurprisingly, the Russia collusion reporting of the *Times* and the *Washington Post*—which together were the primary drivers of the biggest Fake News story of our lifetime—were jointly awarded the 2018 Pulitzer Prize for national reporting. Just look at the award citation: "For deeply sourced, relentlessly reported coverage in the public interest that dramatically furthered the nation's understanding of Russian interference in the 2016 presidential election and its connections to the Trump campaign, the President-elect's transition team and his eventual administration."[85] The news just doesn't get any more fake than that.

The media's obsessive coverage of the Russia hoax crowded out almost all other news. In the first five weeks after Robert Mueller was appointed special counsel to head up the witch hunt, the broadcast networks spent 55 percent of their coverage of the Trump administration on the investigation, of which one-third was anonymously sourced. There was barely any room left for reporting on Trump's governing agenda—withdrawing from the Paris climate treaty and the Iran nuclear deal, negotiating better trade agreements, kick-starting energy production, deregulation, expanding pipeline projects, promoting religious liberty, reforming veterans' care, and nominating constitutionalist federal appellate judges, to name a few.[86]

How important was the Russia hoax to the mainstream media? Speaking with his staff about the Russia collusion investigation shortly after Robert Mueller's disastrous public testimony to Congress, *New York Times* executive editor Dean Baquet admitted, "We built our newsroom to cover one story."[87] Think about that. The nation's most prestigious newspaper organized its entire reporting operation to cover a single story—and it was a hoax!

As you would expect, the *Times* was put in a tough spot when Mueller found no evidence to vindicate its reporting on the dominant story of the previous two years. Here's what Baquet told his demoralized employees: "The day Bob Mueller walked off that witness stand, two things happened. Our readers who want Donald Trump to go away suddenly thought, 'Holy sh*t, Bob Mueller is not going to do it.' And Donald Trump got a little emboldened politically, I think. Because, you know, for obvious reasons. And I think that the story changed. A lot of the stuff we're talking about started to emerge like six or seven weeks ago. We're a little tiny bit flat-footed. I mean, that's what happens when a story looks a certain way for two years. Right?"[88]

You have to love Baquet's choice of words here. Let me translate:

- "Our readers who want Donald Trump to go away suddenly thought, 'Holy sh*t, Bob Mueller is not going to do it.'"— *Our rabid Trump-hating subscribers were shocked that Mueller was not going to overthrow our duly elected president.*
- "And Donald Trump got a little emboldened politically, I think. Because, you know, for obvious reasons."— *Unfortunately, Donald Trump benefited when the coup attempt against him failed.*
- "And I think that the story changed."—*Our reporting was exposed as a hoax.*
- "A lot of the stuff we're talking about started to emerge like six or seven weeks ago. We're a little tiny bit flat-footed."— *Our leakers on the Mueller team told us six or seven weeks ago that Mueller had no evidence of collusion. We're the biggest frauds in American journalism.*
- "I mean, that's what happens when a story looks a certain way for two years. Right?"—*I mean, that's what happens when you wildly distort a story for two years. Right?*

The media mob met with more humiliation in this saga due to its coverage of Congressman Devin Nunes's memo revealing that the FBI used unverified allegations from the Steele dossier to get FISA warrants to spy on Trump campaign aide Carter Page. First they and their Deep State allies warned that releasing the memo would endanger national security. "People must understand what is at stake by release of the bogus, contrived Nunes memo," said disgraced Obama attorney general Eric Holder. "It uses normally protected material and puts at risk our intel capabilities in order to derail a legitimate criminal investigation. This is unheard of—it is dangerous and it is irresponsible."[89] Not to be outdone, CNN political analyst Brain Karem warned that Nunes was a threat to the republic, claiming that publishing the memo "is a tipping point for our democracy. Are we going to be a democracy after today, or is this going to be demagoguery and despotism?"[90]

Once the memo was released, the American people could see for themselves that there was no threat to democracy in revealing how the FBI faked evidence to spy on Carter Page. So the hate-Trump media moved to their next storyline: the memo was a dud. We were supposed to believe that it was just no big deal that the Obama administration perpetrated a fraud on the FISA court and used fake information to get warrants to spy on its political opponents. And you almost have to admire the media's messaging discipline while making this insane argument. Just look at the headlines:

- *New York Times*: "Devin Nunes's Nothingburger"[91]
- *Salon*: " 'Worse Than a Nothing Burger': The Nunes Memo Lands With a Thud"[92]
- *Washington Monthly*: "Devin Nunes and the Nothing Burger Memo"[93]
- *Esquire*: " 'Nothingburger' Doesn't Do This Memo Justice"[94]
- *The Hill*: "Press: The GOP'S Giant Nothing Burger"[95]

Finally, the Fake News outlets rallied around the counter-memo put out a few weeks later by Congressman Adam Schiff, a congenital liar, leaker, and hoax artist. Filled with slimy insinuations that Carter Page is a Russian agent, the Schiff memo denied there were any abuses at all in the Page FISA warrants. Schiff claimed the Department of Justice made only "narrow use" of the Steele dossier in the warrant applications; that the FBI had "undertaken a rigorous process" to vet Steele's allegations; that there were no omissions in the applications; and that the FISA contained "additional information obtained through multiple independent sources that corroborated Steele's reporting."[96] The media triumphantly announced that the Schiff memo was "the nail in the coffin" for the Nunes memo.[97]

But Schiff and his Fake News mouthpieces were catastrophically wrong. The report by DOJ inspector general Michael Horowitz showed that the FBI had perpetrated a premeditated fraud on the FISA court by misrepresenting bogus dossier information, just as Nunes had said. The report shredded every aspect of the Schiff memo that the media had championed, finding *seventeen* major problems in the FISA warrants.[98] When asked if he'd admit he was wrong, Schiff claimed he simply didn't have the evidence that the inspector general found and he didn't know about the abuses.[99] That's hard to believe, considering Nunes told everyone. As for the media, nearly all of them reported Horowitz's findings without noting how it brutally murdered the Schiff memo and vindicated the Nunes memo, which they had universally denounced as a fraud, a dud, and a threat to our national security.

"THE CAMPAIGN TO IMPEACH PRESIDENT TRUMP HAS BEGUN"

The media have tried to get President Trump impeached since his first day in office. I'm not exaggerating—a *Washington Post* report on January 20, 2017, Trump's inauguration day, had the blaring headline

"The Campaign to Impeach President Trump Has Begun." Trump had done nothing at that point but swear the oath of office, but the *Post* wanted Americans to know about a campaign to build public support to impeach him launched by two liberal activist groups using the website ImpeachDonaldTrumpNow.org. The story also quoted the American Civil Liberties Union, which it said "plans to wield public-records requests and lawsuits as part of an aggressive action plan aimed at protecting immigrants and pushing for government transparency, among other issues." [100]

So the left was planning an all-out campaign of harassment to stop Trump even before he took office. The truth is, the left's mad crusade to impeach Trump never had anything to do with his conduct. The unforgivable crime he committed was beating Hillary Clinton, and that's why the campaign to impeach him began on his first day in office. The fact that he was elected on vows to implement a strong, conservative agenda made it even more urgent for the left to get rid of him. As the *Washington Post* story noted, the impeachment push "comes as Democrats and liberal activists are mounting broad opposition to stymie Trump's agenda." [101]

From the beginning the Democrats have been in hot pursuit of any conceivable pretext to impeach Trump, and every bogus impeachment effort they've launched has reflected their bad faith. Just imagine if Hillary Clinton had won the election and Republicans carried out a nonstop effort to frame her and impeach her for imaginary crimes beginning on her inauguration day. We all know the media would cast Republicans as hate-filled, partisan sexists. Yet they not only supported the impeachment drive against Trump, but with their daily production of "bombshell" leaks featuring anonymous sources describing some phony Trump misconduct, it'd be perfectly accurate to say they *led* it. The media, who hold themselves out as stewards of our democracy, actively conspired with Democrats to remove a duly elected president and thereby dismantle the republic they pretend to be saving.

In truth, the media was fantasizing about impeachment even *before*

Trump's inauguration. Two days after the election—November 10, 2016—*Good Morning America* ran through a whole series of supposed Trump outrages that have since formed the basis of impeachment demands. ABC's George Stephanopoulos discussed various civil suits pending against Trump, insisting, "If he takes the risk of going to trial and he's convicted, that could be seen as an impeachable offense." Aside from Stephanopoulos's embarrassing use of the criminal term "convicted" in discussing civil cases, he apparently was unaware that a president cannot be impeached for actions taken before he became president, as noted by the network's legal analyst, Dan Abrams.

Stephanopoulos also interviewed correspondent Brian Ross, who reported on "dozens of cases" involving Trump that might get the president in trouble. One of the urgent matters Ross raised was—you guessed it—Russia! "Trump has extensive ties with several Russian oligarchs close to Vladimir Putin," said Ross. "He and his children have sought investments with controversial overseas figures." And to round things out, Stephanopoulos and Ross invoked their go-to issue—vague allegations that Trump may have violated tax laws.[102]

Despite years of endless investigations of these issues in Congress and elsewhere—including the years-long Russia collusion hoax—the Democrats couldn't find anything strong enough to use as a basis to impeach Trump. Finally, they jumped on the Ukraine whistle-blower issue contrived by Adam Schiff. In many ways, the Ukraine hoax was an even weaker pretext for impeachment than the parade of idiotic allegations that preceded it. That's why media deceptions were crucial to impeachment from the very beginning. The first report on the content of the whistle-blower complaint was a September 18, 2019, story in the *Washington Post* that revealed the complaint was related to a conversation between President Trump and a foreign leader. Exactly as we've come to expect, there was a giant lie at the beginning of the story, with two anonymous sources claiming the complaint related to a "promise" Trump made to Zelensky.[103] Once the White House published the transcript of the call, everyone could see there was no promise at all, but by then impeachment hysteria was already unstoppable.

The media also stoked a frenzy surrounding the depositions given by witnesses behind closed doors at Schiff's House Intelligence Committee. It became a daily ritual that shortly after a witness finished testifying, the media would publish a slew of Democrat leaks from anonymous sources designed to portray the testimony in the most incriminating light possible. As we all learned much later when the witness transcripts were made public, all the exculpatory testimony was left out of the leaks.

The media continued in this vein throughout the impeachment charade. They showed little interest in learning all the details of the secret coordination between Schiff's staff and the whistle-blower, which no one knows to this day. They also denounced Republican concern about Ukrainian meddling in U.S. elections as a "conspiracy theory" despite Alexandra Chalupa's admission to *Politico* that she cooperated with Ukrainian officials to smear the Trump campaign.[104] Working with foreign officials to sabotage an opposing campaign, of course, is the exact false accusation that was made against Trump throughout the Russia collusion hoax. But for some reason when a Democrat *admitted* doing it, the media did not demand FBI investigations. In fact, they couldn't seem to have cared less.

In the end Trump beat the coup attempt. The media's best efforts to gin up support for impeachment failed miserably because they had already lost all credibility with tens of millions of Americans. The coverage was so biased that Devin Nunes dedicated an entire opening statement at one of the televised impeachment hearings to media malpractice. As Nunes said, "The media, of course, are free to act as Democrat puppets, and they're free to lurch from the Russia hoax to the Ukraine hoax at the direction of their puppet masters. But they cannot reasonably expect to do so without alienating half the country who voted for the President they're trying to expel. Americans have learned to recognize fake news when they see it, and if the mainstream press won't give it to them straight, they'll go elsewhere to find it—which is exactly what the American people are doing." [105]

I have consistently defended the First Amendment rights of everyone in this country, including members of the media and Hollywood elite whose opinions I find repugnant. I can give you chapter and verse on my defending various liberal figures to voice their most noxious views. I've taken some heat for that, but principle is principle. We must not confuse their inalienable right to free speech, however, with immunity from criticism. We have a duty to criticize politicized and dishonest journalism, and I have tried to do my part. The liberal media fraudulently hides behind the First Amendment when caught in their lies. And they use it to intimidate their honest critics, cynically depicting them as authoritarian speech suppressors. By deliberately spreading disinformation on a daily basis and dedicating all their considerable power to ousting a democratically elected president, the mainstream media has well earned the moniker "enemy of the people."

I'm not trying to pat myself on the back too hard for getting right so many stories that the Fake News Media got wrong either out of incompetence or bias. But I am proud of my team, who worked diligently to pursue and report information that you couldn't find anywhere else. My show didn't start out with much investigative reporting, but we had to turn in that direction when the Fake News tried to destroy President Trump and their phony stories weren't being exposed. We decided we weren't going to stand aside and watch the liberal media and the Democratic Party pulverize this remarkable president and turn the lights out on America's liberty. I like to think we are filling the role the media is supposed to play—shining a disinfecting light of truth on corruption, bias, and abuses of power. The media itself are now major perpetrators of this misconduct, possibly even more than politicians are. So until CNN, the New York Times, the Washington Post, and the rest of the Fake News constellation start trying to inform the American people instead of indoctrinating them, we will continue to hold them to account and do so without apology.

CHAPTER EIGHT

"Organized Destruction": The Left's Assault on Free Speech

THE CENSORIOUS LEFT

I have detailed the dire threat the Democratic Party poses to America if it regains control and implements its leftist agenda. But it can continue to do plenty of damage outside government as well. The left has a stranglehold on the media, our academic institutions, Hollywood, and social media. This means that even if we beat back the Democrats' effort to win the presidency and control of Congress, they'll continue to impose their lunacy through the culture. Yes, we must work hard to elect conservatives at the local, state, and national levels, but we can no longer afford to neglect the culture battlefield.

Leftists are a totalitarian, intolerant bunch who now look to shut down opposing viewpoints in both the public and private sectors. In the private sector, we've seen the left bully Chick-fil-A for its founder's biblical views on marriage. Though the restaurant chain withstood that pressure for years, it finally succumbed and withdrew funding for the Salvation Army and the Fellowship of Christian Athletes— Christian charities that have also come under withering attack from the left. Note that neither of the charities was accused of discriminating against gays or anyone else—they've simply voiced politically incorrect viewpoints on issues like gay marriage, so they are subjected to a torrent of left-wing abuse and boycott demands regardless of the tens of millions of downtrodden people they've assisted. So for the left, helping the poor is all well and good, but if you don't mouth the right political platitudes, there's no place for you in society.

Inside the policy arena, through laws and regulations, they are limiting our First Amendment freedoms. Outside the policy arena, through political correctness and cultural shaming, they are policing thought and speech, and in many cases, using violent means to do so. They readily suppress our speech, religious liberties, and freedom of assembly. The left has become so intolerant that even some progressives—such as popular blogger Dave Rubin, political commentator Kirsten Powers, and comedian Bill Maher—have denounced this tendency among their own comrades.[1]

On college campuses the left shuts down debates inside and outside the classroom. Among younger students they set up "zero tolerance" crusades, where kids are punished for such benign activities as forming their breakfast pastry into the shape of a gun.[2] They claim to preach tolerance but outwardly practice bigotry against Christians and conservatives.[3]

They have long since seized control of Hollywood, which serves a steady diet of leftist insanity in the guise of entertainment while actors who express any conservative sentiments get shamed and blackballed. It's hard for the left to resist jamming their politics in our faces, even in entertainment venues with no logical connection to politics—because for the left, everything is political. Everything. It's hard to find a television series free of leftist preaching, let alone any of Hollywood's self-congratulatory awards shows. During the 2020 Golden Globes, even after host Ricky Gervais preemptively mocked the celebrities' hypocritical political preaching and obliviousness to the concerns of everyday Americans, they *still* proved his point by droning on with self-righteous political speeches before jumping into their limos and returning to their gated palaces.

Progressives control social media as well—Facebook, Twitter, YouTube, Google, etc.—and are censoring conservatives. These giant corporations wield enormous power over speech on their respective platforms, where First Amendment protections do not apply. It's arguable that these social media giants—not the government—now pose the biggest threat to free expression.[4]

Progressives are often guilty of the very thing they accuse conservatives of doing. Take the *New York Times'* Adam Liptak, for example, who paints conservatives as the real enemies of free expression. He claims the conservative Supreme Court has weaponized the First Amendment to "justify unlimited campaign spending, discrimination against gay couples and attacks on the regulation of tobacco, pharmaceuticals and guns." He points to the Court's ruling prohibiting the state of California from forcing faith-based crisis pregnancy centers to provide pregnant women with information about obtaining an abortion. Of course, far from weaponizing the First Amendment, the ruling affirmed it, by preventing the government from forcing people to advocate for things they don't believe in. Progressives, in fact, are the ones "weaponizing" free speech, such as when campus radicals claim a First Amendment right to disrupt and shut down speakers with dissenting views.[5]

Liptak's distorted argument is hardly shocking as leftists routinely corrupt language, twisting words into the opposite of their true meaning. They use the term "inclusion," for example, to mean "exclusion." "Inclusion is merely the new soft, cottony term for marginalizing, shutting down, and kicking out the disfavored," writes *National Review's* Kyle Smith. "Look at Harvard, which brought the hammer down on all single-gender groups in the name of inclusion, then exempted female groups, saying it was okay for them to be 'gender-focused.' " Smith cites other examples of this leftist hypocrisy, such as a Catholic high school removing statues of Jesus and Mary to be "inclusive"—wholly ignoring those who liked the statues.[6]

The left is also increasingly dogmatic on gender. If you dare to state there are only two genders, you are a bigot. At last count there are more than seventy possibilities. Jon Caldara, a *Denver Post* columnist, learned this the hard way. In a Facebook post he said he "supports gay rights" and is "strongly pro–gay marriage," but that wasn't enough—he was fired after insisting on the biological fact that there are only two sexes. "There was a time when the liberals in the press fought hard to protect free speech," wrote Caldara. "Now they fight hard to mandate speech because, heaven forbid, someone be offended or have their feelings hurt. [It's] okay people get offended. In fact, I encourage it. It means we are being challenged. It's not hate speech. It's speech. It used to be [what] the press was all about."[7]

The left is willing to criminalize certain expressions, even those that a substantial percentage of people—perhaps even a majority—find harmless. The New York Commission on Human Rights, for instance, adopted guidelines that allow government authorities to impose fines up to $250,000 on people who "misgender" a person, meaning to refer to a person by something other than their chosen pronoun. You violate the guidelines if you call someone "he" or "she" instead of using their preferred gender-neutral terms, such as ze/hir.[8] To many people this sounds insane, but that's not the point. The point is that the left will use the force of government to compel you to pay homage to their ideas, even the obviously crazy ones.

Senators Bernie Sanders and Elizabeth Warren showed an Orwellian urge for censorship by signing a letter to the Federal Communications Commission requesting it to "investigate Sinclair Broadcasting's news activities to determine if it conforms to the public interest." The senators claim Sinclair had forced its local news anchors to read scripts warning of "one-sided news stories plaguing our country." "As strong defenders of the First Amendment guarantees of free speech and freedom of the press, we are alarmed by such practices. . . . Must-run dictates from Sinclair harm the freedom of the press guaranteed in the First Amendment by turning local journalists into mouthpieces for a corporate and political agenda," the letter read.[9] So in the name of free speech, they asked the government to investigate the content of private news broadcasts.

Can you believe this? What do they think CBS, NBC, ABC, NPR, MSNBC, CNN, and the rest of the leftist media are, if not mouthpieces for a political agenda? FCC chairman Ajit Pai declined the request, saying the agency has no authority to revoke licenses based on the content of a particular newscast. "I understand that you disliked or disagreed with the content of particular broadcasts, but I can hardly think of an action more chilling of free speech than the federal government investigating a broadcast station because of disagreement with its news coverage or promotion of that coverage," said Pai.[10]

I can't emphasize strongly enough how dangerous the suppression of free speech is to our republic. We must never forget that liberty is what makes America unique. The framers placed free expression at the beginning of the Bill of Rights because it's central to all our other liberties. But the left is so focused on imposing their grand socialist schemes that freedom takes a backseat. They either do not see or do not care that their quest to muzzle the expression of certain ideas, even abhorrent ones, is more dangerous than the ideas themselves.

CANCEL CULTURE

Who but the radically intolerant left could even come up with such a heartless and unforgiving idea as "cancel culture"? The term is defined by dictionary.com as "The popular practice of withdrawing support for (*canceling*) public figures and companies after that they have done or said something considered objectionable or offensive. *Cancel culture* is generally discussed as being performed on social media in the form of group shaming." It's kind of like saying, "If you say something politically incorrect, you're dead to us—forever." Such sweethearts, these leftists. The term, says author and commentator Roger Simon, is "used by the self-anointed 'woke' for boycotting—essentially turning into non-persons and erasing from public life—people (usually celebrities, but plebes aren't exempt) who have exhibited what they deem questionable behavior or written something untoward on social media." Simon notes that the cancelers went after Ellen DeGeneres just for having a friendly chat with former president George W. Bush, and actor Vince Vaughn was targeted for talking and shaking hands with President Trump and First Lady Melania Trump at a football game.[11]

Cancel culture is one negative consequence of the wonderful explosion of free expression the internet affords. While the Web has allowed ordinary people a public voice, it has also created an opportunity for social media mobs to destroy people and ruin their livelihoods. It can play to our darkest side because the cancelers have nothing to gain except pleasure in hurting others—they used to call that sadism. T. J. Roberts disputes claims that cancel culture makes people accountable for their misconduct and offensive statements. If it "implied accountability, then there would be an avenue for redemption," says Roberts. "When the mob controls justice, there is no means by which you can gain their respect."[12] That's right. It's not about accountability, it's about empowering virtue-signaling scolds to project themselves as morally superior, which, come to think about it, is pretty much what leftists always do.

Even progressives are not exempt if they stray from leftist orthodoxy. Harry Potter author J. K. Rowling objected to the firing of a British woman from a think tank for saying that there are two sexes and no one can really change their sex. Rowling would have to be canceled, as would her fictional characters Harry, Ron, Hermione, and Hagrid.[13] You'll notice, though, that not many people get canceled for offending conservatives—because we aren't totalitarian censors.

Columnist Douglas Murray doesn't just blame the bullies for this climate but the people who allow them to get away with it. "The problem is not that the sacrificial victim is selected," writes Murray. "The problem is that the people who destroy his reputation are permitted to do so by the complicity, silence and slinking away of everybody else."[14] I agree, and I've been pretty outspoken in calling for a second chance

even for people who've said stupid things. We've all made mistakes—
even the cancelers themselves.

UNIVERSITIES: LEFTIST INCUBATORS

Universities, which mainly seem to produce speech-suppressing leftists, regularly betray their stated commitment to academic freedom
and free expression. Instead, they promote a radical closing of the
mind and hostility to all dissenting ideas. And they do it deceptively,
publicly championing the very principles they systematically abuse.
Columbia University president Lee Bollinger unwittingly makes my
point in his piece denying the obvious truth that university campuses
are bastions of selective censorship. Bollinger ridiculed President
Trump's executive order withholding federal funding to colleges and
universities that deny speech protections as "a transparent exercise in
politics. Its intent was to validate the collective antipathy that many
Trump boosters feel toward institutions of higher learning."[15]

Notice the little dig there, echoing Obama's previous disparaging
comments about conservatives—Trump supporters are bitter, Bible-
clinging, pickup-driving, education-hating lamebrains whose concerns about free speech are really a front for their hatred for institutions
of higher learning themselves. Bollinger then incoherently defends
academic censorship on the grounds that Americans have long "been
grappling with basic questions about offensive speech for decades . . .
[and] exchanges over the boundaries of campus speech should therefore be welcomed rather than reviled when they take place."[16] In other
words, the fact that universities allow discussions of their censorship
policies proves that they cherish free speech.

Bollinger protests too much. Polls show that 73 percent of Americans support free speech assurances on university campuses, yet
according to the National Association of Scholars (NAS), more than
90 percent of colleges "substantially restrict freedom of speech and

association." "Higher education is the special place in society set aside for the freedom to seek the truth—but that freedom is under assault," said the organization in a statement signed by more than 440 professors, scholars, writers, and representatives of civil and academic organizations. "We call on Congress to cease subsidizing unlawful behavior by public colleges and universities, and to protect freedom of speech on college campuses." [17]

Unsurprisingly, the Obama administration made matters much worse. Just as Obama's Education Department had conditioned federal funding on schools stripping students and staff of due process protections in sexual misconduct cases,[18] his Justice Department conspired with the University of Montana in settling a case to redefine sexual harassment to limit protected speech. Greg Lukianoff, president of the Foundation for Individual Rights in Education (FIRE), argued that the administration mandated a definition of sexual harassment so broad that it exposes all students to harassment claims and effectively imposes unconstitutional speech codes at universities throughout America.[19]

The government imposed these new rules on all campuses by decreeing that the Montana findings should serve as a "blueprint for colleges and universities throughout the country." Henceforth, said Lukianoff, "only a stunningly broad definition of sexual harassment— 'unwelcome conduct of a sexual nature'—will now satisfy federal statutory requirements. This explicitly includes 'verbal conduct,' otherwise known as speech." Campuses would now have "an obligation to respond to student-on-student harassment" even when it occurs off campus. "In some circumstances . . . universities may take 'disciplinary action against the harasser' " before the case is completed. "In plain English: Students can be punished before they are found guilty of harassment." [20]

The Obama administration further sought to deny the accused the right to question the accuser in sexual harassment cases— because the accuser might find it traumatic or intimidating. As liberal

George Washington University Law School professor Jonathan Turley observed, "Notably, the Supreme Court stated in 2004 that 'dispensing with confrontation because testimony is obviously reliable is
akin to dispensing with a jury trial because the defendant is obviously
guilty.' "[21]

When U.S. education secretary Betsy DeVos reversed Obama's
unconstitutional policy, Texas attorney Rob Ranco said he'd "be okay"
if DeVos were sexually assaulted. Charming. That's the thanks conservatives get from progressives for, to quote Turley again, "restoring
minimal rules of due process for the investigation of sexual misconduct."[22] Turley notes that liberals are imposing a false choice between
due process for students accused of sexual harassment and full protection for their alleged victims.

Leftist professors have infected their students, including journalism students, with an alarming tolerance for censorship. When
violent leftist protesters at Middlebury College in Vermont silenced
visiting speaker Charles Murray, a conservative thinker, and pulled
the hair and injured the neck of the professor trying to shield him,
the school's paper, the *Middlebury Campus*, refused to denounce the
protestors, and most of the opinions solicited and printed by the paper
defended them. When another violent mob at the University of California, Berkeley blocked Milo Yiannopoulos from speaking, the *Daily
Californian's* student journalists defended the mob, claiming that the
university had "invited chaos" by giving a platform to "someone who
never belonged here."[23] Twelve of the university's professors had sent
a letter asking the administration to cancel the speaking event before
it occurred, with nearly ninety more professors later signing on. In an
email to the paper, one of the letter's authors, David Landreth, argued
the professors "wholeheartedly" support free speech *but* Yiannopoulos engages in "personal harassment," so he should be silenced.[24]

Progressives frequently justify their censorship by labeling certain opinions "hate speech." "Free speech is no longer sacred among
young journalists who have absorbed the campus lessons about 'hate

speech'—defined more broadly—and they're breaking long-standing taboos as they bring 'cancel culture' into professional newsrooms," writes New York journalist John Tierney. They are "terrified of seeming insufficiently 'woke.' Most professional journalists, young and old, still pay lip service to the First Amendment, and they certainly believe it protects their own work, but they're increasingly eager for others to be 'de-platformed' or 'no-platformed,' as today's censors like to put it—effectively silenced."[25]

Tierney is right about these "younger progressive journalists" who try to get their conservative counterparts fired and banned from social media platforms, lobby Amazon to ban conservative books, and organize advertising boycotts against conservatives, which we Fox primetime hosts are routinely subjected to. Tierney makes a point I often make: "They equate conservatives' speech with violence and rationalize leftists' actual violence as . . . speech."[26] These virtue-signaling liberals are ever more dangerous to free expression in this country, blissfully unaware that eviscerating free speech for conservatives will inevitably, someday, boomerang back against the left.

GENERATION SNOWFLAKE

Discrimination against campus conservative groups is another leftist ploy to suppress speech. Trinity University's student government denied funding to bring conservative author Heather Mac Donald to campus because she has been an outspoken critic of universities' diversity mania. One student senator commented that if Mac Donald was "going to come to our campus and tell us that, like campus rape culture isn't a thing, I think that would make a lot of people on this campus feel unsafe." Another said that inviting her would be "the equivalent of inviting a climate change denier."[27] You got that? It endangers students if someone denies leftists' claims that rape is a common and socially acceptable occurrence on campuses, and allowing that kind of speech is just as bad as allowing someone to deny that we're all going to die from global warming.

Often led by extremely high-salaried bureaucrats, university "diversity" programs are a colossal waste of resources that drive up tuition rates. But hearing that is simply unbearable on many campuses. There is only one acceptable opinion. This is the type of leftist intolerance that courses through the Democratic Party and threatens our First Amendment freedoms.

It's no wonder campus thought police resent Mac Donald, a leading critic of campus censorship. In *City Journal*, she cited numerous outrageous examples. At Claremont McKenna College, in October 2015, a Hispanic student complained in an op-ed about the school's "western, white, cisheteronormative upper to upper-middle class values" that make minority students feel out of place. In response, the dean of students attempted to accommodate the student, asking her to meet with administrators to assist them to "better serve students, especially those that don't fit our CMC mold." Boy, did that backfire— though minority students had themselves used the phrase "not fitting the mold," they launched protests, hunger strikes, and marches demanding that the dean resign for supposedly insulting them. Unable to appease them despite an hour's worth of apologizing, the dean quit.[28] Mission accomplished! Leftist hate vindicated!

I've covered a few examples of this kind of student tyranny on my show, including Mac Donald's own experience with Claremont McKenna, where agitators cut short her speech using what she called "brute totalitarian force." I also told you about a student group protesting a proposed Chick-fil-A restaurant at Duquesne University in Pennsylvania, claiming it could jeopardize the school's "safe spaces." There are endless other examples.

At Emory University, in March 2016, minority students demanded that the university's president protect them from "Trump 2016" slogans written in chalk on sidewalks, which made them "afraid." Groveling university president James Wagner said, "I learn from every conversation like the one that took place yesterday and know that further conversations are necessary." Wagner announced a plan to "honor" the students' complaints, to include reviewing the sidewalk Trump slogans. Like a good leftist, he invoked the language of inclusion to announce exclusionary measures. "As an academic community, we must value . . . the expression of ideas . . . [But] at the same time, our commitment to respect, civility, and inclusion calls us to provide a safe environment that inspires and supports courageous inquiry." " 'Safety,' " Mac Donald comments, "is a code word for suppression."[29]

Do schools even question the merits of such complaints anymore? Think about the supposed offense here—advocating the election of someone who was promising to improve living conditions for minorities (and the president has kept that promise). That anyone, let alone the administration of an institution of higher learning, would treat this as threatening is appalling and alarming. Since we're talking about safety, who is attending to the safety of Trump-supporting students? Wouldn't they have more reason to feel unsafe on campus, being surrounded by intolerant leftist students, professors, and administrators?

At Evergreen State College, in May 2017, students screamed obscenities at biology professor Bret Weinstein for refusing to comply with an order from the school's director of First Peoples Multicultural Advising Services that all white professors must cancel their courses for a day and not enter the campus. The students shouted, "F--- you, you piece of s---." "Get the f--- out of here." "F--- what you have to say." "This is not a discussion." Weinstein, notes Mac Donald, is a lifelong progressive.

The radical students also cursed out the university's president, who then *praised* the students' misbehavior. "Let me reiterate my gratitude for the passion and courage you have shown me and others," said President George Bridges. "I want every one of you to feel safe on this campus and be able to learn in a supportive environment free from discrimination or intimidation. . . . For a long time, we've been working on the concerns you've raised and acknowledge that our results have fallen short. . . . This week, you are inviting us into the struggle you have taken up." Mac Donald informs us that "Weinstein and his biologist wife, Heather Heying, were eventually hounded out of Evergreen." This, my friends, is leftism at work. This is the future if we don't fight and win. Our universities are molding a generation of Stalinist leftists and enabling their fanatical behavior.[30]

Abortion is another hot-button issue for campus leftists. Colorado State University denied a "diversity grant" for its Students for Life chapter "to educate students on the differing perspectives surrounding the abortion argument and encourage students to take a stand on the issue." But as you well know, "diversity" doesn't mean diversity of ideas. Campus Activities Program coordinator Tyrell Allen informed the group that the Diversity Grant Committee denied the request because the "speaker's content doesn't appear entirely unbiased as it addresses the topic of abortion," and the "committee worries that folks from varying sides of the issue won't necessarily feel affirmed in attending the event."[31]

So a university denied a voice to a conservative group because the mere expression of a contrary view might make leftist students feel uncomfortable, unsafe, or unaffirmed. Welcome to our world! Conservative students feel unaffirmed and uncomfortable every day at their close-minded leftist universities. Take for instance a Purdue University employee who denounced Purdue Students for Life as "vile, racist idiots" on Facebook for distributing pro-life brochures on campus with the slogan "Hands up, don't abort"—a takeoff on a Black Lives Matter slogan. How's that for unaffirming? The students said they found the comments disturbing and were concerned for their safety on campus.[32] For once, it seems students had legitimate safety concerns as opposed to using such concerns as a smoke screen for silencing opposing viewpoints.

"ECHO CHAMBERS OF ORTHODOX CREEDS"

Progressive students are dutifully learning the ways of their leftist mentors. For example, the University of Scranton student government refused to recognize a chapter of Turning Point USA, a conservative group. The Foundation for Individual Rights in Education (FIRE) asked the university's president to recognize the group in accordance with its commitment to free expression or to provide a viewpoint-neutral reason for its refusal. According to FIRE, the university sent an unsatisfactory response and has not provided clarification despite further requests.[33]

The student government president seemed hell-bent on denying recognition to the group. He insisted the student government has the right to consider a prospective group and say, "Yikes, nope, denied." He added that "in the slim chance" the student senate does approve the group, he has the power to veto that decision.[34] I can honestly say that conservatives don't think like this. While we strongly disagree with leftists—obviously—we wouldn't deny their right to form a student group even if we had the power to do it. But many leftists who doubtlessly consider themselves progressive, enlightened, and tolerant have no qualms denying conservatives a voice, even if those rights are guaranteed by the university to the students.

While liberals downplay this disturbing trend, there were more than fifty attempts to disinvite speakers from college campuses in 2018 and 2019.[35] Possibly even more egregious, more than 120 colleges and universities have campus speech codes that restrict what students may say,[36] even though courts have consistently held these to be unconstitutional.[37] Some of the examples are almost too bizarre to believe. At Kellogg Community College in Battle Creek, Michigan, three students were *arrested and jailed* for distributing pocket copies of the United States Constitution in the process of forming a campus chapter of Young Americans for Liberty. It seems that the conservative students had ventured outside the university's "speech zone" and were violating the school's Speech Permit Policy by "engaging [students] in conversation on their way to education places" without a permit.[38]

Can you believe they pay adults to spend their time harassing students like this? At this school, officials have total discretion to deny students permission to speak on campus if the content of their speech doesn't "support the mission of the school or the mission of a recognized college entity or activity," said Travis Barham, an attorney with Alliance Defending Freedom, the law firm that represented the aggrieved students after they sued the university. Barham said the school's policy is so restrictive that it prohibits spontaneous conversations anywhere on campus.[39] The lawsuit was eventually settled, with the college agreeing to change the policies that led to the students' arrest—after a federal judge indicated he believed the school's policies were unconstitutional.

FIRE defines speech codes as "any university regulation or policy that prohibits expression that would be protected by the First Amendment in society at large. Any policy—such as a harassment policy—can be a speech code if it prohibits protected speech or expression." FIRE points out—chillingly—that "if universities applied these rules to the letter, major voices of public criticism, satire, and commentary would be silenced on American campuses, and some of our greatest authors, artists, and filmmakers would be banned." These codes harm some students through censorship, and they lead other students to believe they can go through life free of being offended, embarrassed, or made to feel uncomfortable. Our universities are desensitizing students to our liberties, and as FIRE notes, "A nation that does not educate in freedom will not survive in freedom, and will not even know when it has lost it."[40]

It is particularly dangerous that universities, which are supposed to be bastions of academic inquiry and free expression, are leading the charge against free speech. In *Speak Freely: Why Universities Must Defend Free Speech*, author Keith Whittington sounds the alarm. "The current crisis of free speech on college campuses," writes Whittington, "is both symptom and cause of a larger threat to the maintenance of liberal democracy itself." Free speech is intrinsically part of what universities are about. "Likewise, free speech is bred into the bones of a modern university, and any institution that sets those principles aside can no longer be meaningfully regarded as a proper institution of higher education."

Unfortunately, Whittington argues, many universities have abandoned their responsibilities and become "mere facades that camouflage a campus culture that has rejected liberal tolerance and free inquiry in favor of dogma and indoctrination." Universities, he notes, are essential to the communication of ideas in our society and so must honor free expression. "Sacrificing speech subverts the very rationale for having a university and hampers the ability of universities to achieve their most basic goals."[41] But to honor their mission, universities must "preserve the college campus as a sanctuary for serious debate of unorthodox ideas and avoid succumbing to the temptation to make" universities "echo chambers of orthodox creeds."[42]

Thankfully, most speech codes that have been challenged in court have been struck down.[43] But as I've told you, leftists never rest. Instead of tucking their tails between their legs, they double down. George Mason law professor Jon Gould observes that "hate speech policies not only persist, but they have actually increased in number following a series of court decisions that ostensibly found many to be unconstitutional."[44] Enterprising progressives simply began to craft their speech codes more narrowly. "Many of the provisions that used to be called speech codes are now being wrapped into anti-harassment policies," according to University of Pennsylvania law professor Robert Richards.[45]

Campus speech codes arose during the 1980s and early 1990s supposedly to address discrimination and harassment, with more than 350 public colleges and universities adopting codes to regulate "hate speech" by 1995. In typical Orwellian fashion, far-left professors argued that these assaults on free speech were needed to protect free expression, particularly of minorities, who they said were made unsafe by exposure to hate speech.

Naturally, it didn't take long for a wide range of conservative advocacy to be classified as hate speech, which it turns out is just another term leftists distort to muzzle conservatives. Simply expressing support for President Trump—as noted earlier—is now grounds for accusations of hate speech and threatening students' safety.

The opposition to free speech has jumped from academic misfits to the Democratic Party. For example, in a *Washington Post* column former Obama official Richard Stengel advocated a federal ban on hate speech, citing dismay among Arab diplomats that Americans are not arrested for burning the Koran. Stengel bemoans that American jurisprudence even protects hateful speech that can lead to violence, calling it a "design flaw" in the First Amendment. Law professor Jonathan Turley responded that this so-called design flaw is free speech itself. Noting that the Democratic Party has "abandoned its historic fealty to free speech," Turley fears the willingness of leftist politicians like AOC to coerce social media companies into regulating speech—"to do what the government cannot do under our Constitution." "It seems Democrats have fallen out of love with free speech and lost all tolerance for opposing views," wrote Turley.[46]

In light of the left's growing intolerance, it was predictable that leftists would begin a campaign to harass and intimidate conservatives in public. Kirstjen Nielsen, Sarah Huckabee Sanders, and Ted Cruz, among many other prominent conservatives, have been verbally abused and run out of restaurants. In years past Democrats would have denounced this thuggery, but after each of these incidents you hardly heard a peep of condemnation out of them.

All this fanaticism reaches its natural endpoint in Antifa. On my show I covered the despicable tactics of Antifa in Portland, where they blocked traffic, assaulted pedestrians, and threatened commuters. According to *USA Today*, Antifa's "primary goal is to stop neo-Nazis and white supremacists from gaining a platform."[47] In plain

English, this means Antifa aims to use violence to stop their political opponents—including conservatives and Trump supporters, all of whom Antifa labels as neo-Nazis—from speaking publicly. Once again, the Orwellian element is undeniable here—in the name of opposing fascism, Antifa acts exactly like fascists do, violently attacking their political opponents in the street in order to deny them any means of expressing their beliefs.

Antifa already has a long, sick record of violent assaults. In fact, the group managed to get one of its own killed in Tacoma, Washington, on July 13, 2019, after one of their supporters set fire to a car outside an ICE detention facility for illegal immigrants. The attacker, Willem Van Spronsen, then opened fire on the building with an AR-15, hurled Molotov cocktails, and attempted to blow up a propane tank. Police shot Van Spronsen when he aimed his rifle at them and ignored their commands.[48]

The most recent (and egregious) example of Antifa's incitement was the plague of riots following the death of George Floyd. The president tweeted that moving forward, Antifa will be recognized as a terrorist organization.

There can be little doubt Antifa will be responsible for more casualties unless authorities take a much stronger approach to their violent acts and adopt a much more proactive policy of defending the free speech rights of the group's targets.

DEMOCRAT DIGITAL DOMINANCE

America's social media giants are mostly owned and run by leftists, and it's common knowledge, except among leftists who deny common knowledge, that they are discriminating against conservatives on their platforms. Actually, I find it amusing that leftists deny they discriminate against conservatives on social media while simultaneously defending their right and even their duty to do it—supposedly to protect users from hate and misinformation. They'll make up some pretext or another for suspending or suppressing conservatives—violation of terms of service, using "manipulated" images, etc.—but everyone understands what's really going on here. When conservatives, like *Daily Caller* reporter Chuck Ross, get suspended from Twitter for tweeting "learn to code" at liberal journalists—meant to point out the heartlessness of leftists who say laid-off workers in disfavored industries should simply learn a new trade—it's obvious social media is cracking down on one political camp and protecting the other.[49]

Twitter CEO Jack Dorsey adamantly denied that Twitter bases its decisions to rank content or enforce its rules on political ideology. "We believe strongly in being impartial, and we strive to enforce our rules impartially," Dorsey told Congress.[50] But the facts show otherwise. Richard Hanania, a postdoctoral research fellow at Columbia University, assembled a database of prominent, politically active Twitter users who were temporarily or permanently suspended. "My results make it difficult to take claims of political neutrality seriously," wrote Hanania. "Of 22 prominent, politically active individuals who are known to have been suspended since 2005 and who expressed a preference in the 2016 U.S. presidential election, 21 supported Donald Trump."[51]

Hanania also notes that conservatives are often punished for certain types of speech that liberals engage in with impunity. He cites Sarah Jeong, an editorial writer for the *New York Times*, who posted many tweets expressing her contempt for white people. Twitter had no problem with those tweets, but it suspended conservative Candace Owens when she copied some of Jeong's tweets and changed "white" to "Jewish" to make a point. And it's not just Twitter, Hanania points out. He noted that if you type "Sarah Jeong" in a Google search box, it will not provide auto-complete suggestions that refer to her controversial tweets, whereas Bing and Yahoo both suggest "Sarah Jeong racist." (As I write this, Bing no longer suggests "Sarah Jeong racist," though it does suggest "Sarah Jeong Jews.") "While one could argue that individuals' worst moments shouldn't follow them around forever, it is difficult to imagine a big tech company suppressing unflattering information about a conservative in a similar manner," said Hanania.[52]

At Facebook, company officers don't go to particularly great lengths to disguise their political preferences. In fact, Chief Operating Officer Sheryl Sandberg publicly endorsed Hillary Clinton in the 2016 presidential election right on her platform. "Tonight, I am hopeful thinking about what it means for my children to watch Hillary Clinton accept the Democratic nomination for president of the United States and for me to be able to tell them #ImWithHer," Sandberg posted on Facebook.[53] Oops—guess that was a little premature. But Sandberg's announcement was especially brazen given that Facebook had just recently been accused of suppressing conservative stories, and several of their executives, including CEO Mark Zuckerberg and Sandberg herself, had met with conservative commentators to try to convince them of Facebook's political neutrality.[54]

At Google, a window opened into the company's culture when a software engineer, James Damore, sent around a memo proposing that biological differences between men and women could explain the gender gap in tech companies, since women are more prone to "empathizing" and men to "systematizing." In response, Google CEO Sundar Pichai sent a memo to employees beginning with his assurance that "we strongly support the right of Googlers to express themselves"— and then he completely undermined that guarantee by whining about how Damore's memo made his snowflake employees feel "under threat" and unsure whether they can "safely" express their views. Soon after that, Damore was fired.[55]

Similarly, in 2014, before "Cancel Culture" was even a thing, Brendan Eich was hounded into resigning as CEO of Mozilla when it became known that years before, he'd contributed to California's Proposition 8, affirming that marriage is between one man and one woman. There was no tolerance, no mercy, and no forgiveness for Eich, just naming, shaming, and unceasing harassment until he could no longer continue in his job.[56]

I've often featured James O'Keefe on my show to highlight his incredible investigative reporting of abominable leftist behavior. His Project Veritas organization interviewed whistle-blowers from Pinterest and Google, revealing that these companies intentionally suppress conservative content in an effort to promote the left's agenda and prevent another "Trump situation" in 2020.[57] Proving O'Keefe's point, YouTube and Vimeo blocked access to the interviews.[58]

FREE SPEECH AS A THREAT

Even Ravelry, a presumably apolitical knitting website, banned pro-Trump messages and users from its site, claiming Trump's message is racist.[59] Notice the telltale nod to inclusiveness as Ravelry drummed out political dissidents from their knitting club: "We cannot provide a space that is inclusive of all and also allow support for open white supremacy."[60] Why would a knitting site take such a polarizing political stance? The answer, as I've told you, is that the left politicizes everything. Leftism is their religion. It is their constitution. It is their be-all and end-all. You'd think they'd enjoy bringing people of various political views together to share their common hobby, but no, *everything* is subservient to left-wing politics.[61]

Brad Parscale, the Trump campaign's digital guru, explains that "Democrats view free speech as a threat to their political ambitions."[62] They "are extremely concerned about the power of social media to circumvent the standard media channels they control. Legacy media outlets such as CNN and *The New York Times* are vital to the Democrats' political power, using their influence to create an 'echo chamber' in support of liberal viewpoints," said Parscale, referring to Ben Rhodes's media manipulations, as I detailed earlier.

The left has employed this strategy often during Trump's term, with their media mob acting in unison to undermine Trump and his agenda, such as their despicable smearing of Supreme Court justice

Brett Kavanaugh. "Today's mainstream media act more like public relations firms on the payroll of the Democratic Party than independent seekers of truth," Parscale explains. But President Trump counters the Fake News attacks through his "revolutionary use of social media." This has terrified Democrats, who aren't used to competing on a level playing field, "so they want social media companies, especially Twitter and Facebook, to carry water for them just like the legacy press has done for so long," says Parscale.

Oftentimes, these social media giants do just that. For example, Twitter used fake-news CNN and the *Washington Post*, of all newspapers, as their fact checkers, which is laughable.

Parscale notes that Democrat presidential candidates urged Twitter to ban Trump permanently, and congressional Democrats are trying to intimidate Facebook into policing "hate speech," meaning conservative speech. Democrats support Twitter's decision to ban political advertising, says Parscale, "because social media executives are in bed with the Democrats and most of their employees are far-left ideological zealots" who use their power "to undermine conservatives and advance a radical liberal agenda" while claiming they are promoting "fairness." [63] The Democrats have no real regard for fairness or free speech protections, which are just platitudes they invoke when it helps promote their agenda or stifle conservative policies.

Several remedies have been proposed to curtail the unfair treatment of conservatives. Section 230 of the Communications Decency Act shields certain internet platforms from liability for posts their users publish. The law's rationale is that these social media platforms are like phone companies—neutral platforms, not content providers, and they allow people to post regardless of their political views. But some Republicans, including Senator Ted Cruz, argue these companies censor conservative content, so their status should be revoked. Senator Josh Hawley introduced the "Ending Support for Internet Censorship Act," which would amend Section 230 to provide that social media companies will lose their immunity from liability unless they submit to an external audit to show that their content removal practices are politically neutral.[64]

President Trump has suggested looking into antitrust action against these companies by the Department of Justice and the Federal Trade Commission. After all, the reason a few Silicon Valley firms have been able to suppress the conservative message is that they have near-monopolies. "No one cares who gets kicked off MySpace," writes Peter Van Buren. "If you end the monopolies, you defang deplatforming."[65]

Liberals have been outraged at the prospect of losing their media monopoly since the birth of the alternative media. And the advent of social media, even with its current biases, is particularly threatening to the media mob, empowering any old Dick or Jane to post along-side the "professionals" and possibly see their contribution go viral. The hate-Trump media mob has reacted by calling for more speech suppression—they want filters, more censoring of "hate speech," and the positioning of media outfits as arbiters to rule on the truthfulness of users' posts.

WEAPONIZING CAMPAIGN FINANCE

It particularly frosts Democrats that Republicans oppose campaign finance reform on free speech grounds and that the Supreme Court's 2009 *Citizens United* decision vindicated that view, holding that the First Amendment protects political speech, which includes corporations spending money on political advocacy. At issue in the case was whether the Federal Election Commission could ban a movie criticizing Hillary Clinton, then running for president in the Democratic primaries, from distribution by a nonprofit company.[66]

The reasoning is that freedom of speech is meaningless in elections if Congress can prevent you from spending money to communicate your message. "If the First Amendment has any force, it prohibits Congress from fining or jailing citizens, or associations of citizens, for simply engaging in political speech," wrote Justice Anthony Kennedy in his majority opinion. "The government may not suppress political speech on the basis of the speaker's corporate identity." The Court made clear that "it is our law and our tradition that more speech, not less, is the governing rule."[67]

What part of "Congress shall make no law" do people not understand? The Democrats tried and failed to secure a constitutional amendment to overturn *Citizens United* and narrow the First Amendment by empowering Congress to limit fund-raising and spending on election campaigns and independent political speech.[68] Gaining the support of fifty-four Democrat senators,[69] the proposed amendment, instead of "leveling the playing field," as Democrats falsely claimed, would hurt candidates trying to unseat incumbent congressmen and limit ordinary Americans' expression of their views about candidates. By an amazing coincidence, it would also benefit Democrats, who have a built-in advantage with the liberal media. So under the amendment, the media mob could continue dedicating their huge resources to promoting Democrats, while spending would be constricted for conservatives trying to counter those messages.[70]

But the left never gives up. Our friend Adam Schiff has proposed another constitutional amendment to overturn *Citizens United*.[71] And the Democrats have launched a separate attack through H.R. 1, a bill deceptively called the "For the People Act" but more accurately described by Senator Mitch McConnell as the "Democrat Politician Protection Act."[72] The bill would encroach on free speech rights by empowering Congress to "regulate the raising and spending of political money." Ted Cruz noted that the legislation would give "Congress power to regulate—and ban—speech by everybody."[73] Even the left-wing American Civil Liberties Union warned the bill would "unconstitutionally infringe the freedoms of speech and association" and "silenc[e] necessary voices that would otherwise speak out about the public issues of the day."[74] Yes, exactly—that's the point of the bill, and that's the aim of the Democratic Party.

THE LEFT'S ASSAULT ON RELIGIOUS LIBERTY

Let's now turn our attention to the left's assault on religious liberty. Many leftists are outwardly anti-Christian. The left denies they're anti-religious, and I don't challenge the sincerity of progressives who are professing Christians. But there is no disputing that liberalism by and large today is hostile to Christian values and religious liberties. They oppose homeschooling and can't seem to tolerate Christian-based symbols like Christmas trees or even candy canes on public property. They revile Vice President Mike Pence and his wife, Karen, for their Christian faith.

The Democrats showed their true colors when they booed God at their 2012 convention. That was no one-off incident—it's part of a deliberate effort to diminish Christianity and champion atheism. In August 2019, the Democratic National Committee unanimously passed a resolution celebrating the religiously unaffiliated, noting—nonsensically—that they're the "largest religious group" among Democrats. The resolution also affirmed that they "overwhelmingly share the Democratic Party's values" and "have often been subjected to unfair bias and exclusion in American society." The Secular Coalition of America, a lobbying group for atheists, agnostics, and humanists on public policy, praised the resolution as the first time a major party "embraced American nonbelievers."[75] Sarah Levin, director of affairs from the Secular Coalition of America, said the resolution would help "to ensure that policy is driven by science and evidence, not sectarian beliefs," implying that one must choose between one's religious beliefs on the one hand, and science and evidence on the other.[76] Annie Laurie Gaylor, copresident of the Freedom from Religion Foundation, touted the resolution as a "political landmark" that is "long overdue."[77]

The resolution maligns believers and denounces their alleged abuse of religious liberty to infringe on certain groups' civil rights. "Those most loudly claiming that morals, values, and patriotism must be defined by their particular religious views have used those religious views, with misplaced claims of 'religious liberty,' to justify public policy that has threatened the civil rights and liberties of many Americans, including but not limited to the LGBT community, women, and ethnic and religious/nonreligious minorities," the resolution reads.[78]

What conservatives have long understood is that the left is not just trying to convince people of their arguments but to suppress opposing views. We saw that in the Masterpiece Cakeshop case, in which a gay couple sued the owner, Jack Phillips, not because he refused to serve gays in general but because he refused, based on his religious beliefs, to make a cake celebrating a same-sex wedding. We saw the same impetus in Beto O'Rourke's demands to strip Christian educational institutions, churches, and other charities of their tax-exempt status unless they recognize same-sex marriage.

The Obama administration targeted Christian adoption agencies for trying to place orphans with Christian parents and sought to compel Catholic nuns to comply with an Obamacare mandate to provide access to contraceptives and abortifacients as part of their health-care package.[79] Obamacare enforcers also came after Hobby Lobby, which refused to comply with the mandate because of its founders' religious convictions. NARAL, a pro-abortion group that supports Democratic candidates, opposes conscience laws that permit medical doctors and other providers to opt out of activities, such as abortion or euthanasia, that violate their religious convictions.[80]

The Democrats are also trying to advance this agenda through the Equality Act, which was introduced in the House in March 2019 and would add sexual orientation and gender identity to the 1964 Civil Rights Act. "This would essentially remove any legal protections that small business owners, nonprofits, churches, schools, and private individuals currently enjoy to live and operate according to traditional and deeply held religious beliefs about sex, the human family, and human dignity," writes Rev. Joseph D'Souza, founder of Dignity Freedom Network.[81] "This is not a good-faith attempt to reconcile competing interests," said University of Virginia law professor Douglas Laycock. "It is an attempt by one side to grab all the disputed territory and to crush the other side."[82]

Fortunately President Trump strongly defends America's religious liberty. "On every front, the ultra-left is waging war on the values shared by everyone in this room," he said at the 2019 Values Voter Summit. "They are trying to silence and punish the speech of Christians and religious believers of all faiths. . . . They are trying to use the courts to rewrite the laws, undermine democracy, and force through an agenda they can't pass at the ballot box. They are trying to hound you from the workplace, expel you from the public square and weaken the American family and indoctrinate our children. They resent and disdain faithful Americans who hold fast to our nation's historic values. And, if given the chance, they would use every instrument of government power, including the IRS, to try to shut you down. . . . We know that families and churches, not government officials, know best how to create strong and loving communities. . . . And above all else, we know this: in America, we don't worship government, we worship God."[83]

Trump haters accuse the president of cynically promoting religious liberty to pander to Christian voters, but has any president since Ronald Reagan been such an outspoken proponent of Christian liberties? Would a fair-weather supporter of Christianity have taken this message to the United Nations as President Trump did, declaring that religious liberty is not just an American constitutional right but a God-given right that should be respected by all nations?

Just a month after Trump's remarks at the UN, Attorney General William Barr delivered an impassioned speech in support of religious liberty at the University of Notre Dame.[84] Barr argued that we are witnessing much more than merely a pendulum swing against religious liberty in America. "First is the force, fervor and comprehensiveness of the assault on religion we are experiencing today. This is not decay, it is organized destruction. Secularists, and their allies among the 'progressives', have marshaled all the force of mass communications, popular culture, the entertainment industry, and academia in an unremitting assault on religion and traditional values," said Barr. "These instruments are used not only to affirmatively promote secular orthodoxy, but also drown out and silence opposing voices, and to attack viciously and hold up to ridicule any dissenters." Barr also noted the irony that the "secular project has itself become a religion, pursued with religious fervor. It is taking on all the trappings of a religion, including inquisitions and excommunication."[85]

In light of the left's antagonism to Christianity, it's unsurprising that leftist academics are increasingly questioning the need for religious liberty itself. University of Chicago Law School professor Brian Leiter's *Why Tolerate Religion?* asks why religion is singled out for preferential treatment in both law and public discourse.[86] Micah Schwartzman, University of Virginia School of Law professor, argues in his piece "What If Religion Is Not So Special" that "[l]eading accounts of the First Amendment's Religion Clauses fail to provide a coherent and morally attractive position on whether religion warrants special treatment as compared with secular ethical and moral doctrines."[87]

As we've seen with the Democrats' full embrace of identity politics, what begins as bizarre left-wing theorizing on college campuses often makes its way into the Democratic Party. Rejecting the very concept of religious liberty may be a fringe position now, but time will tell how long that remains the case.

CHAPTER NINE

Trump Triumphs

As I've shown, the left consistently displays undisguised contempt for everyday Trump supporters. We've seen this going back to President Obama and his insulting comments about working-class midwesterners: "They get bitter, they cling to guns or religion or antipathy to people who aren't like them or anti-immigrant sentiment or anti-trade sentiment as a way to explain their frustrations."[1]

That was a bad mistake by Obama—the *Guardian* called it "an uncharacteristic moment of loose language."[2] Back then, politicians weren't supposed to insult huge parts of the American population. But that's all changed when it comes to Trump supporters. When they're not comparing us to Nazis, well, we're the smelly Walmart people that FBI agent Peter Strzok called us, or the irredeemable deplorables that Hillary Clinton called us.

The left is determined to destroy Donald Trump and his administration. They hate him, and deep down, they hate us—the people who voted for him. For example, look at this gem from long-serving Democratic congressman Hank Johnson. "Americans elected an authoritarian, anti-immigrant, racist strongman to the nation's highest office. Donald Trump and his Make America Great Again followers—who want to return America back to a time when white men and white privilege were unchallenged, and where minorities and women were in their place—these folks now control the highest office in the land," said Johnson, who went on to compare Trump to Hitler.[3]

The left hates us because we empowered Trump, and they hate Trump because he disempowered *them*. That's why they deny or conceal his amazing record of presidential accomplishments—nothing good can come from the man who interrupted what was supposed to be another eight years of Democratic rule. Even if Trump singlehandedly cured heart disease and gave every American millions of dollars today, they would still hate him just as much—because he represents the greatest obstacle to them regaining power.

The media have systematically downplayed President Trump's stunning record of success, but I do what I can to highlight the good news—and there's a lot of it. I've chronicled it on my shows, and I want to do a deep dive into these triumphs in this chapter as a testament to how great Americans and America can be when we have a president who implements policies that liberate them from the stranglehold of government and encourage them to create and produce in the free market. This book is not just an urgent warning about the dangers of the Democrats regaining power, but a reminder of how terrific things can be—and have been—under President Trump.

Granted, things have changed dramatically since the coronavirus pandemic hit our shores, but can you imagine how much worse our economy would be now if it hadn't been so strong when the virus broke out? Further, it is horrifying to contemplate how much worse the virus's impact would have been had a Democrat president been in office at the time, paralyzed by political correctness from issuing travel bans, unwilling to reject bureaucratic obstacles as Trump has done, and incapable of coordinating the public and private sectors to manage this crisis.

Some Americans had forgotten just how unique this nation is. Some had given up on our entrepreneurial spirit and the unlimited potential of our economy. Well, under Trump their memories were jogged, as all witnessed the dramatic change just three years could make. Our spirit of patriotism was reborn with this superpatriotic president—a patriotism that has served us well in battling the pandemic and should continue to do so through our economic recovery.

Under Trump's economic policies, the lives of millions of forgotten men and women were strikingly improved. We saw record-setting tax cuts, lucrative trade deals, energy independence that we never dreamed of, regulatory reforms, a boom in manufacturing, prison reform, national security successes, and the confirmation of scores of conservative judges, including two Supreme Court justices. We had the best employment numbers in fifty years and an economy that was booming and breaking records like never before, with millions of people being moved off food stamps and out of poverty.

Some of you, my conservative friends, doubted me when I told you Donald Trump was a conservative. Well, do you believe me now? We haven't seen someone govern this conservatively since Ronald Reagan. I told you he would deliver on his campaign promises, and his accomplishments now speak for themselves. If people become familiar with his record, he will win reelection handily. So let's now look at the state of the union under President Trump as it stood prior to the pandemic. Let's look at the economy and jobs, deregulation, energy, national security and defense, foreign policy, the courts, life and religious liberty, immigration, health care, and more, with apologies in advance for the impossibility of covering everything this president has accomplished. Most important, let's see why President Trump's amazing economic record before the coronavirus makes him the single most qualified person to lead our post-virus recovery.

TRUMP'S BOOM ECONOMY

While the coronavirus had a devastating economic impact on America, that does not change the *fact* that Trump's economic policies before the virus were enormously successful. They led to one of the greatest booms in American history, and resuming them is essential to leading us out of the virus-induced recession and to future growth. It should go without saying, but as Democrats are famous for exploiting crises, it needs to be said, that the economic meltdown beginning in the first quarter of 2020 was not due to Trump's economic policies prior to the virus, but to the restrictions on movement and commerce enacted at the local, state, and federal levels in an effort to reduce the virus's spread.

Prior to the onset of the pandemic here, were Americans better off than they were four years ago? Well, let's remember where we were at the end of the eight-year-long Obama presidency. Back then, we had a perpetually sluggish economy, companies shutting down and moving overseas, the war on coal and other sources of domestic energy, wasteful and failed experiments in alternative energy, environmental radicalism, the Obamacare nightmare, the lowest home ownership rate in fifty-one years, the worst recovery since the 1940s, 13 million more Americans on food stamps, 8 million more Americans in poverty, and of course he accumulated more debt than every other president before him combined.

Remember the orchestrated malaise from Obama and his team of doomsayers, including his Treasury secretary Jack Lew, who said slow growth was our permanent destiny, and Obama himself, who said Trump would need a magic wand to improve manufacturing? Remember the downsizing of the military, the Benghazi debacle, and a lead-from-behind foreign policy catering to Iran and condescending to Israel? How about Obama's war on religious liberty, his expansion of the welfare state, his leftist judges, his explosion of rules and regulations, his lawless executive orders, his use of the IRS to harass conservative organizations, and his lax border policies?

When a Republican president replaces a Democrat, there is usually just a temporary pendulum swing back to the right. Rarely do we experience the kind of dramatic turnaround we've seen in President

Trump's first term. Let's start by looking at some of the Trump-era economic indicators.

The Tax Cuts and Jobs Act, signed into law by President Trump in December 2017, was the biggest tax reform bill in thirty years,[4] providing tax relief for 80 percent of middle-class families and fiercely igniting the economy. It doubled the Child Tax Credit, almost doubled the standard deduction, simplified the tax filing process for millions, and cut taxes by 20 percent on small businesses. It lowered individual rates, included a long-overdue reduction in the corporate tax rate from 35 percent to 21 percent, and reduced state and local deductions. It repealed the Obamacare individual mandate and expanded college savings accounts.[5]

The pre-coronavirus economy soared under President Trump. Obama's economy rarely saw substantial growth, but annual growth now regularly nears or exceeds 3 percent.[6] The Bureau of Labor Statistics (BLS) reported that in 2018 the economy reached 3 percent growth (3.1 percent) for a one-year time period—from the fourth quarter of 2017 to the fourth quarter of 2018—for the first time in thirteen years. By contrast, Obama was the first president in history who never reached a year of 3 percent growth.[7]

In February 2020, Obama tweeted, "Eleven years ago today, near the bottom of the worst recession in generations, I signed the Recovery Act, paving the way for more than a decade of economic growth and the longest streak of job creation in American history." Hours after Obama posted his tweet, President Trump's team issued a statement to Fox News refuting Obama's absurd claim. "President Trump reversed every single failed Obama-era economic policy, and with it, reversed the floundering Obama/Biden economy," read the statement.[8]

Trump's boom was not part of a continuing arc of growth as Obama claims. If the pre-2017 growth trend had continued, growth would have been about 2 percent in 2017 and 2018. In fact, economic output was $280 billion more than it would have been under the earlier trends.[9] It's a bit rich for Obama to hijack credit for Trump's record, since Larry Summers, Obama's National Economic Council director, ridiculed the idea that Trump's policies could generate 3 percent growth. "Apparently, the budget forecasts that U.S. economic growth will rise to 3.0 percent because of the administration's policies—largely its tax cuts and perhaps also its regulatory policies," wrote Summers in May 2017. "Fair enough if you believe in tooth fairies and ludicrous supply-side economics."[10] Do you remember Summers retracting his "ludicrous" statement and apologizing? Me, neither!

As of July 2018, 155,965,000 Americans were employed, the most in our history.[11] In April 2019, the unemployment rate dropped to 3.6 percent, the lowest since December 1969, according to BLS.[12] As of December 2018, for the first time on record, there were more job openings than unemployed Americans, showing the economy's remarkable strength. Usually, the number of unemployed far exceeds job openings, but job openings had increased to a record-high 7.3 million, and unemployment was at an extraordinary low of 4 percent.[13] A BLS household survey showed unemployment at 3.7 percent in August 2019, representing the eighteenth consecutive month the unemployment rate was below or equal to 4 percent.[14] January 2020 marked the twenty-third consecutive month—the longest such streak in fifty years.[15]

Factors contributing to Trump's boom included the tax cuts, deregulation, and trade reform, but let's not overlook the wave of optimism Trump brought into the Oval Office. A Gallup poll of early 2019 showed that 50 percent of Americans believed they were better off than a year before when the boom was kicking in, and 69 percent expected their personal finances to improve over the next year—the most economic optimism Americans (of both parties) had expressed in sixteen years. "Though Republicans' expectations rose after Trump took office and Democrats became less optimistic, majorities from both parties said they expected to be better off in the coming year in both the pre-Trump election polls and the post-Trump-inauguration ones," said Gallup.[16] A quarterly survey by the National Association of

Manufacturers (NAM) in the last half of 2018 showed renewed optimism among America's manufacturers, with 93 percent of them projecting expansions for their businesses. "We used to be happy when that number would get up to the mid- and high-50s," said NAM's chief executive officer, Jay Timmons.[17]

In its pre-2016 election forecast, the Congressional Budget Office (CBO) projected 14,000 new jobs per month by September 2019, but the growth was almost ten times higher for that quarter. The economy had added 6.3 million jobs since the president was elected, dwarfing by 4.5 million the CBO's predictions.[18] As of January 2020, 7 million jobs had been added in the thirty-eight months since Trump's election.[19] For perspective, there were only 2.45 million jobs added between 2007, the peak employment year under President George W. Bush, and the end of Obama's second term in 2017.[20] And there was some additional tremendous news: the unemployment rate for historically disadvantaged groups—African Americans, Hispanic Americans, and Asian Americans—hit all-time lows. Unemployment levels for those with no high school degree and those with disabilities also reached record lows.[21] The African American unemployment rate was 5.5 percent, the African American adult female unemployment rate was 4.4 percent, the African American teen unemployment reached historic lows, and Hispanic unemployment was 4.2 percent.[22] In the summer of 2018, the unemployment rate for women reached its lowest level in sixty-five years.[23]

Once thought dead and gone, manufacturing bounced back in the Trump economy. (Obama said, "those jobs ain't coming back." Well, they came back.) As of March 2019, 480,000 manufacturing jobs had been added since Trump's election.[24] "In terms of the percentage of manufacturing job increases, the gains made thus far under the Trump administration surpass the performance in the first term of every president since the 1970s," wrote Justin Haskins.[25] Trump's manufacturing jobs record should be compared to President Clinton's last three years in office, when more than 430,000 manufacturing jobs were lost. That trend continued under President George W. Bush, when millions more manufacturing jobs were lost even before the 2008 crash, and during Obama's eight years, with some 300,000 manufacturing jobs lost.[26]

The *Wall Street Journal* reported at the end of 2019 that wages were rising for rank-and-file workers, that is, nonsupervisory employees, who make up 82 percent of the workforce, at the quickest pace in more than a decade—even at a faster rate than for their bosses.[27]

These stunning numbers disprove Democrats' claims that only the rich benefited from this economic growth. Failed presidential candidate Elizabeth Warren even claimed that "America's middle class is under attack." But the Heritage Foundation's Stephen Moore put it in perspective. "Real median household income—the amount earned by those in the very middle—hit $65,084 (in 2019 dollars) for the 12 months ending in July," wrote Moore. "That's the highest level ever and a gain of $4,144, or 6.8%, since Mr. Trump took office. By comparison, during 7½ years under President Obama—starting from the end of the recession in June 2009 through January 2017—the median household income rose by only about $1,000. . . . the median income continued its decline almost all of his first term and rose only slowly in his second term—the weakest recovery from a recession since the 1930s." Under Trump, said Moore, "the middle class not only isn't shrinking, it's getting richer."[28]

Trump labor secretary Eugene Scalia noted that workers' wages were growing faster than their bosses', which was reducing income inequality. "At the end of the Obama administration" what we saw is wage growth for the high wage earners [and] slow wage growth for the low wage earners," said Scalia. "We've flipped that in this economy." This change was partly a result of decreasing unemployment and a reduction of regulations, Scalia argued.[29] Likewise, the White House reported that wealth inequality declined following the passage of Trump's tax cut—the net worth of the bottom 50 percent of households increased, while the share of the top 1 percent decreased.[30]

As of August 2019, median family income had risen almost $5,000 since Trump took office—from about $61,000 in January 2017 to $65,976 in August 2019.[31] Yet CBS declared, "Two years after Trump tax cuts, middle class Americans are falling behind." Moore described this as possibly "the most dishonest news story headline of recent times," as median income had risen substantially. "So how in the world did CBS mangle the universally good news to come up with an opposite conclusion?" asked Moore. They did it with "a classic head fake," by comparing the gains of the middle class only to those of the wealthiest 1 percent. "Even though the middle class had a bigger income boost under Trump than anytime in 20 years, the middle class is now allegedly suffering a decline since the rich saw even faster gains. This appears to be an intentional distortion of economic reality."[32] Moore noted that CBS used similar trickery to downplay middle-class income growth by comparing it to income for the poor, which grew strongly.[33]

President Trump achieved a number of other economic successes. Some $1 trillion returned to America from overseas after he passed his tax cut bill. He instituted Opportunity Zones to stimulate growth in poorer communities. His administration designated artificial intelligence, quantum information science, and 5G as emerging technologies and as national research and development priorities.[34] He reported in his 2019 State of the Union address that "as a result of my administration's efforts, in 2018 drug prices experienced their single largest decline in 46 years."[35] He worked to expand apprenticeship programs, with more than 660,000 apprentices getting hired. He established the National Council for the American Worker to develop a workforce strategy for future jobs. More than 370 companies signed Trump's "Pledge to America's Workers," in which they vowed to provide more than 14.4 million employment and training opportunities. And he signed an executive order on Cyber Workforce Development aimed at giving America the most skilled cyber workforce in the twenty-first century.

DEREGULATION

Deregulation is another area where the Republican Party, prior to Trump, was more talk than action. Convinced that regulations were burdening the economy and restricting our liberty, President Trump acted. The Competitive Enterprise Institute estimates that federal regulations cost $1.9 trillion annually, which amounts to a hidden tax of almost $15,000 per household.[36] Trump promised to cut two regulations for every new one imposed and has far exceeded that pledge. As of January 2020, President Trump had signed sixteen bills to deregulate various aspects of the economy, slashing 8.5 regulations for every new one passed[37] and saving nearly $50 billion.[38] The Council of Economic Advisers reported that twenty major regulatory actions the administration implemented would save American consumers and businesses some $220 billion per year, raise real incomes by $3,100 per household annually, and increase U.S. gross domestic product (GDP) by 1.0 to 2.2 percent over the next decade.[39]

The administration formed the Governors' Initiative on Regulatory Innovation to expand Trump's model for regulatory reform to local and state governments. The initiative seeks to reduce outmoded local and state regulations, cut costs, advance occupational licensing reform, and align federal and state regulations.[40] Trump also signed an executive order to reduce obstacles small company employees face in participating in retirement plans.[41]

In October 2019, Trump signed two executive orders to increase transparency in the federal regulatory process. One bars federal agencies from skipping a cost-benefit analysis and avoiding public comment. The other protects people from unexpected penalties arising from interpretations of obscure regulations, by ensuring they are given advance notice of the agency's jurisdiction and the applicable legal standards. This is designed to shelter people from major fines for conducting innocuous activities on their own property, such as building a pond. "Today, we take bold, new action to protect Americans from out-of-control bureaucracy and stop regulations from imposing secret rules and hidden penalties on the American people," said President Trump at the signing ceremony for the orders.[42]

The administration also rolled back the "Waters of the U.S." rule, an Obama-era order that empowered the federal government to regulate even swamps and wetlands on private property, subjecting farmers to heavy fines and uncertainty. The rule change would prevent landowners from spending thousands of dollars on permit costs. Other federal and state regulations would still apply, but repeal of this rule, says EPA administrator Andrew Wheeler, "would mean that farmers, property owners and businesses will spend less time and money determining whether they need a federal permit."[43]

Importantly, President Trump rejected environmentalist fearmongering and terminated President Obama's reckless war on the coal industry. The administration's greenhouse gas emissions plan aims to boost production from coal-fired power plants. The plan allows states to develop their own initiatives to increase the efficiency of their power plants.[44] Trump also signed a bill repealing the Obama administration's Office of Surface Mining's Stream Protection Rule, which effectively banned mining in portions of Appalachia,[45] saying the elimination of this "terrible job killing rule" would save "many thousands of American jobs, especially in the mines."[46]

Leftist environmental extremists always force us to falsely choose between the environment and the economy, demonizing conservatives as enemies of the planet. In fact, conservatives believe in good stewardship but reject the radical solutions offered by leftists, which don't work, savage our domestic energy sources, and financially burden consumers. As such, Trump's Environmental Protection Agency (EPA) replaced the Obama administration's overreaching "Clean Power Plan" with an "Affordable Clean Energy" (ACE) rule, which allows states to reduce emissions while still providing affordable energy for consumers.[47]

In August 2018, the administration also recommended freezing the extreme miles-per-gallon standard for cars and light trucks at their 2020 level, instead of implementing Obama's unrealistically stringent standards. Wheeler stated that the EPA seeks to strike "the right regulatory balance" between cost, safety, and environmental concerns. The change will prevent vehicle prices from increasing by an average of $2,340.[48] The administration also seeks to replace Obama-era fuel economy regulations with the SAFE Vehicles Rule to make cars cheaper and "substantially safer."[49] In compromise, the Trump administration agreed to increase fuel economy standards by 1.5 percent per year from 2021 through 2026 instead of freezing them at 2020 levels.[50] Of course, that wasn't enough to please environmentalists, who won't be satisfied until we return to the horse and buggy—and even then, they'd probably object to exploiting horses.

Trump also signed a bill rolling back bank rules of the Dodd-Frank Act of 2010, which was passed in the wake of the 2008 financial crisis. Trump's bill lifted onerous rules on small and medium-sized lenders and was designed to spur economic growth. Trump was adamant that Dodd-Frank was crippling community banks and credit unions. Despite progressive angst over the bill, seventeen Senate Democrats voted for it.

On June 25, 2019, Trump established the White House Council on Eliminating Regulatory Barriers to Affordable Housing, saying that "federal, state, local and tribal governments impose a multitude of regulatory barriers—laws, regulations, and administrative practices— that hinder the development of housing," impede America's economic growth, and harm low- and middle-income Americans.[51]

ENERGY

President Trump dramatically reversed Obama-era energy policies— with amazing effect. In April 2017, he issued an executive order to expand offshore oil and gas drilling in the Arctic and Atlantic Oceans and open more leases to develop offshore drilling. This was just four months after Obama withdrew these areas from development. At the signing ceremony Trump touted America's abundant offshore oil and gas reserves, lamenting that the federal government had kept 94 percent of these areas closed from exploration and production. "We're opening it up," said Trump.[52] In March 2019 an Alaska district judge blocked Trump's order, declaring that presidents have the power under federal law to remove lands from development but cannot revoke those removals.[53] In May, the Trump administration appealed the ruling.[54] Separately, the Department of the Interior and Bureau of Ocean Energy Management announced they would offer 78 million acres in the Gulf of Mexico for oil and gas leasing in March 2019.[55]

President Trump signed a bill to open the Alaskan Arctic National Wildlife Refuge to domestic energy production, with the Bureau of Land Management offering leases on 1.6 million acres.[56] Trump also signed executive orders to permit the building of the Dakota Access and Keystone XL oil pipelines, which had been blocked by the Obama administration. Keystone would be almost 1,200 miles long and pass through six states, shipping more than 800,000 barrels of petroleum daily from Canadian oil sands through Nebraska and on to the Gulf coast. The Dakota pipeline would transport crude oil from North Dakota through South Dakota and Iowa and on to Illinois.[57] The projects would create 42,000 temporary jobs and generate a projected $2 billion in earnings.[58] In April 2020, however, a Montana federal judge ordered the Army Corps of Engineers to suspend all filling and dredging activities on the pipeline pending proof that it complies with the Endangered Species Act.[59]

In June 2017 Trump approved construction of a new petroleum pipeline between the United States and Mexico to boost American exports.[60] The Trump EPA also rescinded Obama's methane emissions rule that would cost energy companies a projected $530 million annually.[61]

As a result of Trump's systematic reversal of Obama's energy agenda, the United States, as noted, has become a net exporter of natural gas for the first time since 1957 and for the first time since 1973 is the world's largest producer of oil and natural gas, having surpassed Saudi Arabia and Russia.[62] More good news on this front came in April 2020 when it was reported that Pantheon Resources PLC, an oil exploration firm, discovered a deposit of some 1.8 billion barrels in Alaska's North Slope region, south of Prudhoe Bay.[63]

TRADE

Initially many people mistakenly assumed President Trump was a protectionist, but as I've said from the beginning, his goal is not to isolate America from the rest of the world or restrict our international trade but to secure better trade deals that stop other nations from taking advantage of us. Fulfilling his campaign promise, Trump imposed a 25 percent tariff on steel imports and a 10 percent tariff on aluminum imports from the European Union, Canada, and Mexico, believing these industries had suffered from unfair trade practices that reduced our production of those products and imperiled our national security.[64]

From the beginning of his term, Trump sought better trade deals with our trading partners. Early on, by executive order, he withdrew the United Sates from the Trans-Pacific Partnership (TPP), billed as a free trade agreement between the United States and eleven other countries. Critics of the agreement believed it was a regulatory nightmare that did more to advance non-trade special interests than to promote free trade.[65] "Great thing for the American worker what we just did," said Trump as he signed the order ending our participation in the deal that was a central part of President Obama's Asia policy.

In July 2018, Trump reached an agreement with the European Union to work toward zero tariffs, zero non-tariff barriers, and zero subsidies on non-auto industrial goods. The EU agreed to purchase billions of dollars in American exports such as soybean and natural gas, and to cooperate on reforming international trade rules. "The European Union is going to start almost immediately to buy a lot of soybeans—a tremendous market . . . from our farmers in the Midwest primarily," said Trump.[66] In September 2019 Trump announced he had struck a deal in which Japan would cut tariffs on $7 billion worth of American agricultural products and the United States would lower tariffs on many Japanese industrial goods. The deal would also increase digital trade between Japan and the United States, but did not resolve existing or additional U.S. tariffs on Japanese autos.[67]

Trump honored his promise to roll back the Obama administration's favorable trade and travel policies with Cuba that bolstered the regime while harming the Cuban people. Trump reimposed certain travel and trade restrictions but did not sever diplomatic or commercial ties or close the U.S. embassy in Havana. He continued to allow commercial flights from the United States and to permit Americans to bring Cuban goods into the United States.[68] In October 2019, he imposed new sanctions on Cuba because of its human rights violations and for supporting Venezuelan president Nicolás Maduro.[69]

President Trump kept his promise to renegotiate the North American Free Trade Agreement (NAFTA), which he believed damaged midwestern industries by undermining the bargaining power of American workers and stalling the expansion of the middle class.[70] Trump also completed the United States–Mexico–Canada Trade Agreement (USMCA) in early 2020. USMCA revises Mexico's labor laws, encourages greater North American car production, and pries open Canadian markets for American dairy farmers.[71] Despite widespread resistance from Democrats to reopening NAFTA negotiations in the first place, eventually they overwhelmingly joined Republicans in approving the revised deal in both the House and the Senate.

President Trump has taken strong and unprecedented moves against predatory behavior by communist China. An investigation he initiated found that China was engaged in numerous unfair trade practices against the United States, including stealing technology and intellectual property from the computer networks of U.S. companies, using licensing procedures to pressure technology transfers to Beijing, and imposing substantial restrictions on the investments and activities of American companies. In March 2018 Trump announced that in response, he would impose tariffs on various Chinese products, pursue action against China in the World Trade Organization, and restrict China's U.S. investments.[72] He has also limited the ability of Huawei, a government-backed Chinese telecom equipment manufacturer, to operate in the United States.[73]

In the summer of 2019, the administration placed 25 percent tariffs on some $250 billion worth of products that benefit from China's unfair industrial policies.[74] He later announced he would impose 10 percent tariffs on another $300 billion worth of goods, effective September 1, 2019.[75] When China threatened to retaliate with increased tariffs on American products, Trump threated to raise tariffs to 30 percent on the initial $250 billion worth of goods and 15 percent on the additional $300 billion worth of goods, effective October 1, 2019.[76]

Although the Democrats denounced Trump for sparking a "trade war" with China, his hardball tactics have paid off. After further negotiations, Trump and China reached a phase-one deal, whereby the United States would leave the 25 percent tariffs in place and impose 7½ percent tariffs on $120 billion of the remaining $300 billion worth of goods.[77] In exchange China agreed to make substantial purchases of American goods and to adopt structural reforms in intellectual property, technology transfer, agriculture, financial services, and currency and foreign exchange.[78] In December 2019 President Trump said that at Beijing's request, "phase two" talks with China would begin soon. In this phase Trump aims to eliminate even more of China's malign trading activities.[79]

REBUILDING OUR DEFENSES

To fully appreciate President Trump's revitalization of our military, you have to understand that President Obama deliberately engineered a decline in our military, which I pointed out as it was happening. Obama expanded our military commitments for both military and nonmilitary purposes while gutting its funding. President Trump has taken the opposite approach—to disentangle our forces from unnecessary wars and assignments while building up our defense capabilities to deter future wars and increase our readiness should they occur.

Soldiers themselves testified to Obama's fecklessness toward the military. A *Military Times*/Institute for Veterans and Military Families poll showed that more than half the troops had an unfavorable opinion of Obama and his military leadership, while just 36 percent approved.[80] Service members seemed to doubt his military priorities—maybe, for example, because of incidents such as Obama using a commencement speech to West Point cadets to tout his global warming agenda, which he called a "creeping national security crisis."[81] "There's no question that this era will go down as the third 'hollow' army, and it's the president's fault," said the Heritage Foundation's James Carafano, speaking of Obama. "For all his promises, the operations tempo hasn't gone down as much as he hoped, and he has invested little in the military."[82] The Obama administration's failure to reinvest in our military was the "biggest factor" in our allies' underinvestment in defense, says Carafano. Writing in 2017, he noted that "the defense budget has been cut by 25 percent over the last five years."[83]

Obama's disarmament is shown by "defense-spending arithmetic," says Thomas Donnelly of the American Enterprise Institute. The Pentagon lost $250 billion in purchasing power from Obama's changes to the five-year defense plan he inherited from the prior Bush administration. In 2009, right off the bat, Obama ordered defense secretary Robert Gates to cut $300 billion from Pentagon programs, which effectively eliminated several major weapons acquisitions projects, says Donnelly. A particularly damaging cut was the F-22 fighter, which was designed to employ stealth technology to ensure America's air superiority. Obama and Gates terminated the program at 187 planes—just one-fourth of the 750 the Air Force planned.[84] The Navy and Air Force have also retired ships and planes without replacing them. The Defense Department planned to build 300 F-35 fighters per year to replace the lightweight fighters in the Air Force, Navy, and Marines—but they built less than 10 percent of the planned number. Obama also significantly cut our troop numbers from 560,000 to around 450,000.[85]

The progressive media and other assorted leftists deny that Obama gutted our defenses. You'd actually think they'd be proud of it, since they constantly advocate downsizing military spending in favor of social programs. But even an NPR fact-check article in 2016 conceded that military "spending is down; the force is smaller than when Obama took office and its equipment is aging."[86]

Mark Moyar, author of *Strategic Failure: How President Obama's Drone Warfare, Defense Cuts, and Military Amateurism Have Imperiled America*, argues that President Obama's goal from the start was to shrink the military.[87] Republicans recaptured the House in 2010 promising fiscal conservativism. With free-spending Democrats controlling the White House and the Senate, an impasse was inevitable. To entice Congress to raise the debt limit, Democrats agreed to Republican demands for spending cuts, which led to the Budget Control Act of 2011. This imposed compulsory spending caps—called sequestration—to be triggered if the parties couldn't reach an agreement on a spending plan to reduce the deficit. Somehow President Obama managed to secure a deal that allocated half the sequestration cuts to defense when defense constituted only 20 percent of spending.[88]

National-security-oriented Republicans like John McCain naively believed Democrats would agree to a compromise, forestalling major defense cuts.[89] That didn't happen due to Obama's insistence on huge tax hikes, so sequestration kicked in and military spending was slashed. "Though President Obama denounced sequestration, his actions suggest that at the very least he was comfortable with its gutting of the defense budget," writes Moyar. "During the 2011 negotiations the White House had already begun to work on a new national-security strategy to accommodate drastic defense cuts."[90]

The Republicans' weakness and defeat in this battle is the type of thing that led to conservative grassroots discontent, and ultimately their embracing Donald Trump. Thankfully, President Trump is far more supportive of the military than Obama was. Within about a year of taking office, Trump and the Republican-controlled Congress increased defense spending projections by more than $200 billion for fiscal years 2017 through 2019.[91] In 2018, the Trump administration signed a $700 billion National Defense Authorization Act, the largest defense bill in our history, which added 20,000 more troops and included a 2.4 percent pay raise for the military, the biggest increase since 2010. "History teaches us that when you weaken your defenses, you invite aggression," said Trump on signing the bill. "The best way to prevent conflict of any kind is to be prepared. Only when the good are strong will peace prevail."[92]

Under President Trump, this upward trend in defense spending continued—by design. His National Defense Authorization Act of 2020 included a record-high $738 billion for defense spending, a 3.1 percent pay increase for our troops, and the first-ever paid family leave allowance.[93] During his 2020 State of the Union address Trump proudly reported on his military buildup. "To safeguard American liberty, we have invested a record-breaking $2.2 trillion in the United States military," said Trump. "We have purchased the finest planes, missiles, rockets, ships, and every other form of military equipment— all made in the United States of America."[94]

President Trump is committed to modernizing our military. He has made the U.S. Cyber Command a wartime concern to advance our efforts in cyberspace.[95] He also announced the creation of the United States Space Command in late August 2019. As the eleventh U.S. combatant command and drawing forces from existing military branches, the command defends our nation's interests in space, which Trump calls "the next warfighting domain." "Those who wish to harm the United States, to seek to challenge us, in the ultimate high ground of space, it is going to be a whole different ballgame," he said. "Our freedom to operate in space is also essential to detecting . . . any missile launches against the United States. Ultimately, we have no choice if we are to remain the world's greatest superpower."[96] Trump eventually overcame congressional resistance to establish the U.S. Space Force as America's sixth military service, beginning with 16,000 active-duty military personnel and civilian staffers, with more people to be added over time.[97]

Trump has been concerned for years about inadequate health care for U.S. military veterans. On June 6, 2018, he signed the VA Mission Act, which significantly improved veterans' access to VA health care, including allowing veterans to receive urgent care in their own cities and improving their overall quality of care.[98] The administration has also improved veterans' access to telehealth services, including serving patients at home, outside a hospital or clinic, whereas before, these services mostly involved connecting clinicians and patients from different medicine facilities.[99] The administration passed the Veterans Affairs Accountability and Whistleblower Protection Act of 2017 "to improve VA's ability to hold employees accountable and enhance protections for whistleblowers."[100] Also in 2017, the president signed the Veterans Appeals Improvement and Modernization Act to streamline the appeals process for veterans.[101] Trump created a White House veterans hotline, which opened in June 2017 and within two years had fielded more than 250,000 calls.[102] In June 2019, the Department of Veterans Affairs and White House launched a veteran suicide prevention task force.[103] In August 2019, President Trump signed a presidential memorandum to ensure that veterans receive expedited access to student loans and educational benefits available to them.[104]

Finally, due to the Trump boom, the jobless rate for all veterans dipped to an eighteen-year low of 3.5 percent in 2018.[105]

FOREIGN POLICY

President Trump has reversed Obama's lead-from-behind foreign policies that benefited our adversaries and punished our allies. He has shifted our policy from an America-last to an America-first emphasis. Trump succeeded in securing an agreement from NATO members to increase their defense spending by $130 billion.[106] He has directed millions of dollars in U.S. aid to Christians and other minorities persecuted by Islamic terrorists. With input from Vice President Pence, Trump redirected U.S. funds originally planned for more general distribution by the United Nations toward Christians, Yazidis, and other minorities targeted by ISIS.[107] Trump has supported democracy throughout the Western Hemisphere, imposing severe sanctions on repressive regimes in Cuba, Venezuela, and Nicaragua.

In a November 2017 trip to Asia, President Trump visited five nations—Japan, South Korea, China, Vietnam, and the Philippines—and attended the APEC CEO Summit in Da Nang and the U.S.-ASEAN Summit. His remarks on his trip capture his no-nonsense, patriotic approach to foreign policy and stand in sharp contrast to Obama's disgraceful apology tour. "When we are confident in ourselves, our strength, our flag, our history, our values—other nations are confident in us," said Trump. "And when we treat our citizens with the respect they deserve, other countries treat America with the respect that our country so richly deserves. During our travels, this is exactly what the world saw: a strong, proud, and confident America."[108]

During the trip, American representatives agreed to provide advanced military equipment to South Korea and Japan, and those countries agreed to more closely collaborate with the United States on defense. Trump also promoted stronger cooperation with India and Australia, and expressed America's commitment to promote security and prosperity in Asia, especially by developing financial institutions.[109]

Trump also attended two historic summits in North Korea and

became the first U.S. president to cross the DMZ into North Korea. Though criticized for negotiating with Kim Jong-un, Trump has kept the pressure on the North Korean dictator. He has imposed sanctions on people and companies that helped North Korea evade sanctions;[110] refused to give North Korea sanctions relief without a full denuclearization first;[111] and has led both the Treasury Department and the United Nations Security Council to implement and maintain sanctions on North Korea.

One of President Trump's most significant reversals of Obama foreign policy involves America's relationship with Israel. Unlike other presidents who glibly promised to recognize Jerusalem as the capital of Israel, President Trump fulfilled his promise and moved the U.S. embassy there, opening it on May 14, 2018. "For many years, we have failed to acknowledge the obvious, plain reality that the [Israeli] capital is Jerusalem," said Trump. A grateful Israeli prime minister Benjamin Netanyahu said, "President Trump, by recognizing history, you have made history. . . . Today the embassy of the most powerful nation on earth, our greatest ally, the United States of America, today the United States embassy opened here. What a difference." [112] Trump also withdrew America from UNESCO, the UN's cultural arm, citing its pervasive anti-Israel bias. "It sends a strong message that we need to see fundamental reform in the organization, and it raises everyone's awareness about continued anti-Israel bias," said a State Department official.[113]

On March 25, 2019, Trump formally recognized Israeli sovereignty over the Golan Heights. "Israel has never had a better friend than you," Netanyahu told Trump, citing America's withdrawal from the Iran nuclear deal, his reimposition of sanctions on Iran, and his recognition of Jerusalem as Israel's capital along with moving our embassy there. "This is truly an historic day," said Netanyahu, noting that it had taken half a century "to translate our military victory into a diplomatic victory. Your recognition is a two-fold act of historic justice. Israel won the Golan Heights in a just war of self-defense, and the Jewish people's roots in the Golan go back thousands of years." [114] The administration also declared that Israeli settlements in the West Bank do not violate international law.

Also in furtherance of our national security, the Trump administration issued an executive order to strengthen America's industrial base through the first whole-of-government assessment of America's manufacturing and defense supply chains since 1950.[115]

Trump has taken the offensive against terrorists around the world, destroying ISIS's caliphate and recapturing all territory subsumed by ISIS in Iraq and Syria. In the process, ISIS founder and leader Abu Bakr al-Baghdadi, one of the most murderous terrorists in the world, killed himself during a raid by U.S. commandos in northwestern Syria.

Trump has also taken strong action against Iran, the world's leading state sponsor of terrorism. In addition to killing Iran's terror mastermind Qasem Soleimani, he pulled out of the disastrous nuclear deal and replaced it with a "maximum pressure" campaign of sanctions on more than one thousand Iranian individuals, companies, and organizations. These were later enhanced with additional sanctions targeting Iran's oil, banking, and shipping sectors. "We are striking at the heart of the regime's inner security apparatus," said Secretary of State Mike Pompeo.[116] The administration has also pursued military action against Iran's ally, the Assad regime in Syria, in retaliation for using chemical weapons against its own people, and Trump authorized sanctions against nations affiliated with Syria's chemical weapons program.[117]

President Trump has employed a new approach in Afghanistan to prevent terrorists from reestablishing a terrorist base there and to finally enable the United States to bring our troops home. He is increasing pressure on the Taliban to enter into a peace settlement with the Afghan government and is pressuring neighboring Pakistan to stop harboring militants and terrorists.

Trump has taken a personal interest in securing the release of Americans unjustly imprisoned in foreign countries. He has forced the release of Ziyue Wang, an American doctoral student imprisoned in Iran; Aya Hijazi, an Egyptian-American imprisoned in Egypt; four prisoners held by North Korea—although one of them, Otto Warmbier, had slipped into a coma under suspicious circumstances and died shortly after being returned home;[118] and Danny Burch, an American oil worker held in Yemen.[119]

Finally, President Trump has lived up to his "America First" pledge by rejecting self-defeating international treaties and defending American sovereignty. He announced that the United States would withdraw from the Paris Climate Agreement, a product of environmental zealotry whose draconian provisions would kill American jobs and destroy U.S. competitiveness without appreciably reducing global temperatures.[120] He also declared that the United States would never ratify the United Nations 2014 Arms Trade Treaty, which was signed by Obama's Secretary of State John Kerry and sent to the Senate on December 9, 2016. The treaty provides an end run around the Second Amendment by imposing regulations and conditions on the transfer and possibly the possession of any weapon.[121] "This treaty threatened your . . . rights. . . . Under my administration, we will never surrender American sovereignty to anyone," Trump told the National Rifle Association. "We will never allow foreign bureaucrats to trample on your Second Amendment freedom."[122]

JUDGES

The president has treated the appointment of originalist judges as a top priority.[123] As of early March 2020, Trump had appointed 193 federal judges, including two Supreme Court justices (Neil Gorsuch replacing Antonin Scalia and Brett Kavanaugh replacing Anthony Kennedy), fifty-one judges for the United States Court of Appeals, 138 United States District Court judges, and two judges for the United States Court of International Trade. This was more than any other president in modern history at this point in their presidency.[124]

Most notably, Trump showed steadfast support for Supreme Court nominee Brett Kavanaugh during the despicable smear campaign run by the left and the Democrats, which included an escalating series of false allegations of sexual assault. Some of the most outlandish accusations were made by disgraced lawyer Michael Avenatti, with whom CNN's Brian "Humpty Dumpty" Stelter showed a strange infatuation back then.

While people focus mostly on Supreme Court appointments, lower federal court appointments are extremely important, especially considering the small percentage of cases that actually make it to the Supreme Court. (The Supreme Court decides fewer than eighty cases per year, while the thirteen Circuit Courts decide tens of thousands.) Since judges have lifetime tenure, Trump has intentionally appointed younger judges, once boasting that "the average age of my newly appointed circuit court judges is less than 50."

Senate Majority Leader Mitch McConnell, who has been instrumental in shepherding the confirmation of these judges, also intends for these appointments to have a lasting, beneficial impact on the judiciary and the nation. "My goal is to do everything we can for as long as we can to transform the federal judiciary, because everything else we do is transitory," said McConnell. "The closest thing we will ever have an opportunity to do to have the longest impact on the country is confirming these great men and women and transforming the judiciary for as long into the future as we can."[125] In some cases—such as the United States Courts of Appeals for the Second, Third, and Eleventh Circuits—Trump's appointments have flipped key courts to a majority of Republican-appointed judges.[126]

PROTECTING LIFE

President Trump has compiled an astonishing record in defending life. Those who scoffed at his campaign commitment to these causes have egg on their faces. True to his campaign promise to appoint pro-life judges,[127] within days of taking office Trump issued an executive order reinstating and expanding the "Mexico City Policy," which he renamed the Protecting Life in Global Health Assistance Policy, to ban federal funding of abortion-providing groups abroad. "President Trump is continuing Ronald Reagan's legacy by taking immediate action on day one to stop the promotion of abortion through our tax dollars overseas," said Marjorie Dannenfelser, president of the Susan B. Anthony List, a pro-life group. "President Trump's immediate action to promote respect for all human life, including vulnerable unborn children abroad, as well as conscience rights, sends a strong signal about his administration's pro-life priorities."[128]

As I've shown, however, there is no denying the pro-abortion extremism of the Democratic Party. In January 2019, while most were focusing on the border wall debate, House Speaker Nancy Pelosi pushed through the Democrat-controlled House a measure repealing the Protecting Life in Global Health Assistance Policy so that funding could be resumed for abortionists like International Planned Parenthood Federation, which performs abortions in foreign countries.[129] The bill did not pass the Senate, but Democrats continue to press to repeal the policy while Republicans seek to close a loophole in the law that allows nongovernmental organizations incorporated in the United States that perform or support abortion to receive federal funds.[130]

In April 2017, the State Department announced it was ending funding for the United Nations Population Fund because it "supports, or participates in the management of a program of coercive abortion or involuntary sterilization."[131] That same month, the administration cut all funding for the UN's Family Planning Agency, which the administration believes has supported China's oppressive population control activities, such as coercive abortions and involuntary sterilizations.[132] He also cut funding for international groups that provide abortions.[133]

Also in April 2017, President Trump overturned an Obama administration rule and allowed states to defund Planned Parenthood of family planning funds under Title X, which serves low-income

Americans.[134] In February 2019 the administration finalized its Protect Life Rule, which substantially cuts Title X funds being distributed to abortion providers, including an estimated $50 million–$60 million cut per year for Planned Parenthood. In January 2018 the Trump administration rescinded Obama's 2016 policy that prevented states from defunding Planned Parenthood of Medicaid funds. "President Trump and his administration have taken . . . an important step toward getting American taxpayers out of funding the abortion industry, especially Planned Parenthood," said Dannenfelser.[135]

On March 4, 2019, the Department of Health and Human Services (HHS) finalized a rule change to lift the Clinton-era provision of the Title X family planning program that requires organizations receiving Title X funding to counsel women about abortion and give them referrals for abortion services. Under the amended rule, providers would not be required to talk about abortion, though they would not be forbidden to, according to the administration.[136]

In June 2019 the Trump administration announced the government will no longer conduct research using fetal tissue obtained through elective abortions. The Trump administration has "once again done the right thing in restoring a culture of life to our government," said Kristan Hawkins, president of Students of Life for America.[137]

In January 2020, HHS reversed another Obama administration policy and granted the state of Texas a Medicaid waiver to fund the Healthy Texas Women program, which excludes abortion businesses like Planned Parenthood. Also that month, the HHS declared it would take action against California for violating the Weldon Amendment, which prohibits discrimination against groups that don't provide abortion coverage in their health-care plans.[138]

On January 24, 2020, President Trump became the first sitting president to address the annual March for Life rally in person in Washington, D.C. "Every child is a precious and sacred gift from God," said Trump. "Together, we must protect, cherish, and defend the dignity and sanctity of every human life. . . . Unborn children have never had a stronger defender in the White House. And, as the Bible tells us, each person is 'wonderfully made.' "[139] During his State of the Union address on February 4, President Trump urged Congress to ban late-term abortions.[140]

PROMOTING RELIGIOUS LIBERTY

In the last chapter I detailed many of the pressing threats to Americans' religious liberty. President Trump's record shows he understands the danger and is taking strong action against it. On May 4, 2017, Trump issued an executive order, "Promoting Free Speech and Religious Liberty," that fulfilled a campaign promise to dismantle the Johnson Amendment, which banned tax-exempt entities such as churches and nonprofits from engaging in political speech and activities. Trump's order relaxes federal enforcement of the ban, but only Congress can repeal it.[141] The order instructs the Internal Revenue Service (IRS) to "not take any adverse action against any individual, house of worship, or other religious organization" for endorsing or opposing candidates. "We are giving churches their voices back," said Trump. The order also instructs the Departments of Treasury, Labor, and HHS to consider changing Obamacare regulations requiring employers to provide contraception coverage in employee insurance plans.[142]

The Trump administration further demonstrated its commitment to religious liberty when its Department of Justice filed an amicus brief with the Supreme Court in support of the religious freedom of baker Jack Phillips to decline to make a wedding cake for a gay couple in what became the Masterpiece Cakeshop case.[143] In May 2018, the president issued an executive order establishing a White House Faith and Opportunity Initiative.[144]

Trump's HHS has been particularly active on this issue. It has proposed two regulations to exempt organizations with moral or religious objections from being required to buy insurance coverage for contraceptives and abortifacients, and has launched a Conscience and Religious Freedom Division. It also finalized a rule to prevent federal agencies from discriminating—and to deny federal funding for state and local governments that discriminate—against health-care organizations based on their refusal to provide or participate in abortion services. The rule protects health-care entities and individuals from being forced "to provide, participate in, pay for, provide coverage of, or refer for, services such as abortion, sterilization, or assisted suicide." "Finally, laws prohibiting government funded discrimination against conscience and religious freedom will be enforced like every other civil rights law," said Office for Civil Rights director Roger Severino. "This rule ensures that health care entities and professionals won't be bullied out of the health care field because they decline to participate in actions that violate their conscience, including the taking of human life. Protecting conscience and religious freedom not only fosters greater diversity in health care, it's the law." [145]

The State Department has hosted two Ministerials to Advance Religious Freedom, in which world leaders met to discuss and promote religious liberty.[146] The Department of Justice has also engaged in religious freedom matters, having formed a Religious Liberty Task Force to issue explicit legal guidance for all executive agencies on how to apply the religious liberty protections under federal law.[147] More recently, Attorney General William Barr warned government officials that during the coronavirus outbreak, they cannot impose restrictions on religious activity that don't also apply to similar nonreligious activity.[148]

The DOJ also filed an amicus brief with the Supreme Court arguing that a memorial to forty-nine World War I veterans in the form of a cross on public land in Bladensburg, Maryland, does not violate the Constitution's Establishment Clause.[149] The Trump administration has filed amicus briefs supporting religious liberty in many other cases—in fact, it has filed more such briefs than either the Obama or the George W. Bush administrations.[150]

President Trump is the first American president to convene a meeting at the United Nations solely on the topic of religious liberty. In a speech to the UN General Assembly exclusively on religious liberty, he called for ending religious persecution throughout the world.[151] Trump backed up his words by dedicating $25 million to protect religious sites and houses of worship across the globe, and also established a coalition of top business leaders to promote religious liberty in the workplace.[152] Shortly thereafter, HHS secretary Alex Azar declared to the UN General Assembly, "There is no international right to an abortion." Furthermore, he denounced efforts to provide global access to abortion and condemned the UN's use of euphemisms for abortion such as "sexual and reproductive health and rights."[153]

The Trump administration, through nine federal agencies including the Education Department, HHS, and DOJ, has issued guidance to protect voluntary prayer in public elementary and secondary schools. The administration also proposed a rule to facilitate the acquisition of federal funds by religious groups that provide social services, which would eliminate an Obama executive order forcing religious entities, such as health-care providers, child welfare organizations, and medical nonprofits, to inform people they may receive the same service from secular providers.[154]

In a recent action on religious freedom, on February 5, 2020, Secretary of State Mike Pompeo inaugurated the International Religious Freedom Alliance to promote religious liberty and fight religious persecution, especially by terrorists and violent extremists. "The Alliance is intended to bring together senior government representatives to discuss actions their nations can take together to promote respect for freedom of religion or belief and protect members of religious minority groups worldwide," said Pompeo.[155]

BORDER SECURITY

President Trump has acted energetically to secure our border despite determined resistance from open-borders Democrats and judges who sympathize with them. As soon as he entered office, President Trump honored his signature campaign promise by calling on Congress to fully fund a wall on our southern border, close loopholes in immigration laws, and end chain migration and the visa lottery program. He also issued several executive orders to enhance border security. In his first week in office, on January 25, 2017, he imposed penalties on sanctuary cities and made them ineligible for certain federal grants. Having driven the left berserk, the order was challenged in court and ultimately upheld by the Second U.S. Circuit Court of Appeals in Manhattan. Following the ruling President Trump announced that the federal government would begin withholding funding from sanctuary cities.[156] The president's order also called for the hiring of 5,000 border patrol agents and 10,000 more Immigration and Customs Enforcement (ICE) agents,[157] and for deporting those who "pose a risk to public safety or national security."[158]

Another executive order called for the construction of a border wall on our southern border and building additional detention facilities to house those entering the country illegally.[159] Yet another order suspended the refugee admission program for 120 days, indefinitely stopped the admission of refugees from Syria, and asked for a review of the refugee admission process. The order also limited the number of refugees in 2017 to fewer than 50,000 and banned travelers from Iraq, Iran, Libya, Somalia, Sudan, Syria, and Yemen from entering the country for at least ninety days, to improve security screening for terrorists and criminals.[160]

From the beginning, however, federal judges partially thwarted Trump's border enforcement efforts. Federal district judge Ann M. Donnelly of the federal district court in Brooklyn enjoined the government from removing people arriving in the United States from the covered countries.[161] Federal district judge James Robart blocked key parts of the travel ban, and his ruling was upheld by the United States Court of Appeals for the Ninth Circuit on February 9, 2017.[162]

As announced by UN ambassador Nikki Haley, the Trump administration refused to sign the United Nations' Global Compact for Safe, Orderly and Regular Migration, because it would cede sovereignty over U.S. immigration decisions to an international body. The compact would extend asylum rights and provide access to government benefits beyond those allowed by U.S. immigration law. "No country has done more than the United States, and our generosity will continue," said Haley. "But our decisions on immigration policies must always be made by Americans and Americans alone. We will decide how best to control our borders and who will be allowed to enter our country. The global approach in the New York Declaration is simply not compatible with U.S. sovereignty." [163]

Department of Homeland Security secretary John Kelly signed a memorandum revoking Obama's Deferred Action for Parents of Americans and Lawful Permanent Residents (DAPA), which provided a pathway to citizenship for illegal immigrants whose children are United States residents or citizens. Obama's plan was never formally implemented, having been blocked in 2015 by a federal district court, whose order was affirmed by a three-member panel of the Fifth Circuit in November 2015. Obama's Justice Department appealed the ruling, but the Supreme Court in June 2016 was deadlocked in a 4–4 tie, which left in place the Fifth Circuit's ruling.[164] Kelly's action formalized the end of the policy.

On December 5, 2017, Trump rescinded President Obama's Deferred Action for Childhood Arrivals (DACA) program, which shielded and provided work permits for "dreamers"—illegal immigrants who were brought to the United States as children. In initially announcing the winding down of DACA, Trump said, "I do not favor punishing children, most of whom are now adults, for the actions of their parents." However, "we must also recognize that we are a nation of opportunity because we are a nation of laws." Thereafter three separate federal district courts blocked Trump's action. In November 2018, the Trump administration asked the U.S. Supreme Court for permission to end Obama's dreamer program. Trump said it was up to Congress, not the executive branch, to establish immigration policy. Then–attorney general Jeff Sessions said the 2012 order that created DACA was "an unconstitutional exercise of authority by the executive branch."[165] As of this writing, the Supreme Court has not yet ruled on the issue.

Early in his tenure as attorney general, Sessions instructed his deputies to prioritize the targeting of the transnational MS-13 street gang.[166] In September 2017, more than 3,800 members of the MS-13 and 18th Street gangs in the United States and Central America were criminally charged as part of Operation Regional Shield, a coordinated law enforcement action.[167]

In April 2018, defense secretary James N. Mattis authorized up to four thousand National Guard troops to be deployed on the southern border.[168] On February 15, 2019, President Trump declared a national emergency at the southern border in order to stop the invasion of illegal aliens, criminal gangs, and drugs. "We're going to confront the national security crisis on our southern border, and we're going to do it one way or the other," said Trump, who was seeking to dedicate billions of dollars allocated to the Defense Department to building a border wall.[169] Another successful element of Trump's approach has been pressuring the Mexican government, which agreed to place six thousand national guard troops throughout Mexico and on its southern border to address the immigration crisis and human trafficking.[170] Such actions helped lead to a 56 percent drop in the number of illegal immigrants crossing into the United States from Mexico as of September 2019.[171]

Despite Democrats opposing every inch of it, Trump has secured funding for about 445 miles of the 722 miles of border wall that he's requested, and under his leadership we've built more than one hundred miles of the wall, with much more under construction. The funding depends on Trump's national emergency and executive actions being upheld in court challenges.[172] Sixteen states sued him in the Ninth Circuit, which issued a permanent injunction against the diversion of funds for construction of the wall,[173] though the Supreme Court later overturned the ruling. In a separate case, a U.S. district court in Texas issued a permanent nationwide injunction blocking Trump's use of $3.6 billion of Defense Department funds,[174] though that injunction too was lifted after an appeal.[175]

In May 2019, President Trump announced an immigration plan for the twenty-first century, which consists of two components. One is the recognition that full border security is essential for our immigration system. The other is the creation of a new, merit-based, legal immigration system that protects American wages and safety net programs, prioritizes immediate families, and creates a "fair and transparent" immigration process.[176]

In fiscal year 2019, the Justice Department prosecuted a record-breaking number of immigration-related cases. The U.S. Attorneys' Offices charged 25,426 defendants with felony illegal reentry in fiscal year 2019 (FY19), an increase of 8.5 percent from FY18. Almost 81,000 defendants were charged with misdemeanor improper entry in FY19, which increased the previous record of FY18 by 18.1 percent. And 4,297 defendants were charged with alien smuggling in FY19, an increase of 15.4 percent from FY18.[177]

President Trump prioritizes combating human trafficking. Federal law enforcement, through the Anti-Trafficking Coordination Team (ACTeam) initiative, has more than doubled convictions of human traffickers and increased by 75 percent the number of defendants charged in ACTeam districts. ICE's Homeland Security Investigations arrested 1,588 criminals associated with human trafficking in FY18.[178]

The administration also continues to increase pressure on sanctuary cities. Attorney General Barr announced that the Justice Department was reviewing actions of certain local prosecutors whom it suspects of charging foreign nationals with lesser offenses to shield them from deportation. "In pursuing their personal ambitions and misguided notions of equal justice, these district attorneys are systematically violating the rule of law and may even be unlawfully discriminating against American citizens," Barr stated.[179]

Many American taxpayers are rightly outraged that illegal immigrants avail themselves of free health care, education, and other government benefits. The Trump administration issued a rule in August 2019, to take effect in about two months, to deny green cards and visas to illegals who use, or who are expected to use, a number of federal, state, and local government benefits, including food stamps, housing vouchers, and Medicaid.[180] The Trump administration asked the Supreme Court to allow the rule to go into effect, which it did in January 2020.[181]

HEALTH CARE

As noted, the administration repealed Obamacare's individual mandate as part of its tax cut bill, which President Trump contends was disproportionately harming lower-income people. The *Wall Street Journal*'s editorial board notes that more than 75 percent of penalized households made less than $50,000 and nine in ten earned less than $75,000.[182] Three Obamacare taxes—the Cadillac tax, the health insurance tax, and the medical device tax—were also repealed.[183]

In October 2017, President Trump issued an executive order promoting health-care choice and competition across state lines.[184] The Department of Labor finalized a rule relaxing restrictions on associated health-care plans to make it easier for small businesses to band together to buy health insurance. A federal district judge, however, struck down the rule, and the administration has appealed the decision.

President Trump has made it a top priority to battle the opioid crisis. In July 2017, the Justice Department achieved a major victory by shutting down AlphaBay, the nation's largest online market for deadly, illegal drugs such as fentanyl and heroin.[185] As a result of such efforts, the number of first-time heroin users ages twelve and older fell by more than 50 percent in July 2017.[186] In October 2017, President Trump ramped up the campaign, declaring the nation's opioid crisis a "national health emergency" and pledging that the country would fight it as a "national family." He directed federal agencies to use all resources to fight the opioid scourge.[187] In a positive sign, from Trump's inauguration until October 2018, high-dose opioid prescriptions fell 16 percent.[188]

In November 2017, U.S. Department of Agriculture secretary Sonny Perdue announced that his department had provided more than $1 billion in fiscal year 2017 to help 2.5 million people in rural communities in forty-one states acquire health-care services.[189]

In January 2018, President Trump signed a bill for a six-year extension of the Children's Health Insurance Program (CHIP), which provides coverage for 9 million children in families who earn too much to qualify for Medicaid but not enough to afford private insurance.[190]

In May 2018, President Trump fulfilled another campaign promise when he signed into law the "right to try" drug bill, which would allow terminally ill patients access to experimental medical treatments not yet approved by the Food and Drug Administration.[191]

In August 2018, the Trump administration announced a rule that would increase competition and help reduce prescription drug prices for many seniors in the Medicare Advantage program.[192] Trump later signed an executive order to improve private Medicare plans. HHS secretary Azar said the president has "directed HHS to take a number of specific, significant steps that will meaningfully improve the financing of Medicare, advance the care American seniors receive from their doctors, and improve the health they enjoy." Among those steps are lowering costs in Medicare Advantage, allowing those beneficiaries to create savings accounts, and accelerating access to the latest medical technologies.[193]

Under President Trump, the Food and Drug Administration (FDA) has approved a record number of generic drugs designed to lower drug prices through competition.[194] The White House reported in November 2019 that prescription drug prices are falling at rates not seen since the 1960s.[195]

In his 2019 State of the Union address, President Trump proposed to spend $500 million over ten years on childhood cancer research.[196] He later signed the Tobacco-Free Youth Act, which raises the federal legal age for buying tobacco and vaping products from eighteen to twenty-one.[197]

CRIME AND CRIMINAL JUSTICE REFORM

President Trump signed the First Step Act, the most significant justice reform legislation in years, with overwhelming bipartisan support. "This legislation reformed sentencing laws that have wrongly and disproportionately harmed the African American community," Trump said in his 2019 State of the Union address. "The First Step Act gives nonviolent offenders the chance to reenter society as productive, lawabiding citizens. Now, states across the country are following our lead. America is a nation that believes in redemption." [198] No one will ever forget when Alice Marie Johnson was released into the arms of her loving family. She's someone I've gotten to know, someone who absolutely deserved a second chance. It took Donald Trump to make it happen.

The president recommitted the nation to implementing the crime prevention strategies involved in Project Safe Neighborhoods and convened the first nationwide meeting of that organization in eight years.[199] In Trump's first two years of office, the homicide rate for the largest U.S. cities dropped 6 percent, which the president attributed to Project Safe Neighborhoods. Trump secured $50 million in funding for the project, which he used in part to deploy almost two hundred new violent-crime prosecutors throughout America.[200]

As you can see, President Trump's first-term accomplishments have been nothing short of remarkable, but if you depend on the extremely dishonest and liberal news outlets for your information, you'd think

Trump's presidency has been a historic catastrophe in which the middle class was driven into poverty as he systematically gave away the nation's wealth to Putin. The media mob hid the fact that by nearly any metric, prior to the coronavirus outbreak, Trump's economic record was the most successful since Reagan's. The coronavirus devastated the economy in the short term, but President Trump has put the nation in the best possible position to bounce back once the virus has run its course and the nation can reopen.

At the time of the outbreak, our manufacturing was staging a major comeback, energy production was at record levels, taxes were lower, corporate money parked overseas was flowing back into America, and unemployment rates were lower than many thought possible. If President Trump could achieve all this in less than four years, imagine what he can do in eight. Let's now take a look at how President Trump deftly managed this wholly unexpected virus that shocked the nation more than any health issue of my lifetime.

CHAPTER TEN

Trump's Response to the Coronavirus and America's Great Comeback

The coronavirus stunned America with its extreme contagiousness and unpredictable lethality. Medical experts will eventually get to the bottom of this when sufficient data is collected and analyzed, but it's important to remember that when the pandemic hit our shores, we didn't know a lot about it. At the time no one could have dreamed that in just a few months we would shut down nearly our entire economy. President Trump was in a tough position because whether he acted cautiously or forcibly, people would get hurt.

It was a perfect position, however, for Trump's critics, because no matter how he responded they could pin the blame on him—and they rose to the task, as they always do. The Democrats are so consumed with their hatred of Trump, and so determined to use any means possible to remove him from office, that their unhinged reaction to the coronavirus was predictable. Remember, this was a deadly virus that spread out of China, where the communist regime's initial reaction was to lie to the entire world about the outbreak, try to cover it up, and arrest doctors who were informing others about the virus.[1] But according to Democratic senator Chris Murphy, "The reason that we're in the crisis that we are today is not because of anything that China did, is not because of anything the [World Health Organization] did. It's because of what [President Trump] did." You got that? China had nothing to do with it—the virus is 100 percent Trump's fault. So many Democrats were scapegoating Trump that a Rasmussen poll found that 60 percent of Democratic likely voters agreed with Murphy's statement.[2]

When he voiced optimism that America would defeat this menace, the left cited it as evidence of his unseriousness. Yet he was serious enough to ban travel from China and then Europe against the advice of almost all his critics and even many in his inner circle. But don't ever expect the haters to give Trump any credit. To hear them tell the story, Trump's inaction and incompetence cost thousands of American lives. But had he listened to them, had he cowered when they accused him of racism for banning travel from epicenters of the outbreak, thousands more Americans would have died, and the economy would have spiraled into further chaos.

As we'll see, Trump and his team consistently took decisive action despite his critics blaming him, after the fact, for failing to take steps they themselves did not contemplate at the time. They were too busy investigating and impeaching him. During the first three Democratic presidential debates—on January 14, February 7, and February 19—the candidates endlessly attacked Trump but uttered only one reference to the coronavirus outbreak: a passing remark made by Pete Buttigieg on February 7. In the February 19 debate, Michael Bloomberg warned about Chinese people dying, but he was referring to climate change, not the virus.[3] True to form, the Democrats were more worried about global warming than a spreading pandemic. In fact, at the next debate on February 25, as the coronavirus was spreading throughout the globe, candidate Tom Steyer argued that "the biggest threat to America right now in terms of our safety of our citizens is climate."[4]

It's particularly hard to explain how the Democrats ignored the virus during the February 7 and February 19 debates, seeing as the Trump administration on January 31 had declared the outbreak a public health emergency and announced the China travel ban. By that time, China had reported more than 34,500 confirmed coronavirus cases and more than 700 deaths.[5] By the February 19 debate, China had reported 74,000 cases and more than 2,100 deaths, and twenty-six other countries had reported a total of 1,070 cases and eight deaths.[6]

President Trump later commented on the Democrats' finger-pointing over the issue when they themselves didn't think the virus was even worth discussing. "That was February 19, that's way after I closed entrance from China into our country," said Trump. "I just thought that was very interesting—because, you know, you hear these people, some of the people, the Democrats, said oh, this, that. It never even was part of their dialogue. Now they bring it up because you see what happens now. But they didn't bring it up. But I brought it up."[7]

The Biden campaign reacted to all this with its typical mix of befuddlement and hypocrisy. Just after the travel ban was announced, Ever-Forgetful Joe denounced Trump's "record of hysterical xenophobia and fear mongering." But in April he had a change of heart, bravely sending a staffer to tell CNN that, in fact, Biden supported the ban.[8]

This was no surprise—despite Democrats' reflexive accusations of racism, the American people quickly understood, as the coronavirus rapidly spread worldwide, that banning travel from China was a commonsense defensive measure. In fact, at the end of April, Nancy Pelosi tried to diminish the credit Trump was getting for having instituted the ban. When asked about it on CNN, Pelosi sputtered that the travel ban "wasn't as it is described, this great moment" because "tens of thousands of people were still allowed in from China. . . . If you're going to shut the door because you have an evaluation of an epidemic, then shut the door."[9] As Pelosi herself acknowledged, those people entering America from China after the ban were American citizens and green-card holders. So suddenly, the problem wasn't that Trump adopted an unnecessary, racist travel ban, it was that *the ban was too weak and didn't stop Americans from returning home.*

The Democrats' hypocrisy could give you whiplash. On April 19, while interviewing Pelosi, my Fox News colleague Chris Wallace noted that she was accusing Trump of failing to respond to the virus in January and February, yet Pelosi herself went to San Francisco's Chinatown on February 24 and announced, "We think it's very safe to be in Chinatown" while encouraging tourists to go there. Dodging the issue of her hypocrisy, Pelosi claimed she "was saying that you should not discriminate against . . . Chinese-Americans" and outrageously accused the "the President and others" of "making Asian-Americans a target of violence across the country." It's noteworthy that Pelosi issues press releases nearly every day, often multiple times a day. But the day of her Chinatown visit—February 24—was the first time she issued a press release mentioning the virus. And far from warning of its dangers, the release was an interview she did in Chinatown in which she cited empty fashion shows in Italy and claimed such fears were "unwarranted" in America because of the "precautions" people were taking—all this as she urged public gatherings of tourists.[10]

In fact, while Democrats were ranting about Trump's xenophobia, he was taking vital steps to manage this crisis, beginning with the travel ban and continuing in February and beyond. Democrats accuse Trump of adopting a racist travel ban in January and then doing virtually nothing in February. HBO's Bill Maher pushed this narrative when interviewing Congressman Dan Crenshaw, who set him straight. Crenshaw reminded him that Trump requested funding from Congress to combat the virus in February, but the only vote Pelosi allowed at the time was a bill to ban flavored tobacco. "We were in a fact-finding mode in February. People forget this," said Crenshaw. "People keep calling February this lost month, but it's really not. That's an easy and cheap accusation, because there's no big bold moves taken like there was in January or like there was in March. But the reality is our government was working to create that test. . . . By March 3, there was only 102 cases in the United States and yet I'm hearing criticism that we should have been locked down weeks earlier, but do you think the American people would have accepted that with only 100 cases in the United States?"[11]

Democrats tried to portray Trump as incompetent throughout the pandemic. But at daily press briefings he demonstrated, despite a barrage of comically hostile and often personally nasty questions from the politicized White House press corps, his intimate knowledge of all aspects of the government's response and showed he was fully in charge. He had become a wartime commander in chief, leading the nation, bringing together the public and private sectors, and working with state governors to implement his nationwide plan to slay this invisible enemy. Without delegating major decisions, he demonstrated prudent leadership by regularly conferring with business leaders, pharmaceutical companies, airline officials, health insurers, retail and grocery store representatives, and bank leaders.

Millions of Americans voted for Trump because they believed he could bring his business acumen and common sense to the White House, and they have been vindicated. His exceptional management of this effort showed his enormous talent for leadership and for inspiring capable people at all levels to work together to win this war. I am confident that even many of his critics were shocked—and disappointed—by how well he performed. President Trump was made for a time like this, and he outdid himself. This was not the caricature that the Democrats, the media, and Never Trumpers had projected for four years. This was not some ill-prepared Washington politician but a wise, sober leader calmly and effectively steering the ship of state through treacherous waters.

They tried to manufacture a wedge between Trump and his two principal medical advisers, Dr. Anthony Fauci and Dr. Deborah Birx, but he was working in close cooperation with them every step of the way. When these doctors were encouraged to criticize Trump and say he was contradicting their advice, they refused to take the bait. All three worked in synch with each other, and both doctors emphasized that Trump was an attentive listener and quick learner and was following their advice.

President Trump was proactive throughout the outbreak. He was accessible and responsive to state governors and demonstrated foresight in managing the supply chain, securing necessary equipment for distribution to states and localities most in need. Respectful of federalism, he often encouraged states to make their own decisions based on local conditions and emphasized that the federal government would serve as a backstop, not a dictator. He alluded to what he believed to be his plenary power during this state of emergency, and he mentioned invoking this power if necessary, but he rarely used the federal whip hand.

Let's now take a closer look at the timeline of the Trump administration's actions to combat the outbreak. This abbreviated list conclusively rebuts false claims that Trump didn't respond aggressively to the outbreak.

December 31, 2019: China reported its discovery of the coronavirus to the World Health Organization, confirming more than forty infections. "Reportedly, most patients had epidemiological links to a large seafood and animal market," according to the Centers for Disease Control. "The market was closed on January 1, 2020." [12] While the CDC suspected a "zoonotic origin to the outbreak," Fox News later reported that the virus may have, in fact, originated in a Wuhan lab as part of China's efforts to compete with the United States. [13] Three days later, CDC director Robert Redfield emailed George Gao, director of the Chinese CDC, and offered to send American scientists to China to investigate the virus. Getting no response, he sent Gao another email on January 5. On January 6 the CDC issued a travel health notice for Wuhan, which it updated on January 11. [14]

January 17: The CDC started public health entry screening at San Francisco, New York (JFK), and Los Angeles airports, as these received the most Wuhan travelers. [15] On January 20, Dr. Fauci reported that the National Institutes of Health was working on developing a vaccine for the virus. [16] On January 21, the CDC directed its Emergency Operations Center to provide support for the virus response. Also on that day the first infection was reported in the United States. [17]

January 21: The day of the first identifiable American coronavirus case in the state of Washington. [18]

January 23: The CDC sought emergency approval from the FDA to permit U.S. states to use a CDC-developed diagnostic test to detect the coronavirus. Though at least sixteen people had close contact with the Washington State man first diagnosed with the virus in the United

States, none of them had yet shown symptoms of the virus by January 23. At that point the virus had killed eighteen people and infected some 650, mostly in China, and the World Health Organization would not yet declare the virus a global health emergency.[19] On January 27, President Trump tweeted that he had made an offer to Chinese president Xi Jinping to send experts to China to investigate the virus, and the CDC urged Americans to avoid nonessential travel to China. On January 29, Trump announced the formation of the President's Coronavirus Task Force.[20]

January 31: With Chinese officials confirming some ten thousand cases of COVID-19 in China, Trump declared the coronavirus a public health emergency and issued a travel ban suspending entry into the United States for foreign nationals who were in China during the fourteen-day period preceding their entry or attempted entry into the United States.[21] The Department of Homeland Security directed that all flights from China and all passengers who had traveled to China within the preceding two weeks be routed through one of seven U.S. airports and expanded entry screening to eight U.S. airports on February 2.[22]

The travel ban prevented more infected people from coming into the United States and gave us time to prepare for the outbreak. But the media mob denounced the ban as unnecessary and racist, while House Democrats that very day proposed the "No Ban Act" to require that any future travel ban be temporary and subject to congressional oversight.[23] As late as March, Democrats were still blistering Trump for the ban. Calling Trump xenophobic, Bernie Sanders declared that he wouldn't consider closing the U.S. border to prevent the spread of the virus.[24]

Early to mid-February: Trump promised in his State of the Union address on February 4 to "take all necessary steps" to protect Americans from the virus. Meanwhile, Democrats were focused on voting the next day in President Trump's impeachment trial in the Senate. Also in early February the administration began briefing and working with state governors, and the U.S. shipped test kits for the virus to some thirty nations. The Department of Health and Human Services began to work with private companies to develop a coronavirus vaccine and treatment for infections. Later in February the Food and Drug Administration permitted certified labs to develop coronavirus testing kits. In mid-February the CDC began working with five labs to conduct "community-based influenza surveillance" to study and detect the spread of the virus.[25]

Late February: On February 23, the administration raised travel advisory levels for Japan and South Korea. On February 24, it asked Congress for $2.5 billion to fight the virus, but Nancy Pelosi delayed a vote on the measure. On February 26, Trump discussed virus containment efforts with Indian prime minister Narendra Modi and appointed Vice President Mike Pence to lead his Coronavirus Task Force.[26] The next day, Pence appointed Dr. Deborah Birx to serve as the White House Coronavirus Response Coordinator. On February 29, the administration issued a travel ban for Italy, South Korea, and Iran.[27]

Early March: The administration announced it would buy some 500 million N95 respirators over the next eighteen months, and President Trump signed an $8.3 billion bill to target the outbreak, with $7.76 billion to be distributed to federal, state, and local agencies.[28] Trump and Pence met with major insurance companies to persuade them to waive copays for COVID-19 testing. The administration directed the Small Business Administration to issue low-interest loans to small businesses affected by the outbreak and asked Congress to increase this fund by $50 billion.[29] The Education Department eased rules to provide colleges and universities more flexibility to conduct online classes during the outbreak.[30]

March 12: Trump imposed a thirty-day travel ban on travelers from Europe. The next day he declared a national emergency to access $42 billion to fight the virus. Through the emergency declaration, President Trump asked every state to set up emergency operations centers immediately and every hospital to activate its emergency preparedness plan. He explained that the declaration would allow the HHS secretary to "waive provisions of applicable laws and regulations to give doctors, hospitals . . . and healthcare providers maximum flexibility to respond to the virus."[31] He also announced that the public and private sectors were working together to open drive-through testing collection sites.[32] In mid-March the White House worked with the private sector to start a website to provide free access to online education technologies for families, students, and educators during the outbreak.[33]

March 16: President Trump announced national guidelines to slow the spread of the coronavirus, which stressed social distancing. It urged Americans to avoid gatherings of more than ten people, discretionary travel and social visits, eating and drinking in bars, restaurants, and public food courts, and to refrain from visiting nursing homes or long-term care facilities. Americans were urged to work from home if possible and homeschool their children. The guidelines advised older people and those with underlying health conditions to stay home and encouraged Americans to frequently wash their hands and avoid touching their face. Those who felt sick or had tested positive for the virus were encouraged to stay at home.[34] The president predicted that the nation might get the outbreak under control by July or August at the earliest.[35]

March 17: Treasury secretary Steve Mnuchin met with lawmakers to consider a stimulus and relief bill for businesses, industries, and workers suffering economically due to the virus. The Department of Defense announced it would make 5 million respirator masks and 2,000 ventilators available to the HHS. Also, agriculture secretary Sonny Perdue announced collaboration with the Baylor Collaborative on Hunger and Poverty, McLane Global, PepsiCo, and other firms to deliver almost 1 million meals per week to rural school students.[36]

March 18: The Federal Reserve announced the establishment of a new Money Market Mutual Fund Facility to provide liquidity for the financial system.[37] President Trump also announced that the Department of Housing and Urban Development would suspend all foreclosures and evictions until the end of April. HUD later said the FHA would extend the moratorium for single-family homeowners with FHA-insured mortgages for sixty days. The Federal Housing Finance Agency and Fannie Mae and Freddie Mac adopted the same policy.[38]

On the same day, President Trump announced the temporary closure of the U.S.-Canada border to nonessential traffic and also said he planned to invoke the Defense Production Act to enable production of the necessary supplies to fight the virus. He also reported that the navy would deploy the *Comfort* and *Mercy* hospital ships.[39] Also on March 18, President Trump signed into law the Families First Coronavirus Response Act, effective April 1, which funded free coronavirus testing, fourteen-day paid leave for workers affected by the virus, and additional food stamp funding. The bill also provided funding and flexibility for emergency nutritional assistance for the elderly, women, children, and low-income families.[40]

March 19: The State Department issued an advisory urging Americans to avoid all international travel.[41] President Trump also announced that the antimalaria drug hydroxychloroquine had shown encouraging progress in fighting the virus. He directed FEMA to lead the federal government's coronavirus response effort. Vice President Pence reported that tens of thousands of ventilators had been located that could be converted to treat virus patients.

March 20: The United States and Mexico agreed to restrict nonessential cross-border traffic. Secretary Mnuchin reported that President Trump had moved tax filing day from April 15 to July 15 for American taxpayers. The Department of Education suspended standardized testing requirements for the rest of the school year and suspended interest rates on federally held student loans for sixty days.[42] Also that day, to help protect hospital workers, the president signed legislation removing restrictions that prevented manufacturers from selling industrial masks directly to hospitals.[43]

March 23: Attorney General William Barr announced the formation of a National Task Force meeting on hoarding and price gouging and said all ninety-three AG offices were appointing lead prosecutors to prevent hoarding. On March 24, Trump stated that the Army Corps of Engineers and the National Guard were building four hospitals and four medical centers in New York. Also, Vice President Pence reported that FEMA sent New York 2,000 ventilators, which became 4,000 the next day. He urged those who had recently been in New York to self-quarantine for fourteen days. Dr. Birx reported that the United States had conducted more tests in the previous week than South Korea had in eight weeks.[44]

March 27: Trump signed the Coronavirus Aid, Relief, and Economic Security (CARES) Act into law, providing almost $2 trillion, including direct payments to individuals and families, loans for small businesses and distressed companies, unemployment benefits, aid to states and cities, and monies for hospitals to obtain equipment and infrastructure.[45] Democrats delayed passage of the bill while attempting to blackmail Republicans to agree to a slew of left-wing provisions with no connection to the coronavirus, including increased collective bargaining powers for unions, increased fuel emission standards for airlines, expansion of wind and solar tax credits, requirements for same-day voter registration and early voting, publication of corporate pay statistics by race and race statistics for all corporate boards, an increase of the minimum wage to $15 per hour for all companies receiving aid, funds to study climate change mitigation efforts in the aviation and aerospace industries, and an expansion of the Obamaphones program.

"Pelosi & Schumer are willing to risk your life, your job, your retirement savings for a radical, left-wing wish list that has nothing to do with this virus," Senator Tom Cotton tweeted. "Disgraceful."[46] Republicans killed most of these obnoxious demands, though the Democrats secured $75 million each for PBS stations, the National Foundation on the Arts and Humanities, and the National Endowment for the Humanities; $50 million for the Institute of Museum and Library Services; $25 million for the Kennedy Center for Performing Arts; $75 million for the Smithsonian Institution; and $400 million to states for "election security grants."[47]

March 29: President Trump reported that the Army Corp of Engineers had completed construction of a 2,900-bedroom temporary hospital at the Javits Center in New York. Also on that day Trump, saying the death rate from COVID-19 was expected to peak in the next two weeks, announced the extension of CDC guidelines to limit the spread of the virus through April 30. He formally extended the guidelines on March 31.[48] Trump also reported that 1,100 patients in New York were being treated with hydroxychloroquine for coronavirus and that Cigna and Humana had agreed to waive copays for coronavirus treatment. A few days later Vice President Pence announced that Blue Cross Blue Shield would be waiving out-of-pocket costs for coronavirus treatment. Pence further reported that more than 17,000 National Guard troops had been activated to assist in the coronavirus response, and that number expanded to 29,600 by April 10. Also, the HHS accelerated the clinical trial for a coronavirus vaccine developed by Janssen Research and Development.[49]

April 2: The administration announced that the Paycheck Protection Program from the CARES Act would be launched the next day to begin providing $350 billion in small business loans. The FDA approved the first coronavirus antibody test, developed by Cellex. Secretary Pompeo reported that the State Department had brought home 30,000 Americans stranded overseas due to the virus and by April 8 they had repatriated 50,000. On April 3, the administration announced voluntary CDC guidelines recommending that Americans wear non-medical, fabric or cloth face masks. That day Trump also announced that Anthem would waive copays for coronavirus treatment for sixty days. He further reported that the administration had secured from hoarders 200,000 N95 masks, 130,000 surgical masks, and 600,000 gloves for distribution to health-care workers.

April 5: President Trump said the administration had stockpiled 29 million doses of hydroxychloroquine. FEMA sent 19.1 million doses to cities across the country by April 14. On April 6, Trump announced that FDA had approved Inovio's potential vaccine for a clinical trial and that ten potential coronavirus therapeutic agents were in active trials and another fifteen were in plans for clinical trials. By April 9, there were nineteen potential therapies being tested and another twenty-six in active planning for clinical trials. Also on April 6, HHS said it would purchase fifteen-minute coronavirus tests from Abbott for the Strategic National Stockpile.[50]

April 9: The Federal Reserve announced new lending programs of up to $2.3 trillion for businesses and state and local governments.[51] Further, the USDA announced that farmers would be given one year to repay marketing assistance loans to protect them from having to sell crops to make loan payments.[52]

April 10: President Trump reported he would convene a bipartisan council of business and medical leaders, called "Opening Our Country Council," to advise the administration on reopening the economy.[53] On April 11, he approved a major disaster declaration for Wyoming, making it the first time in American history that a major disaster had been declared for all fifty states. On April 13, Trump announced that infection rates had remained flat over the weekend in America and that 3 million tests had been completed, with 150,000 new tests being conducted each day.[54]

April 14: Trump said that the biggest decision he would ever have to make was when and how to reopen the country.[55] Two days later, believing the nation had "passed the peak" in new cases, he announced a three-phase plan with new federal guidelines to restart the economy, saying, "To preserve the health of Americans, we must preserve the health of our economy. We are not opening all at once, but one careful step at a time."[56] The guidelines were approved by Dr. Birx, Dr. Fauci, and FDA head Dr. Stephen Hahn. Under the guidelines, state governors would be given wide latitude to reopen based on local conditions.[57]

Each state's opening would progress in three phases. To advance to the next phase a state must show a downward trajectory of cases for fourteen days and demonstrate hospital capacity sufficient to handle any flare-ups. At the time the administration announced these guidelines, some twenty-nine states were already eligible for phase one, though the decision would be left up to their governors.

Under all phases people should continue to practice good hygiene and the sick should stay at home. The guidelines for phase one would be slightly more relaxed than those already in place. Vulnerable people (the elderly and those with serious underlying health conditions) should continue to remain home as much as possible, and members of households with vulnerable residents who reenter society should be careful to isolate from them. Socializing in groups of more than ten people would be discouraged unless social distancing could be maintained. Nonessential travel should be minimized. Telework should be encouraged, and returning to work should occur in phases. Common areas in workplaces should be closed. Schools, day care centers, and bars should remain closed, but restaurants, movie theaters, sporting venues, places of worship, and gyms could be opened provided strict physical distancing is maintained. Elective surgeries could resume on an outpatient basis.[58]

During phase two, vulnerable people should remain at home and those living with them should be careful to isolate from them within the home. People should still maximize physical distance from others, and social settings of more than fifty people should be avoided unless social distancing can be practiced. Nonessential travel can resume. Telework would still be encouraged and common areas in workplaces should still be closed. Schools, day cares, and camps could be opened. Visits to senior care facilities and hospitals should be prohibited. Large venues—restaurants, movie theaters, sporting venues, and places of worship—can operate by observing moderate physical distance protocols. Gyms can operate under strict physical distancing and sanitation protocols, and bars may open "with diminished standing-room occupancy, where applicable and appropriate."[59]

Under phase three, vulnerable individuals could go back out in public but must practice physical distancing. Visits to hospitals and nursing homes could resume, though people who interact with patients and residents must diligently practice hygiene. Unrestricted staffing of work sites could resume. Restaurants, movie theaters, sporting venues, and places of worship could now operate under limited physical distancing protocols. Bars could operate with increased standing-room occupancy.

• • •

President Trump's approach to reopening the economy was balanced, seeking to reignite growth without reexposing Americans to unnecessary risk. But there's no satisfying the left—because they don't want to be satisfied. Never weighing Trump's actions fairly, they reflexively oppose everything he does, and they were true to form here as well—as Trump was adhering to the scientists' guidance, Nancy Pelosi dismissed him as a science denier. Why anyone pays attention to this hyperpartisan attack rhetoric is a mystery to me. For every Trump action, they seem to have a pre-crafted denunciation just waiting to drop. They are destructive agents incapable of contributing solutions to the nation's problems.

The left was determined to keep the economy closed regardless of the damage it was causing the very people whose interests they pretend to represent. As unemployment skyrocketed due to the shutdown, they showed shocking disregard for the plight of American workers who were increasingly anxious about how they'd pay the next month's rent. New York governor Andrew Cuomo cavalierly dismissed desperate people protesting the shutdown, saying, "If you want to go to work, go take the job as an essential worker. Do it tomorrow."[60] AOC did her part, calling for a national boycott in which Americans would categorically refuse to go to work.[61] Meanwhile, as the Democrats were delaying Republican attempts to replenish depleted emergency funds for small businesses, Queen Pelosi released a video of herself showing off the gourmet ice cream collection in her deluxe refrigerator-freezer.[62]

The Democrats' primary focus before the general election was on destroying Trump. In their minds they had no choice. Impeachment had backfired, and Trump was flying high before the virus fell into their laps like a political gift from the gods. They had to capitalize on it and cripple Trump enough to defeat him in November.

Never forget the Democrats' abominable behavior when they parade themselves as the party of compassion. I've always told you that they are the opposite, and they vindicated me again.

President Trump's masterful leadership during this entire timeline shows his instincts as incredibly superior to his partisan, opportunistic critics. Ten days after the first known case in the United States, he instituted the travel ban on China. Then he instituted the first quarantine in more than fifty years, followed by subsequent travel bans. It is incalculable how many more Americans would have contracted the virus and died had he not done so. Remember that Joe Biden called the travel ban "hysterical, xenophobic, and fearmongering." Following these crucial actions, President Trump implemented the largest and fastest medical mobilization in the history of mankind. Democrats were too busy impeaching him to even pay attention.

Meanwhile, Democrats made the deadliest decisions in this entire saga. Governor Andrew Cuomo issued a directive on March 25 that nursing homes must take in COVID-19 patients, followed by Governor Tom Wolf's same decision in Pennsylvania on March 29, followed by Governor Phil Murphy in New Jersey on April 6, Governor Gretchen Whitmer in Michigan on April 15, and Governor Gavin Newsom in California on April 24.

THE MEDIA MOB GOES
ALL IN ON THE "TRUMPVIRUS"

You might think the spread of a pandemic would provoke the media to temporarily drop their constant Trump bashing and inform the American public about the relevant facts needed to protect their health. But you'd be wrong. As the coronavirus spread, the media marched in lockstep with the Democrats, reporting the story through the warped prism of attacking Trump. "Let's Call It Trumpvirus," declared *New York Times* columnist Gail Collins on February 26, following that headline with the subhead "If you're feeling awful, you know who to blame." [63] "Trump Makes Us Ill," wrote her fellow *New York Times* columnist Maureen Dowd three days later. [64] *New York Times* columnist Bret Stephens labeled the coronavirus "Trump's 'Chernobyl.'" [65] The

New Yorker graced their cover with a drawing of Trump screaming with a medical face mask around his eyes.[66]

The media's amnesia is unbelievable—they themselves systematically downplayed the virus for months after the outbreak. Here's just a sample of the early coverage:

- "Why we should be skeptical of the Chinese coronavirus quarantine."—*Washington Post*, January 24, 2020
- "Don't worry about the coronavirus. Worry about the flu."—*BuzzFeed*, January 29, 2020
- "Is this going to be a deadly pandemic? No."—*Vox* (now-deleted tweet), January 29, 2020
- "Get a grippe, America. The flu is a much bigger threat than coronavirus, for now."—*Washington Post*, February 1, 2020
- "Who Says It's Not Safe to Travel to China?"—*New York Times*, February 5, 2020
- "Coronavirus, with zero American fatalities, is dominating headlines, while the flu is the real threat."—*Daily Beast*, February 7, 2020
- "Coronavirus is not going to cause a major issue in the United States."—Dr. David Agus, *CBS This Morning Saturday*, February 8, 2020
- "The risk [of coronavirus in America] is low. The risk, however, for the flu is through the roof."—Dr. Jennifer Caudle, *CNN Newsroom*, February 15, 2020
- "So if you're freaked out at all about the coronavirus, you should be more concerned about the flu."—Anderson Cooper, CNN, March 4, 2020

Once the virus's impact became undeniable, the blame-Trump media brigade changed course and decided the outbreak was a historic catastrophe caused by Trump. Because they believed the deeper the crisis was, the more damage it would do to the president. Shockingly, many of them sounded like cheerleaders for the virus. MSNBC host Nicole Wallace claimed the virus could have a "silver lining" because it caused "all of the president's sins from his first three years to catch up with him."[67] They'd even show contempt for the American people and denigrate our whole country when it was useful for bashing Trump. Referring to media reports that Trump once referred to certain places as "sh*thole countries," GQ Magazine's Julia Ioffe asked, "Who's the sh*thole country now?" while retweeting a report that America had the world's highest number of confirmed coronavirus cases.[68] It's like the media was trying to prove me right that they're a purely destructive force for the country.

The coronavirus crisis came at just the right time for the media mob, because they were in desperate need of a new line of attack on the president. They had failed in two separate efforts to remove Trump from office—once through the Russian collusion hoax and once through the appalling impeachment on the Ukraine hoax. The coronavirus outbreak presented a third opportunity to get rid of Trump, this time by making him unelectable in 2020 by blaming the virus on him.

And the mob went all in. An analysis of the first hundred days of coronavirus-related stories on the Washington Post's front page showed that negative stories about Trump outnumbered positive ones by an incredible 25–1 ratio. "Trump's error-filled speech rattled rather than reassured" and "70 days of denial, delays and dysfunction" were typical attacks—and mind you, these were supposedly news stories, not opinion columns—while the only two positive stories did not even focus on the president but on Dr. Anthony Fauci and Treasury secretary Steven Mnuchin.[69] The Post also argued that the economic damage of the virus shutdown somehow diminished Trump's previous stellar economic record, claiming, "The Coronavirus crisis is exposing how the economy was not as strong as it seemed."[70]

The get-Trump strategy was clear in the media's hysterical response to the China travel ban. Citing critics warning that travel bans "are unnecessary and could generate a racist backlash against Chinese people," the Atlantic warned that Trump might now "double down on xenophobic suspicions."[71] CNN also worried that the ban would have the "backfire" effect of "stigmatizing countries and ethnicities."[72] Apparently, travel bans are politically incorrect, and as always, political correctness takes priority over everything else for the media, including even Americans' health and safety. Trump's later travel ban on Europe was harder to portray as being racist, but the media attacked it anyway, with CNBC reporting, "Trump's travel ban on many European countries is 'politically motivated,' analysts say."[73]

The media's racism accusations reached a comical extreme. Trump haters were outraged when Secretary of State Mike Pompeo called the virus the "Wuhan coronavirus," referring to the Chinese city where the outbreak began. They were also crazed by House Minority Leader Kevin McCarthy's tweet referring to the "Chinese coronavirus." "Academics have ranted the practice leads to stigma and racism," reported the *Guardian*.[74] Ferreting out the real important news as a deadly virus was spreading worldwide, CNN published an article denouncing the "lack of diversity" in a photo of officials briefing President Trump on the pandemic.[75]

When Congressman Paul A. Gosar announced on Twitter that he would self-quarantine after having been exposed to someone who had tested positive for the "Wuhan Virus," the race-obsessed media mob went ballistic. Apparently unaware that the mainstream media had been using the term "Wuhan virus" for weeks, MSNBC's Chris Hayes called Gosar's tweet "astoundingly gross," and David Gura called it "racist."[76] The media also exploded when Trump referred to the coronavirus as a "foreign virus"—which of course it is. CNN's Jim Acosta raised the specter of "xenophobia,"[77] while *New Yorker* staff writer Susan Glasser took offense at Trump's "militaristic, nationalistic language."[78] Amazingly, after China somehow birthed this virus, covered it up, and lied about it, the American media viewed it as an abomination to talk about its origins in China.

When Trump justifiably denounced the Democrats' politicization of the virus as "their new hoax," the media widely misreported Trump as having said the virus itself was a hoax. During a presidential press conference on the virus, *Daily Caller* writer Chuck Ross noted that reporters asked Trump two questions about his use of the term "hoax" and asked no questions of the assembled experts about how the disease might spread through the United States. "This press conference is insane," Ross said.[79]

Ross was right. Trump's daily press conferences were an object lesson in media bias. While the president and his experts tried to inform the American people about the virus's trajectory, the government's economic assistance efforts, and prospects for reopening the economy, many reporters were busy trying to pin the blame for the virus directly on Trump. In one exchange, *New York* magazine correspondent Olivia Nuzzi asked Trump, "If an American president loses more Americans over the course of six weeks than died in the entirety of the Vietnam War, does he deserve to be re-elected?"[80] Former White House spokesman Ari Fleischer criticized Nuzzi's question on Twitter, noting that it was designed purely to "provoke," not to provide any useful information to viewers. Showing the class and restraint typical of the mob, Nuzzi replied by tweeting at Fleischer, "Oh shut the f*ck up."[81]

Reporters in the briefings were completely indistinguishable from Resistance activists. They developed a strategy of trying to drive a wedge between Trump and his medical experts, Dr. Fauci and Dr. Birx, by encouraging the doctors to contradict the president or disagree with his policies or actions. At an April 13, 2020, press conference, Dr. Fauci tried to clear the air after the media attacked Trump over a comment Fauci had made indicating that more lives would have been saved if mitigation efforts had been enacted earlier. Fauci explained he was not accusing Trump of a late response—in fact, he said, Trump enacted strong mitigation measures after the first time Fauci recommended them. Robbed of another get-Trump narrative, a reporter asked Fauci if he was providing that explanation voluntarily or if Trump put him up to it. Disgusted, Fauci put his hands up and said, "Everything I do is voluntarily—please, don't even imply that."[82] The press conference enraged CNN, which displayed these captions on the screen:

- "Trump uses task force briefing to try and rewrite history on coronavirus response"
- "Trump melts down in angry response to reports he ignored virus warnings"
- "Trump refuses to acknowledge any mistakes"
- "Trump attacks media after series of reports he ignored warnings as virus spread"
- "Angry Trump uses propaganda video produced by government employees at taxpayer's expense"
- "Angry Trump turns briefing into propaganda session"[83]

So CNN was angrily melting down as it accused Trump of having an angry meltdown.

The mob was also provoked by Dr. Birx, who had the audacity to express agreement with the president and support his policies. For the media, that's over the line. The only acceptable position toward Trump *on every issue and every controversy* is outright condemnation— anything short of that is treason against the press corps. When Dr. Birx questioned predictions of a shortage of ventilators and hospital beds— a shortage that never happened—reporters tried to smack her back into line. The *New York Times'* Noah Weiland and Maggie Haberman claimed Dr. Birx has "accommodated herself to the political winds with the kind of presidential flattery that Mr. Trump demands from aides."[84] In a tweet pitching her story, Haberman all but portrayed Dr. Birx as having been brainwashed. "An astute Trump adviser once described the president as 'turning' people so they start to adopt his views, in a binary Trump sees as him vs media. Some fear Dr. Deborah Birx is the latest example," she said.[85] More bluntly, when Dr. Birx praised Trump's attention to detail and understanding of the relevant data, *Vox's* Aaron Rupar denounced her comments as "shocking, hackish stuff."[86] Viewing Trump as some sort of superhuman force for evil, *Mother Jones's* David Corn chimed in, "Trump ruins everything and everyone he touches."[87]

Later, when Dr. Birx criticized the media for blatantly taking out of context Trump's comments about studying the possibility of using disinfectants and ultraviolet light to fight the virus inside infected patients, *Rolling Stone*'s Peter Wade accused her of "pandering." "The public's need to trust the media during a pandemic is of utmost importance, and one of America's top health officials sowing seeds of distrust is dangerous," Wade warned.[88] You got that? That's the media warning you that no one should question the media.

In case that point is too subtle, the *Atlantic* ran a story by two professors in which the authors approvingly cited increased online censorship of coronavirus topics and argued for Chinese-style internet censorship in America. "In the great debate of the past two decades about freedom versus control of the network," they said, "China was largely right and the United States was largely wrong. Significant monitoring and speech control are inevitable components of a mature and flourishing internet, and governments must play a large role in these practices to ensure that the internet is compatible with a society's norms and values."[89]

Who can argue with that Orwellian "logic"—that we need "significant monitoring and speech control" to have a "flourishing internet"? Seeing the American media argue *for* censorship is shocking, but they obviously think it'll be their political opponents who will be censored, not them. And I'm sure that would be true at first. But this is a dangerous door to open, and it's easy to imagine how what begins as "limited" speech restrictions against conservatives will expand and eventually boomerang against the mainstream media in one way or another.

The unhinged media tried again and again to get Americans to understand that President Trump was responsible for people *dying*. They sounded ghoulishly gleeful when an Arizona woman claimed her husband had died after the pair responded to Trump's hopeful comments about hydroxychloroquine by drinking a fish tank cleaner containing a chemical with a similar name. The woman stated that they drank the chemical after seeing Trump on "every channel" on TV saying it was "basically pretty much a cure." She warned afterward, "Don't believe anything the President says."[90] The media understood that was their cue. "The president has blood on his hands. There's literally no debate about it," said the *Intercept*'s Mehdi Hasan.[91]

For the get-Trump media, the story was too good to check. But in interviews with the *Washington Free Beacon*, people who knew the couple cast doubt on the story. One said it was hard to believe the man would foolishly swallow fish tank cleaner since he was an intelligent, retired mechanical engineer.[92] It also seems strange that the woman would drink hydroxychloroquine supposedly at Trump's command, considering she had donated thousands of dollars to *Democratic* causes and candidates during Trump's presidency. Although she initially blamed her own actions on Trump, she later backpedaled and told the *Beacon*, "We weren't big supporters of [Trump], but we did see that they were using [hydroxychloroquine] in China and stuff." Police are now investigating the incident, and I wouldn't be surprised if there is more to come on this story.[93]

It was inevitable that the mob would extend these accusations to Fox News—the only network that didn't blame Trump for a virus spreading out of China. In a column titled "Fox's Fake News Contagion," the *New York Times*' Kara Swisher accused Fox News generally and me personally of spreading "dangerous misinformation" in the early days of the coronavirus crisis. Using her own elderly mother as a prop for the story, Swisher explained that her mom refused to believe Swisher's warnings about the danger of the virus because of misinformation her mother heard on Fox News. Her mom got her information on the virus exclusively from Fox, Swisher said, to the point that "it sometimes feels like Fox News is eating my mother's brain." But don't worry, the story had a happy ending because eventually her mom began disbelieving Fox, even though she continued watching it.[94]

You almost have to admire the nerve Swisher shows in completely rewriting history just a few months after the fact. First, any Fox viewer knows that our coverage from the beginning was informative and reflected the best scientific understanding of the virus as it broke out and spread. I had three different physicians including Dr. Fauci on my January 28 radio show to discuss the virus's likely trajectory, the challenges of tracking its spread, the incubation period, and its asymptomatic transmission. This was my whole approach to the virus from the beginning—to get out the facts. But Swisher, and a lot of the rest of the media herd, portrayed any criticism of the media's get-Trump coverage of the virus as an evil attempt to "play down" the threat. This is the real misinformation, but you know that only if you actually watch Fox News or listen to my radio show, which the target audience for this propaganda do not regularly do.

In her hit piece, Swisher totally ignored huge parts of the public record that contradict her imaginary world where Fox downplayed the virus while the mainstream media got it right. There's no mention of *Vox* guaranteeing there would be no pandemic, or *BuzzFeed*, the *Washington Post*, the *Daily Beast*, and Anderson Cooper insisting the flu was a bigger threat, or Swisher's fellow *New York Times* columnist denouncing Trump's China travel ban and asking whether it was even necessary. There was no reference to Nancy Pelosi encouraging tourists to congregate in San Francisco's Chinatown at the end of February, the same time Swisher claims she was so concerned about her mom. No, in Swisher's fake universe, none of that happened, and everyone reported responsibly except the brain-eating conservatives at Fox News who were corrupting her helpless mother.

The Democrats and the media mob are working overtime to ensure the virus brings down Trump's presidency and torpedoes his reelection. But his handling of this crisis, in fact, has been his finest moment. Can you imagine if Sleepy Joe Biden were in charge of the response? They'd trot him out once a week to mechanically read a dumb speech off a teleprompter, and meanwhile no one would have any clue who was really calling the shots. With Trump, it's crystal clear who's in charge. And if you look outside the mainstream media, it's also clear how incredibly effective his response has been.

CONCLUSION

When I began writing this book the coronavirus had not yet reached pandemic proportions, but the American left's rapid acceleration toward socialism had long since begun. While President Trump's America-first, capitalist agenda was making great strides in beating back this socialist menace, the national emergency fed the left's enthusiasm for an expansion of federal powers. They eagerly exploited the crisis to try to cram their massive leftist agenda down our throats, including a smorgasbord of transformative Green New Deal items that had zero connection to the virus. Nancy Pelosi even said the coronavirus should open the door to adopting a universal basic income.[1] Their response to the crisis should have focused on saving lives and minimizing the economic damage, but it only whet their appetites for more federal control over our money and our lives.

As the virus was approaching peak levels in America, with hundreds of thousands being infected and tens of thousands dying, President Trump urged governors to take charge of their own states, assuring them that the federal government would provide adequate production and stockpiling of equipment for distribution to the states as needed. Some criticized Trump for being too authoritative while others were demanding he be more so. Though Trump threatened to put the federal hammer on certain recalcitrant companies to up their production

of certain supplies, the threats themselves were usually effective without further action, and throughout he assured Americans he strongly
preferred to defer to the governors to manage their own states.

So even during a declared federal emergency, President Trump's
conservative instincts guided him to resist exercising excessive
power—and this applied not just to management of the medical supply chain but also to decisions to shut down and reopen economies,
which he largely left to the discretion of the states. While the success
of Trump's approach validates our federalist constitutional structure,
Democrats will argue that only the federal government could keep the
nation financially afloat during this period, and that this proves the
glories of central planning.

The left will look back on this dark period as evidence of the wonders of federal power without lamenting the loss of individual liberty
that always ensues. Conservatives, by contrast, will regard it as a time
that conclusively shows that the American private sector—small and
large businesses, individual entrepreneurs, manufacturers and industries, and white- and blue-collar workers throughout the land—is the
lifeblood of the American economy; not the public sector, which creates no wealth on its own. Conservatives will reflect with pride on the
American spirit and the essential role of the private sector in ramping
up production to meet government needs. They will celebrate Americans' eagerness to reopen the economy and resume their lives as proof
of their dedication to liberty and their precious constitutional rights.
Though President Trump has been given little credit for this, the virus
exposed America's precarious dependence on foreign nations for necessary essentials and vindicated Trump's long-held determination to
restore America's self-sufficiency as a manufacturing powerhouse.

You get the point. The left is relentless in pushing their extreme
agenda. They were horrifyingly committed to statism before the virus;
they are even more so today. You can count on it, which makes this
year's presidential and congressional elections exponentially more
important than they already were. The left has now fully unmasked

itself. The American electorate will face a clear choice in November between those who love America and want to protect it, and those who resent it and want it to become another failed socialist state. The Democrats' media machine may try to downplay the party's extremism, but there's no longer any denying it, as I've shown throughout these pages.

Prior to the virus, we watched Democrats and the media deny the spectacular success of the American economy under President Trump. Their message during the post-virus recovery is predictable: they'll say the economy was a disaster waiting to happen and the virus just hastened the inevitable. Or they'll admit that there were signs of growth but that they benefited only the rich—despite all the evidence to the contrary. But we can't let them get away with it.

No matter how much devastation the virus caused, it in no way erases Trump's phenomenal economic record. Without it, we wouldn't have been able to absorb those losses. This makes resuming his agenda even more important going forward. Just as he led the fight against the virus, he has been leading the fight to unleash our economy once again.

President Trump knows America can recapture its economic vitality—and he leaped into action to prove it. Having fulfilled his campaign promises on economic growth and demonstrated decisive crisis leadership, hasn't he earned our trust? Having resurrected the American economy when ill-informed economic policies had driven it into the dirt, how much more so will he lead us to recovery?

Not only must President Trump's economic agenda be reinvigorated, but his contagious spirit of hope and optimism is every bit as essential. His patriotism, his love for the American people, his faith in the American worker, and his unwavering belief in the free market are indispensable to America's recovery.

The left, of course, will portray Joe Biden as a steady hand, ready to deliver this nation from chaos, in stark contrast to the volatile and combative Trump. Biden, they'll say, is a moderate, perfectly situated to heal our deep divisions. But as we've seen, Joe Biden is no moderate.

He is a chameleon—willing to be whomever he needs to be and say whatever he needs to say to win votes. While wooing his party's base, he is an untrustworthy panderer—moving further to the left with each passing moment, even if he conveniently veers back to the center as the election nears. If elected he'll either push, or be a pawn of others who will push, a leftist agenda.

Media propaganda aside, Biden is not a seasoned force of stability and leadership. He is a walking gaffe machine who should be nowhere near the Oval Office. He is light-years away from the person Democrats portray. In reality, he doesn't even know what office he's running for. On February 25, 2020, he mistakenly proclaimed himself "a Democratic candidate for the United States Senate." Apparently believing that some family member of his was also a candidate, he said if you don't like him you should "vote for the other Biden."[2]

Nor is President Trump the unstable monster his obsessed haters depict. He rose to the unique challenge the outbreak presented, outperforming even his strongest supporters' best expectations. No president in modern history could have better led the nation through this crisis, coordinating the public and private sectors and balancing health and economic concerns to produce the best possible results amid an unprecedented catastrophe not of his making.

It's unsettling to consider what would have happened if Biden had been in power during the crisis. He would have been wholly ill-equipped to lead America even under normal circumstances, and would certainly be ill-suited to lead during possible future outbreaks. Biden at his best would be a disaster for these times, but his obviously declining mental condition—and I say this without malice but with deep concern—makes the prospect of his presidency foreboding and alarming. We have no idea who will really be pulling the strings if he's elected. It is inconceivable that the Democratic leadership is unaware of Biden's incapacity to handle the demands of the most powerful position on the planet, but they found themselves without any other viable option when Bernie survived as his last remaining rival. If the Democrats finally throw Biden overboard because of his incompetence or allegations of sexual assault, we can be sure that his replacement—to pass muster with the leftist Democrats and their base—will be equally disastrous for the nation.

My fellow patriots, I trust that you understand as well as I do the gravity of the times we are living in. As such, I implore you to get engaged and work harder than you ever have to reelect President Trump and deliver Republican majorities in both houses of Congress. The fate of this nation and of my children and yours depends on this election. Let not your hearts be troubled. Have faith and work hard. We can and will make this happen. God bless you and God bless America.

ACKNOWLEDGMENTS

I always said I would never do another book, yet here I am. We are at a pivotal point in our nation's history, and I felt compelled to lay out what is at stake, which I hope I have accomplished to your satisfaction.

It takes tremendous time and effort to write a book, especially one as comprehensive in scope as this one. With my incredibly busy schedule I had to rely on the research assistance from my radio and television teams, and advice from certain valued friends, without which I simply wouldn't have been able to complete this project as efficiently. As such I want to sincerely thank my radio team: Lynda McLaughlin, James Grisham, Blair Cullen, Jason Mosse, Eric Stanger, Ethan Keller, and Katie Holcomb; and my television team: Tiffany Fazio, Porter Berry, Robert Samuel, Ben Miller, Christen Bloom, Andrew Luton, Drew Lynch, Stephanie Woloshin, Tim Rhodes, Irena Briganti, Carly Shanahan, and Hayley Caronia.

Thank you to everyone at Fox News for their consistent support, including Rupert and Lachlan Murdoch, Suzanne Scott, and Dianne Brandi. Much appreciation also to the radio executives with iHeartMedia whose support is also invaluable, including Bob Pittman, Rich Bressler, Julie Talbott, and Dan Metter.

Thanks to the entire team at Threshold Editions of Simon & Schuster, who believed in this book from the beginning. Specific thanks to my editor, Natasha Simons, publisher Jennifer Bergstrom, associate publisher Jennifer Long, executive publicist Jennifer Robinson, editorial assistant Maggie Loughran, production editor Al Madocs, managing editor Caroline Pallotta, art directors Lisa Litwack and John Vairo, copyeditor Tom Pitoniak, and interior designer Jamie Putorti.

Thanks also to my long-time friends Mark Levin and David Limbaugh, who reviewed the manuscript and offered valuable feedback.

Thank you to my family, who are always loving, supportive, and understanding of my long work hours and job demands.

And as always, thank you to the American people who join me in this fight to preserve America as the greatest nation in history.

NOTES

CHAPTER 1: "A REPUBLIC—IF YOU CAN KEEP IT"

1. Larry Schweikart and Michael Allen, *A Patriot's History of the United States, From Columbus's Great Discovery to the War on Terror* (New York: Sentinel, 2004), xxiv.
2. Kay Cole James, Terry Miller, et al., "2019 Index of Economic Freedom," Heritage Foundation, 2019, https://www.heritage.org/index/book/chapter-4.
3. Robert Kagan, "Benevolent Empire," Carnegie Endowment for International Peace, June 1, 1998.
4. History.com Editors, "The Marshall Plan," History.com, December 16, 2009; Paul Johnson, *A History of the American People* (New York: HarperCollins, 1997), 812.
5. Sam O'Brien, "Questioning the Marshall Plan in the Buildup to the Cold War," *University of New Hampshire Inquiry Journal*, Spring 2014.
6. Jean-Louis Panne, Andrzej Paczkowski, et al., *The Black Book of Communism: Crimes, Terror, Repression* (Cambridge, MA: Harvard University Press, 1999).
7. Kagan, "Benevolent Empire."
8. Ibid.
9. Paul K. MacDonald and Joseph M. Parent, "Trump Didn't Shrink U.S. Military Commitments Abroad—He Expanded Them," *Foreign Affairs*, December 3, 2019.
10. Leo Shane III and Joe Gould, "The Military Could See Big Changes if Democrats Win Control of Congress," *Military Times*, October 23, 2018.
11. Maegan Vazquez, "NY Gov. Andrew Cuomo Says America 'Was Never That Great,' " CNN.com, August 16, 2018.

12. Ian Schwartz, "Eric Holder to Trump: 'Exactly When Did You Think America Was Great?' " *Real Clear Politics*, March 27, 2019.
13. Ronald Reagan, "Farewell Address to the Nation," Reagan Foundation, January 11, 1989.
14. Dinesh D'Souza, *What's So Great About America?* (Washington, DC: Regnery, 2002), 32–33.
15. Wilfred M. McClay, *Land of Hope: An Invitation to the Great American Story* (New York, London: Encounter Books, 2019), 428.
16. Reagan, "Farewell Address to the Nation."
17. Ibid.
18. McClay, *Land of Hope*, 26.
19. The Editors of Encyclopaedia Britannica, "Mayflower Compact," *Encyclopaedia Britannica* (Encyclopedia Britannica, Inc., November 14, 2019), https://www.britannica.com/topic/Mayflower-Compact.
20. Peter Marshall and David Manuel, *The Light and the Glory* (Grand Rapids, MI: Fleming H. Revell, 1977), 120.
21. Paul Johnson, *A History of the American People* (New York: HarperCollins, 1997), 302.
22. The Editors of Encyclopaedia Britannica, "Mayflower Compact"; M. Stanton Evans, *The Theme Is Freedom* (Washington, DC: Regnery, 1994), 188, 193.
23. Alice M. Baldwin, *The New England Clergy and the American Revolution* (London: Forgotten Books, 2018).
24. Governor John Winthrop, "A Model of Christian Charity," 1630. From the Collections of the Massachusetts Historical Society (Boston, 1838, 3rd series: 7:31-48), https://history.hanover.edu/texts/winthmod.html.
25. Evans, *The Theme Is Freedom*, 194.
26. Baldwin, *The New England Clergy and the American Revolution*.
27. Verna G. Hall, ed., *The Christian History of the Constitution* ([n.p.]: American Christian Constitution Press, 1962), 253.
28. Marshall and Manuel, *The Light and the Glory*, 251–52.
29. Johnson, *A History of the American People*, 116.
30. D. James Kennedy and Jerry Newcombe, *What if the Bible Had Never Been Written?* (Nashville, TN: Thomas Nelson, 1998), 90.
31. Benjamin Franklin, "Constitutional Convention Address on Prayer," American Rhetoric Online Speech Bank, https://www.americanrhetoric.com/speeches/benfranklin.htm.
32. Evans, *The Theme Is Freedom*, 231–32.
33. Thomas Jefferson, *The Life and Selected Writings of Thomas Jefferson* (New York, New York: Modern Library Classics, 2004), 656.
34. Michael Novak, *On Two Wings: Humble Faith and Common Sense at the American Founding* (San Francisco: Encounter Books, 2002), 38, 42.
35. McClay, *Land of Hope*, 41.

36. "The Originality of the United States Constitution," *Yale Law Journal*, June 1896, 239.

37. W. David Stedman and La Vaughn G. Lewis, eds., "Our Ageless Constitution," National Center for Constitutional Studies, https://nccs.net/blogs/our -ageless-constitution/our-ageless-constitution.

38. Alexander Hamilton, "Introduction," Federalist No. 1, https://avalon.law .yale.edu/subject_menus/fed.asp.

39. McClay, *Land of Hope*, 76.

40. M. E. Bradford, *A Worthy Company* (Marlborough, NH: Plymouth Rock Foundation, 1982).

41. Edwin J. Feulner, Ph.D., "Preventing 'The Tyranny of the Majority,'" Heritage Foundation, March 7, 2018.

42. Novak, *On Two Wings*, 42.

43. David Barton, *Celebrate Liberty! Famous Patriotic Speeches & Sermons* (Wallbuilder Press Kindle Edition, 2013), Kindle Locations 2044-2048.

44. Stedman and Lewis, eds., "Our Ageless Constitution."

45. Ibid.

46. Abraham Lincoln, "Fragment on the Constitution and the Union (Jan. 1861), in *The Collected Works of Abraham Lincoln*, Roy P. Basler et al., eds., 1953, 168–69.

47. Abraham Lincoln, "The Gettysburg Address," November 19, 1863, https:// www.historynet.com/gettysburg-address-text.

48. McClay, *Land of Hope*, 181.

49. "We the People: The American Constitution After 200 Years, Celebrating the Nation's Charter as Problem and Solution," *Los Angeles Times*, September 13, 1987; "Rediscovering the Ideas of Liberty," National Center for Constitutional Studies, https://nccs.net/pages/resources, 2020.

50. President Ronald Reagan, "Remarks at the Annual Convention of Kiwanis International," July 6, 1987, Reagan Foundation, https://www.reaganfounda tion.org/media/128817/kiwanis.pdf.

51. McClay, *Land of Hope*, 240.

52. Ibid., 240.

53. David M. Kennedy, Lizabeth Cohen, and Thomas A. Bailey, *The American Pageant: A History of the American People* (Boston: Wadsworth, Cengage Learning Center), Kindle ed., location 14603 of 25194.

54. Ibid., location 14603–14620 of 25194.

55. Larry Schweikart and Michael Allen, *A Patriot's History of the United States: From Columbus's Great Discovery to the War on Terror* (New York: Sentinel, 2004), xxiv.

56. David Davenport, "Rugged Individualism: Dead Or Alive?" *Defining Ideas, A Hoover Institute Journal*, January 10, 2017; Kennedy, Cohen, and Bailey, *The American Pageant*, location 14603 of 25194.

57. John Burgess, *The Foundations of Political Science* (New York, 1933), 89, 90.
58. William A. Schambra and Thomas West, "The Progressive Movement and the Transformation of American Politics," Heritage Foundation, July 18, 2007.
59. C. Edward Merriam, *A History of American Political Theories* (New York: Macmillan, 1903), 311; William A. Schambra and Thomas West, "The Progressive Movement and the Transformation of American Politics."
60. Merriam, *A History of American Political Theories*, 307.
61. John Dewey, *Liberalism and Social Action* (New York: Prometheus Books, 2000), 34.
62. Ibid., 27; Schambra and West, "The Progressive Movement and the Transformation of American Politics."
63. Daniel J. Flynn, *A Conservative History of the American Left* (New York: Crown Forum, 2008), 131.
64. Schambra and West, "The Progressive Movement and the Transformation of American Politics."
65. Ronald J. Pestritto, "The Progressive Rejection of the Founding, Introductory Remarks," *The U.S. Constitution: A Reader* (Hillsdale, MI: Hillsdale College Press, 2012), 617.
66. McClay, *Land of Hope*, 246–47.
67. Madeline Osburn, "The Progressive Movement Rejected the Founders' Model for Lawmaking," *Federalist*, February 1, 2019; McClay, *Land of Hope*, 247.
68. Flynn, *A Conservative History of the American Left*, 131.
69. McClay, *Land of Hope*, 247.
70. Madeline Osburn, "The Progressive Movement Rejected the Founders' Model for Lawmaking."
71. Johnson, *A History of the American People*, 636.
72. Flynn, *A Conservative History of the American Left*, 132.
73. Schambra and West, "The Progressive Movement and the Transformation of American Politics."
74. Johnson, *A History of the American People*, 633.
75. Schambra and West, "The Progressive Movement and the Transformation of American Politics."
76. M. J. Heale, *The Sixties in America: History, Politics and Protest* (Edinburgh: Edinburgh University Press, 2001), 13–14.
77. D'Souza, *What's So Great About America?*, 147.
78. Evans, *The Theme Is Freedom*, 42.
79. Flynn, *A Conservative History of the American Left*, 132.
80. David Davenport, "Rugged Individualism: Dead or Alive?" *Defining Ideas: A Hoover Institution Journal*, January 10, 2017.

81. James Madison, "Notes on the Debates in the Federal Convention," Tuesday, September 17, 1787, Avalon Project, Yale Law School, https://avalon.law.yale.edu/18th_century/debates_917.asp.

CHAPTER 2: RISE OF THE RADICALS

1. Nathaniel Sheppart Jr., "Chicago Home of a Friend Was Refuge for Miss Dohrn," *New York Times*, December 5, 1980, A22.
2. John Kifner, "A Radical 'Declaration' Warns of an Attack by Weathermen," *New York Times*, May 25, 1970; "Women on FBI's Most Wanted List," CBS News, https://www.cbsnews.com/pictures/women-on-fbis-most-wanted-list/4/; FBI's Former Ten Most Wanted Fugitive #314, https://www.fbi.gov/wanted/topten/topten-history/hires_images/FBI-314-BernardineRae Dohrn.jpg/view.
3. Stanley Kurtz, "Obama and Ayers Pushed Radicalism on Schools," *Wall Street Journal*, September 23, 2008; Bernie Quigley, "Obama and Bill Ayers: Together from the Beginning," *Hill*, September 24, 2008.
4. Mort Kondracke, "Democrats' Far-Left Lean Risks More Than the Presidency," *Real Clear Politics*, July 18, 2019.
5. Hunter Schwarz, "Obama's Latest 'Evolution' on Gay Marriage: He Lied About Opposing It, Axelrod Says," *Washington Post*, February 10, 2015.
6. Ben Smith, "Obama Rejects Single Payer," *Politico*, June 15, 2009, and "Barack Obama on Single Payer in 2003," Physicians for a National Health Program, June 4, 2008, http://www.pnhp.org/news/2008/june/barack_obama_on_sing.php.
7. Amy Chozick, "Obama: 'If They Bring a Knife to the Fight, We Bring a Gun,'" Washington Wire, *Wall Street Journal*, June 14, 2008.
8. Barack Obama, "Obama Says 'Argue with Neighbors, Get in Their Face,'" YouTube, September 18, 2008.
9. Mark Knoller, "Obama Casts Republicans as Slurpee Sippers," CBS News *Political Hotsheet*, October 8, 2010.
10. Susan Jones, "'Spread the Wealth Around' Comment Comes Back to Haunt Obama," CNS News, October 15, 2008.
11. Kent Hoover, "4 Reasons Why 'You Didn't Build That' Still Haunts Obama," *Biz Journals*, July 20, 2012.
12. Angie Drobnic Holan, "Lie of the Year: 'If you Like Your Health Care Plan, You Can Keep It,'" PolitiFact, December 12, 2013.
13. Editorial Board, "The Democratic Divide," *Wall Street Journal*, July 31, 2019.
14. Lydia Saad, "U.S. Still Leans Conservative, but Liberals Keep Recent Gains," Gallup, January 8, 2019.
15. Stephan Dinan, "'It's about COVID': Nancy Pelosi Retreats on Stimulus 'Wish List,'" *Washington Times*, March 24, 2020.

16. Nicole Darrah, "Pelosi Plays Down Influence of AOC Wing of Democrats, Says It's 'Like 5 People,' " Fox News, April 14, 2019.

17. Karine Jean-Pierre, "MoveOn: 2020 Democratic Nominee Must be Unapologetically Progressive," USA Today, January 6, 2019.

18. Donica Phifer, "Congresswoman Rashida Tlaib Refers to Donald Trump in Speech, Tells Crowd 'We' Will 'Impeach This Motherf---Er,' " Newsweek, January 4, 2019.

19. Scott Jennings, "Reps. Alexandria Ocasio-Cortez, Rashida Tlaib Are Honest Democrats. And Their Party Can't Stand It," USA Today, January 10, 2019.

20. Ibid.

21. Ibid.

22. Brett Samuels, "Joe Lieberman Says He Hopes Ocasio-Cortez Is Not 'the Future' of Democratic Party," Hill, January 10, 2019.

23. Morgan Gstalter, "Ocasio-Cortez Responds to Joe Lieberman's Criticisms: 'New Party, Who Dis?' " Hill, January 11, 2019.

24. Joe Heim, "Nancy Pelosi on Impeaching Trump: 'He's Just Not Worth It,' " Washington Post Magazine, March 11, 2019.

25. Jonathan S. Tobin, "Ocasio-Cortez, Tlaib, and Omar Are Driving Democrats' Agenda," National Review, January 10, 2019.

26. David Siders, "You Don't Just Get to Say That You're Progressive': The Left Moves to Defend Its Brand," Politico, December 9, 2018.

27. Ibid.

28. Ibid.

29. "Bernie Sanders No Such Thing as a Pro-Life Dem, 'Being Pro-Choice Is An Absolutely Essential Part," GOP War Room YouTube channel, February 8, 2020, https://www.youtube.com/watch?v=r-QgmvSx1Cs&feature=youtu.be.

30. Sean Illing, " 'We're Losing Our Damn Minds': James Carville Unloads on the Democratic Party," Vox, February 7, 2020, https://www.vox.com/policy -and-politics/2020/2/7/21123518/trump-2020-election-democratic-party -james-carville.

31. Juana Summers, "Obama Says Democrats Don't Always Need to Be 'Politically Woke,' " NPR, October 31, 2019.

32. J. M. Rieger, "Trump Says Democrats Used to Be for New Border Barriers. He's Right," Washington Post, January 19, 2019.

33. Reid J. Epstein and Linda Qiu, "Fact-Checking Trump's Claims That Democrats Are Radical Socialists," New York Times, July 20, 2019.

34. Ibid.

35. James S. Robbins, "Progressive Democrats Let Their 'Policy Freak Flags' Fly, Want to Take Party to Far Left," USA Today, January 15, 2019.

36. Thomas B. Edsall, "How Far Left Is Too Far Left for 2020 Democrats?" New York Times, April 10, 2019.

37. "Political Polarization in the American Public," Pew Research Center, June 12, 2014.

38. Tim Haines, "Elizabeth Warren: Men Who Oppose Gay Marriage Should 'Just Marry One, Woman,' 'If You Can Find One,' " *Real Clear Politics*, October 11, 2019.

39. Ibid.

40. Caleb Parke, "Beto Threatens Tax-Exempt Status of Churches if They Don't Support Gay Marriage," Fox News, October 11, 2019.

41. Tucker Higgins, "Joe Biden Says He Now Supports Federal Funding of Abortion, in Second Apparent Reversal," NBC, June 6, 2019.

42. Emily Ekins, "Millennials Don't Know What 'Socialism' Means," *Reason*, July 16, 2019.

43. Kathleen Elkins, "Most Young Americans Prefer Socialism to Capitalism, New Report Finds," CNBC, August 14, 2018, http://www.cnbc.com/2018/08/14/fewer-than-half-of-young-americans-are-positive-about-capitalism.html.

44. Mohamed Younis, "Four in 10 Americans Embrace Some Form of Socialism," Gallup, May 20, 2019.

45. Ibid.

46. Scott Rasmussen, "Is Socialism a Threat to America, to Democrats or Both?" *Townhall*, February 21, 2019, https://townhall.com/columnists/scottrasmussen/2019/02/21/is-socialism-a-threat-to-america-to-democrats-or-both-n2541951.

47. Peter Beinart, "Will the Left Go Too Far?" *Atlantic*, December 2018.

48. Ibid.

49. Ibid.

50. Ibid.

51. Ibid.

52. J. Edward Moreno, "Nadler Calls Trump a 'Dictator' on Senate Floor," *Hill*, January 24, 2020.

53. Marc A. Thiessen, "Trump Isn't the Biggest Threat to the Constitution. Democrats Are," *Chicago Tribune*, March 22, 2019.

54. Ryan Saavedra, "Breaking: Democrats Introduce Bill to Eliminate Electoral College," *Daily Wire*, January 3, 2019.

55. Li Zhou, "Senate Democrats Introduce a Constitutional Amendment to Abolish the Electoral College," *Vox*, April 3, 2019.

56. Daniel Davis, " 'Save Our States' Is Fighting to Keep the Electoral College Alive," *Daily Signal*, November 13, 2019.

57. Ibid.

58. Ibid.

59. Rea Hederman and David Azerrad, Ph.D., "Report: Poverty and Inequality, Defending the Dream: Why Income Inequality Doesn't Threaten Opportunity," Heritage Foundation, September 13, 2012.

60. Ibid.
61. Council of Economic Advisers, "President Trump's Policies Continue to Benefit All Americans, Especially the Disadvantaged," Whitehouse.gov, September 10, 2019.
62. Ella Nilsen, "Joe Biden Has Been Talking About Income Inequality a Lot Lately—to His Rich Donors," *Vox*, June 24, 2019.
63. Akhil Rajasekar, "Democrats Harp on Income Inequality Because They Don't Know Now to Help the Poor," *Federalist*, November 18, 2018.
64. "Rigging the Election—Video I: Clinton Campaign and DNC Incite Violence at Trump Rallies," Project Veritas YouTube channel, October 17, 2016, https://www.youtube.com/watch?v=5IuJGHuIkzY&feature=youtu.be.

CHAPTER 3: WELCOME TO FANTASYLAND: THE DEMOCRATS' 2020 AGENDA

1. Karl W. Smith, "Trump's Economy Is Working for Minorities," Bloomberg, November 6, 2019.
2. Paul Krugman, "The Economic Fallout," *New York Times*, November 9, 2016.
3. "Full Transcript: Democratic Presidential Debates, Night 1," *New York Times*, June 26, 2019.
4. Editorial Board, "The Democratic Divide," *Wall Street Journal*, July 31, 2019.
5. Ibid.
6. Ibid.
7. https://twitter.com/BarackObama/status/1229432034650722304?s=20.
8. Hannity Staff, " 'Wake Up Call': CNN's Van Jones Says Trump Helping African-American Communities in 'Real Life,' " Hannity.com, February 5, 2020.
9. Editorial Board, "The Democratic Divide," *Wall Street Journal*, July 31, 2019.
10. Griffin Connolly, "The Detroit Trump Diss Track: Debating Democrats Blister the President," *Roll Call*, August 1, 2019.
11. Ibid.
12. Ibid.
13. Lara Bazelon, "Kamala Harris Was Not a 'Progressive Prosecutor,' " *New York Times*, January 17, 2019.
14. Connolly, "The Detroit Trump Diss Track."
15. Ibid.
16. Ibid.
17. Jessica Chasmar, "Nancy Pelosi pre-ripped pages during SOTU speech, Trump campaign says," *Washington Times*, February 6, 2020.
18. Mike DeBonis, "Pelosi Laces into Trump, Defends Tearing Up His State of the Union Speech," *Washington Post*, February 6, 2020.
19. Joe Heim, "Nancy Pelosi on Impeaching Trump: 'He's Just Not Worth It,' " *Washington Post*, March 11, 2019.

20. DeBonis, "Pelosi Laces Into Trump, Defends Tearing Up His State of the Union Speech."

21. John Verhovek and Molly Nagle, "Bernie Sanders Endorses Joe Biden, They Announce 'Working Groups' on Policy Issues," ABC News, April 13, 2020.

22. https://twitter.com/BarackObama/status/1250088269502709762?mod=arti cle_inline.

23. Doug Mainwaring, "Joe Biden: 'Transgender Equality Is the Civil Rights Issue of Our Time'," LifeSite News, January 27, 2020.

24. David Montgomery, "AOC's Chief of Change," Washington Post Magazine, July 10, 2019.

25. Diana Budds, "The Green New Deal Is Really About Designing An Entirely New World," Curbed, September 19, 2019.

26. Benjamin J. Hulac and Elvina Nawaguna, "The ABCs of the Green New Deal," Roll Call, March 25, 2019.

27. Bill McKibben, "The Necessity and Political Savvy of the Green New Deal," Washington Post Magazine, November 12, 2019.

28. Editorial Board, "Vote on the Green New Deal," Wall Street Journal, February 11, 2019; "Cosponsors: H.Res.109—116th Congress (2019-2020)," Congress.gov.

29. Michael Grunwald, "The Trouble with the 'Green New Deal,' " Politico Magazine, January 15, 2019.

30. Ibid.

31. Ibid.

32. Lisa Friedman, "What is the Green New Deal? A Climate Proposal, Explained," New York Times, February 21, 2019.

33. Resolution, Recognizing the Duty of the Federal Government to Create a Green New Deal, 116th Congress, 1st Session, February 5, 2019, https://assets .documentcloud.org/documents/5729033/Green-New-Deal-FINAL.pdf.

34. This partial list was taken from a larger list compiled by Salvador Rizzo, "What's Actually in the 'Green New Deal' from Democrats?" Washington Post, February 11, 2019. The list comes from the resolution itself: https:// assets.documentcloud.org/documents/5729033/Green-New-Deal-FINAL .pdf#page=8.

35. Javier Blas, "The U.S. Just Became Net Oil Exporter for the First Time in 75 Years," Bloomberg, December 6, 2018.

36. Matt Egan, "America Is Now the Largest Oil Producer," CNN Money, September 12, 2018, https://money.cnn.com/2018/09/12/investing/us-oil-pro duction-russia-saudi-arabia/index.html.

37. Resolution, Recognizing the Duty of the Federal Government to Create a Green New Deal.

38. Joseph Curl, "The Laughable, Pathetic, Infantile Green New Deal Sets a New Low for Democrats," Washington Times, February 8, 2019.

39. Rizzo, "What's Actually in the 'Green New Deal' from Democrats?"
40. Timothy Cama, "Ocasio-Cortez Explains 'Farting Cows' Comment: 'We've Got to Address Factory Warming,' " *Hill*, February 22, 2019.
41. Rich Lowry, "Millennial Socialism 101," *Salem News*, January 13, 2019.
42. Resolution, Recognizing the Duty of the Federal Government to Create a Green New Deal.
43. Eliza Relman, "Alexandria Ocasio-Cortez Says Her Green New Deal Climate Plan Would Cost at Least $10 Trillion," *Business Insider*, June 5, 2019.
44. Ari Natter and Bloomberg, "The Green New Deal Would Cost $93 Trillion, Ocasio-Cortez Critics Say," *Fortune*, February 25, 2019.
45. Brittany De Lea, "How Much AOC's Green New Deal Could Cost the Average American Household," Fox Business, July 30, 2019; Paul Bedard, "Green New Deal to Cost Up to $100,000 per Home in First Year," *Washington Examiner*, July 30, 2019.
46. Kevin Dayaratna, Nicolas Loris, and David Kreutzer, "Consequences of Paris Protocol: Devastating Economic Costs, Essentially Zero Environmental Benefits," Heritage Foundation, April 13, 2016.
47. Julio Rosas, "Elizabeth Warren Says the Green New Deal Doesn't Go Far Enough: We Need a Blue New Deal!" Townhall.com, February 14, 2020.
48. Dino Grandoni and Jeff Stein, "Joe Biden Embraces Green New Deal as He Releases Climate Plan," *Washington Post*, June 4, 2019.
49. Ibid.
50. Zachary Evans, "Biden Suggests Dems Push for 'Green New Deal' Provisions in Next Coronavirus Stimulus Bill," *National Review*, March 25, 2020.
51. Brian Riedl, "America Might Be Ready for Democratic Socialism. It's Not Ready for the Bill," *Vox*, August 7, 2018.
52. Megan Henney, "Warren vs. Sanders on Medicare-for-all: How do Their Plans Compare?" Fox Business, November 5, 2019.
53. Tami Luhby, Gregory Krieg, M. J. Lee, and Leyla Santiago, "Elizabeth Warren Releases Plan to Fund Medicare for All, Pledges No Middle Class Tax Hike," CNN, November 7, 2019.
54. Reed Abelson and Margot Sanger-Katz, "Medicare for All Would Abolish Private Insurance. 'There's No Precedent in American History,' " *New York Times*, March 23, 2019.
55. Ibid.
56. Ed Kilgore, "What Biden Can Do About Pressure to Embrace Medicare for All," *New York Intelligencer*, April 13, 2020.
57. Ibid.
58. Elizabeth Warren, "My Plan for Universal Child Care," *Medium*, February 19, 2019.
59. Christina Wilkie, "Elizabeth Warren's Plan to Fund Universal Child Care with 'Millionaire Tax' Hints at Growing Divide Among 2020 Democrats,"

CNBC, February 20, 2019; Aparna Mathur and Abby McCloskey, "Universal Child Care Is the Wrong Approach," AEI, February 22, 2019.

60. David Goldstein, "I Paid Off All My Student Loans. I Still Support Student Loan Forgiveness," *Vox*, June 24, 2019; Riedl, "America Might Be Ready for Democratic Socialism. It's Not Ready for the Bill."

61. Tim Haines, "Voter Challenges Warren's Student Loan Forgiveness Plan: 'Those of Us Who Did the Right Thing Get Screwed?'" *Real Clear Politics*, January 23, 2020.

62. The Editorial Board, "Joe Biden Pivots . . . to the Left," *Wall Street Journal*, April 12, 2020.

63. Riedl, "America Might Be Ready for Democratic Socialism. It's Not Ready for the Bill."

64. "Adding Up Senator Sanders's Campaign Proposals So Far," Committee for a Responsible Budget, May 9, 2016.

65. John O. McGinnis, "The Modern Constitution Empowers Redistribution, the Original One Not So Much," *Law Liberty*, September 18, 2017.

66. Tyler Olson, "What's in Democrats' Coronavirus Bill? Arts Funding, Union Help and More," FoxNews.com, March 23, 2020.

67. Phillip W. Magness, "The Rich Never Actually Paid 70 Percent," American Institute for Economic Research, January 7, 2019.

68. Ibid.

69. Vanessa Williamson, "Alexandria Ocasio-Cortez's 70 Percent Tax on the Rich Isn't About Revenue, It's About Decreasing Inequality," NBC News, January 26, 2019.

70. Laura Davison, "A Guide to Democrats' Plans to Tax the Rich More," *Fortune*, December 4, 2019.

71. Brett Arends, "Elizabeth Warren Wouldn't Be the First to Try a Wealth Tax—How Did the Others Do?" *Market Watch*, December 20, 2019.

72. Bernie Sanders, "The Inclusive Prosperity Act of 2019," Sanders.Senate.gov.

73. Howard Gleckman, "Can the Sanders Financial Transactions Tax Raise Trillions and Cut Speculation," Tax Policy Center, July 1, 2019.

74. Curtis Dubay, "The Economic Case Against the Death Tax," Heritage Foundation, July 20, 2010.

75. Davison, "A Guide to Democrats' Plans to Tax the Rich More."

76. Ylan Mui, "Even Moderate Joe Biden Would Significantly Increase Taxes on the Wealthy if Elected," CNBC, March 5, 2020.

77. Rea Hederman, Guinevere Nell, and William Beach, "Economic Effects of Increasing the Tax Rates on Capital Gains and Dividends," Heritage Foundation, April 15, 2008.

78. Daniel J. Mitchell, "The Overwhelming Case Against Capital Gains Taxation," *Forbes*, November 7, 2014.

79. Maggie Astor, "The Democratic Presidential Candidates Don't Want to Sim-

ply Defend Abortion Rights. They Want to Go on Offense," *New York Times*, November 25, 2019.

80. Caleb Parke and Gregg Re, "Dems Block 'Born Alive' Bill to Provide Medical Care to Infants Who Survive Failed Abortions," Fox News, February 25, 2019.

81. Astor, "The Democratic Presidential Candidates Don't Want to Simply Defend Abortion Rights. They Want to Go on Offense."

82. Ibid.

83. Eric Zorn, "Pelosi Says Border Walls Are 'Immoral.' But That's Not the Conversation We Need to Be Having Right Now," *Chicago Tribune*, January 11, 2019.

84. Dara Lind, " 'Abolish Ice' Shows How Far Left Democrats Have Moved on Immigration," *Vox*, July 9, 2018.

85. Thomas Kaplan and Katie Glueck, "Joe Biden Calls for Immigration Overhaul, Acknowledging 'Pain' From Deportations," *New York Times*, December 11, 2019.

86. Molly Hensley-Clancy and Nidhi Prakash, " 'Abolish Ice' Was the Call of Last Summer. 2020 Democrats Have Moved On," *BuzzFeed News*, May 15, 2019.

87. "Where 2020 Democrats Stand on Immigration," *Washington Post*, February 1, 2020.

88. Alexandra Hutzler, "On Shaky Ground with Native American Community, Elizabeth Warren Supports Reparations for Indigenous People," *Newsweek*, February 23, 2019.

89. Megan Henney, "Here's Where 2020 Democrats Stand on Slavery Reparations," Fox Business, June 20, 2019.

90. "Where Do 2020 Democrats Stand on Question of Reparations for Slavery? It's Complicated," *Newsweek*, June 19, 2019; "Where Democrats Stand: Should the Federal Government Pay Reparations to the Descendants of Slaves?" *Washington Post*, https://www.washingtonpost.com/graphics/politics/policy-2020/economic-inequality/reparations/.

91. David Krayden, "Biden Supports Slavery Reparations Study, Wants Immediate Action on 'Institutional Racism,' " *Daily Caller*, February 29, 2020.

92. Michael Bloomberg, "Updated: Mass Public Shootings Keep Occurring in Gun-Free Zones: 94: of Attacks Since 1950," CrimeResearch.org.

93. John Malcolm, "6 Reasons Gun Control Will Not Solve Mass Killings," Heritage Foundation, March 16, 2018.

94. Tawnell D. Hobbs, "Most Guns Used in School Shootings Come from Home," *Wall Street Journal*, April 5, 2018.

95. "Fact Sheet: Gun Violence," Heritage Foundation, March 12, 2018.

96. John Malcolm, "6 Reasons Gun Control Will Not Solve Mass Killings," Heritage Foundation, March 16, 2018.

97. Gary Kleck, "Did Australia's Ban on Semiauto Firearms Really Reduce Violence? A Critique of the Chapman et al. (2016) Study," *SSRN*, December 20, 2017.

98. Tobias Hoonhout, "Biden Says Beto O'Rourke Will 'Take Care of the Gun Problem with Me,'" *National Review*, March 3, 2020.

99. Zachary B. Wolf, "Democrats Have Spent Years Denying They'll Take People's Guns. Not Anymore," *CNN*, September 12, 2019.

100. Becket Adams, "That Time Eric Swalwell Threatened to Go Nuclear on Gun Owners. Literally," *Washington Examiner*, July 8, 2019.

101. David Marcus, "Yes, Democrats Want to Take Your Guns; Beto O'Rourke Is Just Desperate Enough to Say So," *Federalist*, September 16, 2019.

102. Maggie Haberman and Alan Rappoport, "Trump Tries to Walk Back Entitlement Comments as Democrats Pounce," *New York Times*, January 23, 2020.

103. Kenneth Rapoza, "In Attack Ad, Paul Ryan Kills Grandma in Wheelchair," August 12, 2012.

104. Owen Mason, "Democrats: Your Identity Politics Obsession Will Reelect Trump," *Washington Examiner*, August 2, 2019.

105. Matt Ford, "Biden's Diversity Promises Are Identity Politics at Their Best," *New Republic*, March 16, 2020.

106. Ibid.

CHAPTER 4: SOCIALISM: A HISTORY OF FAILURE

1. Karl-Eugen Wädekin, "Soviet Agriculture's Dependence on the West," *Foreign Affairs*, Spring 1982, and Barry K. Goodwin and Thomas J. Grennes, "Tsarist Russia and the World Wheat Market," *Explorations in Economic History* 35, no. 4 (October 1998).

2. Fabiola Zerpa, Lucia Kassai, and Ben Bartenstein, "Venezuela Weighs Privatizing Oil in Face of Economic Free Fall," Bloomberg, January 27, 2020, https://reason.com/2020/01/29/socialist-venezuela-proposes-to-privatize-its-collapsing-oil-industry/, and https://www.forbes.com/sites/rrapier/2017/05/07/how-venezuela-ruined-its-oil-industry/#578371717399; CEIC, "Venezuela Crude Oil: Production," https://www.ceicdata.com/en/indicator/venezuela/crude-oil-production.

3. Vladimir Lenin, *The State and Revolution* (Harmondsworth: Penguin Books, 1992), 45–46.

4. Michael Bakunin, *Statism and Anarchy* (Cambridge: Cambridge University Press, 1990), 178–79.

5. Karl Marx and Friedrich Engels, *A Communist Manifesto* (New York: Simon & Schuster, 1964), 70.

6. Ibid., 70, 76.

7. Ibid., 116.

8. Dmitri Volkogonov, *Lenin: A New Biography* (New York and London: Free Press, 1994), 69–70.

9. Richard Pipes, *A Concise History of the Russian Revolution* (New York: Vintage Books, 1995), 161–63.

10. Ibid., 369–70.

11. "Gulag," History.com, https://www.history.com/topics/russia/gulag.

12. Dmitri Volkogonov, *Autopsy of an Empire* (New York: Free Press, 1998), 72.

13. Ibid., 73–74.

14. Richard Pipes, *The Russian Revolution* (New York: Vintage Books, 1990), 791–92.

15. Robert Conquest, *The Harvest of Sorrow: Soviet Collectivization and the Terror–Famine* (New York: Oxford University Press, 1986), 306.

16. "The Editorial Notebook; Trenchcoats, Then and Now," *New York Times*, June 24, 1990.

17. Pipes, *The Russian Revolution*, 689.

18. David Remnick, *Lenin's Tomb: The Last Days of the Soviet Empire* (New York: Vintage Books, 1994), 184–5.

19. Ibid., 185.

20. Seth Mydans, "From Russia with Hope: In America to Stay—A Special Report; Seeking Shelter in U.S. After the Soviet Storm," *New York Times*, January 25, 1992.

21. Andy Bellairs, "Defections: Hungary at the Melbourne Olympics 1956, *Vice*, March 14, 2016, https://www.vice.com/en_au/article/ypy3k5/defections-hungary-at-the-melbourne-olympics-1956 and https://www.smithsonianmag.com/history/blood-in-the-water-at-the-1956-olympics-1616787/.

22. Karen Reedstrom, "Victor Belenko," *Full Context* 9, no. 2 (November 1996), https://web.archive.org/web/20010111004300/http://fullcontext.org/people/belenko.htm.

23. Strobe Talbott, ed., *Khrushchev Remembers* (Boston and Toronto: Little, Brown, 1970).

24. "The East German Uprising, 1953," Office of the Historian, U.S. Department of State, https://history.state.gov/milestones/1953-1960/east-german-uprising.

25. James Bovard, "The Daily Hell of Life in the Soviet Bloc," Mises Institute, https://mises.org/wire/daily-hell-life-soviet-bloc.

26. Stephane Cortois et al., *The Black Book of Communism: Crimes, Terror, Repression* (Cambridge, MA: Harvard University Press, 1990), 656.

27. Ibid.

28. Nigel Jones, "It Is a Sad Reflection of Our Time That Che Guevara Is Seen as a Hero," *Guardian*, January 2, 2009.

29. Mark Goldblatt, "Revenge of Che," *National Review*, December 19, 2008, https://www.nationalreview.com/2008/12/revenge-che-mark-goldblatt/.

30. Ibid.

31. Simon Hattenstone, " 'Dammit, This Guy Is Cool,' " *Guardian*, November 29,

2008, https://www.theguardian.com/film/2008/nov/29/benicio-del-toro-che
-guevara.

32. Frank Dikköter, "Looking Back on the Great Leap Forward," *History Today* 66, no. 8 (August 2016).

33. Dr. Li Zhisui, *The Private Life of Chairman Mao* (New York: Random House, 1994), 271–72, 282–83.

34. Cambodia Tribunal Monitor, https://www.cambodiatribunal.org/history /cambodian-history/khmer-rouge-history/.

35. https://newsroom.ucla.edu/releases/ucla-demographer-produces-best-esti mate-yet-of-cambodias-death-toll-under-pol-pot.

36. Kirstie Brewer, "How Two Men Survived a Prison Where 12,000 Were Killed," BBC, June 11, 2015, https://www.bbc.com/news/magazine-33096971.

37. Associated Press, "Venezuela's Chavez call Bush "the devil," NBCNews.com, September 20, 2006, http://www.nbcnews.com/id/14923411/ns/world_news -americas/t/venezuelas-chavez-calls-bush-devil/#.Xp1Ba8hKiCg.

38. Daniel Di Martino, "How Socialism Destroyed Venezuela," Economics21 .org, https://economics21.org/how-socialism-destroyed-venezuela.

39. Michael Albertus, "Chavez's Real Legacy Is Disaster," *Foreign Policy*, December 6, 2018, https://foreignpolicy.com/2018/12/06/chavezs-real-legacy-is -disaster/.

40. Robert Rapier, "How Venezuela Ruined Its Oil Industry," *Forbes*, May 7, 2017, https://www.forbes.com/sites/rrapier/2017/05/07/how-venezuela-ruined -its-oil-industry/#578371717399.

41. Ibid; CEIC, "Venezuela Crude Oil: Production," https://www.ceicdata.com /en/indicator/venezuela/crude-oil-production.

42. Jose Nino, "Price Controls Are Disastrous for Venezuela, and Everywhere Else," *Mises Wire*, August 16, 2016; Di Martino, "How Socialism Destroyed Venezuela."

43. Robert Valencia, "Venezuelans Are Losing a Lot of Weight Amid Money Crisis," *Newsweek*, February 22, 2018, https://www.newsweek.com/venezu elans-are-losing-lot-weight-amid-money-crisis-816886.

44. Julie Turkewitz and Isayen Herrera, "Childbirth in Venezuela, where women's deaths are a state secret," *Chicago Tribune*, April 12, 2020, https://www .chicagotribune.com/featured/sns-nyt-dangerous-childbirth-in-venezuela -20200412-5vh5fmc2wvgdtp3rdmjdjlbcmm-story.html.

45. "Overview: Venezuelan Refugee and Migrant Crisis, Iom.com, https://www .iom.int/venezuela-refugee-and-migrant-crisis.

46. Fabiola Zerpa, "Venezuelan Hyperinflation Explodes, Soaring Over 440,000 Percent," Bloomberg, January 18, 2018, https://www.bloomberg.com/news /articles/2018-01-18/venezuelan-hyperinflation-explodes-soaring-over -440-000-percent.

47. Patricia Laya, "Hyperinflation Left Me Broke in Caracas," Bloomberg,

August 10, 2018, https://www.bloomberg.com/news/articles/2018-08-10
/venezuelan-hyperinflation-makes-a-fast-food-meal-a-nightmare?srnd
=life-in-caracas-venezuela.

48. Patricia Laya, "Where a Bottle of Whisky Costs 16 Years of Wages," Bloomberg, July 16, 2018, https://www.bloomberg.com/news/articles/2018-07-16
/in-venezuela-a-bottle-of-whisky-costs-16-years-of-wages.

49. Andrew Rosati, "Venezuela's Bribing Menu Brings Transparency to Corruption," Bloomberg, November 27, 2018, https://www.bloomberg.com/news
/articles/2018-11-27/venezuela-s-bribing-menu-brings-transparency-to
-corruption.

50. Andrew Rosati, "Life Without Water: Sweaty, Smelly, and Furious in Caracas," Bloomberg, August 27, 2018, https://www.bloomberg.com/news/art
icles/2018-08-27/life-without-water-sweaty-smelly-and-furious-in
-caracas?srnd=life-in-caracas-venezuela.

51. Alex Vasquez, "Everyone I Know is Depressed and Medicated: Life in
Caracas," Bloomberg, January 10, 2020, https://www.bloomberg.com/news
/articles/2020-01-10/crisis-in-venezuela-has-nearly-everyone-depressed
-and-medicated.

52. Katie Porzecanski, "Why I Pick Up Hitchhikers in One of the World's Deadliest Cities," Bloomberg, September 13, 2019, https://www.bloomberg.com
/news/articles/2019-09-13/why-i-pick-up-hitchhikers-in-one-of-the-world
-s-deadliest-cities.

53. Andrew Rosati, Dating in Caracas Is Crazy, Infuriating, and a Little
Scary," Bloomberg, May 17, 2019, https://www.bloomberg.com/news/arti
cles/2019-05-17/tear-gas-and-condom-shortages-what-dating-is-like-in
-chaotic-caracas.

54. Patricia Laya, "Gaunt, Filthy and Scared, Kids Roam the Streets of Caracas," Bloomberg, December 10, 2018, https://www.bloomberg.com/news
/articles/2018-12-10/gaunt-filthy-and-scared-kids-roam-streets-of-caracas
-in-packs?srnd=life-in-caracas-venezuela.

55. Kristian Niemietz, "'But that wasn't REAL socialism!' (Part 3: Venezuela),"
iea.com, August 4, 2017, https://iea.org.uk/but-that-wasnt-real-socialism
-part-3-venezuela/; "Noam Chomsky Meets with Chavez in Venezuela,"
Venezuelanalysis.com, August 27, 2009, https://venezuelanalysis.com/news
/4748.

56. Gordon Dritschilo, "Sanders, CITGO strike deal for oil," *Rutland Herald*,
February 4, 2006, https://www.rutlandherald.com/news/sanders-citgo
-strike-deal-for-oil/article_bd5da44a-e919-51f9-a8ad-501a367ca84c.html.

57. Kevin G. Hall, "Clinton-allied group ties Sanders to Venezuela's Hugo
Chavez," *Charlotte Observer*, September 15, 2015, https://www.charlotteob
server.com/news/politics-government/article35368479.html.

58. James Freeman, "Not Even Socialists Believe in Socialism Anymore," *Wall*

Street Journal, February 11, 2020, https://www.wsj.com/articles/not-even
-socialists-believe-in-socialism-anymore-11581458840.

59. Kerry Jackson, "Denmark Tells Bernie Sanders It's Had Enough Of His 'Socialist' Slurs," *Investor's Business Daily*, November 9, 2015, https://www .investors.com/politics/commentary/denmark-tells-bernie-sanders-to -stop-calling-it-socialist/.

60. Joseph Simonson, "Bernie Sanders praised communist Cuba and the Soviet Union in the 1980s," *Washington Examiner*, June 6, 2019, https://www.wash ingtonexaminer.com/news/bernie-sanders-praised-communist-cuba-and -the-soviet-union-in-the-1980s.

61. Zachary Evans, "Sanders Differentiates Socialism from 'Authoritarian Communism' When Confronted by Russian Immigrant," *National Review*, March 10, 2020.

62. Alexander Burns and Sydney Ember, "Mayor and 'Foreign Minister': How Bernie Sanders Brought the Cold War to Burlington," *New York Times*, May 17, 2019, https://www.nytimes.com/2019/05/17/us/bernie-sanders-bur lington-mayor.html.

63. Michael Kranish, "Inside Bernie Sanders's 1988 10-day 'honeymoon' in the Soviet Union," *Washington Post*, May 3, 2019, https://www.washingtonpost .com/politics/inside-bernie-sanderss-1988-10-day-honeymoon-in-the -soviet-union/2019/05/02/db543e18-6a9c-11e9-a66d-a82d3f3d96d5_story .html.

64. Brendan Cole, "Castro Trends after Bernie Sanders Praises Cuban Leader's Literacy Program," *Newsweek*, February 24, 2020, https://www.newsweek .com/bernie-sanders-fidel-castro-cuba-democrats-60-minutes-1488694.

65. Joseph Simonson, "Bernie Sanders campaigned for Marxist party in Reagan era," *Washington Examiner*, May 30, 2019, https://www.washingtonexam iner.com/news/campaigns/bernie-sanders-campaigned-for-marxist-party -in-reagan-era.

66. Ian Schwartz, "Sanders Campaign Organizer: Free Education, Gulags Needed To 'Re-Educate' You To Not Be A 'F*cking Nazi," *Real Clear Politics*, January 14, 2020, https://www.realclearpolitics.com/video/2020/01/14 /sanders_campaign_organizer_free_education_gulags_needed_to_reedu cate_you_not_to_be_a_fcking_nazi.html; Valerie Richardson, "'Extreme Action:' Project Veritas unearths more radical Bernie Sanders staffers," *Washington Times*, January 28, 2020, https://www.washingtontimes.com /news/2020/jan/28/project-veritas-unearths-more-radical-bernie-sande/.

67. Andrew Kaczynski and Nathan McDermott, "Bernie Sanders in the 1970s urged nationalization of most major industries," CNN, March 14, 2019, https://www.cnn.com/2019/03/14/politics/kfile-bernie-nationalization /index.html.

68. Bill Scher, "No, Coronavirus Isn't Proof We Need Socialism," *Politico*,

March 24, 2020, https://www.politico.com/news/magazine/2020/03/24/cor onavirus-socialism-sanders-144490.

69. Margaret Thatcher, Speech to Conservative Central Council ("The Historic Choice"), March 20, 1976, https://www.margaretthatcher.org/document/102990.

CHAPTER 5: DEEP STATE I:
RUSSIAN COLLUSION—THE HOAX OF THE CENTURY

1. Michael Isikoff, "U.S. Intel Officials Probe Ties between Trump Adviser and Kremlin," *Yahoo News*, September 23, 2016.
2. "These Reports Allege Trump Has Deep Ties to Russia," *BuzzFeed News*, January 10, 2017.
3. Greg Gordon and Peter Stone, "Sources: Mueller Has Evidence Cohen Was in Prague in 2016, Confirming Part of Dossier," McClatchy, April 13, 2018.
4. Franklin Foer, "Was a Trump Server Communicating with Russia?" *Slate*, October 31, 2016.
5. Office of the Inspector General, U.S. Department of Justice, "Review of Four FISA Applications and Other Aspects of the FBI's Crossfire Hurricane Investigation," December 9, 2019, ii.
6. Special Counsel Robert S. Mueller III, Department of Justice, "Report on the Investigation into Russian Interference in the 2016 Presidential Election," March 2019, vol. 1, 5.
7. James Comey, "No 'treason.' No coup. Just lies—and dumb lies at that," *Washington Post*, May 29, 2019.
8. "Minority Views," House Intelligence Committee Democrats, March 26, 2018, 19, https://intelligence.house.gov/uploadedfiles/20180411_-_final_-_hpsci_minority_views_on_majority_report.pdf.
9. Isikoff, "U.S. Intel Officials Probe."
10. Howard Blum, "How Ex-Spy Christopher Steele Compiled His Explosive Trump-Russia Dossier," *Vanity Fair*, March 30, 2017.
11. David Corn, "A Veteran Spy Has Given the FBI Information Alleging a Russian Operation to Cultivate Donald Trump," *Mother Jones*, October 31, 2016.
12. "Christopher Steele, Trump Dossier Author, Is a Real-Life James Bond," NBC News, January 13, 2017.
13. Meghan Keneally, "Comey Says He Believes the Source of the Steele 'Dossier' to Be 'Credible,'" ABC News, April 15, 2018.
14. Kenneth P. Vogel, "Clinton Campaign and Democratic Party Helped Pay for Russia, Trump Dossier," *New York Times*, October 24, 2017.
15. Ibid.

16. Margot Cleveland, "9 Key Points from Newly Declassified Report Details on FISA Abuse," *Federalist*, April 16, 2020.

17. "Former Federal Prosecutor Andrew McCarthy On The 2016 Election Scandal—The Real One," *Hugh Hewitt Show*, February 12, 2018.

18. "James Comey on Clinton Probe, Russia Investigation," Fox News, April 26, 2018.

19. House Intelligence Committee Republicans, "Foreign Intelligence Surveillance Act Abuses at the Department of Justice and the Federal Bureau of Investigation," January 18, 2018.

20. Charles E. Grassley, Chairman, U.S. Senate Committee on the Judiciary, and Lindsey O. Graham, Chairman, Subcommittee on Crime and Terrorism, U.S. Senate Committee on the Judiciary, "Referral of Christopher Steele for Potential Violation of 18 U.S.C. 1001," January 4, 2018.

21. House Intelligence Committee Democrats, "Correcting the Record—the Russia Investigation," January 29, 2018.

22. "Comey: Notion That FISA Process Was Abused Is 'Nonsense,'" *Real Clear Politics,* December 7, 2018.

23. "Deputy AG Rod Rosenstein: 'The Department of Justice Is Not Going to Be Extorted,'" *Real Clear Politics*, May 1, 2018.

24. DOJ IG, Review of FISA Applications, vi.

25. Ibid., viii, xi.

26. Margot Cleveland, "Declassified Info: DOJ, FBI Knew Trump Surveillance Was Based on Russian Disinformation," *Federalist*, April 13, 2020.

27. DOJ IG, Review of FISA Applications, 110.

28. Ibid., 188.

29. Margot Cleveland, "9 Key Points from Newly Declassified Report Details on FISA Abuse," *Federalist*, April 16, 2020.

30. DOJ IG, Review of FISA Applications, xi.

31. Ibid.

32. Ibid., xvii.

33. "James Comey on Clinton probe, Russia investigation," Fox News, April 26, 2018.

34. DOJ IG, Review of FISA Applications, xi.

35. John Solomon, "FBI's Steele Story Falls Apart: False Intel and Media Contacts Were Flagged before FISA," *Hill*, May 9, 2019.

36. DOJ IG, Review of FISA Applications, iii.

37. Ibid., 67.

38. "Inspector General Report on Origins of FBI's Russia Inquiry," C-SPAN, December 11, 2019.

39. "Full Interview: AG Bill Barr Criticizes Inspector General Report on the Russia Investigation," *Real Clear Politics*, December 11, 2019.

40. Office of the Inspector General, U.S. Department of Justice, "A Review of

Various Actions by the Federal Bureau of Investigation and Department of Justice in Advance of the 2016 Election," June 2018, v.

41. Rod J. Rosenstein, "Restoring Public Confidence in the FBI," *Real Clear Politics,* May 9, 2017, https://www.realclearpolitics.com/docs/Rosenstein _Memo.pdf.

42. Office of the Inspector General, U.S. Department of Justice, "Report of Investigation of Former Federal Bureau of Investigation Director James Comey's Disclosure of Sensitive Investigative Information and Handling of Certain Memoranda," August 2019, 60.

43. Jonathan Turley, "No Glory in James Comey Getting Away with His Abuse of FBI Power," *Hill,* December 15, 2018.

44. Greg Re, "FBI discussed interviewing Michael Flynn 'to get him to lie' and 'get him fired,' handwritten notes show," Fox News, April 30, 2020.

45. Byron York, "Memo: FBI recommended Michael Flynn not have a lawyer present during interview, did not warn of false statement consequences," *Washington Examiner,* December 11, 2018.

46. Chuck Ross, "FBI Planned To Close Michael Flynn Investigation, And Then Peter Strzok Intervened," *Daily Caller,* April 30, 2020.

47. House Permanent Select Committee On Intelligence, "Report on Russian Active Measures," March 22, 2018, 54.

48. DOJ IG, Report into Comey's Disclosure, 17–18.

49. Office of the Inspector General, U.S. Department of Justice, "A Report of Investigation of Certain Allegations Relating to Former FBI Deputy Director Andrew McCabe," February 2018, 2.

50. Adam Goldman and Michael S. Schmidt, "Rod Rosenstein Suggested Secretly Recording Trump and Discussed 25th Amendment," *New York Times,* September 21, 2018.

51. Adam Goldman, "Prosecutors Face Increased Pressure to Make Decision in McCabe Case," *New York Times,* October 1, 2019.

52. Daniel Chaitin, "Schumer Warns Trump: Intel Officials 'Have Six Ways from Sunday at Getting Back at You,'" *Washington Examiner,* January 3, 2017.

53. Kimberley A. Strassel, "Brennan and the 2016 Spy Scandal," *Wall Street Journal,* July 19, 2018.

54. Ibid.

55. Matt Zapotosky, "Trump Said Mueller's Team Has '13 Hardened Democrats.' Here Are the Facts," *Washington Post,* March 18, 2018.

56. Eleanor Mueller, "Adam Schiff Wants Mueller to Bring His Report 'to Life,' " *Politico,* July 21, 2019.

57. Naomi Lim, "Matt Gaetz Grills Mueller on Steele Dossier's Role in Russian Disinformation Efforts," *Washington Examiner,* July 24, 2019.

58. "Rep. Schiff on MSNBC: Much More Than Circumstantial Evidence, Wor-

thy of Investigation," Rep. Adam Schiff YouTube channel, March 27, 2017, https://www.youtube.com/watch?v=ftxB-WV58_o.

59. "Adam Schiff on Russia investigation (full interview), CNN's *State of the Union*, December 10, 2017, https://www.cnn.com/videos/politics/2017/12/10/adam-schiff-russia-investigation-entire-sotu.cnn.

60. Ibid.

61. DOJ IG, Review of FISA applications, 12.

62. "Statement of U.S. Attorney John H. Durham," United States Department of Justice, District of Connecticut, December 9, 2019, https://www.justice.gov/usao-ct/pr/statement-us-attorney-john-h-durham.

CHAPTER 6: DEEP STATE II: IMPEACHMENT— THE FAILED ATTEMPT TO DECAPITATE THE TRUMP PRESIDENCY

1. "House Judiciary Committee Unveils Investigation into Threats Against the Rule of Law," House Committee on the Judiciary, March 4, 2019, https://judiciary.house.gov/news/documentsingle.aspx?DocumentID=1502.

2. Joseph A. Wulfsohn, "Rep. Al Green Fears Trump 'Will Get Reelected' if He's Not Impeached," Fox News, May 7, 2019.

3. Cleve R. Wootson Jr., "Hunter Biden Says Role with Ukraine Firm Was 'Poor Judgment' but Not 'Improper,' " *Washington Post*, October 15, 2019.

4. Polina Ivanova, Maria Tsvetkova, Ilya Zhegulev, and Luke Baker, "What Hunter Biden Did on the Board of Ukrainian Energy Company Burisma," Reuters, October 18, 2019.

5. Davey Alba, "Debunking 4 Viral Rumors About the Bidens and Ukraine," *New York Times*, October 29, 2019.

6. Alana Goodman, "John Kerry's Son Cut Business Ties with Hunter Biden over Ukrainian Oil Deal," *Washington Examiner*, August 27, 2019.

7. Paul Sonne, Michael Kranish, and Matt Viser, "The Gas Tycoon and the Vice President's Son: The Story of Hunter Biden's Foray into Ukraine," *Washington Post*, September 28, 2019.

8. Ibid.

9. Ibid.

10. Gregg Re, "State Dept. Official Flagged Hunter Biden's 'Conflict of Interest' in Ukraine, Testimony Shows," Fox News, November 7, 2019.

11. Adam Entous, "Will Hunter Biden Jeopardize His Father's Campaign?" *New Yorker*, July 1, 2019.

12. Ibid.

13. James Risen, "Joe Biden, His Son, and the Case Against a Ukrainian Oligarch," *New York Times*, December 8, 2015.

14. "Foreign Affairs Issue Launch with Former Vice President Joe Biden," Council on Foreign Relations, January 23, 2018, https://www.cfr.org/event/for eign-affairs-issue-launch-former-vice-president-joe-biden.

15. Peter Schweizer, "What Hunter Biden Did Was Legal—and That's the Problem," *New York Times*, October 9, 2019.

16. "1-on-1 with Hunter Biden," ABCNews.com, https://abcnews.go.com/Poli tics/video/hunter-biden-66298958.

17. Kenneth P. Vogel and David Stern, "Ukrainian Efforts to Sabotage Trump Backfire," *Politico*, January 11, 2017.

18. John Solomon, "Let's Get Real: Democrats Were First to Enlist Ukraine in US Elections," *Hill*, September 23, 2019.

19. Telephone conversation with President Zelensky of Ukraine, July 25, 2019, https://www.whitehouse.gov/wp-content/uploads/2019/09/Unclassified 09.2019.pdf.

20. "Trump on Ukraine: I Have an 'Obligation to Investigate Corruption,' " *Real Clear Politics*, October 21, 2019.

21. White House Whistleblower Complaint, August 12, 2019, https://intel ligence.house.gov/uploadedfiles/20190812_-_whistleblower_complaint _unclass.pdf.

22. Sean Davis, "Intel Community Secretly Gutted Requirement of First-Hand Whistleblower Knowledge," *Federalist*, September 27, 2019.

23. Byron York, "Whistleblower Had 'Professional' Tie to 2020 Democratic Candidate," *Washington Examiner*, October 8, 2019.

24. Paul Sperry, "The Beltway's 'Whistleblower' Furor Obsesses Over One Name," *Real Clear Investigations*, October 30, 2019.

25. Julian E. Barnes, Michael S. Schmidt, and Matthew Rosenberg, "Schiff Got Early Account of Accusations as Whistle-Blower's Concerns Grew," *New York Times*, October 2, 2019.

26. Bill McCarthy, "Adam Schiff's False Claim That 'We Have Not Spoken Directly with the Whistleblower," PolitiFact, October 4, 2019.

27. Devlin Barrett, Matt Zapotosky, Carol D. Leonnig, and Shane Harris, "Trump Offered Ukrainian President Justice Dept. Help in an Investigation of Biden, Memo Shows," *Washington Post*, September 25, 2019.

28. Michael D. Shear and Maggie Haberman, " 'Do Us a Favor': Call Shows Trump's Interest in Using U.S. Power for His Gain," *New York Times*, September 25, 2019.

29. Tristan Justice, "Adam Schiff Makes Up His Own Transcript of Call Between Trump and Ukraine President," *Federalist*, September 26, 2019.

30. "Telephone Conversation with President-elect Volodymyr Zelensky of Ukraine," April 21, 2019, https://assets.documentcloud.org/documents /6550349/First-Trump-Ukraine-Call.pdf.

31. Paul M. Krawzak, "OMB: Ukraine Aid Delay Was Consistent with Law, Past Practice," *Roll Call*, December 11, 2019.
32. "Ambassador Sondland Says President Never Told Him of Military Aid Preconditions," C-SPAN, November 20, 2019, https://www.c-span.org/video/?c4831945 /ambassador-sondland-president-told-military-aid-preconditions.
33. Tim Hains, "Sondland Confirms POTUS Told Him: 'I Want No Quid-Pro-Quo," *Real Clear Politics*, November 20, 2019, https://www.realclearpolitics .com/video/2019/11/20/sondland_confirms_potus_told_him_no_quid -pro-quo.html.
34. Tim Hains, "Ukrainian President Zelensky: 'Nobody Pushed Me' To Investigate Biden," *Real Clear Politics*, September 25, 2019, https://www .realclearpolitics.com/video/2019/09/25/ukrainian_president_to_trump _at_un_nobody_pushed_me.html.
35. Mark Moore, "Ukraine's Zelensky Again Denies Quid Pro Quo during Trump Phone Call," *New York Post*, December 2, 2019.
36. "Ukraine Minister Denies Trump Put Pressure on Zelensky during Call: Report," Reuters, September 21, 2019.
37. *Washington Post* Staff, "Transcript: Kent and Taylor public testimony in front of House Intelligence Committee, *Washington Post*, November 14, 2019, https:// www.washingtonpost.com/politics/2019/11/14/transcript-kent-taylor -public-testimony-front-house-intelligence-committee/.
38. Oliver Carroll, "Ukraine President Zelensky Says 'No Blackmail' in Trump Call," *Independent*, October 10, 2019.
39. Christopher Miller, "Ukraine Was Still Checking Its Bank Account for US Aid for a Month After the Trump Call," *BuzzFeed News*, October 2, 2019.
40. Joe Heim, "Nancy Pelosi on Impeaching Trump: 'He's Just Not Worth It,' " *Washington Post Magazine*, March 11, 2019.
41. Tim Hains, "Turley to House Dems: If You Make Going To The Courts An Abuse Of Power, It Is 'Your Abuse Of Power,'" *Real Clear Politics*, December 4, 2019, https://www.realclearpolitics.com/video/2019/12/04/turley_to_congress _if_you_make_going_to_the_courts_an_abuse_of_power_it_is_your_ab use_of_power.html.
42. "Schumer Accuses McConnell Of Plotting 'Most Unfair' Senate Impeachment Trial," NBCNews YouTube channel, December 19, 2019, https://www .youtube.com/watch?v=8HvYREYD7YM.
43. Maggie Haberman and Michael S. Schmidt, "Trump Tied Ukraine Aid to Inquiries He Sought, Bolton Book Says," *New York Times*, January 26, 2020.
44. "Flashback: John Bolton Described the President's conversations with Zelensky as 'warm and cordial,'" Trending Politics YouTube channel, January 29, 2020, https://www.youtube.com/watch?v=DHgkHaLa-x8.

45. Tim Hains, "Audio; Russian Comedians Prank Called Rep. Adam Schiff, Promised Him Naked Photos Of Trump," *Real Clear Politics*, February 6, 2018,

46. Alana Goodman, "Adam Schiff sent his staff to try and collect 'classified materials for the FBI' after Russian pranksters told him Putin has NAKED blackmail pictures of Trump," *Daily Mail*, February 6, 2018.

47. John Solomon, "Let's Get Real: Democrats Were First to Enlist Ukraine in US Elections," *Hill*, September 23, 2019.

48. Stu Cvrk, "Impeachment Trial: Compare and Contrast Two Wildly Different Steele Dossier Explanations," *RedState*, January 31, 2020.

49. Trial memorandum of President Donald J. Trump, January 20, 2020, 24, https://www.whitehouse.gov/wp-content/uploads/2020/01/Trial-Memorandum-of-President-Donald-J.-Trump.pdf.

50. "Transcript: Sen. Cruz praises Alan Dershowitz's 'powerful and compelling' constitutional argument," *Hannity*, January 28, 2020, https://www.foxnews.com/transcript/sen-cruz-praises-alan-dershowitzs-powerful-and-compelling-constitutional-argument.

51. Trial memorandum of Donald J. Trump, 44.

52. Jonathan Easley, "Trump Campaign, RNC Raise Staggering $125 Million in Third Quarter," *Hill*, October 1, 2019.

53. Max Greenwood, "Trump Campaign, RNC Raise $154M in Fourth Quarter of 2019," *Hill*, January 3, 2020.

54. Emily Jacobs, "Trump Approval Rating Hits a High Post-Impeachment," *New York Post*, February 19, 2020.

CHAPTER 7: ENEMY OF THE PEOPLE: THE HATE-TRUMP MEDIA MOB

1. Dori Monson Show, "Howard Kurtz Says Media Mate for Trump is Unprecedented," *My Northwest*, July 12, 2018.

2. Robert J. .Samuelson, "Why Trump Loves to Hate the Media," *Washington Post*, February 22, 2017.

3. Stephen Collinson, "Donald Trump Refuses to Say Whether He'll Accept Election Results," CNN, October 20, 2016.

4. David Zurawik, "Trump's War on Press No Match for Obama's," *Baltimore Sun*, March 4, 2017.

5. Ibid.

6. Art Swift, "Americans' Trust in Mass Media Sinks to New Low," Gallup, September 14, 2016.

7. "Why Trump Supporters Hate the Media," *Fair Observer*, July 1, 2017.

8. "Fourth Estate," *Journalism Encyclopedia*, Open School of Journalism, https://www.openschoolofjournalism.com/resources/encyclopedia/fourth-estate.

9. Bruce Thornton, "A Brief History of Media Bias," Hoover Institution, June 12, 2013.

10. Mike Ciandella, "57 Times More Coverage of Trump's Temporary Ban Than Obama Ending Cuban Refugee Program," NewsBusters, January 30, 2017.

11. Matthew Archbold, "8 Most Hilarious and Unsettling Obama-as-Deity Metaphors," *National Catholic Register*, May 31, 2013.

12. Paul Bedard, "Newsweek: Obama Is the 'The Second Coming,'" *Washington Examiner*, January 19, 2013.

13. Cheryl K.. Chumley, "Barbara Walters Admits 'We' Thought Obama was 'the Next Messiah,'" *Washington Times*, December 18, 2013.

14. Mark Moford, "Is Obama an Enlightened Being? Spiritual Wise Ones Say: This Sure Ain't No Ordinary Politician. You Buying It?" *SFGate*, June 6, 2008.

15. Danny Shea, "Chris Matthews: 'I Felt This Thrill Going Up My Leg,' as Obama Spoke," *HuffPost*, December 6, 2017.

16. For the fullest account of the attack, see the House Select Committee on Benghazi's "Final Report of the Select Committee on the Events Surrounding the 2012 Terrorist Attack in Benghazi," December 7, 2016.

17. Bruce Thornton, "A Brief History of Media Bias," Hoover Institution, June 12, 2013.

18. David Samuels, "The Aspiring Novelist Who Became Obama's Foreign-Policy Guru," *New York Times Magazine*, May 5, 2016.

19. Ibid.

20. Ibid.

21. Ibid.

22. Ibid.

23. Joe Concha, "Where's the Outrage Over Obama's Fake News Peddling?" *Hill*, December 6, 2016.

24. Gideon Resnick, "Trump Won't Denounce KKK Support," *Daily Beast*, February 26, 2016, https://www.thedailybeast.com/cheats/2016/02/28/trump-won-t-denounce-kkk-support.

25. Rich Noyes, "Condemning Republicans, Cheering Democrats: The Media's Biased 2016 Convention Coverage," NewsBusters, July 29, 2016.

26. Jim Rutenberg, "Trump Is Testing the Norms of Objectivity in Journalism," *New York Times*, August 7, 2016.

27. Stuart Rothenberg "Trump's Path to an Electoral College Victory Isn't Narrow. It's Nonexistent," *Washington Post*, October 18, 2016.

28. Ibid.

29. Geoffrey Dickens, "Rigged? Trump Doesn't Have a Single Major Newspaper Endorsement," NewsBusters, October 18, 2016.

30. Rich Noyes, "MRC Study: Documenting TV's Twelve Weeks of Trump Bashing," NewsBusters, October 25, 2016.

31. Jack Shafer, "How Trump Took Over the Media by Fighting It," *Politico Magazine*, November 5, 2016.

32. Kalev Leetaru, "Measuring the Media's Obsession with Trump," *Real Clear Politics*, December 6, 2018.

33. Mike Ciandella, "CNN Spends 78 Percent of Prime Time GOP Campaign Coverage on Trump," NewsBusters, September 17, 2015.

34. John Sides, "Why is Trump Surging? Blame the Media," *Washington Post*, July 20, 2015.

35. Nate Cohn, "The Trump Campaign's Turning Point," *New York Times*, July 18, 2015.

36. Paul Farhi, "The Washington Post's New Slogan Turns Out to be an Old Saying," *Washington Post*, February 24, 2017.

37. Joe Concha, " 'The Washington Post: 'Democracy Dies in Darkness,' " *Hill*, February 22, 2017

38. Editorial, "Do the Media Hate Trump? Yes, and from the Very Start of His Presidency, New Survey Shows," *Investor's Business Daily*, October 3, 2017.

39. AllahPundit, "Pew Media Coverage of Trump Through First 60 Days Vastly More Negative Than Last Three Presidents," *Hot Air*, October 2, 2017.

40. Elizabeth Harrington, "The 'Hate Trump' Agenda by the Democrats Has Gone Too Far," *Hill*, August 6, 2019.

41. "Covington Catholic High School Students Smeared by Mainstream Media Lies—Don't Expect an Apology," Fox News, January 21, 2019.

42. Oliver Darcy, "CNN Settles Lawsuit with Nick Sandmann Stemming from Viral Video," *CNN*, January 7, 2020. https://www.cnn.com/2020/01/07/media /cnn-settles-lawsuit-viral-video/index.html).

43. Anonymous, "I Am Part of the Resistance Inside the Trump Administration," *New York Times*, September 8, 2018.

44. John Gans, "Col. Vindman and the Trumpification of the National Security Council," *New York Times*, February 7, 2020, https://www.nytimes .com/2020/02/07/opinion/alexander-vindman-nsc-trump.html.

45. "Gergen on firings: There's a classy way and the Trump way," *Cuomo Prime Time*, CNN.com, https://www.cnn.com/videos/politics/2020/02/08/vind man-sondland-trump-firings-gergen-cpt-sot-vpx.cnn.

46. Elie Honig, "Trump engaged in witness retaliation. That's a crime," CNN.com, February 12, 2020, https://www.cnn.com/2020/02/12/opinions/trump-vind man-criminal-witness-retaliation-cross-exam-honig/index.html

47. https://twitter.com/SteveScalise/status/1188510478634536962?s=20.

48. Dominic Green, "The Democratic Media Hate Trump More Than They Love Iran—or America," *Spectator USA*, January 7, 2020.

49. Joseph A. Wulfsohn, "Ted Cruz Bashes MSNBC's Joy Reid for Her "Trump's Benghazi' Claim: 'What's Wrong with You?' " Fox News, January 2, 2020.

50. Amanda Prestigiacomo, "MSNBC's Joy Reid Celebrates: 'Trump's Benghazi Unfolds In Iraq,'" *Daily Wire*, Janaury 1, 2020.
51. Sharyl Attkisson, "Media Mistakes in the Trump Era: The Definitive List," updated May 3, 2020.
52. Ibid.
53. Ibid.
54. Ezra Klein, "The Media vs. Donald Trump: Why the Press Feels So Free to Criticize the Republican Nominee," *Vox*, August 16, 2016.
55. Margaret Sullivan, "We Have Entered the Trump Unbound Era—and Journalists Need to Step It Up," *Washington Post*, February 23, 2020.
56. Benjamin Hart, "Jeffrey Lord Isn't on CNN Anymore, but He Still Loves Trump," *New York Intelligencer*, July 21, 2019.
57. Michael M. Grynbaum, "Jeffery Lord, Trump Defender on CNN, Is Fired for Using Nazi Slogan," *New York Times*, August 10, 2017.
58. "High School History Lesson Compares Trump with Nazis, Communists," Associated Press, February 23, 2020.
59. Mike Ciandella and Rich Noyes, "HYPOCRISY: 7X More Coverage for Sessions Debacle than Holder Contempt," NewsBusters, March 3, 2017.
60. Rich Noyes and Mike Ciandella, "TV News vs. President Trump: The First 30 Days," NewsBusters, March 2, 2017.
61. Rich Noyes and Mike Ciandella, "Honeymoon from Hell: The Liberal Media vs. President Trump," NewsBusters, April 19, 2017.
62. Rich Noyes and Mike Ciandella, "Study: The Liberal Media's Summer of Pummeling Trump," NewsBusters, September 12, 2017.
63. Jennifer Harper, "Media Bias at CNN and MSNBC: Just 3% of Questions Friendly to GOP, Says Study," *Washington Times*, August 20, 2019
64. Tim Hains, "MSNBC's Lawrence O'Donnell: 'The President Is A Russian Operative," *Real Clear Politics*, February 23, 2020, https://www.realclearpoli tics.com/video/2020/02/23/msnbcs_lawrence_odonnell_the_president _is_a_russian_operative.html.
65. Ian Schwartz, "Chris Hayes: This Is Not About The Wall, It's About an 'Ethnically Pure America,'" *Real Clear Politics*, January 11, 2019.
66. Curtis Houck, "Matthews: Trump Speech Was 'Hitlerian,' Jokes He Could Fix Nepotism Laws By Hanging Son-in-Law," Newsbusters, January 20, 2017, https://www.newsbusters.org/blogs/nb/curtis-houck/2017/01/20/mat thews-trump-speech-was-hitlerian-jokes-he-could-fix-nepotism.
67. Tim Graham, "Roland Martin on MSNBC: All White Evangelical Trump-Backers Are 'Christian Frauds,'" Newsbusters, March 1, 2020, https://www .newsbusters.org/blogs/nb/tim-graham/2020/03/01/roland-martin-msnbc -all-white-evangelical-trump-backers-are-christian-frauds.
68. Matthew Rozsa, "Joe Scarborough says that Donald Trump is either 'an agent of Russia' or 'a useful idiot,'" *Salon*, November 14, 2019, https://www.salon

.com/2019/11/14/joe-scarborough-says-that-donald-trump-is-either-an -agent-of-russia-or-a-useful-idiot/.

69. Curtis Houck, "'Hardball' A-Block Freaks Over 'Delusional,' 'Strong Man' Trump, Compares Him to John Wilkes Booth," Newsbusters, July 25, 2018, https://www.newsbusters.org/blogs/nb/curtis-houck/2018/07/25/hard ball-block-freaks-over-delusional-strong-man-trump-compares-him; Curtis Houck, "MSNBC's Chris Matthews Compares Trump to Idi Amin, Kim Jong-Un: 'He Loves the Parades!,'" Newsbusters, July 20, 2017, https:// www.newsbusters.org/blogs/nb/curtis-houck/2017/07/20/msnbcs-chris -matthews-compares-trump-kim-jong-un-he-loves-parades; Curtis Houck, "Matthews Suggests Trump Channel Mussolini, Murder Kushner; Compares Him to Ethiopian Dictator," Newsbusters, July 29, 2017, https://www.news busters.org/blogs/nb/curtis-houck/2017/06/29/matthews-suggests-trump -channel-mussolini-murder-kushner-compares.

70. Rich Noyes, "Study: CNN Is Completely Obsessed with Donald Trump— and Not in a Good Way," NewsBusters, May 16, 2017.

71. Ibid.

72. Ken Meyer, "CNN's Stelter Looks Back on Taking Avenetti Seriously: 'Was That Stupid on My Part?' " Mediate, February 16, 2020.

73. "PART 1: CNN Insider Blows Whistle on Network President Jeff Zucker's Personal Vendetta Against POTUS," Project Veritas, October 14, 2019, https:// www.projectveritas.com/2019/10/14/exposecnnpart1/.

74. https://twitter.com/donie/status/1213953640198819847.

75. "CNN Attacks Babylon Bee: 'The Internet Is Only Big Enough for One Fake News Site.'" The Babylon Bee, January 7, 2020.

76. "Press Release: FOX News Channel Dominates Basic Cable for 41 Consecutive Months in Total Day," APNews.com, November 26, 2019, https:// apnews.com/Business%20Wire/537d5013e4ba4c4db10ba941b9ee36a1.

77. Amber Athey, "Fox Wins Cable Battle—CNN Loses To Cartoon Network," Daily Caller, June 5, 2018, https://dailycaller.com/2018/06/05/fox-cnn -cable-ratings-cartoon-network/.

78. Eddie Scarry, "Journalists question Buzzfeed publishing unconfirmed intel report on Trump," Washington Examiner, January 11, 2017, https://www .washingtonexaminer.com/journalists-question-buzzfeed-publishing -unconfirmed-intel-report-on-trump.

79. Chuck Ross, "Emails: Jake Tapper Tore Into 'Irresponsible' BuzzFeed Editor for Publishing the 'Steele Dossier,'" Tennessee Star, February 11, 2019, https:// tennesseestar.com/2019/02/11/emails-jake-tapper-tore-into-irresponsible -buzzfeed-editor-for-publishing-the-steele-dossier/.

80. Mike Ciandella, "Nets Spend 44 Minutes on 'One of the Great Political Smears of All Time,' " NewsBusters, January 11, 2017.

81. Bill D'Agostino, "Yellow Journalism: CNN Spouts Off About 'Pee Tapes' 77 Times in Five Days," NewsBusters, April 16, 2018.

82. Chuck Ross, "WaPo Reporter: FBI and CIA Say They Doubt Major Dossier Allegation," *Daily Caller*, December 16, 2018, https://dailycaller.com /2018/12/16/fbi-cia-doubted-dossier/.

83. Geoffrey Dickens, "CNN Promoted Story Debunked by James Comey," NewsBusters, June 14, 2017.

84. Rowan Scarborough, "FBI-debunked Russia-Trump story helped *New York Times* win journalism award," *Washington Times*, March 1, 2018. https:// www.washingtontimes.com/news/2018/mar/1/fbi-debunked-russia-trump -story-helped-new-york-ti/.

85. "National Reporting," Pulitzer.org, https://www.pulitzer.org/prize-winners -by-category/209.

86. Rich Noyes, "Study: TV News Is Obsessed with Trump-Russia Probe," News-Busters, June 27, 2017; Rich Noyes, "Six Trump Accomplishments the Networks Ignored in 2017," NewsBusters, January 17, 2018.

87. Ashley Feinberg, "The New York Times Unites Against Twitter," *Slate*, August 15, 2019, https://slate.com/news-and-politics/2019/08/new-york -times-meeting-transcript.html.

88. Ibid.

89. https://twitter.com/EricHolder/status/958757841116057600?s=20.

90. Conor Beck, "CNN Analyst Warns Against Releasing Nunes Memo: 'Are We Going to Be a Democracy After Today?'," *Washington Free Beacon*, February 1, 2018, https://freebeacon.com/national-security/cnn-analyst-warns -releasing-nunes-memo-are-be-democracy-today/.

91. Bret Stephens, "Devin Nunes's Nothingburger," *New York Times*, February 2, 2018, https://www.nytimes.com/2018/02/02/opinion/devin-nunes-memo.html.

92. Matthew Rozsa, "'Worse than a nothing burger': The Nunes memo lands with a thud," *Salon*, February 2, 2018, https://www.salon.com/2018/02/02 /worse-than-a-nothingburger-the-nunes-memo-lands-with-a-dud/.

93. "Devin Nunes and the Nothing Burger Memo," *Washington Monthly*, February 2, 2018, https://washingtonmonthly.com/2018/02/02/devin-nunes-and -the-nothing-burger-memo/.

94. Charles P. Pierce, "'Nothingburger' Doesn't Do This Memo Justice," *Esquire*, February 2, 2018, https://www.esquire.com/news-politics/politics /a16306229/nunes-memo-nothingburger/.

95. Bill Press, "The GOP's giant nothing burger," *Hill*, February 5, 2018, https:// thehill.com/opinion/national-security/372439-press-the-gops-giant-noth ing-burger.

96. "RE: Correcting the Record—The Russian Investigation," unclassified memo of the House Permanent Select Committee on Intelligence, Janu-

ary 29, 2018, https://intelligence.house.gov/uploadedfiles/redacted_minor
ity_memo_2.24.18.pdf.

97. Robert Schlesinger, "Nail in the Coffin for Nunes Memo," *U.S. News & World Report*, February 24, 2018, https://www.usnews.com/opinion/thomas
-jefferson-street/articles/2018-02-24/house-intelligences-democratic-rus
sia-memo-finishes-off-nunes-nonsense.

98. "Review of Four FISA Applications and Other Aspects of the FBI's Crossfire Hurricane Investigation," Office of the Inspector General, U.S. Department of Justice, December 2019 (revised), https://www.justice.gov/storage/120919
-examination.pdf.

99. Tim Hains, "Stephanopoulos To Adam Schiff: 'Do You Accept You're your Original Judgments Were Wrong' About FISA Scandal? *Real Clear Politics*, December 15, 2019, https://www.realclearpolitics.com/video/2019/12/15
/stephanopoulos_to_adam_schiff_do_you_accept_that_your_original
_judgments_were_wrong_about_fisa_scandal.html.

100. Matea Gold, "The Campaign to Impeach President Trump Has Begun," *Washington Post*, January 20, 2017.

101. Ibid.

102. Matthew Balan, "ABC's Stephanopoulos: Trump Civil Suit Conviction Could Be 'Impeachable,' " NewsBusters, November 10, 2016.

103. Greg Miller, Ellen Nakashima, and Shane Harris, "Trump's Communications with Foreign Leader are Part of Whistleblower Complaint That Spurred Standoff between Spy Chief and Congress, Former Officials Say," *Washington Post*, September 18, 2019.

104. Kenneth Vogel and David Stern, "Ukrainian Efforts to Sabotage Trump Backfire," *Politico*, January 11, 2017.

105. "Opening Statement for Vindman and Williams Hearing on Impeachment," House Intelligence Committee, November 19, 2019, https://republicans
-intelligence.house.gov/uploadedfiles/nunes_opening_statement_for_vind
man_and_williams_hearing_on_impeachment.pdf.

CHAPTER 8: "ORGANIZED DESTRUCTION":
THE LEFT'S ASSAULT ON FREE SPEECH

1. Dave Rubin, "So You Think You're Tolerant?" *PragerU*, July 8, 2018; Kirsten Powers, *The Silencing* (Washington, DC: Regnery, 2013); David Marchese, "Bill Maher on the Perils of Political Correctness," *New York Times Magazine*, September 30, 2019.

2. "7-Year-Old Suspended for Pointing Gun-Shaped Breakfast Pastry," NBC Washington, March 4, 2013.

3. Kim R. Holmes, Ph.D., "How the Left Became So Intolerant," Heritage Foundation, December 12, 2017.

4. Jim Goad, "The Corporate War on Free Speech," *Taki's Magazine*, March 5, 2018.

5. Scott Jaschik, "Is Heckling Right?," *Inside Higher Ed*, February 17, 2010, https://www.insidehighered.com/news/2010/02/17/heckling-right.

6. Kyle Smith, "Now Inclusion Means Exclusion," *National Review*, March 14, 2018.

7. Joseph Curl, "Denver Post Columnist Says He Was Fired for Saying There Are Only Two Sexes," *Daily Wire*, January 21, 2020.

8. Blake Neff, "New York Can Fine You $250k for 'Misgendering' Somebody," *Daily Caller*, December 28, 2015.

9. Matt Welch, "Bernie Sanders and Elizabeth Warrant Want the FCC to Revoke Sinclair's Broadcast Licenses," *Reason*, April 12, 2018.

10. Ibid.

11. Roger L. Simon, "Time to Cancel the 'Cancel Culture,' " *Epoch Times*, January 15, 2020.

12. T. J. Roberts, "Cancel Culture: Its Causes and Its Consequences," *Advocates*, February 24, 2020.

13. Robby Soave, "The Year in Cancel Culture," *Reason*, December 31, 2019.

14. Douglas Murray, "How to Fight Back Against 'Cancel Culture,' " *The Spectator UK*, January 25, 2020.

15. Lee C. Bollinger, "Free Speech on Campus Is Doing Just Fine, Thank You," *Atlantic*, June 12, 2019.

16. Ibid.

17. "Free to Speak: Reforming the Higher Education Act," National Association of Scholars, April 22, 2019.

18. Jonathan Turley, "Betsy DeVos Is Right to Fix Obama's Campus Sexual Assault Policy," *Hill*, September 12, 2017.

19. "Federal Government Mandates Unconstitutional Speech Codes at Colleges and Universities Nationwide," FIRE, May 17, 2013.

20. Greg Lukianoff, "Feds to Students: You Can't Say That," *Wall Street Journal*, May 16, 2013.

21. Jonathan Turley, "Betsy DeVos Is Right to Fix Obama's Campus Sexual Assault Policy."

22. Ibid.

23. John Tierney, "Journalists Against Free Speech," *City Journal*, Autumn 2019.

24. Gibson Chu, "UC Berkeley Professors Request Cancellation of Milo Yiannopoulos Talk," *Daily Californian*, January 10, 2017.

25. Tierney, "Journalists Against Free Speech."

26. Ibid.

27. Frances Floresca, "VETO: Student Gov. Denies Conservative Group Funding to Host Heather Mac Donald," *Campus Reform*, October 28, 2019.

28. Heather Mac Donald, "Drawing the Line, at Last," *City Journal*, April 22, 2019.

29. Ibid.
30. Ibid
31. Kassy Dillon, "Pro-life Group Sues CSU for Denying Funds Based on Content," *Campus Reform*, January 17, 2017.
32. Anthony Gockowski, "Purdue Staff Member Calls Pro-Life Students 'Vile, Racist Idiots,' " *Campus Reform*, February 8, 2016.
33. "University of Scranton: Denial of Recognition of Turning Point USA," FIRE, https://www.thefire.org/cases/university-of-scranton-denial-of-rec ognition-of-turning-point-usa/.
34. " 'Yikes nope, denied': University of Scranton Stands By as Student Government Denies Recognition to Conservative Group," FIRE, December 5, 2019.
35. Disinvitation Attempts," FIRE, https://www.thefire.org/research/disinvita tion-database/#home/?view_2_sort=field_6|desc&view_2_page =1&view_2_per_page=50.
36. "Free to Speak: Reforming the Higher Education Act," National Association of Scholars, April 22, 2019.
37. "State of the Law: Speech Codes," FIRE, https://www.thefire.org/legal/state -of-the-law-speech-codes/.
38. David Rosenthal, "Another College's Speech Code at Odds with First Amendment Values," Heritage Foundation, January 26, 2017.
39. John Agar, "Kellogg Community College Curbs Student's Free Speech with Arrest, Lawsuit Says," MLive, January 18, 2017.
40. FIRE, "What Are Speech Codes?" FIRE, https://www.thefire.org/resources /spotlight/what-are-speech-codes/.
41. Keith E. Whittington, *Speak Freely: Why Universities Must Defend Free Speech* (Princeton and Oxford: Princeton University Press, 2018), xi, 30, 6.
42. Peter Berkowitz, "Colleges' Central Mission Erodes—and Free Speech with It," *Real Clear Politics*, April 7, 2018.
43. David L. Hudson Jr., First Amendment Scholar, and Lata Nott, Executive Director, First Amendment Center, "Hate Speech & Campus Speech Codes," Freedom Forum Institute, March 2017.
44. Ibid.
45. Ibid.
46. Jonathan Turley, "No, the U.S. Does Not Need European-Style Hate Speech Laws," *USA Today*, November 8, 2019.
47. Doug Stanglin, "What is antifa and what does the movement want?," *USA Today*, August 23, 2017, https://www.usatoday.com/story/news/2017/08/23 /what-antifa-and-what-does-movement-want/593867001/.
48. Anna Giaritelli, "Video Shows Car Set Ablaze by Alleged Antifa Shooter in Attack on ICE Detention Center," *Washington Examiner*, August 16, 2019.
49. Robby Soave, "Yes, You Can Get Kicked Off Twitter for Saying 'Learn To

Code'—Even If It's Not Harasssment," *Reason*, March 11, 2019, https://reason
.com/2019/03/11/learn-to-code-twitter-harassment-ross/.

50. Richard Hanania, "It Isn't Your Imagination: Twitter Treats Conservatives
   More Harshly Than Liberals," *Quillette*, February 12, 2019.

51. Ibid.

52. Ibid.

53. Todd Spangler, "Facebook's Sheryl Sandberg Pulls for Hillary Clinton Presidential Win, Citing Her Kids," *Variety*, July 29, 2016.

54. Ibid.

55. Kara Swisher, "Google Has Fired the Employee Who Penned a Controversial
   Memo on Women and Tech," *Vox*, August 7, 2017.

56. David Crary, Rachel Zoll, and Michael Liedtke, "Mozilla CEO Resignation
   Raises Free-Speech Issue," *USA Today*, April 4, 2014.

57. "Insider Blows Whistle & Exec Reveals Google Plan to Prevent 'Trump Situation" on Hidden Cam," Bitchute, June 24, 2018.

58. Auguste Meyrat, "Here's the Real Reason Most Conservative Elites Ignore
   Concerns About Free Speech," *Federalist*, July 30, 2019.

59. Ben Domenech, "How Tech Bias Became a Kitchen Table Issue," *Federalist*,
   June 25, 2019.

60. Ibid.

61. Ibid.

62. Brad Parscale, "Democrats Want to Limit Free Speech, Regain an Iron Grip
   on 'The Narrative,' " *Townhall*, November 1, 2019.

63. Ibid.

64. Josh Hawley, "Senator Hawley Introduces Legislation to Amend Section 230
   Immunity for Big Tech Companies," Hawley.Senate.gov, June 19, 2019.

65. Peter Ban Buren, "When Censorship Moves Way Beyond Alex Jones," *American Conservative*, June 17, 2019.

66. Ibid.

67. Editorial, "Adam Schiff Renews the Democratic War Against the First
   Amendment," *Washington Examiner*, May 10, 2019.

68. *Citizens United v. Federal Election Commission*, 558 U.S. 310, 2010.

69. Hans A. von Spakovsky and Elizabeth Slattery, "Senate Democrats Again
   Pushing to Silence Freedom of Speech," Heritage Foundation, June 2, 2014.

70. Editorial, "Adam Schiff Renews the Democratic War Against the First
   Amendment," *Washington Examiner*, May 10, 2019.

71. Von Spakovsky and Slattery, "Senate Democrats Again Pushing to Silence
   Freedom of Speech."

72. "Rep Schiff Introduces Constitutional Amendment to Overturn Citizens
   United," Press Release, Office of Congressman Adam Schiff, May 8, 2019,
   https://schiff.house.gov/news/press-releases/rep-schiff-introduces-constitu
   tional-amendment-to-overturn-citizens-united.

73. "Is H.R. 1 Really 'for the People?' " Heritage Action, March 7, 2019.

74. Editorial, "Dems Priority List Includes Attacks on Free Speech and Gun Rights," *Investors' Business Daily*, November 12, 2018.

75. Ronald Newman and Kate Ruane, American Civil Liberties Union, "Letter to Rep. Jim McGovern and Rep. Tom Cole," ACLU, March 1, 2019, https://www.aclu.org/sites/default/files/field_document/2019-03-01_aclu_letter_to_house_rules_committee_on_h.r._1.pdf.

76. Caleb Parke, "Democratic Party Embraces Nonreligious Voters, Criticizes 'Religious Liberty' in New Resolution," Fox News, August 29, 2019.

77. Ibid.

78. Ibid.

79. Democratic National Committee, "Resolution Regarding the Religiously Unaffiliated Demographic," Secular.org, August 2019, https://secular.org/wp-content/uploads/2019/08/DNC-Resolution-on-the-Nonreligious-Demographic.pdf.

80. David French, "Yes, American Religious Liberty Is in Peril," *Wall Street Journal*, July 26, 2019.

81. Casey Chalk, "Religious People Think Democrats Will Strip Our Rights Because It's True," *Federalist*, January 1, 2020.

82. Joseph D'Souza, "Can We Trust the Democratic Presidential Candidates to Defend Religious Freedom," *Washington Examiner*, October 28, 2019.

83. Ibid.

84. President Donald J. Trump, "Remarks by President Trump at Values Voter Summit," Whitehouse.gov, October 12, 2019.

85. Mark David Hall, "Donald Trump and Religious Liberty," Imaginative Conservative, January 20, 2020.

86. Attorney General William Barr, "Remarks to the Law School and the de Nicola Center for Ethics and Culture at the University of Notre Dame," Justice.org, October 11, 2019.

87. Brian Leiter, *Why Tolerate Religion* (Princeton, NJ: Princeton University Press, 2014).

88. Micah Schwartzman, "What If Religion Is Not So Special," *University of Chicago Law Review*, January 11, 2013.

CHAPTER 9: TRUMP TRIUMPHS

1. Ed Pilkington, "Obama angers midwest voters with guns and religion remark," *Guardian*, April 14, 2008, https://www.theguardian.com/world/2008/apr/14/barackobama.uselections2008.

2. Ibid.

3. Tim Marcini, "Democratic Congressman Compares Donald Trump to Hitler, Calls President 'Racist Strongman,' " *Newsweek*, January 3, 2019.

4. "Everything You Need to Know About the Tax Cut and Jobs Act," Tax Foundation, https://taxfoundation.org/tax-reform-explained-tax-cuts-and-jobs-act/.

5. Adam Michel, "Analysis of the 2017 Tax Cuts and Job Acts," Heritage Foundation, December 19, 2017.

6. "President Donald J. Trump's Achievements, Economy and Jobs," Promises Kept, https://www.promiseskept.com/achievement/overview/economy-and-jobs/.

7. Tyler Durden, "Barack Obama Is Now the Only President in History to Never Have a Year of 3% GDP Growth," Zero Hedge, January 27, 2017.

8. Amanda Prestigiacomo, "Obama Tries to Take Credit for Trump's Economy. It Backfires Bigly," *Daily Wire*, February 17, 2020.

9. "Economic Growth Has Reached 3 Percent for the First Time in More than a Decade Thanks to President Donald J. Trump's Policies," WhiteHouse.gov, February 28, 2019.

10. Lawrence H. Summers, "Larry Summers: Trump's Budget is Simply Ludicrous," *Washington Post*, May 23, 2017.

11. Susan Jones, "155,965,000 Employed in July; 11th Record-Setter Under Trump," CNS News, August 3, 2018.

12. Council of Economic Advisers, "Unemployment Rate Falls to Lowest Level in Nearly 50 Years; U.S. Economy Adds 263,000 New Jobs in April," WhiteHouse.gov, May 3, 2019.

13. "US Job Openings Jump to Record High of 7.3 Million," CNBC, February 12, 2019.

14. Council of Economic Advisers, "U.S. Unemployment Rate Remains at Near-Historic Low of 3.7 Percent; African-American Unemployment Rate Hits New Series Low," WhiteHouse.gov, https://www.whitehouse.gov/articles/u-s-unemployment-rate-remains-at-near-historic-low-of-3-7-percent-african-american-unemployment-rate-hits-new-series-low/.

15. Ibid.

16. Paul Bedard, "Boom: Best Economic Optimism in 16 Years, 50% 'Better Off' Under Trump," *Washington Examiner*, February 11, 2019.

17. Joe Williams, "Manufacturing Confidence at All-Time High Despite Workforce Shortage," *Washington Examiner*, October 5, 2018.

18. Council of Economic Advisers, "U.S. Unemployment Rate Remains at Near-Historic Low of 3.7 Percent."

19. Council of Economic Advisers, "Job Market Continues to Crush Expectations in 2020," WhiteHouse.gov, February 7, 2020.

20. Justin Haskins, "Trump's Big Reelection Weapon: A Remarkable Manufacturing Jobs Boom," *Hill*, January 23, 2020.

21. Council of Economic Advisers, "Job Market Continues to Crush Expectations in 2020."

22. Council of Economic Advisers, "U.S. Unemployment Rate Remains at Near-Historic Low of 3.7 Percent."

23. Elaine Parker, "Women Are Winning in the Trump Economy," *Real Clear Politics*, October 2, 2018.

24. Council of Economic Advisers, "U.S. Job Growth Remains Strong, Adding 196,000 Jobs in March and Surpassing Market Expectations," WhiteHouse .gov, April 5, 2019.

25. Haskins, "Trump's Big Reelection Weapon: A Remarkable Manufacturing Jobs Boom."

26. Ibid.

27. Eric Morath and Jeffery Sparshott, "Rank-and-File Workers Get Bigger Raises," *Wall Street Journal*, December 27, 2019.

28. Stephen Moore, "Trump's Middle-Class Economic Progress," *WSJ Opinion*, September 29, 2019.

29. Frank Connor, "Income Inequality Declining Under Trump Policies, Says Labor Secretary," Fox Business, January 24, 2020.

30. Council of Economic Advisers, "The Blue-Collar Labor Boom Reduces Inequality," WhiteHouse.gov, January 15, 2020.

31. Stephen Moore, "It's a Middle-Class Boom," *Real Clear Politics*, October 15, 2019.

32. Stephen Moore, "Contrary to What the Media Reports, Middle Class Americans Are Surging," *Hill*, January 6, 2020.

33. Ibid.

34. Paul Bedard, "Exclusive: Trump List Shows 319 'Results' and Promises Kept in Three Years," *Washington Examiner*, December 31, 2019, https://www.scribd .com/document/441370872/ACFrOgAUTMl8Xt31z9R-Bha0n5a-c1S2g31eEY qYd9r9EG1r7I6PoFo9orDZoay8eaEN1BNbXyne01QqUo19M2cM60XJO 4QgQ2RtpPLz-4-uo9-KQ6EE7HLrMsLpIEs#fullscreen&from_embed.

35. Evie Fordham, "Trump Touts 'Single Largest Decline' In Drug Prices in Nearly 50 Years," *Daily Caller*, February 5, 2019.

36. "Costs and Burden of Federal Regulations Reach $1.9 Trillion," Competitive Enterprise Institute, May 31, 2017.

37. Haskins, "Trump's Big Reelection Weapon: A Remarkable Manufacturing Jobs Boom."

38. Cheryl Bolen, "Trump Touts Regulatory Savings of Nearly $50 Billion for Economy," Bloomberg Law, October 21, 2019.

39. Hayley Sledge, "Trump Deregulation Will Save $3100 Per Household, CEA Reports," Heartland Institute, August 8, 2019.

40. President Donald J. Trump, "President Trump's Historic Deregulation Is Benefitting All Americans," WhiteHouse.gov, October 21, 2019.

41. Kenneth Corbin, "White House Looks to Relax Rules for Workplace Retirement Plans," *Benefit News*, August 31, 2018.

42. Nate Madden, "Trump Takes Aim at 'Out-of-Control Bureaucracy' with 2 New Executive Orders," *Conservative Review*, October 10, 2019.

43. Keith Good, "Trump Administration Rolls Back 'Waters of the U.S.' Rule," *Farm Policy News*, September 19, 2109.

44. Oliver Milman, "Trump Administration Scraps Obama-era Regulation on Coal Emissions," *Guardian*, August 21, 2018.

45. William Yeatman, "Congress Should Eliminate Obama's Stream Protection Rule," Competitive Enterprise Institute, January 31, 2017.

46. Devin Henry, "Trump Signs Bill Undoing Obama Coal Mining Rule," *Hill*, February 11, 2017.

47. "Trump Administration Replaces Obama-era Power Plant Rule, in Boost to Coal," Reuters, June 19, 2019.

48. Todd Spangler and Nathan Bomey, "Trump Administration Wants to Freeze Gas-Mileage Standards, Reversing Obama," *USA Today*, August 2, 2018.

49. Juliet Ellperin and Brady Dennis, "Trump Promised His Mileage Standards Would Make Cars Cheaper and Safer. New Documents Raise Doubts About That," *Washington Post*, January 23, 2020.

50. Tom Krisher and Ellen Knickmeyer, "Trump Ups Mileage Proposal, But It's Well Below Obama Plan," Associated Press, January 24, 2020.

51. President Donald J. Trump, "Executive Order Establishing a White House Council on Eliminating Regulatory Barriers to Affordable Housing," White House.gov, June 25, 2019.

52. Juliet Ellperin, "Trump Signs Executive Order to Expand Drilling off America's Coasts: 'We're Opening It Up,'" *Washington Post*, April 28, 2017.

53. "Judge Throws Out Trump Order That Overturned Obama Offshore Drilling Ban in Arctic," CNBC, March 30, 2019.

54. Elizabeth Harball, "Trump Administration Appeals Ruling That Blocked Arctic Offshore Drilling," Alaska Public, May 28, 2019.

55. "President Donald J. Trump's Achievements, Energy and the Environment," Promises Kept, https://www.promiseskept.com/achievement/overview /energy-and-environment/.

56. Emily Holden, "Trump Opens Protected Alaskan Arctic Refuge to Oil Drillers," *Guardian*, September 12, 2019.

57. David Smith, "Trump Orders Revival of Keystone XL and Dakota Access Pipelines," *Guardian*, January 24, 2017.

58. "President Donald J. Trump Achievements, Energy and Environment," Promises Kept, https://www.promiseskept.com/achievement/overview /energy-and-environment/.

59. Nina Lakhani, "Major Blow to Keystone XL Pipeline as Judge Revokes Key Permit," *Guardian*, April 15, 2020.

60. Timothy Cama, "Trump Approves US-Mexico Pipeline: 'That'll Go Right Under the Wall,'" *Hill*, June 29, 2017.

61. "President Donald J. Trump Achievements, Energy and Environment," Promises Kept, https://www.promiseskept.com/achievement/overview/energy-and-environment/.
62. Matt Egan, "America Is Now the World's Largest Oil Producer," CNN Business, September 12, 2018.
63. "Oil Exploration Firm Claims Discovery of Huge Alaska Deposit," MSN .com, April 10, 2020.
64. David J. Lynch, Josh Dawsey, and Damian Paletta, "Trump Imposes Steel and Aluminum Tariffs on the E.U., Canada and Mexico," *Washington Post*, May 31, 2018.
65. Iain Murray, "Free Traders Shouldn't Mourn the Loss of the TPP," Foundation for Economic Education, January 26, 2017.
66. David Smith and Dominic Rushe, "Trump and EU Officials Agree to Work Toward 'Zero Tariff' Deal," *Guardian*, July 25, 2018.
67. Sergei Klebnikov, "6 Key Takeaways from the U.S.–Japan Trade Deal," *Forbes*, October 8, 2019.
68. "Cuba Denounces Trump's Policy Rollback," BBC News, June 17, 2017.
69. Jessica Campisi, "US Imposes New Sanctions on Cuba Over Human Rights, Venezuela," *Hill*, October 18, 2019.
70. Jeff Faux, "NAFTA's Impact on U.S. Workers," Economic Policy Institute, December 9, 2013.
71. Ana Swanson and Jim Tankersley, "Trump Just Signed the U.S.M.C.A. Here's What's in the New NAFTA," *New York Times*, January 29, 2020.
72. "President Trump Announces Strong Actions to Address China's Unfair Trade," Office of the United States Trade Representative, Executive Office of the President, March 22, 2018.
73. Don Lee, "Trump Bans Huawei in U.S. Markets, Saying Chinese Firm Poses Security Threat," *Los Angeles Times*, May 15, 2019.
74. "Making America Great Again, Trade and Foreign Policy," Promises Kept, https://www.promiseskept.com/achievement/overview/foreign-policy/.
75. Yun Li, "Trump Says US Will Impose 10% Tariffs on Another $300 Billion of Chinese Goods Starting Sept. 1," CNBC, August 1, 2019.
76. Alan Rappeport and Keith Bradsher, "Trump Says He Will Raise Existing Tariffs on Chinese Goods to 30%," *New York Times*, August 23, 2019.
77. Thomas Franck, "Trump Halts New China Tariffs and Rolls Back Some of the Prior Duties on $120 Billion of Imports," CNBC, December 13, 2019.
78. Bedard, "Exclusive: Trump List Shows 319 'Results' and Promises Kept in Three Years."
79. Thomas Franck, "Trump Halts New China Tariffs and Rolls Back Some of the Prior Duties on $120 Billion of Imports," CNBC, December 13, 2019.
80. George R. Altman and Leo Shane III, "The Obama Era Is Over. Here's How the Military Rates His Legacy," *Military Times*, January 8, 2017.

81. Barack Obama, "Read President Obama's Commencement Address at West Point in 2014," *Time*, https://time.com/4341783/obamas-commence ment-transcript-speech-west-point-2014/; http://www.washingtonpost .com/politics/full-text-of-president-obamas-commencement-address -at-west-point/2014/05/28/cfbcdcaa-e670-11e3-afc6-a1dd9407abcf _story.html.

82. Altman and Shane III, "The Obama Era is Over. Here's How the Military Rates His Legacy."

83. James Jay Carafano, "Yes: Obama-Era Cuts Left U.S. Too Weak to Deal with Multiple Global Menaces," Heritage Foundation, March 24, 2017.

84. Thomas C. Donnelly, "Doctrine of Decline," *National Review*, January 23, 2017.

85. Ibid.

86. Philip Ewing, "Fact Check: Has President Obama 'Depleted' the Military?" NPR, April 29, 2016.

87. Mark Moyar, "How Obama Shrank the Military," *Wall Street Journal*, August 2, 2015.

88. Ibid.

89. Ibid.

90. Ibid.

91. Lawrence J. Korb, "Trump's Defense Budget," Center for American Progress, February 28, 2018.

92. Amy Bushatz, "Trump Signs 2018 Defense Bill: Here's What It Means for You," Military.com, December 12, 2017.

93. "Making America Great Again, National Security and Defense," Promises Kept, https://www.promiseskept.com/achievement/overview/national-sec urity-and-defense/.

94. Leo Shane III and Joe Gould, "Trump Praises US Military Buildup but Vows Overseas Troop Cuts in State of the Union Address," *Defense News*, February 6, 2020.

95. "Making America Great Again, National Security and Defense," Promises Kept, https://www.promiseskept.com/achievement/overview/national-sec urity-and-defense/.

96. Nancy A. Youssef and Gordon Lubold, "Trump Announces Creation of U.S. Space Command," *Wall Street Journal*, August 29, 2019.

97. Rachel S. Cohen, "Space Force Established as Trump Signs NDAA," *Air Force Magazine*, December 20, 2019.

98. "VA Mission Act," Military Benefits, https://militarybenefits.info/va-mis sion-act/.

99. Jessica Kim Cohen, "Telemedicine Growth Follows 'Anywhere to Anywhere' Rule at VA," *Modern Healthcare*, November 25, 2019.

100. Geoff Bennett, "Congress Passes Bill to Increase Accountability Among VA Employees," NPR, June 13, 2017.

101. "Veterans Appeals Improvement and Modernization Act of 2017," VFW.org, May 2, 2017.

102. Elizabeth Howe, "The White House VA Hotline Has Answered 250,000 Calls," Connectingvets.com, May 22, 2019.

103. "VA and White House Launch Veteran Suicide-Prevention Task Force," VA.gov, June 17, 2019.

104. President Donald J. Trump, "President Donald J. Trump Is Working Tirelessly to Provide the Benefits and Services That Our Brave Veterans Deserve," WhiteHouse.gov, August 21, 2019.

105. "Latest Employment Numbers," United States Department of Labor, https:// www.dol.gov/agencies/vets/latest-numbers.

106. "NATO Secretary General Stoltenberg After 1:1 Meeting/London, United Kingdom," WhiteHouse.gov, December 3, 2019.

107. Jessica Donati and Peter Nicholas, "With Evangelicals Behind Him, Vice President Mike Pence Takes Prominent Role in Foreign Policy," Wall Street Journal, February 19, 2019.

108. President Donald J. Trump, "Remarks by President Trump on His Trip to Asia," WhiteHouse.gov, November 15, 2017.

109. Steve Holland and Matthew Tostevin, "Trump Brings Tough Trade Message in Vision for Asia," Reuters, November 10, 2017.

110. "U.S. Imposes Sanctions on People, Firms It Says Helped North Korea Evade Sanctions," Reuters, August 30, 2019.

111. Tom O'Connor, "What's Next for Kim Jon Un and Donald Trump? U.S., China and Russia React to North Korea's New Warning," Newsweek, January 3, 2020.

112. Brooke Singman, "US Opens Embassy in Jerusalem, Recognizing City as 'True Capital' of Israel," Fox News, May 14, 2018.

113. Eli Rosenberg and Carol Morello, "U.S. Withdraws from UNESCO, the U.N.'s cultural organization, Citing Anti-Israel Bias," Washington Post, October 12, 2017.

114. Vanessa Romo, "Trump Formally Recognizes Israeli Sovereignty Over Golan Heights," NPR, March 25, 2019.

115. "Presidential Executive Order on Assessing and Strengthening the Manufacturing and Defense Industrial Base and Supply Chain Resiliency of the United States," WhiteHouse.gov, July 21, 2017.

116. Carol Morello, "Trump Administration Hits Iran with Fresh Sanctions After Attack on U.S. Forces," Washington Post, January 10, 2020.

117. "Joined by Allies, President Trump Takes Action to End Syria's Chemical Weapons Attacks," WhiteHouse.gov, April 14, 2018.

118. Kathy Gilsinan, "An American Prisoner Comes Home from Iran," Atlantic, December 7, 2019.

119. John Fritze and Deirdre Shesgreen, "Trump Says U.S. Citizen Danny Burch Held in Yemen Has Returned to Family," USA Today, February 25, 2019.

120. Brady Dennis, "Trump Makes it Official: U.S. Will Withdraw from the Paris Climate Accord," *Washington Post*, November 4, 2019.
121. Thomas L. Mason, "Obama's Parting Shot," *Washington Times*, December 15, 2016.
122. David Brown, "Trump Says U.S. 'Will Never Ratify' Arms Trade Treaty," *Politico*, April 26, 2019.
123. Carle Hulse, "Trump and Senate Republicans Celebrate Making the Courts More Conservative," *New York Times*, November 6, 2019.
124. "Judicial Appointment Tracker," Heritage Foundation, https://www.heritage .org/judicialtracker.
125. Richard A. Arenberg, "The Trumpification of the Federal Courts," *The Hill*, January 6, 2020.
126. Bedard, "Exclusive: Trump List Shows 319 'Results' and Promises Kept in Three Years"; "President Donald J. Trump Is Appointing a Historic Number of Federal Judges to Uphold Our Constitution as Written," WhiteHouse.gov, November 6, 2019.
127. "Donald Trump on Abortion," On the Issues, https://www.ontheissues.org /Celeb/Donald_Trump_Abortion.htm.
128. "Trump Reinstates 'Mexico City Policy' on Abortion," *Long Island Catholic*, January 23, 2020.
129. Jonathan Abbamonte, "House Democrats Push for a Repeal of the Mexico City Policy," Population Research Institute, January 23, 2019.
130. Claire Chretien, "US Still Gives Millions to American Pro-Abort Groups That Work Internationally: New Plan Would Stop It," *LifeSite News*, January 23, 2020.
131. "U.S. Withdraws Funding for U.N. Population Fund," Reuters, April 3, 2017.
132. Jina Moore, "The Trump Administration Just Cut All Funding for the UN's Family Planning Agency," *BuzzFeed News*, April 3, 2017.
133. "U.S. Withdraws Funding for U.N. Population Fund," Reuters, April 3, 2017.
134. Colin Dwyer, "Trump Signs Law Giving States Option to Deny Funding for Planned Parenthood," NPR, April 13, 2017.
135. Jessie Hellman, "Trump Administration Rescinds Obama Guidance on Defunding Planned Parenthood," *Hill*, January 19, 2018.
136. Arian Eunjung Cha, "Is it a Gag Rule After All? A Closer Look at Changes to Title X Funding Regarding Abortion," *Washington Post*, May 23, 2018, and "Statutes and Regulations, Title X Notice of Final Rule," HHS.gov, March 4, 2019.
137. Ricardo Alonso-Zaldivar and Lauran Neergaard, "Trump Halts Fetal Tissue Research by Government Scientists," ABC News, June 5, 2019.
138. "President Trump's Pro-Life Wins," Susan B. Anthony List, https://www.sba -list.org/trump-pro-life-wins.
139. Tim Hains, "Trump Speaks at Annual 'March for Life' Rally: 'Unborn Children Have Never Had a Stronger Defender,' " *Real Clear Politics*, January 24, 2020.

140. Phil Thomas and Clark Mindock, "Trump Calls for Ban to 'Late-term' Abortion During State of the Union Address," *Independent*, February 5, 2020.

141. Ali Vitali, "'Trump Signs 'Religious Liberty' Executive Order Allowing for Broad Exemptions," NBC News, May 4, 2017.

142. Emma Green, "Why Trump's Executive Order on Religious Liberty Left Many Conservatives Dissatisfied," *Atlantic*, May 4, 2017.

143. Jess Bravin, "Trump Administration Backs Baker Who Refused to Make Wedding Cake for Gay Couple," *Wall Street Journal*, September 8, 2017.

144. "Executive Order on the Establishment of a White House Faith and Opportunity Initiative," WhiteHouse.gov, May 3, 2018.

145. "HHS Announces Final Conscience Rule Protecting Health Care Entities and Individuals," HHS.gov, May 2, 2019.

146. "United States Hosts First-Ever Ministerial to Advance International Religious Freedom," U.S. Department of State, July 27, 2018, https://medium .com/statedept/united-states-hosts-first-ever-ministerial-to-advance-inter national-religious-freedom-ff84a3f174c7.

147. Attorney General Jeff Sessions, "Attorney General Sessions Delivers Remarks at the Department of Justice's Religious Liberty Summit," United States Department of Justice, July 30, 2018.

148. Kelsey Dallas, "Justice Department Speaks Out on Church Closures, Condemns Religious Freedom Violations in New Statement," *Deseret News*, April 14, 2020.

149. Devin Dwyer, "Supreme Court to Decide Fate of Cross-Shaped WWI Memorial in Maryland," ABC News, February 25, 2019.

150. Adiel Kaplan, David Mora, Maya Miller, and Andrew R. Calderon, "Trump Admin Files More Briefs in Religious Liberty Cases than Obama, Bush," NBC News, February 24, 2019.

151. Tim Haines, "President Trump at UN Summit: USA Calls On the World to End Religious Persecution," *Real Clear Politics*, September 23, 2019.

152. Samuel Smith, "Trump Announces $25 Million Fund, New Business Coalition to Protect Religious Freedom," *Christian Post*, September 23, 2019.

153. Mary Margaret Olohan, "HHS Secretary Tells UN General Assembly: 'There Is No International Right to an Abortion," *Daily Signal*, September 25, 2019.

154. Moriah Balingit and Ariana Eunjung Cha, "Trump Administration Moves to Protect Prayer in Public Schools and Federal Funds for Religious Organizations," *Washington Post*, January 16, 2020.

155. Ewelina U. Ochab, "U.S. Launches the First-Ever International Religious Freedom Alliance," *Forbes*, February 6, 2020.

156. Mairead McCardle, "Trump Says Federal Government Will Begin Withholding Funds from Sanctuary Cities After Court Ruling," *National Review*, March 5, 2020.

157. Jeremy Diamond, "Trump Orders Construction of Border Wall, Boosts Deportation Force," CNN Politics, January 15, 2017.

158. White House, "Executive Order: Enhancing Public Safety in the Interior of the United States," January 25, 2017.

159. White House, "Executive Order: Border Security and Immigration Enforcement Improvements," January 25, 2017.

160. White House, "Executive Order: Protecting the Nation from Foreign Terrorist Entry into the United States," January 27, 2017.

161. Michael D. Shear, Nicholas Kulish, and Alan Feuer, "Judge Blocks Trump Order on Refugees Amid Chaos and Outcry Worldwide," New York Times, January 28, 2017.

162. Adam Liptak, "Court Refuses to Reinstate Travel Ban, Dealing Trump Another Legal Loss," New York Times, February 9, 2017.

163. Hans A. von Spakovsky, "Why the U.S. Is Right to Refuse to Sign UN Migration Compact," Heritage Foundation, December 11, 2018.

164. Aria Bendix, "Trump Rolls Back DAPA," Atlantic, June 16, 2017.

165. David Jackson, Kevin Johnson, and Alan Gomez, "Trump Winds Down DACA Program for Undocumented Immigrants, Gives Congress 6 Months to Act," USA Today, September 5, 2017.

166. Ron Nixon, Liz Robbins, and Katie Benner, "Trump Targets MS-13, a Violent Menace, if Not the One He Portrays," New York Times, March 1, 2018.

167. "3,800 Gang Members Charged in Operation Spanning United States and Central America," United States Department of Justice, September 29, 2017.

168. DoD News, "National Guard Troops Deploy to Southern U.S. Border," Army .mil, April 9, 2018.

169. Peter Baker, "Trump Declares a National Emergency, and Provokes a Constitutional Clash," New York Times, February 15, 2019.

170. Jose Cabezas, "Mexico Says National Guard Deployment to Southern Border Starts on Wednesday," Reuters, June 12, 2019.

171. "U.S. Border: Mexico Announces 56% Migrant Drop After Crackdown," BBC, September 6, 2019.

172. Saagar Enjeti, "Trump Has Secured Funding for More than Half of Border Wall," Daily Caller, March 7, 2019.

173. Saagar Enjeti, "Trump's Prophecy on Border Wall Lawsuit Comes True," Daily Caller, February 19, 2019.

174. Miriam Jordan, "Judge Issues Nationwide Injunction Blocking Border Wall Funding," New York Times, December 10, 2019.

175. Josh Gerstein, "Appeals Court Lifts Block on $3.6 Billion for Trump Border Wall Plan," Politico, January 8, 2020.

176. President Trump's Bold Immigration Plan for the 21st Century," White House.gov, May 21, 2019.

177. "Department of Justice Prosecuted a Record-Breaking Number of Immigration-

Related Cases in Fiscal Year 2019," United States Department of Justice, October 17, 2019.

178. Fact Sheet, "President Donald J. Trump Has Made It a Priority to Combat the Heinous Crime of Human Trafficking," WhiteHouse.gov, October 29, 2019.

179. Kevin Johnson and Kristine Phillips, "Trump Administration Cracks Down on Sanctuary Communities; AG Touts New Legal Challlenges," *USA Today*, February 11, 2020.

180. Pam Fessler, "Trump Administration Rule Would Penalize Immigrants for Needing Benefits," NPR, August 12, 2019.

181. Nicole Narea, "Trump's Rule Creating a Wealth Test for Immigrants Is Now in Effect," *Vox*, February 24, 2020.

182. Editorial Board, "Obamacare's Tax on the Poor," *Wall Street Journal*, September 22, 2017.

183. Peter Sullivan, "Analysis: Repeal of Obamacare Taxes in Bipartisan Spending Deal Costs $373B," *Hill*, December 17, 2019.

184. President Donald J. Trump, "Presidential Executive Order Promoting Healthcare Choice and Competition Across the United States," WhiteHouse.gov, October 12, 2017.

185. "AlphaBay, the Largest Online 'Dark Market' Shut Down," Justice.gov., July 20, 2017.

186. "Ending America's Opioid Crisis," WhiteHouse.gov, https://www.whitehouse.gov/opioids/.

187. Rema Rahman and Andrew Siddons, "Trump Declares Opioid Crisis a 'National Health Emergency,'" *Roll Call*, October 26, 2017.

188. "Ending America's Opioid Crisis," WhiteHouse.gov, https://www.whitehouse.gov/opioids/.

189. "USDA Invests More than $1 Billion to Improve Health Care in Rural Areas," USDA, November 17, 2017.

190. Julie Rovner, "CHIP Renewed for Six Years as Congress Votes to Reopen Federal Government," *Kaiser Health News*, January 22, 2018; Heather Long, "Let's Remember: 9 Million Kids' Health Insurance Is at Stake in This Budget Fight," *Washington Post*, January 18, 2018.

191. Jessie Hellmann, "Trump Signs 'right to try' Drug Bill," *The Hill*, May 30, 2018.

192. Avik Roy, "Trump's New Medicare Rule to Reduce Prescription Drug Prices Through Competition," *Forbes*, August 7, 2018.

193. Berkeley Lovelace Jr., "Trump Signs Executive Order on Medicare, Says He Won't Let Democrats Steal Your Health Care," CNBC, October 3, 2019.

194. Kate Patrick, "FDA Approves Record Number of Generic Drugs, but Do They Help Lower Drug Prices?" Inside Sources, October 23, 2019.

195. Council of Economic Advisers, "Prescription Drug Prices Are Falling at His-

toric Levels Thanks to Trump Administration Policies," WhiteHouse.gov, November 5, 2019.

196. Jocelyn Kaiser, "Researchers Weigh In on Trump's $500 Million Plan to Share Childhood Cancer Data," *Science Magazine*, August 5, 2019.

197. Madeleine Carlisle, "Federal Legal Age to Buy Tobacco Products Officially Raised to 21," *Time*, December 23, 2019.

198. German Lopez, "The First Step Act, Explained," *Vox*, February 5, 2019.

199. Donald J. Trump, "Remarks by President Trump at the 2018 Project Safe Neighborhoods National Conference," WhiteHouse.gov, December 7, 2018.

200. Melanie Arter, "Trump Credits Project Safe Neighborhoods with Drop in Homicides During His Adminstration," CNS News, February 14, 2019.

CHAPTER 10: TRUMP'S RESPONSE TO THE CORONAVIRUS AND AMERICA'S GREAT COMEBACK

1. Audrey Conklin, "China's 3-week delay in coronavirus response accelerated spread: study," Fox Business, March 19, 2020.

2. "60% of Democrats Blame Trump More Than China for Coronavirus," Rasmussen Reports, April 20, 2020.

3. Dave Sminara, "The Democrats' 2020 Coronavirus Hindsight," *Wall Street Journal*, April 19, 2020.

4. Ibid.

5. Patrick Goodenough, "Coronavirus Was All but Ignored in First Three Democrat Debates of the Year," CNS News, April 20, 2020.

6. Ibid.

7. Ibid.

8. Jake Tapper, "Biden Campaign Says He Backs Trump's China Travel Ban," CNN, April 3, 2020.

9. "Tapper presses Polosi on new coronavirus law," CNN.com, https://www.cnn .com/videos/politics/2020/04/26/sotu-nancy-pelosi-full.cnn.

10. Mairead McCardle, "Pelosi Denies Downplaying Coronavirus by Inviting People to 'Come to Chinatown' in February, Claims She Was Fighting 'Discrimination,'" *National Review*, April 20, 2020; "Chris Wallace grills Pelosi on her own disregard for social distancing," Fox News YouTube Channel, April 19, 2020, https://www.youtube.com/watch?v=R2CJ0PNLNKw.

11. Nick Arama, "Holy Cow: Dan Crenshaw Takes Apart Bill Maher on Trump Response to Virus, Just Leaves Him Wrecked," *Red State*, April 19, 2020.

12. "Emergency Preparedness and Response," Centers for Disease Control and Prevention, Janaury 17, 2020.

13. Bret Baier, "Sources Believe Coronavirus Outbreak Originated in Wuhan Lab as Part of China's Efforts to Compete with US," Fox News, April 17, 2020.

14. "Emergency Preparedness and Response," Centers for Disease Control and Prevention, Janaury 17, 2020.
15. "Press Release: Public Health Screening to Begin at 3 U.S. Airports for 2019 Novel Coronavirus ('2019-nCoV')," Centers for Disease Control and Prevention, January 17, 2020.
16. Elizabeth Cohen, "Vaccine for New Chinese Coronavirus in the Works," CNN, January 20, 2020.
17. "Initial Public Health Response and Interim Clinical Guidance for the 2019 Novel Coronavirus Outbreak—United States, December 31, 2019–February 4, 2020," *Centers for Disease Control and Prevention*, February 7, 2020.
18. CDC Newsroom, "First Travel-Related Case of 2019 Novel Coronavirus Detected in the United States," Centers for Disease Control and Prevention, January 21, 2020.
19. Julie Steenhuysen, "U.S. Health Officials Seek Emergency Approval to Use Diagnostic Test for New Coronavirus," *U.S. News & World Report*, January 23, 2020.
20. "Statement from the Press Secretary Regarding the President's Coronavirus Task Force," WhiteHouse.gov, Janaury 29, 2020.
21. "Proclamation on Suspension of Entry as Immigrants and Nonimmigrants of Persons Who Pose a Risk of Transmitting 2019 Novel Coronavirus," WhiteHouse.gov, January 31, 2020.
22. "DHS Issues Supplemental Instructions for Inbound Flights with Indivdiuals Who Have Been in China," Department of Homeland Security, February 2, 2020.
23. Gabriella Munoz, "House Democrats Schedule Vote on Bill to Dismantle Trump Travel Ban," *Washington Times*, March 7, 2020.
24. Gregg Re, "After Attacking Trump's Coronavirus-Related China Travel Ban as Xenophobic, Dems and Media Have Changed Tune," Fox News, April 1, 2020.
25. "Timeline: The Trump Administration's Decisive Actions to Combat the Coronavirus," DonaldJTrump.com, April 13, 2020.
26. Matthew Choi, "Trump Puts Pence in Charge of Coronavirus Response," *Politico*, March 26, 2020.
27. "Timeline: The Trump Administration's Decisive Actions to Combat the Coronavirus."
28. Caitlin Emma and Jennifer Scholtes, "House Swiftly Passes Bipartisan $8.3B Coronavirus Package," *Politico*, March 4, 2020.
29. "Timeline: The Trump Administration's Decisive Actions to Combat the Coronavirus."
30. Erica L. Green, "Rules Eased on Colleges Seeking to Close Their Campuses Amid Outbreak," *New York Times*, March 10, 2020.
31. Jack O'Brien and Mandy Roth, "President Trump Declares National Emer-

gency Due to COVID-19 Outbreak, Includes Hospital Waivers," Health LeadersMedia.com, March 13, 2020.

32. Saim Saeed, "Trump's Europe Travel Ban Explained," *Politico*, March 12, 2020; "Delivering on President Trump's Promise, Secretary DeVos Suspends Federal Student Loan Payments, Waives Interest During National Emergency," U.S. Department of Education, March 20, 2020, https://www .ed.gov/news/press-releases/delivering-president-trumps-promise-secre tary-devos-suspends-federal-student-loan-payments-waives-interest-dur ing-national-emergency.

33. Dian Schaffhauser, "Updated: Free Resources for Schools During COVID-19 Outbreak," TheJournal.com, April 17, 2020.

34. Dan Mangan, "Trump Issues 'Coronavirus Guidelines' for Next 15 Days to Slow Pandemic," CNBC, March 16, 2020.

35. Kevin Breuninger and Kevin Williams, "Trump Says Coronavirus Crisis Could Stretch Into August, May Look at Lockdown for 'Certain Areas,'" CNBC, March 16, 2020.

36. "USDA Announces Feeding Program Partnership in Response to COVID-19," USDA.gov, March 17, 2020.

37. Aaron Friedman, Phillip Gillespie, Nancy Schroeder, Timothy Silva, and Wilmer Hale, "Federal Reserve Announces Money Market Mutual Fund Liquidity Facility," JDSupra.com, March 20, 2020.

38. Ben Lane, "Fannie Mae, Freddie Mac, HUD Suspending All Forecolsures and Evictions," *Housing Wire*, March 18, 2020.

39. "Timeline: The Trump Administration's Decisive Actions to Combat the Coronavirus."

40. Sean Ludwig, "Families First Coronavirus Response Act: What Businesses Need to Know," U.S. Chamber of Commerce, March 26, 2020.

41. Laura Kelly and Morgant Chalfant, "State Dept. Urges US Citizens to Avoid All International Travel," *Hill*, March 19, 2020.

42. "Timeline: The Trump Administration's Decisive Actions to Combat the Coronavirus."

43. "The Arc's COVID-19 Updates: March 20, 2020," Arc Massachusetts, March 20, 2020.

44. "Timeline: The Trump Administration's Decisive Actions to Combat the Coronavirus."

45. "President Trump Signs into Law the Coronavirus Aid, Relief, and Economic Security (CARES) Act," *National Law Review*, March 29, 2020.

46. Ronn Blitzer, "Republicans Say Dems Blocking Coronavirus Relief Over 'Ideological Wish List,'" Fox News, March 23, 2020.

47. Maxim Lott, "Coronavirus Relief Bill Contains Nearly $12 Billion in Questionable Spending," Fox News, March 27, 2000.

48. "Trump Announces Social Distancing Guidelines Extended to April 30," CBS News, March 30, 2020.

49. Timeline: The Trump Administration's Decisive Actions to Combat the Coronavirus."

50. Ibid.

51. Press release, "Federal Reserve Takes Additional Actions to Provide Up to $2.3 Trillion in Loans to Support the Economy," Board of Governors of the Federal Reserve System, April 9, 2020.

52. "Timeline: The Trump Administration's Decisive Actions to Combat the Coronavirus."

53. Brett Samuels, "Trump to Convene Council Focused on Reopening the Country," Hill, April 10, 2020.

54. "Timeline: The Trump Administration's Decisive Actions to Combat the Coronavirus."

55. Ben Kennedy, "Restrictions Rolled Back in May? Trump Forms Second Task Force to Focus on US Economic Recovery," CBN News, April 14, 2020.

56. Tim Hains, "President Trump Announces Three-Phase Plan to Reopen Economy," Real Clear Politics, April 16, 2020.

57. Adam Edlman, Monica Alba, Hans Nichols, and Peter Alexander, "Trump Unveils Three-Phase Plan for States to Reopen Amid Coronavirus Pandemic," NBC News, April 16, 2020.

58. "Guidelines: Opening Up America Again," WhiteHouse.gov, https://www.whitehouse.gov/openingamerica/.

59. Ibid.

60. Greg Norman, "New York Gov. Cuomo to Protestors Wanting Economy Reopened: 'Get a Job as an Essential Worker,' " Fox News, April 23, 2020.

61. Jennifer Harper, "Rep. Alexandria Ocasio-Cortez Calls for National Work Boycott," Washington Times, April 22, 2020.

62. Emma Colton, " 'You Should Be Ashamed': Critics Unleash on Pelosi for Showing Off Freezer Loaded with Ice Cream," Washington Examiner, April 16, 2020.

63. Gail Collins, "Let's Call it Trumpvirus," New York Times, February 26, 2020.

64. Maureen Dowd, "Trump Makes Us Ill," New York Times, February 29, 2020.

65. "Joseph A. Wulfsohn, "New York Times Columnist Bret Stephens Declares Coronavirus is Trump's 'Chernobyl,' " Fox News, March 11, 2020.

66. Francoise Mouly, "Brian Stauffer's 'Under Control,' " NewYorker.com, February 27, 2020. https://www.newyorker.com/culture/cover-story/cover-story-2020-03-09.

67. Andrew Mark Miller, "MSNBC's Nicolle Wallace: Trump getting hurt politically is 'silver lining' to coronavirus pandemic," Washington Examiner, April 24, 2020.

68. https://twitter.com/juliaioffe/status/1243297913863835648?s=20

69. Rich Noyes, "STUDY: Washington Post Bashes Trump Virus Response with 25-to-1 Negative Headlines," MRCNewsbusters, April 25, 2020.

70. David Lynch, ""The Coronavirus crisis is exposing how the economy was not as strong as it seemed," *Washington Post*, March 28, 2020.

71. Peter Nicholas, "The Coronavirus Outbreak Could Bring Out the Worst in Trump," *Atlantic*, February 18, 2020.

72. Catherine E. Shoichet, "The US coronavirus travel ban could backfire. Here's how," CNN, February 7, 2020.

73. Silvia Amaro, "Trump's travel ban on many European countries is 'politically motivated,' analysts say," CNBC, March 13, 2020.

74. Adam Gabbatt, "Republicans Face Backlash Over Racist Labeling of Coronavirus," *Guardian*, March 10, 2020.

75. Brandon Tensley, "Coronavirus Task Force Another Example of Trump Administration's Lack ofDiversity," CNN, January 30, 2020.

76. Joseph A. Wulfsohn, "MSNBC Journalists Say Calling Coronavirus the 'Wuhan Virus' is 'Racist,' " Fox News, March 10, 2020.

77. Tristan Justice, "CNN: It's Racist to Say the Wuhan Virus Started in China," *Federalist*, March 12, 2020.

78. David Rutz, "Media Balk at Trump Calling Wuhan Virus 'Foreign,' " *Washington Free Beacon*, March 12, 2020.

79. https://twitter.com/chuckrossdc/status/1233835255230029831?s=21

80. "Olivia Nuzzi Asks Trump If a President Deserves to Be Re-Elected after Losing More Americans in Week," Brief News YouTube channel, April 27, 2020, https://www.youtube.com/watch?v=E3ffvwP8fKs.

81. https://twitter.com/Olivianuzzi/status/1254904577981394949?s=20

82. "Dr. Fauci lashes out at media in White House press briefing," Fox News YouTube channel, April 13, 2020, https://www.youtube.com/watch?v=bUFgxduAHaM.

83. Madison Dibble, " 'Propaganda session': CNN mocks 'angry' Trump press conference with critical chyrons," *Washington Examiner*, April 13, 2020.

84. Noah Weiland and Maggie Haberman, "For Dr. Deborah Birx, Urging Calm Has Come With Heavy Criticism," *New York Times*, March 27, 2020.

85. https://twitter.com/maggieNYT/status/1243927133594030088

86. https://twitter.com/atrupar/status/1243556939369496576

87. https://twitter.com/DavidCornDC/status/1243561420853297161

88. Peter Wade, "Dr. Birx More 'Bothered' by Media Than Trump for Injecting Disinfectant Comments," *Rolling Stone*, April 26, 2020.

89. Jack Goldsmith and Andrew Keane Woods, "Internet Speech Will Never Go Back to Normal," *Atlantic*, April 25, 2020.

90. https://twitter.com/HeidiNBC/status/1242241046815354881

91. https://twitter.com/mehdirhasan/status/1246586099981574151

92. Alana Goodman, "Man Who Died Ingesting Fish Tank Cleaner Remem-

bered as Intelligent, Levelheaded Engineer," *Washington Free Beacon*, April 24, 2020.

93. Alana Goodman, "Police Investigating Death of Arizona Man From Chloroquine Phosphate," April 28, 2020, *Washington Free Beacon*, April 28, 2020.

94. Kara Swisher, "Fox's Fake News Contagion," *New York Times*, March 31, 2020.

CONCLUSION

1. Susan Ferrechio, "Pelosi: Time to Consider Providing 'Guaranteed Income,'" *Washington Examiner*, April 27, 2020.

2. Emily Jacobs, "Joe Biden Says He's a 'Candidate for US Senate' in Latest Gaffe," *New York Post,* February 25, 2020.